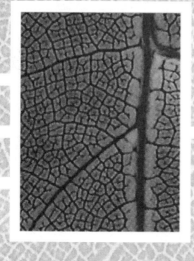

IntranetWare BorderManager

IntranetWare™
BorderManager™

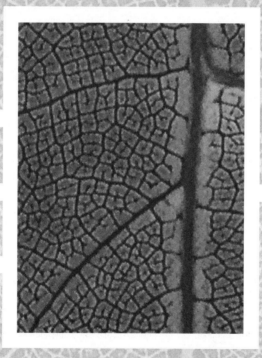

James E. Gaskin

San Francisco • Paris • Düsseldorf • Soest

Associate Publisher: Guy Hart-Davis
Acquisitions Manager: Kristine Plachy
Acquisitions & Developmental Editor: Neil Edde
Editor: Marilyn Smith
Project Editors: Jeff Chorney, Shelby Zimmerman
Technical Editor: Gary Govanus
Book Designer: Patrick Dintino
Desktop Publisher: Susan Glinert Stevens
Production Coordinator: Amy Eoff
Indexer: Matthew Spence
Cover Designer: Archer Design
Cover Photographer: The Image Bank

Screen reproductions produced with Collage Complete.
Collage Complete is a trademark of Inner Media Inc.

Network Press, Sybex, and the Network Press logo are registered trademarks of SYBEX Inc.

TRADEMARKS: SYBEX has attempted throughout this book to distinguish proprietary trademarks from descriptive terms by following the capitalization style used by the manufacturer.

The author and publisher have made their best efforts to prepare this book, and the content is based upon final release software whenever possible. Portions of the manuscript may be based upon pre-release versions supplied by software manufacturer(s). The author and the publisher make no representation or warranties of any kind with regard to the completeness or accuracy of the contents herein and accept no liability of any kind including but not limited to performance, merchantability, fitness for any particular purpose, or any losses or damages of any kind caused or alleged to be caused directly or indirectly from this book.

Library of Congress Card Number: 97-68519
ISBN: 0-7821-2138-1

Manufactured in the United States of America

10 9 8 7 6 5 4 3 2 1

Acknowledgments

Books are wonderful things to hold in your hands and see on bookstore shelves, but they can be painful things to create. Preoccupation with the book while doing family and personal things is one of the hazards of being a writer. I apologize to my family for going, "Huh?" all the time.

As usual, my lovely wife Wendy accepted my strangeness with her usual understanding, and didn't make me sleep on the couch even once. My handsome son Alex, and lovely daughter Laura, always know where to find me: in the office. Thankfully, they come and find me on a regular basis, so I can be amazed at how fast they're growing.

Of course, the cause of all this work and distraction is the group at Novell who designed, developed, and organized BorderManager into the (I believe) winning program it is. Henry Sprafkin, who helped so much with the 4.11/IntranetWare book, helped convince me to write this book, and convinced the rest of the Novell people to provide me with outstanding support and information. Kym Williams, Frank Cabri, and Ron Lee are other Novellians who gave me help, ideas, and encouragement.

Marilyn Smith, my intrepid editor, has now finished her fourth project with me. Before long, she'll have me completely trained. Well, maybe not completely. As long as she does her usual wonderful job, I'm allowed to remain slightly untrained.

Gary Govanus signed on as technical editor of this mighty tome, and I appreciate his help. Gentle reminders of overlooked facets and ideas to better illustrate new concepts came flowing from his direction.

Sybex provided an excellent crew of editors and production folks to make this book the physical object you now hold in your hands. Guy Hart-Davis is now far up the Sybex ladder, but still talks to authors and actually gives the impression he enjoys doing so. Neil Edde organized and shepherded this book from start to finish. Jeff Chorney and Shelby Zimmerman handled production chores quickly and professionally, resulting in a better book because of their hard work. And the production coordinator Amy

Eoff and desktop publisher Susan Glinert Stevens made a book that looks good.

The nice people at Gateway2000 have continued to provide me servers able to digest wild combinations of beta software and experimental configurations. They kept working during all the different times my patience and good humor quit.

Perhaps most important, let me thank you for buying this book, and pass on the thanks from the Novell group for trying BorderManager. I hope both will make you a happier person and better network manager.

Contents at a Glance

Table of Contents

Introduction

BorderManager is many things, some of which are new to NetWare, and some of which are improvements to NetWare 4.11/IntranetWare. There are so many new features, in fact, that there are rumors of making BorderManager the second version of IntranetWare—that's a lot of improvements.

BorderManager is also a new area to traditional NetWare customers, who may not be used to worrying about the Internet, proxy servers, firewalls, and subnet addresses. As the world pushes NetWare users into Internet connections, these customers need something familiar, such as standard Novell utilities and management tools, to take them into this new world. And that's what BorderManager provides, both for NetWare clients and non-NetWare TCP/IP clients.

As its name suggests, BorderManager is designed for managing borders. For our purposes, a *border* is anywhere two systems meet. Your network to the Internet is the easiest border to visualize, but your network has many borders. Links to other networks in the building and the company are all borders, as are internal connections to TCP/IP-based hosts and networks.

Every place two of anything meet creates friction, whether you're talking about matches and sandpaper or your network and the Internet. BorderManager helps manage that friction, at least enough to stop a firestorm from destroying your network.

Who Should Read This Book?

Every author has the same answer to this question: everyone. Well, honestly, we authors only care if everyone in the world buys the book. You don't all need to read it immediately.

Less outrageously, I hope that all the NetWare and IntranetWare managers interested in the Internet or intranets take a look at this book. Every NetWare network doesn't need to become Internet-enabled overnight, but many do.

Unless you have experience with TCP/IP, Unix, or other Internet technologies, relying on your NetWare experience will not be enough. There are plenty of new things to learn in BorderManager, as well as new areas to manage. The idea that BorderManager, for the first time, allows you to manage and control non-NetWare clients is a big step forward.

Even if you're not getting an Internet connection right away, many of the BorderManager features described in this book will become part of IntranetWare itself in the next version. Code named Moab, the upgrade to IntranetWare will include full TCP/IP client-to-server communications (if the rumors are true; and they always are, aren't they, except when they're not?)

You won't find a bigger fan of IPX than I, yet everything says that TCP/IP has won the protocol wars. IPX will continue, and I believe it offers some excellent performance and security advantages when used with BorderManager, but we must all learn more about TCP/IP. Sections of this book will, I hope, teach you some TCP/IP details that will help you in network business.

When your boss says the Internet is a priority, then BorderManager will be at the top of your required software list. Between your NetWare experience, the solid performance of BorderManager, and this book, even your boss will wind up being satisfied with the end result.

The Politics of BorderManager

When your boss does say that the Internet is a priority, your network thinking must change. Internet access brings a host of legal, ethical, and personnel decisions that must be made. Luckily, your boss will be the one to make many of those decisions. Unluckily, you'll be the only one up to date on the issues, so your boss will try to push the decisions onto your desk.

The most common borders you see are fences. Every fence has a gate, and that gate allows traffic to flow in and out of the confined area. Your network borders are exactly like that fence and gate, in sort of a metaphysical, virtual way. Sometimes the borders are minimal and easy to see through, like a chain-link fence. Sometime the borders are rigid and tough, like a wall and fortified gate.

Every border has a gate, and every gate allows traffic to leave and traffic to enter. Those that enter get the most press, as the nontechnical world is alternately frightened and fascinated by hackers. Your boss will no doubt be worried about hackers getting into your network and stealing information. Your boss should worry more about insiders carrying your information out through the gate, or insiders that create untenable situations inside the company.

Internet access will be eagerly accepted, and you will have the unhappy job of telling people that there are restrictions on access. A large part of BorderManager focuses on controlling insider access to TCP/IP hosts and network resources. There is a reason for this focus: Control is necessary.

Stopping outsiders from getting inside is much easier with Border-Manager than with any other comparable product available today. That's positive, but also a bit of a misnomer. There are no other products that offer the range and control you get with BorderManager, which is good, because you'll need all the help you can get.

Expect your management to waffle on Internet access restrictions, policies, goals, and budget. Many NetWare users have yet to gain full-time access to the Internet, and both users and managers have a lot of learning to do. And you, of course, are the guide for their voyage of discovery.

How This Book Is Organized

First, for those new to NetWare, IntranetWare, TCP/IP, IPX, or the Internet, we help you get up to date. All the pieces just listed are part of your network now, and you need to have a ready reference for those technologies that you don't use on a regular basis. This is the purpose of Part I, Background for BorderManager.

You also get a bird's eye view of BorderManager. Much of the feature set may not make an impression in these early chapters, because you won't know why you need it or how it will help you. That comes later, after all the assorted background is filled in.

Part of the background includes a chapter on IPX/IP gateways. I feel that the gateway function is critical to the success of BorderManager in your network (but I'm biased toward gateways, personally). This important information is presented in Part I, because the Novel IPX/IP Gateway is included in IntranetWare. But please note, your BorderManager package includes an upgrade of the Novell IPX/IP Gateway, which I highly recommend.

Part II, Improving Security and Performance with BorderManager, starts the hard-core BorderManager descriptions, explanations, examples, and commentary. Features like Network Address Translation (NAT), proxy servers, proxy cache servers, packet filtering, and virtual private networks (VPNs) are all new to NetWare networks. This middle section covers the core of BorderManager technology, and should induce a combination of curiosity and excitement as you realize the networking power you gain with BorderManager.

Part III, Providing Content with BorderManager, finishes up with some existing technologies you may or may not have used in your network already, such as Web servers, Web client applications, e-mail servers, and Windows NT systems. All these are much more solidly integrated into BorderManager than they were in the NetWare and IntranetWare packages. Since your conception of how some of these technologies apply to your network will change as you add BorderManager, you will find real-world value in these chapters.

Finally, the book has three appendices and a glossary. The first appendix includes some case studies of BorderManager use. Not surprisingly, Novell itself provides the best case study, and you'll read how parts of Border-Manager were developed to help Novell's Web server first, and applied to customer networks later. The next appendix deals with Cyber Patrol, an add-in program that helps control network user access to the Internet. The final appendix provides an easy reference to all the Web addresses for various products (and other resources) mentioned throughout the book. And the glossary, of course, defines terms related to the subject of this book.

Special Features of This Book

I like lots of screen shots, and I hope you do as well. You'll find plenty of those from various NetWare, IntranetWare, and BorderManager pieces, as well as from other software.

Although some may argue whether my writing style counts as a feature, I think it does. Many computer books do double duty as sleep aids, and I hate to see that happen. I hope the little asides, jokes, pokes, and boss roastings scattered throughout make the information go down a little more smoothly.

At the end of each chapter is a "Wrap" session. Here, in TV talk, I address the audience directly. These are the details about the just-finished chapter I would tell my best friends about, if they were crazy enough to go into the networking business. Sometimes the most important pieces are technology, and sometimes they are dealing with the people at the end of every network cable. Either way, each chapter ends with some words of wisdom, solace, comfort, or humor.

Scattered throughout the book you'll find notes, tips, and warnings related to the topic at hand. There are also plenty of sidebars to hold information that I felt was important or interesting, but that I wasn't smart enough to weave into the fabric of the chapter. All these little tidbits are clearly marked in the page margins. If you want, you can read all of these rather than the text, and you'll get a truly bizarre idea about networking in general and BorderManager in particular.

Hardware and Software Used for This Book

Many companies have been generous with their hardware, software, and expertise in order to make this book possible.

The hardware I used includes two Gateway2000 P5-120s, each equipped as follows:

- 120MHz Pentium processor

- 32MB RAM

- 1.6GB hard disk

- 8x CD-ROM drive

- 3Com 3C509 10Base-T network adapter

- 3Com LinkBuilder TP/8 wiring concentrator

- Thomas Conrad TC5055 10Base-T wiring concentrator

The software I used includes the following:

- NetWare 4.11, IntranetWare, and BorderManager from Novell, Inc.

- Collage Complete 1.1, screen capture/catalog software from Inner Media, Inc.

- Windows 95, Windows NT, and Windows 3.1 from Microsoft (Word 7, and the Microsoft Office Suite, was used for writing every word of this book)

How to Contact the Author

Send good news and bad; examples of success or frustration; and tears, cheers, or (unlikely, I hope) jeers to:
james@gaskin.com

Enjoy BorderManager and this book. There are no marauding aliens in this book, chased by men wearing black or any other color, but that's okay. Sometimes just making your network run properly is just as exciting as space travel.

PART

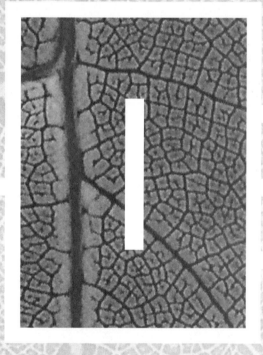

I

BACKGROUND FOR BORDERMANAGER

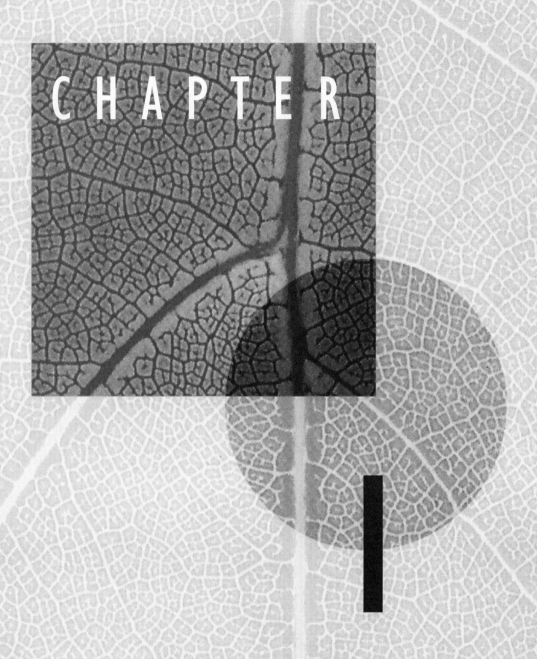

CHAPTER 1

How NetWare Became IntranetWare

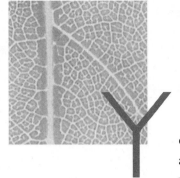

You know NetWare, you love NetWare, and you're comfortable with NetWare. So what is this IntranetWare stuff? Will you ever love it like you love NetWare?

Absolutely, because IntranetWare is just NetWare with some more "stuff" added on. Some of the new stuff may not impact you and your network, but some will. BorderManager, as shipped today, is separate from IntranetWare, but that may change.

Before we cover the migration from NetWare to IntranetWare and BorderManager, we should establish some common language and background. If you are an experienced NetWare administrator, you may already know some of this information. If you are new to NetWare or Internet technologies, this will be new. Since technologies such as extranets and virtual private networks are new to everyone, we need to agree on what they are before talking about how to use them. We'll even back up and define what makes up an intranet, just to cover all our bases.

LAN versus Intranet versus Extranet versus VPN

Life was once simple in the network business: You had either a LAN (local-area network) or a WAN (wide-area network). The two systems were connected by either a bridge in the early days (mid-1980s) or a router. The division was clear: If the LAN left the building in some way, it was a WAN.

There are examples of CANs (campus-area networks) and MANs (metropolitan-area networks), where some special fiber or microwave connections linked sites that weren't exactly long distance but were too far to reach with a patch cable. Some marketing types dreamed up cute names for networks with some wireless components, but since the *W* was already take from *wide*, the wireless folks had to settle for just plain *wireless*.

All these designations referred to the connection method of the network, not what was carried on the network. If physical wires connected your systems, you had a LAN. If telephone links were needed, you had a WAN. Wasn't that simple?

Defining by Protocol: From LAN to Intranet

Now you understand the classic difference between LAN and WAN, and have seen the tangents, CAN and MAN. All of these were defined by their physical connections. Protocols had nothing to do with these definitions.

When we get to the Internet, however, protocols play a huge part. The Internet is technically a network of networks, meaning we have LANs and WANs connected to a separate, shared WAN. By Internet law, the only protocol allowed on the Internet is TCP/IP. Here's the first difference for you: A WAN becomes part of the Internet when it shares connections and the TCP/IP protocol suite, including all the various tools and utilities (we'll get to the details of TCP/IP later in this chapter).

That difference is magnified when we discuss LAN versus intranet. It is absolutely possible to take a LAN, with every one of 50 computers (for example) tied together with physical cable and restricted to one floor of one building, and turn it into an intranet. How? After all, we didn't change the cable, we didn't add a WAN, and we didn't connect fiber across a campus or across town.

The flip answer? An intranet is a LAN with better PR. But the differences run deeper.

TCP/IP makes the biggest difference. When you add TCP/IP and all the attendant other Internet-developed tools, particularly parts of the WWW (World Wide Web), you get an intranet.

Yes, you still have the same PC, Macintosh, and Unix clients, and you still have the same NetWare servers, but now you also have Web and Internet-spawned client and server software. You may add a few other servers, particularly some servers running Window NT and some flavor of Unix, just to add a little more spice to your new dish. But you don't need to pull a single new wire, or add a single new telephone link, to call your old LAN a new intranet.

Extending to an Extranet

What do we add to make an extranet? Many look at this term for the first time and guess we're now talking about a WAN with TCP/IP and Web technologies added. That is a logical guess, but this is the computer biz, and few things are logical.

An extranet adds the *extra* modifier to designate an outside company gaining access to your internal network. This is different from the Internet mode of connecting networks to a shared network backbone, so everyone can see everyone else. On the Internet, companies want to be seen, but only on their own terms; every intelligent company has a strong firewall separating the Internet from its internal network. This is true even if their internal network can rightly be called an intranet.

Again, the *extra* in extranet refers to outside companies that are invited inside your intranet. That's correct—the other company's clients can see inside your firewall, with access to some of your network resources. This is the same as giving your next door neighbor a key in case you lose yours, and then offering your neighbor free run of your garage and kitchen for anything he may need, without asking permission for each visit.

Why would you do this with another company? The reason is to speed information exchange between the two of you. What could be faster than actually sharing the same databases on your Web server? If the other company is your biggest customer, why wait for management to blunder along and figure out what's needed, if you and your equivalent others can communicate directly?

Linking Your Company with VPNs

If you're an old-timer with your last few gray hairs barely clinging to your scalp, you may remember when commercial traffic on the Internet was taboo. Vehement arguments flew around the Internet whenever a commercial enterprise of any kind began to connect to the sacred, nonprofit Internet.

Boy, how times change. The Internet, primarily because of the Web traffic starting in late 1993, is the world's largest billboard today. Whoever coined the term "information highway" must have foreseen the virtual billboards lining the virtual highway in numbers far higher than ever seen in real life.

The next step in the "Internet as commercial network" progression is for companies to rely on the Internet for all their remote computing needs. We're no longer speaking of strictly Web server connections or Telnet sessions to remote hosts, but for any and all computing beyond the walls of the company.

The *virtual private network* (VPN) is an idea becoming more popular every day. After all, if you're already paying for an Internet connection, why buy a second high-speed data line to reach your remote offices? Can't the Internet be used for this connection? Of course, within your comfort level concerning security. Do you care if anyone in the world looks at your data packets as they wind their way across the Internet? If so, your paranoia may make you too uncomfortable. The vast majority of Internet packets are ASCII, readable by any text editor or word processor.

Early on, all Internet packets were required to be ASCII because of router limitations. Non-ASCII characters were used for router programming, meaning any non-ASCII packets would cause the router great confusion. This almost always meant the router crashed, taking your Internet access down with the ship. Encryption now enables ASCII packets full of gobbledygook to zoom across the Internet. No longer viewable yet not crashing routers, the new generation of Internet traffic maintains security even across the most public of networks.

Novell defines a VPN as a way to securely combine various remote networks into your existing enterprise network, using the Internet for connections. Do you have offices in Dallas, Chicago, and Boston? Link them all over the Internet connections already in use in every office. Encryption between servers keeps the packets private during their Internet trip.

Protocol Wars: TCP/IP versus IPX/SPX

Part of the reason for IntranetWare and BorderManager is the growing importance of TCP/IP-dependent applications. You can thank the Internet for this. As the Internet becomes more and more a consumer item, company management demands connection, and that means TCP/IP support.

Much of the Protocol Wars has been fought on the marketing front rather than by technology, which is unfortunate. TCP/IP is not the harbinger of peace on earth, or even peace on networks. It is a fairly old protocol, developed originally with government research funds for military applications. There are serious problems facing the TCP/IP community, even as the world is racing to add TCP/IP to everything up to and including the building security system.

Microsoft folks take credit for pushing TCP/IP to the PC LAN world, but they shouldn't. Their implementation of TCP/IP for Windows client to Windows server is not a pure TCP/IP network, but a mish-mash of loading NetBEUI (Network BIOS Extended User Interface, which is just as proprietary as NetWare's protocols) onto an incomplete TCP/IP stack. Next time a Microsoftie takes credit for "inventing" TCP/IP, be kind, because they know not what they say. If it matters, Novell supported TCP/IP on its server with version 3.11 much better and about two years earlier than Microsoft supported TCP/IP on its server.

Life would be simpler if this lemming-like rush to TCP/IP happened two years in the future, after IPv6 (the next version of TCP/IP, designed to solve the address crunch among other things) was complete and implemented, or IPv6 had been finished two years ago. Current TCP/IP software has major problems with security, available addresses, and quality of service guarantees for time-dependent packets such as audio and video. IPv6 could almost be considered a patch consolidation update for the current version of TCP/IP.

None of this matters, however, since the market is pushing TCP/IP ubiquity over common sense. Our job today is not to decide whether TCP/IP is the proper move for your network, but how to integrate and support TCP/IP with your NetWare and IntranetWare clients and servers.

That said, I counsel against moving a working IPX/SPX network over to TCP/IP just for the symmetry of your network protocols. IPX was developed for local network applications, and runs faster and jumps higher than TCP/IP when tested locally. Besides, why change something that works, when you have so much more on your plate?

TCP/IP: The Internetworking Leader

Regardless of your feelings toward TCP/IP and your network, you must acknowledge that the developers of TCP/IP did many more things right than they did wrong. The protocol of tomorrow was complete in 1982, and covered all the important considerations nearly a decade before that.

My flippant definition for open systems used to be "Unix on Ethernet." Now, my flippant answer to the open systems question is "A TCP/IP-enabled anything is an open system." Neither of these quips is a correct definition, of course, but they both illustrate an important truth. The concept of open systems today concerns the operating system less than the networking capabilities of the system in question.

How did TCP/IP assume the role of internetworking protocol leader? By design, believe it or not. Early design goals included tolerating poor WAN connections, voice traffic using packet radio, and a fault-tolerant network. Remember, this was a military project at the beginning, and maintaining communications in the worst possible situation, namely a nuclear attack, was the goal of the developers.

The Internet became TCP/IP-only on January 1, 1983, and TCP/IP remains the only protocol allowed on the Internet for today and the foreseeable future. Local network implementations of TCP/IP were initially limited to Unix systems, because those were the smallest systems with enough memory and protocol support to run TCP/IP software. Now, of course, every network-compatible device made has a TCP/IP option.

TCP/IP Building Blocks

TCP/IP, like IPX/SPX, is a combination of many job-specific protocols organized into a coherent communications software suite. Let's take a look at the important protocols that make up the TCP/IP suite:

- **TCP (Transmission Control Protocol):** Adds reliable, connection-oriented and full-duplex packet delivery between hosts using IP as the transport.

- **IP (Internet Protocol):** Provides internetwork datagram routing through best effort (not guaranteed).

- **UDP (User Datagram Protocol):** Provides unreliable, connectionless packet delivery service between clients over IP.

- **FTP (File Transfer Protocol):** As a file transfer protocol between hosts, carries ASCII, binary, and EBCDIC file formats.

- **DNS (Domain Name System):** Provides a hierarchical naming scheme with domain subnames separated by periods.

- **HTTP (HyperText Transfer Protocol):** Serves as a transport protocol used for Web server communications.

- **SMTP (Simple Mail Transfer Protocol):** Provides rules for exchanging ASCII electronic mail between different systems.

- **Telnet:** Provides remote terminal connection services.

- **ICMP (Internet Control Message Protocol):** Reports errors and responds to queries about remote conditions. ICMP is an integral part of IP.

- **ARP (Address Resolution Protocol):** Maps Internet addresses to physical network addresses.

- **RARP (Reverse Address Resolution Protocol):** Maps physical network addresses to Internet addresses.

- **RIP (Routing Information Protocol):** Keeps a list of reachable networks for internetwork packets.

This big block of protocols is why people refer to the TCP/IP protocol "suite" rather than just a single protocol called TCP/IP. When you buy a TCP/IP suite, you get all the above, plus a few more of these fairly invisible protocols. You also get applications, including an e-mail client, a terminal-emulation package built on Telnet, a graphical FTP utility, and the like.

Although the components mentioned here constitute the TCP/IP building blocks, not every software box labeled "TCP/IP" includes the same stuff. For example, what happens when you get TCP/IP "free" from Microsoft with Windows 95 or NT? Being "free" as part of the operating system means you don't get the same level of TCP/IP suite you get when you buy a separate package. Also left out of the free TCP/IP bag are utilities and applications that every other system includes.

Microsoft says you get all you need, because Internet Explorer (the Web browser built into the latest Windows 95 and NT versions and available as a free download for earlier releases) includes rudimentary e-mail and news reader clients. Do you get enough TCP/IP "free" from Microsoft to participate in a TCP/IP-based network? It's close, depending on how your network is configured. Do you get anywhere near as many utilities, applications, and documentation as you do when you buy a separate TCP/IP package? No.

What do you get when the package comes from Novell? For the server, you get all the TCP/IP protocols and addressing software necessary to put your server on the Internet. If you install NetWare/IP (which allows Net-Ware clients and NetWare servers to communicate using the TCP/IP protocol suite rather than IPX/SPX; you'll find details in Chapter 3), you get all the client protocol blocks, but not fancy applications. After all, the purpose of NetWare/IP is to replace IPX on your local network, not become completely TCP/IP-enabled. If you wish to go that far, the IPX/IP Gateway (which is server-based software that converts IPX network packets into TCP/IP packets; more on this in Chapter 6) that comes with Intranet-Ware works perfectly well. If all this fails to satisfy your boss, go for a network license of the LAN WorkPlace application, and you'll get one of the leading TCP/IP application suites on the market.

TCP/IP and the OSI Model

The rules for networking book authors demand that there be at least one copy of the OSI (Open Systems Interconnection) model be shown. Let's fulfill that duty here, and overlay the TCP/IP protocol suite over the seven layers of the OSI model (this is required language, sorry). Match the TCP/IP building blocks presented earlier to the diagram in Figure 1.1, and the TCP/IP system will become a bit clearer for you.

There, we've satisfied the rules. I put in the diagram, and you will probably skip over it. Our roles have been played properly. But I'll go one step further and ask you to take a quick look at it to get an idea about the relationships. Notice which block sits atop which other block. You can't have TCP until you have IP, as the diagram shows and as I said earlier. All the utilities and applications on the first layer depend on either a reliable transport (TCP) or a best-effort transport (UDP). If a TCP packet is lost, the network software will automatically ask for the packet to be resent. If a UDP packet is lost, it's up to the application, not the network software, to realize the loss and request a repeat packet.

Do you need to know every detail about TCP/IP in order to receive BorderManager advantages in your network? No, but the more you know

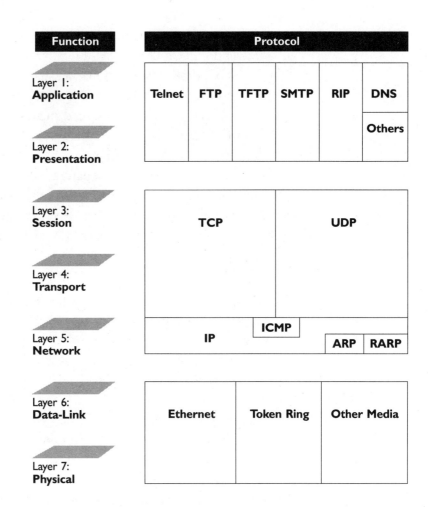

FIGURE 1.1

TCP/IP building blocks stacked beside the OSI layers

about your new protocol best friend, the better. You will spend more time installing, configuring, and cursing TCP/IP than you ever did IPX. So it's best you know what you curse, and why it is often so vexing. You'll get more details about TCP/IP in upcoming chapters.

IPX/SPX: The Popular Standby

NetWare purists may wonder why I listed TCP/IP before IPX/SPX. Isn't that backwards to the way Novell has always thought of these protocols?

Yes, but that's the past. The future is clear, for Novell and every other network vendor: TCP/IP or bust—literally. If IBM can't keep the SNA (Systems Network Architecture) market share up, when it completely controls the mainframe market, what chance does Novell have forcing IPX on the world? Every time you read an article about connecting mainframes via TCP/IP, realize the bad news is shared by IBM and every other vendor relying on a non-TCP/IP protocol.

However, inertia is the strongest natural force, which is why the sun will expire in about twelve billion years. Inertia also explains why IPX/SPX will be around for years to come. Just because you can technically use TCP/IP for a network connection doesn't always mean that's the best option.

IPX/SPX Building Blocks

IPX corresponds to IP, if you remember the chart from the previous section. In fact, the *I* in IPX stands for Internetworking, and the *I* in IP stands for Internetwork. The primary goal of both protocols is to traverse multiple networks and deliver packets if at all possible. Both protocols assume that there is more than one network involved, and handle the internetwork routing properly.

SPX corresponds to TCP, with the network operating system handling any errors across the network. SPX rides on IPX, letting the lower protocol handle the internetwork addressing problems. Since SPX is a reliable protocol, it is used to establish a permanent connection between two named devices. If you have any server tape backup software that works with network workstations, SPX is the protocol used for the tape operations.

Like TCP/IP, IPX/SPX consists of a batch of various protocols clumped together into a protocol suite. RIP is used in IPX/SPX just like in TCP/IP, and for the same reasons. SAP (Service Advertising Protocol) is unique to IPX/SPX, and is used by all servers to broadcast their address every 60 seconds. TCP/IP people hate broadcasts, and SAP use is one of the major reasons IPX/SPX has fallen out of favor in the open systems (read TCP/IP) community.

NCP's Role

The workhorse protocol for NetWare is NCP (NetWare Core Protocol). NCP is a higher-layer protocol proprietary to Novell, providing the Presentation and Application layer interface for the OSI model. It runs over IPX or SPX, depending on the application. This protocol handles all the file access, print sharing, and application program support. NCP functions include:

- Create service connection.

- Request (to server).

- Reply (from server).

- Destroy service connection.

- Request being considered (from server).

You can see that all the common file and print handling requests from a client rely on NCP. This is the protocol that requires each packet to be acknowledged before the next packet will be sent. This ping-pong or ack-ack syndrome brings sneers from TCP/IP loyalists who state that IPX/SPX is obviously not a prime-time protocol. Not only are the TCP/IP fans incorrect, they are inaccurate and out of date. NCP requires the acknowledgments, not IPX/SPX, and Novell long ago added Packet Burst Mode protocol to send multiple packets and acknowledge them with a single packet in return, just like TCP/IP does.

In spite of these protocol "failures," as some would say, IPX/SPX has well over 3000 applications written specifically for this protocol, making it by far the most popular protocol. Developed for local and reliable networks, IPX/SPX does away with much of the overhead of TCP/IP, because there's no need to worry as much about unreliable connections between nodes when all of them are connected by the same cable system. Across the Internet is a different story, of course, which is where TCP/IP really shines.

The Arguments against a Single Protocol

There are two primary arguments against a single protocol, particularly when the single protocol is TCP/IP. Since TCP/IP is the wave of the future, let's list the arguments against having each and every device run TCP/IP. The main issues are security and workstation resources.

Threats to Security

With TCP/IP as your only protocol, security becomes a serious concern. This applies primarily to Internet connections, where the nontechnical press seems to believe every Internet user is a pornography-dealing, software-stealing, hacker outlaw bent on invading your network. True? Only slightly.

Yes, there are hackers on the Internet, and you must take precautions. You lock the doors to your building when you're gone, don't you? Your network must have the same attitude, and let in friendly people but lock out unfriendly and/or unknown people.

With the IPX/IP Gateway, your internal network remains based on IPX/SPX. The gateway converts IPX/SPX packets into TCP/IP for use on the Internet. Outsiders, both legitimate TCP/IP clients and hackers, see only the single gateway IP address shared by all gateway users. Since TCP/IP stops at the gateway, no outsider can see a single IPX/SPX NetWare resource, whether host or client (if your gateway is installed properly, of course).

How does this work? We'll go into the details in Chapter 6, but rest assured it does work and work reliably. Just realize that if there are no TCP/IP-enabled devices within your local network, no one can see past your gateway into your local network.

You may ask if security is really that much of a problem both from outside hackers and inside miscreants. The answer is that serious breaches are statistically unlikely, but can be devastating when they happen. Outsiders may be merely curious, or they may be searching for corporate information. Using the same protocol inside your network as on the Internet makes it simple for insiders to hack into your systems. After all, the secrets to the TCP/IP protocol are an open standard, and the details and programming tools to hack TCP/IP are freely available on the Internet and at your bookstore.

Configuration and Workstation Resource Demands

Another consideration is that TCP/IP still requires much more configuration and workstation resources than IPX/SPX. If your network consists of nothing but 32-bit clients such as Unix, OS/2, and Windows 95 and NT, then workstation resources may not be a contributing factor to your protocol choice. If you're still struggling with plenty of Windows 3.1 and even DOS stations, taking more RAM from your workstations becomes a critical issue. In other words, your clients will scream at you for sucking scarce resources from their systems.

Lacking the SAP and RIP method of discovering network information, TCP/IP requires particular stations to become name and address servers for other network systems. Each of these addresses must be configured in each workstation's TCP/IP configuration files. If you have 50 workstations, that's a pain. If you have 5000 workstations, the pain becomes unbearable.

Yes, there are ways to automatically boot TCP/IP at your workstation and have it receive an IP address from a DHCP (Dynamic Host Configuration Protocol) server. This stops you from configuring the individual IP address in each and every workstation, but you still must configure the DHCP client portion at each node. Then, of course, you must set up and configure the DHCP server (your NetWare server can be your DHCP server, if you wish) to supply your network clients with the proper IP address.

Is this a lot of work? Yes, especially at the beginning. All this is possible, but will make you yearn for the good old days of adding IPX/SPX nodes and not needing to configure any client network addresses, router addresses, default gateway addresses to reach the Internet, or subnet masks for your TCP/IP segments. Don't let anyone ever tell you a TCP/IP station is easier to install than an IPX/SPX station, because it just isn't true.

The Arguments for a Single Protocol

Money, convenience, management, and monitoring head the list of reasons for standardizing on TCP/IP for your network. Novell executives always said that one or two large customers were behind the push for NetWare/IP because of their WAN needs. Boiled down, this means that some large companies can save money if they run only TCP/IP on their WAN.

Simpler Single Protocol Support

Saving money is certainly not a bad thing. The convenience of having all network clients use the same network transport protocol is considerable, especially when speaking of companies with many routers that cost extra when supporting a second protocol. Management tools tend to be for a single protocol, so that having two protocols means two separate tools to buy, two products to learn, and two places to look while troubleshooting. Monitoring a single protocol is simpler than monitoring two or three, and careful monitoring is becoming increasingly important.

Improvements in TCP/IP Tools

Security for TCP/IP networks is getting stronger and cheaper all the time, making even paranoid managers a bit more comfortable. The new generation of firewalls and proxy servers, even from Novell as you'll see soon, clamp down hard on security holes and provide monitoring of internal employee actions as well. Tracking who does what on the Internet is a popular management requirement, and TCP/IP tools are starting to make this information available for less money.

One of the advantages of BorderManager is the addition of NAT (Network Address Translation), sometimes referred to as the IP/IP Gateway. Many local TCP/IP networks didn't follow the Internet numbering sequence, and therefore couldn't get on the Internet without renumbering every TCP/IP device on their network. NAT tools automatically change the internal IP address to an acceptable external address before allowing packets out on the Internet. TCP/IP now has utilities to correct almost every early design and implementation flaw, making TCP/IP a good choice for local and remote networks.

Standardize Now Rather than Later

When the TCP/IP world upgrades to IPv6, many companies will need major time to install, configure, and debug the new software. Better to upgrade everyone at once than fight the possible incompatibilities among your existing IPX software and the new TCP/IP protocol stack. Novell doesn't yet have the same type of real-time data delivery capabilities of IPv6, and may not even when IPv6 is delivered.

Besides all the technical reasons for standardizing on a single protocol, marketing makes a big difference. People want to be part of the leading group, and TCP/IP is certainly leading the protocol parade lately. Who today wants to admit having a Betamax rather a VHS VCR? After all, everyone agreed that Betamax provided better pictures, but VHS marketing overwhelmed the Betamax camp.

Novell and the Lure of the Web

This is where it all starts, isn't? The Web has captured the imagination of the public like no other computer technology since HAL 9000 in *2001: A Space Odyssey*.

Novell engineers were working with Web browsers since the first version of Mosaic hit the Internet in late 1993. Using the foundation of NetWare/IP and LAN WorkPlace, Novell network clients have always had Web access, at least in the Novell labs.

Novell's Marketing department missed this boat, unfortunately, and let Microsoft advertisers take the high ground and claim their products were the proper connection to the Internet in general and the Web in particular. The fact that Web server software was available for Windows NT systems a year or more earlier than for the NetWare server emphasized that point. Pilot Windows NT servers that were gradually worming their way into NetWare customer networks became the focus of the Web excitement, leaving NetWare in the shadows.

Although late, Novell has leveled out the playing field quite a bit between the IntranetWare operating system and Windows NT regarding Web server platforms. There are still many more options for Web servers on the Windows NT platform, but Novell servers also have multiple options. There is a certain purity in running the Web server on the same operating system where all your files exist.

Taking a page out of Microsoft's book of tricks, Novell decided to include the Web server software and support pieces in the IntranetWare package for no extra cost. In other words, your IntranetWare package includes both the best file and print network server and an excellent, high-performance Web server. As more people discover the value and security of the NetWare Web server software, the focus may swing back toward NetWare servers and away from Windows NT boxes.

Sure, you can use BorderManager without connecting any of your clients to the World Wide Web. You can connect remote branches into your company network across the Internet, rather than through leased lines, and not necessarily allow your network clients to see the rest of the Web. You can block all that from their view if you wish. But you won't. After all, the Internet zoomed to public consciousness because the Web is so exciting, inviting, and just plain fun. Your bosses and clients all want to research, investigate, and leverage the Web to better your own company.

Of course, employees also want to check out playboy.com, playgirl.com, the latest stock quotes, news from Hollywood, and how cheaply they can buy a stereo over the Web. Unless your company is unusual, none of these activities will "leverage the Web to better your own company," if you know what I mean.

You'll see in later chapters how you can allow your network clients to use the Web to their (and your company's) advantage without turning the Web into a corporate playground. I'll also show how you can monitor employee activities, and reduce your company's liability for employee misdeeds. But the point of this section is to emphasize the joy of the Web and the pull it has had over Novell's development cycle.

Refocusing with IntranetWare and BorderManager

Novell launched its major Web and Internet attack with IntranetWare and NetWare 4.11. Formally announced during BrainShare in late March, 1997, BorderManager refocused Novell on the Internet. All the new products seem aimed at improving NetWare-to-Internet connections and security. I'm sure some Novell developers are still working on improving the traditional file and print services, but when they go to lunch, they may all fit into one car (joke—laugh now).

Focusing outward, Novell developed BorderManager to improve the following:

- **Security**: NDS (NetWare Directory Services) becomes the hub of Internet security and access for users and guests.

- **VPNs (virtual private networks):** These allow secure, encrypted interoffice communications across the Internet.

- **Proxy services**: These services speed performance and access to the Web by utilizing the same award-winning caching techniques used for years by NetWare.

There are plenty of details within each of these sections, of course, but you should see from here that these services are outside the traditional NetWare area. Even printing improvements, promised in the next version of IntranetWare, focus on printing to TCP/IP devices and across the Internet. No part of NetWare is safe from the Internet hordes actively remaking the product.

Appointing Eric Schmidt the CEO in March of 1997 also indicates more Novell focus on the Internet and the Web. Schmidt, for years the CTO (Chief Technical Officer) of Sun Microsystems, was one of the strongest proponents of Java while at Sun. If not for Schmidt, Java would likely have remained an obscure programming toolkit buried in the huge catalog of Sun products. Schmidt has always focused on the Internet and remote computing, and there's no indication that will change while he is at Novell. Even before Schmidt was appointed CEO, Novell executives made deals with Netscape to better support SuiteSpot Web servers on IntranetWare platforms. They went so far as to start a separate company, Novonyx, just to develop and market compatible NetWare/Netscape products.

Java, the hot language of the Web world, will run on NetWare servers before the end of 1997. Novell engineers will officially release Java tool-kits to run Java directly on NetWare server NLMs (NetWare Loadable Modules), updating the control of the NetWare server. Novell has always supported Java applications on the Web server software, so the addition of a JIT (Just-In-Time) compiler and the Java Virtual Machine set of support NLMs will turn an IntranetWare server into a multimedia, hopping, bopping, animated—and no doubt noisy—Web server.

The 3.11/IntranetWare Correlation

Many critics say Novell NetWare became a workhorse operating system with NetWare 3.11. By then, all the promises made for NetWare 3.0 were actually delivered and working. If Novell executives had been smart, they would have made a bigger noise about 3.11 than just upgrading one-hundredths of a point. Being somewhat embarrassed about the delay in providing promised features, however, the executives soft-pedaled the upgrade as if all these details were always in the box, and the critics and customers just missed them.

A direct correlation between NetWare 3.11 and IntranetWare should be made here. Novell embraced TCP/IP at the server with NetWare 3.11. Novell servers could sit on the Internet, communicate with remote servers across the Internet through IP tunneling, and even be controlled through Telnet connections with XConsole. This was unheard of in the PC LAN world, no matter how much Microsoft's PR people may squeal that they did it first. They didn't. Novell did. And with IntranetWare, Novell still does.

NetWare/IP, for example, was first shipped as a separate product with a substantial price tag attached. When NetWare 4.10 came out, NetWare/IP was still an optional part of the NetWare package. With NetWare 4.11, NetWare/IP was included, although some nameless Novell people say they were forced to include it because of a mistake. The Web server software was already on the 4.11 CD-ROM when the decision was made to separate the product into Net-Ware and IntranetWare. The time for testing a new CD-ROM file layout would have delayed the product release, so the Web server remained in the package. The same was said of NetWare/IP.

To be fair, NetWare/IP may have been slated for NetWare 4.11 no matter what. After all, Microsoft was busy blasting Novell for "not supporting" TCP/IP between clients and servers. Never mind that Windows NT uses a hokey TCP/IP-NetBIOS network transport that's no more standard than IPX. Remember, it's not reality that counts, it's marketing papers that define product features today. To combat Microsoft's marketing, Novell likely felt compelled to include NetWare/IP to allow comparison shoppers to check off "TCP/IP client transport" on their comparison charts.

The IPX/IP Gateway, also labeled the NetWare Internet Access Server, did help differentiate between NetWare 4.11 and IntranetWare. Although the Web server was included in NetWare 4.11, a simple way to reach that Web server for all the millions of existing IPX clients was not in the box. Yes, you could install NetWare/IP and wrestle that into supporting the browser and hence the Web server, but that is a struggle.

How did all these products wind up in their current configurations? Not being a Novell employee, I was not part of the decision-making process. That doesn't stop me from guessing what happened and why, however, and it certainly helps isolate me from any retribution when I say Novell made mistakes here and there. Employees who lambaste their employers in print tend to become ex-employees, and I don't need to worry about that. What I tell you may not be exactly accurate, but it is not filtered by any fear on my part. Some may suggest only a little intelligence was used in the filtering process as well, but my mother resents that remark. Besides, I like IntranetWare and BorderManager, and this book will help you and your company learn to like them, as well.

How BorderManager Fits with IntranetWare

Notice that these BorderManager services mentioned in the previous section are facing outward, but retain the essential privacy of your own network. The first step for integrating NetWare with the Internet came with the first wave of IPX-to-TCP/IP gateways from a dozen different third-party vendors. Novell waited for the market to settle, then included its own IPX/IP Gateway product with IntranetWare. The NetWare version carried fewer bells and whistles, but was integrated into NDS and controlled by the NetWare Administrator program (NWAdmin).

Perhaps Novell's goal is to stretch your NetWare network as far as necessary, using the Internet for transport. If true, you would expect Novell to make Web servers easy to load and manage (done), add more security for networks connected to the Internet (done), and manage everything through NWAdmin or programs created in that vein (done again).

Hmm... Novell must be looking to make wide-area networking as simple as local-area networking, and using BorderManager to make this happen. My first clue was the press release announcing BorderManager, labeled "Novell Extends Corporate Networks to the Internet, Outlines New BorderManager Product." See, years of writing networking books gives you the ability to read press releases.

If I had written the press release headline, I would have focused on extending corporate networks *across* the Internet. This wording would point attention to the MPR (Multi-Protocol Router) software that connects to the Internet, the encryption software that keeps packets private, and the management to control all these technologies. But I didn't write it, although the basic ideas certainly fit here with this book, don't they?

Think of BorderManager as a "booster pack" for IntranetWare, able to turbo-charge the operating system to run faster, protect better, and connect with more remote networks more reliably than ever before. Unlike some operating system booster packs (which shall remain nameless), BorderManager won't fill your hard disk full of junk and trash your existing WINSOCK.DLL program.

Corporate Intranet Politics

Before we move on to the specifics of BorderManager and setting up your intranet or extranet, let's take a few moments to consider the effects your new system can have on your new company. Not the improved communications, increased productivity, or technological breakthroughs—we'll get to all those in the next chapters. What I'm speaking of now is the ever-present corporate politics and what happens when you throw in this new element.

If you're new to the Internet, you may be surprised to learn that some people feel strongly about the material that is available on the Internet. Let's just say that there is a constant struggle between Internet access and appropriate business material.

Your intranet will have less of this problem, but there will still be questions. When your intranet connects to either the Internet at large or just a few other affiliated companies, you are thrust into a public forum. How you, and your network clients, behave in public should be different than how you behave in private.

Whether you are the Web Master or not, you will likely be involved in some area of Web server content and access to the Web server. Both areas have some delicate aspects, which should be considered before you jump into the Web business. This need for caution doubles when you are connected to outside companies through an extranet.

Equal Access for Everyone

This heading echoes the civil rights struggle for a reason—everyone will want equal access to everything possible. Although equal access is the law of the land, it is not the law of your company, or any other company for that matter. Management is perfectly within its rights, and the law, to restrict some or all employees from reaching some or all of the Internet, your intranet, or the extranet. Simply put, you have no "right" to Internet access at work. This is not a free speech issue; this is a matter of employment. Your employer decides what you should and shouldn't have access to, period.

Of course, you don't want to state this quite so harshly for your network clients. No one likes to be told to "shut up and work," even if that's the underlying message to "we'll get access to your department as soon as we can."

That said, plan for everyone possible to get as equal access as management and technology allow. If your company is large enough to require a rollout of Internet or intranet access, tell everyone the schedule for implementation. Adding access to one department, without informing the other departments of their implementation date, will start tongues wagging all over the company. I'm sure your company has enough idle gossip running around already, so you should keep a lid on the gossip caused by your job.

Many companies encourage competition between departments. If your company does so, providing varying levels of system access may be seen as an insult or a devious plot for competitive advantage. It won't be, of course, but that doesn't mean people won't get upset.

What's the best way to deal with these problems? Provide a full schedule of the rollout to all the departments, with explanations if necessary. Do you like the Boston office more than you like the Chicago office? Probably not, but the Chicago people may feel hurt if Boston gets online first. Explaining that the new dedicated connection to the Chicago ISP (Internet service provider) will take two weeks longer than the link to the Boston ISP should soothe some feelings. The Chicago folks may still hold a slight grudge, but at least you won't be contributing to the problem.

Display Appropriate Material Only

This should go without saying, but companies get in trouble every day for mistakes and oversights. If your intranet or Internet Web site is for business use, make sure that only business material is displayed. If there's any doubt concerning some material, leave it out. You are more than welcome to put anything you wish on your personal Web site at home, but keep the company site clean and beyond reproach.

Keep Private Information Private

Appropriate can mean more than just "not dirty" of course, particularly when working on an extranet. Does your intranet server detail material you want your associated companies to read? Are your discussions about new products appropriate for outside eyes?

Intranets encourage departments to show off a bit, and place plenty of material on an intranet Web server that should remain within the family. When you open the doors to associated companies with your extranet, verify what the outsiders can and can't read. Allow full access to one Web server only, if possible, and use the excuse that it's easier to manage just one server at the start of the relationship. There's no reason to allow an outside company, even a closely associated company, a chance to peek into every corner of your company.

Make Sure It's Legal

Copyright infringement is rampant on the Web, and will be no different on your intranet. If you don't have control of images and text, don't put them up on any Web server. Pulling images from another Web server and displaying them on yours as if they were local images still requires copyright permission. You can't assume that any image on the Web is owned by the company supporting the Web page. You can only guarantee that your site falls within the letter of the copyright laws.

A common advertising ploy is to reprint good reviews about your company or products on your Web page. Clear that copy with the owner, which in most cases is the magazine in which the review appeared. Until you get permission, provide a link to the source material rather than copying the material to your site. Yeah, it takes longer, but it's less likely to expose you to hostile lawyers bearing bad news.

Need we speak of pirated software? Any illegal software found on a Web server should receive the same treatment as any other stolen property. In other words, the software should be returned or deleted, and the miscreant should be reported and punished.

Monitoring Is Legal

Again, free speech doesn't cover your actions as an employee during the workday. The company has the right to monitor your activities pursued in the normal task of performing your job. If you say or do something stupid, you can be fired by, not jailed by, your employer. That's why it's not a free speech issue.

That means your telephone calls may be monitored, even if you aren't told this is possible. Most companies inform the employees that telephone monitoring is possible, but bury the information deep in the employee handbook everyone loses within the first week on the job. Other companies just decide no warning is legally necessary, so they don't tell you about the monitoring possibility.

Courts have extended the right for companies to monitor telephone calls to include all electronic communications, including e-mail, faxes, and files on any company computer. Let me repeat: e-mail is *not* private. All e-mail you send or receive may be viewed by authorized management personnel. You may be asked to help provide random e-mail messages for this monitoring.

Don't get all bent out of shape over the "rights" you think you have lost. When you use company equipment on company time, the company has every right to ensure that you are using that time and equipment properly.

Be prepared for some users to become upset if and when they hear about this. To head off trouble, it's best for the company to spell out the policy regarding monitoring in a document given to each employee using the system. Most lawyers suggest each employee sign a document listing the rules and stating that the employee understands said rules. Some companies are too large to handle managing the documents if they are returned, so post the material so each and every employee will have no excuse for not knowing the situation.

Wrap

NetWare begat IntranetWare, and IntranetWare begat Border-Manager. Technically, IntranetWare opened the doors to the Internet, requiring BorderManager.

This is, I believe, the correct way to regard BorderManager. As the scope of your network grows, so do your needs to protect and manage your network. BorderManager adds the extra protection you need to connect to the Internet, your intranet, or an extranet, with full confidence.

Sure, some of this stuff is new and weird looking, but so what? You and I both were new and weird looking at one time, and we came out okay. Well, I did, and I'm assuming you did, since you're reading this book.

Hang on, and prepare to have some fun as we learn and explore Border-Manager together.

CHAPTER

2

BorderManager Overview

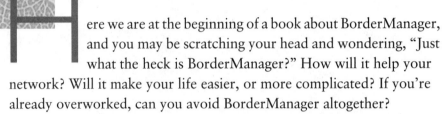

ere we are at the beginning of a book about BorderManager, and you may be scratching your head and wondering, "Just what the heck is BorderManager?" How will it help your network? Will it make your life easier, or more complicated? If you're already overworked, can you avoid BorderManager altogether?

BorderManager is IntranetWare software for Internet, intranet, and extranet connections. We'll get to a more specific definition shortly. Will it help your network? In almost all cases, yes. The only companies with little need of BorderManager are those companies not connected to the Internet or any other companies. In other words, if your network doesn't touch the Internet, a supplier, a contractor, or a remote office, then you can skip BorderManager for the most part.

However, if you need strong security options when communicating outside your network, BorderManager will help. If your Internet clients complain about slow Web performance, both internally and externally, BorderManager will help. If you have more network than time to manage that network, BorderManager will help.

Can you avoid BorderManager? Not if you're smart. Novell worked hard to engineer BorderManager to eliminate the three *W*'s from computing: worry, waste, and wait. With BorderManager, you won't worry about what your employees are doing on the Internet, employees won't waste time doing things they shouldn't, and the Proxy Server will eliminate much of the wait for remote Web pages to download.

Defining BorderManager

These services were originally called "Border Services" to illustrate where they function: at the connecting points between your network and other networks. In other words, they work at the border between your private area and other network areas.

This border may separate your network from the Internet, which is the most common method. You want to provide Internet access for network users, and publish content on the Internet through Web and other servers. Therefore, you need both incoming and outgoing controls, much like the border crossing guards at national borders checking every person going from one country to another.

Intranets become borders as well, but more like relaxed borders between states in the United States than between the United States and other countries. There are no travel restrictions moving from Texas to Oklahoma, for instance, just as there may be no impediments to your network clients using some of the resources of another department's network. However, the laws are different in Texas and Oklahoma, and a state judge in Oklahoma has no authority over Texas and Texas residents. Similarly, you may have access to some network resources in a neighboring network, but no control over security or server setup on the remote network.

As networking expanded, and Internet technologies (and clumsy naming terms) started expanding your private networks, more borders arrived. Your company and your principal supplier will need more communication than you and a semi-regular customer. It's common for your supplier to allow you access to some internal Web servers, and you may allow some of that company's employees to peruse some internal marketing plans involving their products. There are still two separate companies, but enhanced communications provide benefits for both parties.

The "Great Wall of China" mind-set doesn't work well in these modern times. It's not enough to block out everyone not geographically connected to you. Your own networks will spread to other sites, perhaps in other cities, and yet you still want to treat them like a local connection. Thus comes the VPN (virtual private network) part of BorderManager.

Another Great Wall problem is making room for allies. A wall doesn't know which person is an enemy and which is a friend. Luckily, Border-Manager can tell the difference between a key supplier and an outsider. Thus comes the extranet part of BorderManager.

Within the Great Wall, everyone had equal access. That may have worked in ancient China, but not today in your company. Other departments have no reason to access your department's private information, yet they may still need access to many documents, files, and other network resources. Thus comes the intranet part of BorderManager.

Does it sound like BorderManager is many things? Perhaps all things to all people? Well, maybe my enthusiasm paints too grand a picture. No single product can solve the entire world's problems (in spite of what Microsoft promises for its next version). BorderManager doesn't make miracles, but it does make better networks. And even more exciting, it makes your existing NetWare networks faster and more secure while using the NetWare management tools you use already.

How BorderManager Can Help Your Network

When you ask your bosses what type of Internet connectivity your network should support, you're liable to get much more input than you wanted. Let me save you the trouble, and tell you what they want:

- **Insiders accessing Internet resources.** Every white-collar worker in America has come to expect Internet access on the job, just like employees expect a computer and a telephone. Even the blue-collar workers with unions are putting Internet access on their bargaining platforms (well, they could be, if I bothered to check). Hyperbole on my part or not, users need Internet access, and you need to control and manage that access.

- **Allow remote users into the company network.** The problem travelers and remote offices have with a LAN is the first part: *local*. A LAN requires a cable to reach all systems in the network. Remote users, and particularly travelers, have a hard time getting access to internal network resources. The few options that exist are plagued by performance and security problems.

- **Turn your LAN into a seamless WAN cheaply.** WANs with high performance are easy to build—order T1 lines between all the offices. Unfortunately, the price is even higher than the performance. Your bosses want to know why you have leased lines and links to the Internet in every office. Can you eliminate one or the other? With BorderManager, you can.

Not much of a list, is it? Ha ha ha—isn't it easy to demand so much with so few words? Oh, by the way, your bosses say to do all this without changing the network, the primary software, and most important, without compromising security in the least.

BorderManager and Security

It always comes down to security sooner or later, doesn't it? So it has once again.

Novell questioned customers while developing BorderManager, and the overwhelming concern companies had for Internet and extranet connections was security. That makes sense, when you examine the situation. After all, you want to extend some hospitality, not expose your business to being plundered.

Fortunately, Novell engineers listened to the security requests of their customers. There are a variety of ways Novell increased security with BorderManager.

NOTE   You and I may understand that every IP address doesn't shelter a hacker, but your boss may not. After all, the only information executive management gets is by reading executive newspaper and magazine articles written by those who don't quite "get" the Internet. Remember the Carnegie Mellon fiasco in 1995, when some fool boasted he had "surveyed the net" and found an enormous amount of pornography? Turns out the idiot was checking sexually oriented sites only, so of course he thought the entire Internet world was inundated by pornography.

NAT or IP/IP Gateway

One area new to NetWare users is NAT (Network Address Translation), also called the IP/IP Gateway. Novell users have had little reason to worry about their NetWare IP addresses not being officially assigned and unique on the Internet in the past, but as more customers connect, more address problems will arise.

Each IP address on the Internet must be unique in the world. When you contract with an ISP (Internet service provider), the provider will give you a block of IP addresses for your use only. No one else in the world will have those same addresses. That's the theory, anyway. Realistically, many companies set up an internal TCP/IP network without ever imagining that their network will one day connect to the Internet.

Oops. A vice president comes through one day, telling you to order a router and call the minute the router is to be connected to the Internet. You call an ISP to make service connections, only to find that your internal network addresses clash with the world. Will you tell the VP that Internet connections are impossible, or reconfigure each and every device running TCP/IP in your company? Or will you leave town during the night?

You can avoid leaving town by using BorderManager's NAT, and letting the NAT software translate your internal IP address to an Internet-legal address on outgoing packets. As far as the Internet is concerned, each client is using a perfectly "legal" and unique IP address. Inside your network, each client may still be running with the default IP addresses shipped with the TCP/IP software, but at least you can get on the Internet now.

Many security experts suggest using NAT no matter what. After all, if outside hackers don't know your internal IP addresses, they have a terrible time trying to hack into your network. When they try the common trap doors for your legal IP address, they will get nothing worthwhile back. If they can't see your servers, they can't hack your servers.

NAT works well to protect inside resources from outsiders, and the IP/IP Gateway protects your intranet using NAT. We'll go into the details about NAT in Chapter 7.

The Proxy Server

What if you don't have any address translation in place, can Border-Manager help protect your network? Absolutely, by using the Proxy Server. The Proxy Server is the most common example of firewall services familiar to Unix-based network managers. Three levels of security are available: packet filters, circuit-level proxies, and application-level proxies. One or all of these three options can be used to authenticate outsiders trying to gain access. Packets in response to an internal client, such as a Web page for an internal browser application, are authenticated as proper response packets and allowed through the proxy. Packets that don't fit that profile can be refused without concern.

Some commentators (including your humble narrator) have mentioned the apparent lack of concern Microsoft has shown for TCP/IP security problems. Putting TCP/IP in the operating system on millions of PCs destined for corporate desktops without any disclaimers or restrictions on TCP/IP server applications compromises security to an unacceptable degree. Microsoft is poorly serving users by not informing them of the potential dangers of connecting to the Internet without safeguards in place.

How much trouble is it to configure your IntranetWare clients to use the Proxy Server? Simply add the Proxy Server name and IP address in the appropriate configuration field in your Desktop browser, and you're finished. Once done, all requests will be relayed through the configured Proxy Server. Chapter 8 is where we cover the Proxy Server details.

Client Control

In Chapter 1, I mentioned that you can let your users get to some parts of the Internet and keep them out of other areas. I also said that monitoring employees as they work is standard business practice. Every client going through the IPX/IP Gateway, the IP/IP Gateway, or the Proxy Server, can be monitored and controlled. That should include every client in your network, if you wish to configure your network to control non-NetWare clients as well. We'll cover the improvements in client software in Chapter 5 and client configurations for various security measures in the appropriate chapters.

Encryption

As explained in Chapter 1, encryption now makes it possible to send private packets between two sites on the Internet. While the debate with the government concerning the level of encryption companies are allowed to include within their products rages on, VPNs require just enough encryption to thwart casually prying eyes.

A few high-priced routers add this capability, but are limited by communicating only with the same brand of router on the other side. This means you are severely limited in product choice and must replace your existing routers.

IntranetWare's VPN service solves these problems by using encryption at the IntranetWare server rather than the router. Your existing router will work perfectly well, and both IP and IPX packets can be routed across the Internet when enclosed in the encrypted packets.

Tunneling is the process used, and provides both a secure link and easy management. PPTP (Point-to-Point Tunneling Protocol) offers a way to connect geographically dispersed networks using the Internet for connection. The encryption included within Novell's VPN software makes the link trustworthy. This security extends to single users accessing the system while traveling. The leading encryption standards, such as IP SEC, are used for virtual networks and electronic commerce.

Multiple LANs can be connected via IntranetWare VPN services. Will your users be inconvenienced? Not at all. Your users, who don't care what trouble you must go to in providing their network access, will be able to use remote network resources without learning anything new. They merely use NDS to locate network resources, just as they do today. The fact that a document is located six states away will never become an issue.

Managing multiple VPNs and remote sites can be bothersome when keeping track of the encryption keys used. The IntranetWare VPN technology uses a master/slave relationship to simplify key management. More details on this later, but believe me, this management option is better than most. Just like in the real world, keeping track of keys can be a problem. IntranetWare VPN services goes a long way toward making VPN management painless.

Authentication

NDS is tied into all parts of your IntranetWare network. Is it secure across virtual networks? Certainly, because NDS controls both ends of the network connection, and authenticates each and every resource request from each and every client. Again, traveling users are supported by the same rigorous security controls when dialing in remotely as they are when connected directly to your intranet.

Security has always been a strong point in NetWare networks. The features added by BorderManager increase, rather than decrease, the security level in IntranetWare.

Performance to Please Users

Security is a wonderful thing in a network, but let's face it, your users don't care about security. They equate security with passwords they can't remember, and probably even complain about having a minimum password length for their NDS sign-on.

Performance is a different story: Everyone wants more. Talk about cars or computers, but speed is the key ingredient to happiness. No matter how fast your network is, people complain. No matter how large a pipe you have to the Internet, people complain.

Delays Impact Productivity

One might say (correctly) that some people complain about something all the time. While this is true, performance of the network and Web access does impact the productivity of your staff. Texas Instruments did research in the early 1980s and found that a screen-update delay longer than half a second gave the user time to start wandering in thought. Once the user got tired of waiting for the screen to update and started daydreaming, the time required to pull the user back to work piled up quickly.

You know this already, of course, since your bosses and users always complain about network performance. In fact, you yourself get bored waiting for NWAdmin to start or programs to load. We all want our computers to run faster and jump higher.

Proxy Server Caching

Your task to improve Web performance crashes into your lack of high-speed WAN connections. Even if you have a full T1 running at 1.544Mbps, your internal network probably runs at least six times faster, at 10Mbps. There's no way you can make the Web seem fast facing this bottleneck, even discounting the traffic problems of the Internet. Congestion will reduce your 1.544Mbps throughput down to that of a fast modem, and all you can do is grind your teeth.

That was the past; the future is now here. BorderManager applies Novell's award-winning cache software to the Web, through the Proxy Cache Server. Applying the same file-caching intelligence used at the NetWare server to the Web delivers up to ten times the performance of traditional Web connections.

Other proxy server caching services are based on the CERN caching guidelines. While the CERN folks are the originators of the Web protocols, they are still using first-generation caching technology. The Proxy Cache Server is based on the next-generation Harvest/Squid cache research, developed to maximize performance in an open standards environment.

CERN (Conseil European pour la Recherche Nucleaire) is a Geneva-based research center for advanced physics research. CERN researchers developed the protocols for the World Wide Web.

The IntranetWare Proxy Cache Server supports HTTP versions 1.0 and 1.1, FTP, and Gopher protocols. HTTP 1.0 handles all the Web page interaction, and is notorious for requiring multiple requests across the Internet to retrieve a single page. HTTP version 1.1 addresses these issues, but is not yet generally available. By using the Proxy Server, users make their repeated load requests to a local server (the caching server) across your local network at local speeds.

Files are transferred from Web servers with FTP as the underlying protocol in most cases. The Proxy Cache Server increases the performance of FTP, as well as the Gopher search and directory listings. When files are transferred using HTTP, the pre-fetching of full pages and related links speeds local performance even more. Many companies rely on the same few Web pages or network resources for most of their information. By caching those requested pages on the Proxy Server, performance jumps for each local network client.

BorderManager and Business Models

What do we mean by "business models"? Are these the young and gorgeous men and women sitting at desks in the office supply catalogs?

Yes, but here we're talking about ways to model your business communications around your business needs, not abnormally attractive people in pictures. BorderManager provides ways for you to mold your network to your business, rather than restrict your business to the limited capabilities of your network.

Everyone wants the tools they use to increase their performance by making tasks quicker, or enable them to perform tasks they couldn't perform without the tools. IntranetWare BorderManager fulfills both these goals.

We've discussed ways that IntranetWare and BorderManager will help your business by increased security and performance. VPNs allow your company to rely on the Internet as an inexpensive, but secure, means of communicating with remote offices all over the world.

Can a combination of VPN and security create an extranet? Absolutely. Allowing another company to communicate directly with your network, and you with theirs, often provides outstanding improvements in your business relationship. While you can already send e-mail simply and easily to anyone on the Internet, seeing their files, servers, documents, and databases takes the next step in cooperative business relationships.

Does security apply? Yes. You can control exactly how much of your network the outsiders can see, and vice versa. The Proxy Server packet, circuit, and application filters work perfectly well with extranets. NDS will be in charge of your network guests, and controls their actions depending on your security configuration.

A study done in 1996 by the publisher of *Information Week*, *Communications Week*, and *Network Computing* showed that nearly three-quarters of all companies hoped to allow customers access to some, but not all, network resources by the end of 1997. These figures may actually be conservative; companies have found that better communications between suppliers and customers help maintain profit margin, customer loyalty, and improve efficiency.

VPN technology helps with another critical concern of business today: the traveling user. PPTP allows a remote user to communicate with the company intranet using the Internet as the connecting network. Connections are available through many ISPs in the country, or directly to the servers over the long-distance network. Either way, the remote user becomes another node on the network, and has all the access privileges allowed by NDS.

NDS—Your Continuing Control Center

You may be thinking that NDS is the critical component in all of the IntranetWare BorderManager offerings. You are correct.

Centralized administration tools power BorderManager, and all rely on the security and authentication features of NDS. Your NWAdmin graphical administration utility grows more and more powerful with each passing update. All BorderManager controls appear within NWAdmin, providing you one dashboard for driving your network into the future (sorry, marketing speak crept in when I turned my head).

Silly as it may seem, the intent of NWAdmin is exactly as stated in the last paragraph. Everything runs through NDS, and NDS is controlled by NWAdmin.

You need to update your clients to take advantage of BorderManager features, don't you? Set that up using the Automatic Client Upgrade facility. Do you want to group users for Internet and intranet access profiles? Use NWAdmin. How do you check security for individuals? Use NWAdmin. Can you control outsider access to your network? Yes, with NWAdmin.

All IntranetWare BorderManager servers share a single set of access control rules from NDS. These rules then spread across all BorderManager servers active on the network, guaranteeing that users won't have escape hatches available (we'll talk more about how NDS handles client control in Chapter 5).

Unlike domain-based security systems (read Windows NT), a distributed and comprehensive directory service such as NDS controls the entire network from a single administrative console. And that console is NWAdmin, so get used to playing with browser windows and properties.

What New Network Plumbing Do You Need for Your Intranet?

Is this a trick question? After all, didn't I say in Chapter 1 that an intranet was just a LAN with good PR? And doesn't a LAN presume infrastructure?

Yes, but there's a bit more to it than that. Your LAN was cobbled together over the last decade or more, and many administrators before you made poor decisions (and yes, your successors will complain about your poor decisions, too—there are parts of your network you never show the new executives during their Data Group inspections, aren't there?).

You have a good chance to make some improvements in your network during the installation of IntranetWare and BorderManager. Many new pieces of your basic network should be upgraded at least every three years, and adding BorderManager is a handy lever to use to pry some extra consideration from your boss's budget. Let's take a look at the places you should have upgraded two years ago, just in case you do get the money you need.

Do You Need Cabling?

No, this isn't a trick question either. Yes, IntranetWare and BorderManager will run over any existing NetWare system cabling. Novell has always supported a wide variety of network interface cards running over a variety of cable types.

That said, however, realize that your intranet (and extranet) will demand more from your cabling than basic file and print services. Part of the beauty of using Web technologies within the company walls is audio, video conferencing, streaming video playback across the network, and high-speed connections to internal Web servers.

This means your cable plant may need to be upgraded as part of your IntranetWare and BorderManager installation. Do you have any network cabling system in place other than Ethernet or Token Ring? Replace it, no matter what it is.

When you replace your old ARCnet, you will be forced to upgrade the network interface card in each machine. You may even have the need to upgrade (excuse me, replace) the machine itself. After all, a PC equipped with an ARCnet connection has likely been in place for more years than you want to admit.

Take a look at your remaining Ethernet and Token Ring physical cables. Are any of the Ethernet segments still coaxial cable (coax)? It's time to dump them. Coax doesn't support the bandwidth necessary for some of the new goodies your boss will want on the company intranet. Besides, thin coax BNC connectors get brittle with age, and they are a constant source of network errors. Dump that cable now.

You Token Ring fans aren't off the hook, either. Shielded twisted-pair (STP) cabling belongs on the Death Star with Darth Vader, not on your new network. The problem comes when dealing with the VP who originally followed the IBM specifications to the letter, budget buster or not. If that VP is still in your company, you'll have some trouble updating your network cabling.

The trick in this case is to use the VP's desire for more IBM systems to bolster, not hinder, your case. Doesn't IBM offer new hubs for unshielded twisted-pair (UTP)? Essentially, the new network cabling looks like 10Base-T Ethernet, no matter what signals are actually carried across the wires. Use the new IBM literature to start the VP's technological ego racing to keep up with desktop ATM and the like. You don't have to tell the VP that desktop ATM is probably a dead issue until after you get your new cabling installed.

And what, you ask, is the cabling of choice? UTP labeled Category 5. This is two grades above the cabling quality needed for telephone connections, because data signals require much cleaner connections than analog telephone calls. Cat 5 cable, as it is often called, is rated for 100Mbps transmission rates for 330 feet (technically, 100 meters) from each powered device.

If your company is large, you may have a telecommunications department, or people within the MIS group responsible for all telephone technology questions. Work with this group to get your cabling upgrade approved. While old-fashioned analog telephone calls don't require Cat 5 cable, they run perfectly well over the higher-quality connection. New digital telephone systems do require better cabling, and Cat 5 is the high watermark for UTP wiring.

Let's put things as starkly as possible: If your network doesn't run across UTP Cat 5 cabling with four pairs of wires to each location, you will be forced to upgrade soon. Put it in your budget now.

> Not to be a troublemaker here, but you and the telecom folks should work together on cabling issues. Telephone systems and computer networks have more in common today than at any time in history, and the network merge trend is continuing. By the year 2000, you won't be able to tell a new computer system from a new telephone system by the wiring, management, or optional connections.

Should You Replace Your Servers?

Now that I've just told you the cabling you use every day is probably not good enough, you're really worried about what I'll say about your network servers. Relax, it's not so bad. In many cases, the servers you have now will work fine for IntranetWare, your intranet, and BorderManager. Not every time, but most times.

Java and MPR Considerations

There are two cases where a stronger server is needed. First, any new Java applications running on the server will suck CPU cycles big time. Just as you used a beefier server in the past when running Btrieve database applications, you should take the same approach with Java applets. Yes, I know that Novell and Microsoft both promise great performance even in Java's "interpreted execution space." And you can believe that just like you believe the last batch of politicians really did streamline government and lower our taxes.

The second concern is for machines running the MPR (Multi-Protocol Router) software along with internal communications boards. Any communications board in a server generates millions (literally) of processor interrupts during connection sessions. Those processor interrupts slow file and printing support response, as you might expect. It's a lot to ask for an already overloaded server to add any new jobs at all, much less one of these two applications.

Gateway Use

You may need more power for external routers, but how about for internal gateways? There isn't much server load from the IPX/IP Gateway, because Novell engineers take care of that translation fairly far down into the operating system kernel. Novell people can do that, of course, since they know the engine so well. But my testing has shown that even third-party gateway software runs fairly well. None of the NetWare-based gateways seem to add much of a load to the server, at least not with moderate gateway traffic.

Web Server Requirements

What about the requirements of the Web server software—are they excessive? Not at all. For Web servers on the Internet, the transmission delay will be so great that your server delay will never be seen, unless you have your server processing thousands of application lines for each Web page. After all, if your server is a bit slow, but the client is at the end of a 28.8Kbps modem, how will that user know?

Excessive loading can overwhelm a server, no matter how slow the connection speed. You may ask how we can overload a server through a slow link, which is a good question, but I'm working to illustrate a point here, not cover reality in all the gory detail. Servers taking thousands of Web client hits per day should be watched carefully, and upgraded when the load becomes too great.

Local Web server applications are a different matter. Instead of a maximum throughput of 1.544Mbps to a remote site, your LAN may pump between 10Mbps to 100Mbps for the fast Ethernet technologies. In these cases, an underpowered server will certainly be noticed, even before you have scores of concurrent active sessions. Graphic Web pages take time to download, even over a local network. Local customers will complain, because they will expect instantaneous response.

While you have no doubt improved the performance of your disk channel as you upgrade servers, the Web server software will put even more load on the disk channel. Active Web clients will put more load on the server than a word processor occasionally saving or reading files. You should regard your Web servers as database servers, and configure them appropriately.

Does the Client Software Change?

Your NetWare 4.11 client software must change in one way or another, no matter whether you use an internal or external option to connect those clients to TCP/IP hosts. If you add a full TCP/IP protocol suite to each station, that's a tremendous change. If you use Novell's IPX/IP Gateway from IntranetWare, the Client32 upgrade will include the client components necessary to communicate to the gateway and on to TCP/IP hosts. Even if you use a third-party IPX-to-TCP/IP gateway, special client software is required.

Client32 will be covered in some detail a bit later (in Chapter 5), but be prepared. You must upgrade, no matter how paranoid you or your boss are about client upgrades in general. Not only must you upgrade your client to include the ability to communicate with TCP/IP hosts, but you add extra management and monitoring capabilities with the newer software.

Versions of Client32 are available for Windows 3.1, 95, or NT. Believe it or not, even your DOS workstations are covered, using the Windows 3.1 software that loads before Windows starts. Your machine's memory profile is lowered in most cases, and performance doesn't suffer terribly. Some features, such as the improved host auto-reconnect, will make your network users happy. And that, ladies and gentlemen, is always a good thing to do.

Wrap

Before long, the idea of separate BorderManager services will become passé, as everyone automatically assumes these features are available in a quality operating system environment. Novell may well fold Border-Manager into the base IntranetWare operating system, but I doubt it. My guess is that Novell will continue to split the NetWare and Intranet-Ware product lines, based on client networks and their needs. After all, if you don't need Internet connections, why buy the connections services for all your networks?

Using BorderManager will appear as a new world for many of you experienced NetWare administrators. My goal remains to build upon your existing NetWare knowledge while explaining and detailing the new functions available to you and your network. Hang on, because the new world starts in the next chapter.

CHAPTER

3

TCP/IP and NetWare/IP

etWare/IP is the name for what many considered a Net-Ware abomination: complete communication between NetWare client and NetWare server using the TCP/IP protocol suite rather than IPX/SPX. So tightly was NetWare bound to its own protocol, IPX/SPX, that even the idea of running client-to-server communications over TCP/IP was considered heretical by many Novell supporters.

This being the modern world, however, what was once heretical is now touted on the feature list. Such is the fate of NetWare/IP. Novell proudly announces that your network, should you decide to configure it, can run completely without IPX/SPX. Rumors are that IntranetWare II (or whatever they call it) will set the default to IP rather than IPX, but no one has said that on the record.

Part of this trend is marketing, of course, since TCP/IP is the latest over-night success, fueled by the explosive growth of the Internet. Anything involving TCP/IP is considered better than anything involving a non-TCP/IP protocol suite. This forces designers working on new-generation net-working, such as ATM (Asynchronous Transfer Mode) and Gigabit Ethernet, to design around the limitations of TCP/IP. Developing a new protocol, or modifying TCP/IP to fit the faster transport capabilities of the new network hardware, would be considered proprietary, unusable, and hostile to the installed base. So TCP/IP continues on, even within your local NetWare network.

TCP/IP not only continues, it will grow and connect more devices, both local and remote, until non-TCP/IP protocols become a minor frac-tion of the market. Is this good? It's rarely good for any one technology to dominate and close the door on improved competitors. Is there anything you or I can do about it? Not a thing. Learn to make your peace with TCP/IP soon, or change careers. In fact, if you must choose, know TCP/IP better than you know DOS. This chapter will help you get a start toward that goal. We'll go over some background, and then get to the specifics of TCP/IP server installation and configuration, which is required for NetWare/IP. Finally, we'll go through the NetWare/IP installation and configuration procedures. But be sure to read the "NetWare/IP Warning" section before you follow those instructions.

IPX, TCP/IP, and NetWare/IP: History and Overview

How did we get to this point, where IPX is shunned in favor of TCP/IP, even within local networks? We discussed the growth of the Internet, fueled by TCP/IP, but that doesn't explain why local NetWare networks have the option to run TCP/IP between NetWare clients and NetWare servers. Place the blame on a few large (well, huge) NetWare customers demanding that Novell help them reduce the number of protocols across their WAN.

The story told around computer conference campfires is that one huge auto manufacturer paid an outsourcing company to run its WAN. This company paid by the protocol: $500,000 per year per supported WAN protocol. Mainframes demanded SNA, engineering and control systems demanded TCP/IP, and NetWare demanded IPX/SPX. Who do you think the company tagged as the easiest vendor to persuade to change its protocols? That's right, Novell.

Of course, Novell could see the growing importance of TCP/IP in the PC networking business as well. By the time this protocol push began, NetWare had already been ported to run over Unix hosts and communicate with NFS (Network File System) clients and servers. Novell developers knew that TCP/IP would play a larger and larger part in their future, even before Microsoft tried to claim the high road for including a TCP/IP transport layer option back in Windows for Workgroups.

The Birth of NetWare/IP

Novell became a player in the TCP/IP business when it purchased Excelan in 1989. LAN WorkPlace, a client-based TCP/IP protocol suite for PCs, was one of the biggest benefits of that purchase. TCP/IP fans who criticize Novell for ignoring TCP/IP tend to overlook the fact that Novell, at one time, had the leading market share for client TCP/IP software.

The combination of marketplace and technical forces forged NetWare/IP. Today, your NetWare network can run almost every piece of software written for IPX/SPX over the NetWare/IP protocol suite. The exceptions are a few network management packages that require NetBIOS broadcasts for node discovery. This small limitation should not hinder your network management at all, since few NetWare networks depend on, or use, NetBIOS.

Novell engineers faced a tough task when undertaking NetWare/IP development. While "modular programming" is all the rage today, back in 1981, NetWare developers were limited by available protocols (TCP/IP wasn't ready yet, so Novell based IPX on Xerox's XNS, or Xerox Network Services) and the constraints of running within DOS on a primordial IBM PC. Modular programming's benefits notwithstanding, packing functionality into the client software using Assembler was necessary. Niceties went out the window to shrink the client footprint as small as possible.

Cramming functions into the client software meant IPX was woven tightly into all the functions of NCP (NetWare Core Protocol). It was difficult to tell which was a protocol and which was an operating system command. It was so restricted at the beginning that each interface card type had its own client software. Layered protocols for network interfaces? They didn't exist in the early 1980s.

Novell made the big move away from Assembler, finally, in 1989 when NetWare 3.0 was rewritten in the C programming language. Only the parts dealing with the server hardware remained in Assembler for speed. Only when NetWare 3.11 was released did the initial promises for TCP/IP support at the server become a reality. No client software touched the TCP/IP protocol stack until NetWare/IP was released, which was after NetWare 3.11 was on the market for a bit.

Broadcasts versus Configuration

Most problems in the world of computing (and the real world as well) have multiple and roughly equivalent solutions. Preferences between the solutions are a matter of personal taste in many situations. Need to get to work sooner, but keep getting stuck in traffic? There are two quick choices: leave earlier or take a different route. If you hate getting up early, you'll look for another route. If you hate driving farther to reach the same place, you'll set the alarm clock back just a bit, hoping to beat the traffic. So, too, do IPX and TCP/IP differ significantly in their approach to receiving network information.

IPX's Broadcast Query-and-Response System

IPX, built for a local network with essentially unlimited bandwidth (8-bit Ethernet cards in an 8MHz IBM PC would never fill a 10Mbps network) utilizes a broadcast query-and-response system. When a client wants to know which servers are available, it sends a packet addressed to every station listening, asking for the servers to identify themselves. To help stations keep current information, NetWare servers broadcast their names, addresses, and some other details every 60 seconds.

Are these a lot of broadcasts? No, not at all, when you check their percentage of available bandwidth used. An Ethernet network can support a maximum of 10Mbps, and these packets are infrequent and usually hold less than 1000 bits. The percentage of bandwidth used is too small for many calculators to display.

The primary advantage of the broadcast query-and-response method is ease of configuration. Network identification numbers are tracked by the NetWare network segment number, which is set at the server, and the default address on the network interface card. Ethernet, the most popular network card, uses a unique address indelibly linked to each individual card. When placing a new Ethernet node on a NetWare network, the identifying numbers are set automatically, and the card is guaranteed not to conflict with other cards. When started, the client software will broadcast queries to discover which server can accept the login packets and get the user up and running.

TCP/IP's Configuration File System

TCP/IP, if you remember, was not designed with the luxury of a high-bandwidth and a reliable network transport layer. The military specified that TCP/IP must work over radio links, telephone lines, and satellite connections, along with a local Ethernet network. Part of the design goal was to make TCP/IP workable across pretty crummy conditions, and the designers succeeded. TCP/IP performs relatively well across low bandwidth and noisy connections, which is why this protocol suite became the foundation of the fledgling Internet.

Now, if your network nodes can't find any network resources without receiving answers back from broadcasts, new nodes may be out of luck if a lousy connection drops the broadcast query packets. One thousand bits of query packet takes much more of a 9600bps network connection than it does over 10Mbps. Obviously, some other method of identifying nodes and network resources was necessary.

Thus appeared the configuration file for each TCP/IP client. By listing the server's address, along with that of the default router, the station can find the resources necessary to start working. The station's IP address is listed in the configuration file as well, so the client doesn't undergo an identity crisis.

Here we have a fundamental difference between NetWare's IPX/SPX and TCP/IP: preconfigured network information versus broadcasted queries. In many ways, these are completely opposite approaches to the same problem.

Which Is Better?

Hard feelings abound, but mostly the TCP/IP camp believes the IPX/SPX camp to be unworthy. The IPX camp counters by listing the lower management overhead of IPX, especially concerning IP address management.

Is either side "right?" No, not really; they're just two solutions to a similar problem. Which one is better depends on what traits your network shows and your personal preferences. Few IPX folks can convince TCP/IP fans to change their minds, and the reverse is true as well.

Of course, the market is changing the minds of the IPX fans, or at least their network protocols. This doesn't mean that TCP/IP is better—just more popular.

DSS Levels the Differences

Novell engineers faced a hard question: How best to replace the SAP (Service Advertising Protocol) method of broadcast queries and responses that provided network information to clients and servers alike? Without certain pieces of network information, the client couldn't even log in. And the problem wasn't restricted to clients, because all types of servers and software applications relied on the traditional broadcast-and-response technology.

The answer came in the guise of another server function, called the DSS, for Domain SAP Server. No, this has nothing to do with distilling Maple tree ooze into pancake syrup. It does have everything to do with special software to answer client software queries that were once broadcast, but now are sent to a particular server. Each client has the IP address of its local DSS configured in the client software.

The *Domain* in the SAP Server means something similar to a TCP/IP domain, but not exactly the same. The names of the SAP and IP domains must be slightly different, and the DSS can't have subdomains. (No application software will fail because of your DSS coverage area, however.) You also need to set a separate network address for the NetWare/IP virtual network segment, but the system will supply that during installation.

Don't confuse DSS with DNS, the Domain Name Service. Used by TCP/IP to help locate nodes across a hierarchical network, a DNS server of some type is still required for NetWare/IP to function. After all, your DSS can't help much if your clients can't find it.

One or more NetWare servers running DSS may be configured as "gateways" back to the world of IPX. Assuming your network won't completely convert from IPX to NetWare/IP in one day, Novell created a gateway function so that all network resources, regardless of transport protocols used, can be visible from all segments of the network. In other words, your IPX clients can still see and use network resources even in the NetWare/IP domain, and vice versa. Many companies use NetWare/IP for only a portion of their network, and this translation gateway is valuable to keep the company network from fragmenting into two separate and unfriendly pieces.

Your NetWare/IP Warning

If you can avoid using NetWare/IP, do so.

Before you start, let me remind you of one important detail: You don't need NetWare/IP in order to take advantage of any other NetWare systems. NetWare/IP doesn't automatically make it easier to connect to the Internet or an intranet server. NetWare/IP doesn't improve management or security. Worst of all, NetWare/IP takes more station resources, slows down communications, and requires extra management of clients and servers.

If you can avoid using NetWare/IP, you will be a happier administrator. Not only will you avoid a painful installation fraught with disaster at every turn, you will also avoid plunging into more TCP/IP details than you ever imagined existed.

Do you read the trade magazine articles talking about the horrors of IP addressing? I hope so, because I've written some of them. With NetWare/IP, you need to worry about IP addressing problems with NetWare. If you can, back up and check your other options before installing NetWare/IP.

You can easily support TCP/IP on the NetWare server without running NetWare/IP. In fact, you can run the Web server software on your NetWare server without installing NetWare/IP. None of the BorderManager features demands that NetWare/IP be loaded and running.

Is this clear enough? Stay away from NetWare/IP if you can. Only if you have a real need for Novell's TCP/IP software suite for your server-to-client communications (such as a corporate mandate to use TCP/IP everywhere) should you continue.

Novell has hinted that "native" IP will be part of the Moab product, which should be IntranetWare II. It could well be that the only changes are for the installation program to default to NetWare/IP rather than IPX, which isn't much of a change. It could well be that the complete philosophy of NetWare's network transport protocol will change, and the DSS, DNS Server, and DHCP (Dynamic Host Configuration Protocol) will become discrete parts of the IntranetWare server operating system.

If that happens, many of my reasons for suggesting that you avoid NetWare/IP will be eliminated. If that doesn't happen, I may still be recommending you use IPX/SPX for all local network communication, and the IPX/IP Gateway for connecting to TCP/IP-based resources, both inside your company and on the Internet.

Brand new networks, of course, don't have the upgrade headaches associated with existing networks. If your company is installing a completely new set of servers and client computers, my recommendation against NetWare/IP should be moderated considerably. You will still have a network that is slightly slower and more resource-intensive than native IPX, but since each new client station is installing the software from scratch, life won't be appreciably more difficult for you, the installer.

You will discover that Novell's original method of using IPX/SPX for network communications was an excellent choice. IPX is faster than TCP/IP in a local setting, takes fewer client resources, requires less server involvement in client control and network configuration, and requires no client addressing overhead for the installation team. So why is Novell dumping IPX for TCP/IP? What is the problem with IPX? The problem is that IPX is not TCP/IP. Marketing forces, not technical reasons, have shifted the world toward TCP/IP, and we, meaning Novell users and supporters, must go with the flow.

TCP/IP Server Installation and Configuration

Unlike NetWare/IP, NetWare TCP/IP support at the server is critically important to all that follows in this book. I put this section here, because you must enable TCP/IP at the server before you install NetWare/IP. If you can just install TCP/IP on the server and skip the NetWare/IP part, you'll be better off. But I've whacked that deceased stallion enough, so let's go forward with the TCP/IP server support software.

TCP/IP must be installed, configured, and running on your NetWare server before beginning the NetWare/IP installation sequence. Yes, the installation routine allows you to install TCP/IP on the server during the NetWare/IP installation, but it won't work properly. I don't know exactly why it doesn't work, but I have a feeling that some server software must be running before you can effectively configure some other server software. Regardless, we must proceed in two separate steps, so let's start with the TCP/IP server software.

Of course, you may have loaded TCP/IP during server setup, since NetWare gives you that option. If not, you may believe you should head to the INSTALL program, which runs on the server console, or use the remote version under DOS, called RCONSOLE. You may do that if you wish, but you won't find an option for TCP/IP installation in the INSTALL utility. NetWare is now so TCP/IP-friendly that the server software loads during installation and waits to be activated.

I'm not going to cover every basic detail for installing and configuring a network board here. Why not? If you're interested in BorderManager, you aren't a beginning administrator, so you don't need all the basics. If you are a beginning administrator, pick up my book, *The Complete Guide to NetWare 4.11/IntranetWare*, at the same place you bought this book. Inside those 1500+ pages, you'll get all the gory details to every menu choice in the NetWare INETCFG program (and all the other utility programs).

Activating TCP/IP

You can activate TCP/IP through NetWare's Internetworking Configuration utility, INETCFG. From the server console or remote connection, type **LOAD INETCFG** to get started.

You will notice the screen display's low resolution is matched by the lack of color control. Welcome to the C-Worthy interface, a blight on computer networking administration. I halfway believe that many reviewers rate Windows NT server so highly just because they're so relieved they don't need to deal with the C-Worthy interface as they do on NetWare servers. No matter what, this DOS-style interface was an embarrassment a decade ago.

Enough complaining (as if you were the one complaining)—let's get to work. If INETCFG hasn't been used before, you will get an odd message asking if you wish to move all your server protocol details from the AUTOEXEC.NCF file to INITSYS.NCF and NETINFO.CFG. These files are stored in the SYS:\ETC directory, rather than in the SYS:\SYSTEM directory, as is the AUTOEXEC.NCF file. Why put them in a different place? My guess is that NetWare engineers are trying to stay consistent with Unix file layout conventions, where stuff like this is put in the /etc directory most of the time.

If the /etc looks like a mistake, and you think I meant \ETC, then you need to pick up a Unix primer before delving too deeply into the Internet. The editor and I pay close attention to slashes, backslashes, and the differences between Unix and DOS-based file systems. That doesn't mean we won't make a mistake sometime, but we triple-check these areas. Chances are, if you think something is written incorrectly, that something has a Unix root, and you're behind the learning curve on Unix file-naming conventions.

Do you have any choice about moving the file contents to these new files? No. I don't know why Novell engineers pretend to give you a choice, because you have none. Accept the new files and continue.

Opening Menu Options

Here's the opening menu for INETCFG:

Since this menu is your internetworking portal, you should know what the options do:

- **Boards:** Adds a new network interface card (hardware) or modifies parameters of existing boards.

- **Network Interfaces:** Configures WAN (wide-area network) boards, if there are any in your server. Used by the MPR (Multi-Protocol Router) most often, and not used for LAN boards at all.

- **WAN Call Directory:** Presents connection information for remote site links. This information is media-specific.

- **Backup Call Associations:** Provides a backup calling information database linked to the WAN Call Directory, in case a primary connection method fails.

- **Protocols:** Allows you to enable, configure, or modify protocols used by network interface cards installed in the server.

- **Bindings:** Associates a configured protocol to an installed network interface.

- **Manage Configuration:** Allows you to configure network parameters (including SNMP), export and import copies of the configuration, enable remote access to the server (including setting the password), and edit the AUTOEXEC.NCF file.

- **View Configuration:** Lets you view, but not edit, the existing configuration details.

- **Reinitialize System:** New with NetWare 4.11, this menu option unloads then reloads the configuration, implementing any changes.

- **Go To Fast Setup:** Another option that is new with NetWare 4.11, this setup choice offers a simplified set of menus for common configurations.

A Configuration File Warning

After loading INETCFG for the first time, avoid manually changing protocols by editing the configuration files directly. In other words, make all your changes through the INETCFG program, and don't ever touch these files:

- AURP.CFG

- TCPIP.CFG

- IPXSPX.CFG

- NLSP.CFG

- NETINFO.CFG

- INITSYS.NCF

Mess with these at your own risk. The last file is new with NetWare 4.11, but the other files may have escaped your notice when working with earlier NetWare versions. If you touch these files, prepare to spend hours of overtime fixing or reconfiguring your network.

Enabling TCP/IP

While the Fast Setup option is handy and quick, let's be old-fashioned and enable TCP/IP manually. After all, you must know as many details as possible, and Fast Setup hides most of those details from you.

Assuming you're using an existing board that already supports IPX/SPX for TCP/IP protocols, choose the Protocols menu option in INETCFG. (If you're planning on configuring TCP/IP when you install NetWare for the first time, you need this information during that initial installation phase.)

Next, choose TCP/IP on the Protocol Configuration menu to open the TCP/IP Protocol Configuration window. Unless your network is complex, you'll need to change only one field here and configure some DNS information.

Highlight the TCP/IP Status field and press Enter to pop up your two choices, then pick Enabled, as shown in Figure 3.1.

The default for IP Packet Forwarding is Enabled, and that's what you want in most cases. If you're using this server as the single Web server for your intranet, you could set this to Disabled, and no TCP/IP packets would go beyond the server. Aha, you say, a security option. Yes indeed,

FIGURE 3.1

TCP/IP Status has two choices, and you want Enabled.

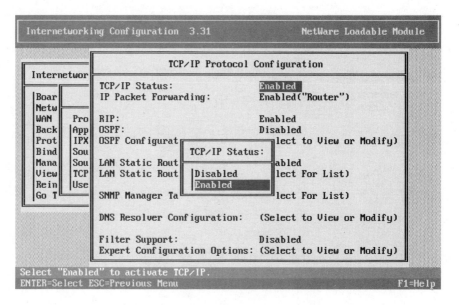

and stopping TCP/IP packets at certain points will become a cornerstone of BorderManager, as you'll see in Part 2 of this book.

Notice that we don't set the IP address here; that's done in the BIND statement later. Once the Enabled choice is set, you can move down to the DNS Resolver Configuration field.

Configuring Your DNS Server Address

What is a DNS Resolver, and why should you want to configure it? DNS works by replicating portions of a network hierarchical name database on multiple systems. Often, local systems know just enough to support their local clients and connect to an upstream name server. That's the ticket for us: local support, then refer other names to our ISP (Internet service provider) name server.

Do as the screen suggests, and select the field highlighted, DNS Resolver Configuration, to set your DNS information. As you can see in Figure 3.2, the window that opens allows you to set the domain name and three name servers. Your domain name may be anything you like, unless you're going to connect to someone else in the world. Once your network moves beyond an

---

FIGURE 3.2

My domain name, the NetWare server as name server, and my ISP's name server as backup

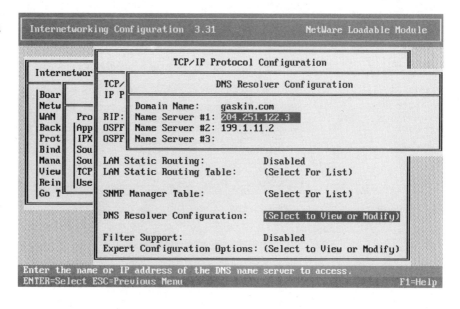

internal intranet, the domain name matters a great deal. In other words, get a registered domain name from your ISP, or put your ISP's domain name in this spot. This is easy to change if you're now waiting for domain name approval.

Nothing forces you to run a name server if your network is limited in scope. However, since name server software comes free within Intranet-Ware, you might want to look into running your own name server, particularly to support e-mail and your own Web servers. If you're running a strict intranet, you'll need a name server to avoid complications with e-mail and certain browser functions.

Your ISP should register your domain name as part of your network connection contract, or at least for a nominal fee. The name service registry charges $100 for the first two years, and $50 a year thereafter, so don't feel swindled when your ISP asks for at least $100 at the beginning of this process. Name service registry is becoming a political hot potato, so don't be surprised if the price drops, and you have more domain name options by next year.

In my case, as the caption for Figure 3.2 says, I have my own domain name, duly registered and paid for: gaskin.com. If you remember, I solicited your e-mail comments in the introduction via the address of james@gaskin.com.

The first IP address, 204.251.122.3, is of my test server, a Gateway2000 Pentium 120 named, coincidentally, GATEWAY2000. According to our process here, I have yet to assign that address to this server, but I will in the "Binding" section coming up. The lack of server IP address won't be a problem, because you'll get there and define one before you lock in the configuration.

The 199.1.11.2 is the IP address of the name server at my ISP, OnRamp Technologies, Inc. If the name server software on GATEWAY2000 isn't working, any DNS queries will be routed to OnRamp for resolution. My ISDN (Integrated Services Digital Network) connection is made through an Ascend Pipeline 50 dial-up router, which automatically dials OnRamp whenever an IP packet must leave my network.

Notice you could have a third name server listed. Most ISPs have at least two name servers themselves, as should you. Listing your two name servers and your ISP's primary name server should keep your DNS queries in good shape. If all these systems are down, you probably have more network problems than you can handle, and won't be reading this book during the crisis.

Now, back up by pressing the Escape key, and save the TCP/IP configuration if you wish. You can wait and save everything at once, but incremental saving helps the configuration proceed more smoothly. Don't worry about rebooting the server and resetting all these protocol configurations. We'll do that when we finish working inside INETCFG.

Binding TCP/IP to Your Network Interface

Now it's time to set the IP address for the TCP/IP server. From the INETCFG main menu, pick the Bindings choice, and the obtusely labeled window, Protocol to Network Interface/Group Bindings, appears. The *Group* part is new with IntranetWare, in case you're wondering.

Press the Insert key, and choose which protocol you wish to bind to a LAN interface—TCP/IP in this case. To NetWare, a *LAN interface* is both the physical board and the virtual boards supporting different frame types, so don't start thinking the network gremlins added some boards to your server box while you were sleeping. Pick the LAN interface you want to use, and press Enter. If you mess up, just don't save the choice later when the system asks if you want to update the TCP/IP configuration.

Another new touch is the ability to bind the chosen protocol to a single network interface, or each interface in a group. Group? Yes, a group of WAN interfaces. You can't bind a protocol to a group as well as an individual interface within that group, so make your decision before you start binding.

The network interface chosen can't be modified in this screen, so the cursor (of sorts) starts on the Local IP Address field. Enter the IP address for your server here. Figure 3.3 shows the screen, with the local IP address for my server already filled in, for the sake of illustration.

FIGURE 3.3

Setting the server
IP address

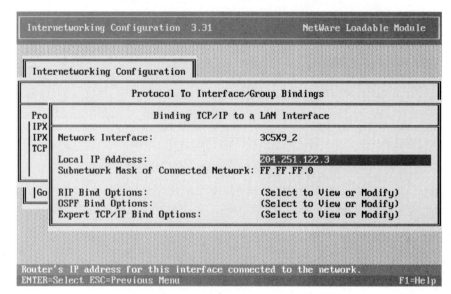

Novell, for some reason, insists on portraying the subnetwork mask in hexadecimal rather than decimal. The FF.FF.FF.0 listed in the Subnetwork Mask of Connected Network field in this window is the same as 255.255.255.0, so don't let that bother you. If you forget to fill in this bit of information, the system will put in that default subnet mask for you.

RIP Binding Options

Next on the list for binding TCP/IP is the RIP Bind Options field. You should be able to leave these options set at the defaults, but let's take a look anyway. Figure 3.4 shows the RIP Bind Options window, with the Status field set to Enabled, the default. The Network Interface field can't be changed from here (just as it can't be changed from the preceding window), and the Interface Group field once again refers to the WAN groups you can set up to handle remote network connections.

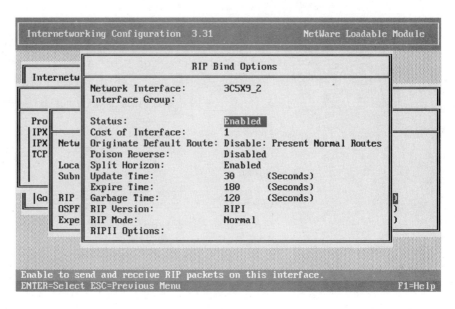

The other options may seem strange to you. What are these things? Let's discuss each, starting after the Status field.

- **Cost of Interface:** The range allowed is 1 to 15; the higher the number, the more the "cost." If you want to discourage using a line, such as a backup WAN connection, set a high number. When the primary line with a cost of 1 is down, then the cost of 15 for the backup will be tolerated.

- **Originate Default Route:** When enabled, RIP advertises only this interface as the default router for the network, and doesn't advertise any other routes. You will normally want to leave this disabled.

- **Poison Reverse:** An improvement to RIP helping to eliminate router loops by sending a packet in reverse through a route, indicating the route is to be avoided like poison.

- **Split Horizon:** A technique to reduce router loops by telling the router to ignore a route relying on the same port where the route information arrived. In other words, a router won't advertise network reachability to the router that just supplied that network information.

- **Update Time:** RIP routers send updates periodically, just as NetWare servers advertise their services every 60 seconds. The default update time is 30 seconds, giving 6 tries every 30 seconds, for a total of 180 seconds waiting time for a response before the route is listed as inactive. The maximum time is 10,992 seconds.

- **Expire Time:** Six times the Update Time number of seconds. The number is supplied automatically when the previous field is changed upwards, but not downwards.

- **Garbage Time:** Four times the Update Time number, so the default is 120. For the set time, a route will try to reappear after that route is down.

- **RIP Version:** In this new and improved world, you now have a choice for RIP I or RIP II, using subnetwork masks in the routing information. Of course, all routers must be RIP II to trade information if you set this to RIP II. You can set either RIP version, or both, using this field.

- **RIP Mode:** The choices are Normal, Receive Only, and Send Only. Obviously, Normal is the default, and will handle both RIP I and RIP II packets.

- **RIP II Options:** This is available only if RIP II is enabled separately or together with RIP I. It asks for authentication and password information to ensure that the router communicates only with other routers using the same authentication key.

OSPF Binding Options

Looking back at the Binding TCP/IP to a LAN Interface window (Figure 3.3), you might guess that the OSPF (Open Shortest Path First) Bind Options handle the same type of information as the RIP options. You are correct, although the different technology does add its own spin to the settings. You may set an ID for each area in your network, a separate priority, and authentication again for network communications between routers.

NAT Note

The last option on the Binding TCP/IP to a LAN Interface window, Expert TCP/IP Bind Options, adds two new twists. One option that you'll see when you choose this is Network Address Translation (NAT), which is brand new and performs a critical management and security function.

We'll go into plenty of depth in Chapter 7 about NAT, so don't get too involved yet. However, since this is so new, and right here where we are now, let's take a quick look at what is being offered.

I've mentioned several times that only registered and "legal" IP addresses are allowed on the Internet. If your network was configured strictly as an intranet, then the decision was made to connect to the Internet, you faced a huge renumbering project. Another addressing problem came when companies merged departments internally, or merged with other companies. Suddenly, two legitimate networks must somehow appear as one network. Other network administrators use a Class A address, 10.0.0.0, to make segmenting the network simple. That network address is reserved for just such an idea, but must be translated to a legitimate address when used on the Internet. NAT provides the solution.

You would think that as part of BorderManager, NAT would have a higher profile than this. After all, you can't even enable NAT until the fifth layer down in INETCFG. That doesn't look like a valuable technology, buried way down there, does it?

Yet NAT is extremely valuable for both management and security. Do you have address problems internally? Use NAT for all your outside communications, and your network address problems drop from mountain-sized to molehill. Do you want to keep outside hackers away from your TCP/IP-based internal network resources? Even the best firewalls spring leaks and leave internal targets exposed.

But what if your internal network numbers are completely different from the numbers seen by the world? How will anyone outside the company know what the addresses are? Once again, it's hard to attack what you can't see.

New twist number two is provided for networks supporting multicast IP packets. The Multicast Override IP Address window, which you can get to when you select Expert TCP/IP Bind Options, sets the default address (255.255.255.0) for broadcasts, or allows you to direct packets to a particular server. Although IP multicast is becoming more important, Novell recommends that you leave the Multicast Override IP Address field blank for now. As this technology becomes more available, and you have specific servers supporting multicast IP, this field will be ready and waiting.

Here we find treasure, buried deep within a cascading set of menus. One would think that the NAT technology would be mentioned on the main menu, but not on my version of the software.

Testing Your Server

Save your TCP/IP configuration by pressing Escape and accepting the offer to save the configuration. You may be tempted to use the Reinitialize System menu option in the INETCFG main menu, but I suggest you save everything, exit INETCFG, and down the server completely. After all, you changed multiple interface card settings, and there are plenty of places to derail your new, TCP/IP-enabled server. Booting is the safest way to go.

You should never change something before testing to see if your previous changes helped or hurt. Adding new protocols works exactly the same way. Watch all the console messages carefully while rebooting, to make sure the new protocols and bindings put things where they belong.

Now, since your system booted completely clean and wonderful, you think you're ready to leave and move on. Not so fast, buddy. Let's test this system before turning you loose in a new protocol.

Testing the Protocol Binding

The first test is that all the new protocols are bound properly. Just because you didn't notice any startup errors doesn't mean there weren't a few.

At the server console (local, or via RCONSOLE), move to the colon prompt, type **CONFIG,** and stand back.

The first block of information will give the server name and the internal NetWare IPX network information, listing a frame type of VIRTUAL_LAN. That's fine, but you're looking for the last block of information, with an LAN Protocol of IP. You may also have an LAN Protocol of ARP, and that's okay, too.

The IP address should be listed, as well as the subnet mask and the number of interfaces active with TCP/IP. If this information is not here, you may have a problem, Houston or no Houston.

PING Tests

After you've checked the configuration, go to a TCP/IP-enabled system connected to the same network segment your server is on, and start the PING program. Give the IP address of your server as the host address to ping, and see if you make contact. You should, but if you don't, verify that you are on the same network segment, and that there are no strange subnet masks to configure, instead of the default you used.

You can ping from the server, too, which is a fairly recent utility addition. At the server console, type **LOAD PING.** A screen showing just the New Target window, as in Figure 3.5, will appear. Type in the IP address of the IP device to ping. This should be a system close at hand, so you can verify that it is working properly. Pressing Enter then Escape will start the ping process, and display the results seen in Figure 3.5.

The top window in Figure 3.5 appears during the PING program. *Node* refers to the system you're pinging. The number of packets sent and received are listed next. For performance testing use, the next five headings describe times between when the packet was sent and when it was received back.

Listed first in Figure 3.5 is a local station, another Gateway2000 running Windows NT 4.0. The High time is almost always the first packet that takes a bit of time to be sent and for the target station to respond.

FIGURE 3.5

Ping and ping again

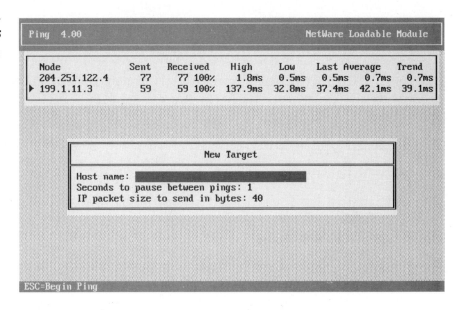

The Last and Average times are more important than the other times, unless the time range wanders quite a bit.

Listed second in Figure 3.5 is the mail server at my ISP, OnRamp Technologies. The High time includes the time required for the ISDN router, an Ascend Pipeline 50, to make connection to the network. Even with the long delay on the first packet, the average time seems respectable.

A DNS server is queried before the first packet is sent when you put a qualified domain name, rather than an IP address, in the Target field. In this test, I listed "mailhost.onramp.net" as the target, and the server queried the DNS name server for the IP address of the system, then listed that address in the top window rather than the name.

What does this test? My server can now send TCP/IP packets, receive those packets, and query the listed name server. Does that cover most of the concerns for a TCP/IP system on my network (and yours)? It's certainly a strong indication that all is well on this server, and that TCP/IP is up and running. You may have other problems appear, but you're on the right track.

NetWare/IP Installation

As someone fairly familiar with NetWare/IP, I can tell you I still can't install it correctly every time, no matter how simple the installation parameters for my network.

If you don't believe me, try following the Novell installation instructions. Go ahead, I'll wait here. Aha, the instructions don't work right, do they? You didn't get NetWare/IP installed properly, did you? I told you to skip NetWare/IP and avoid teeth gnashing and hair pulling.

You say it can't be avoided? Okay, if we must, let's dive into this NetWare/IP mess and get going. Well, it's not exactly a mess, but it can be difficult and frustrating, because TCP/IP networking is difficult and frustrating. What's the reason all the TCP/IP network administrators want the world to go TCP/IP? Misery loves company. You don't believe me? Wait until we're finished here, and tell me what you think.

I'm assuming you didn't install NetWare/IP during your initial server setup. If you did, you're probably still in the middle of the initial installation, pulling your hair out. The smart move is to install NetWare/IP later, as we're doing now.

Loading NetWare/IP Components

To begin, go to the server console (or RCONSOLE) and type **LOAD INSTALL**. Choose Product Options, then Choose an Item or Product Listed Above from the main INSTALL menu.

NetWare will ask for the path to the NetWare/IP installation files on your CD-ROM. Provide the proper storage directions to an internal CD on the server, or some other server and its mounted CD-ROM drive.

UNICON (UNIx CONsole) and NWIPCFG (NetWare /IP ConFiGuration) will be loaded by the program, along with a batch of NLMs that will zoom by. It won't hurt to have TCP/IP active on the server when you load the NetWare/IP components. Don't be surprised at the number of files being added to your system, because there are quite a few.

The "Lucky 13" Steps to a Successful NetWare/IP Installation

The first time I tried this, I trusted the installation routine when it offered to install NetWare TCP/IP for me—big mistake. If you want my advice, bounce out of the installation routine and follow the "Lucky 13" plan I have. If you want to be one tough network administrator, follow Novell's installation routine. If it works for you, congratulations. If not, feel free to follow the trail I've blazed through this jungle during several aggravating installations.

Here is the list of steps to a successful NetWare/IP installation and configuration:

1. Configure TCP/IP on the server.

2. Reboot to start TCP/IP on the server.

3. Configure the DNS server with appropriate TCP/IP addresses and host names.

4. Initialize the DNS master database.

5. Configure the DSS server.

6. Configure the NetWare/IP server.

7. Rename the NetWare/IP domain from the default (gaskin.com, for me) to add nwip (nwip.gaskin.com).

8. Reboot the server to activate the new settings.

9. Start the DNS server.

10. Start the DSS server.

11. Start the NetWare/IP server.

12. Install the client.

13. Communicate over TCP/IP.

TCP/IP must be loaded before starting NetWare/IP. Since installing and testing TCP/IP is critical to the success of NetWare/IP, I put these requirements at the top of the list. You know that TCP/IP is running, since you tested pings in and pings out in the last section. Your job begins at number 3 on the list of 13; you can start by configuring the DNS server software.

Your DNS Server Configuration

A DNS name server must be available for your NetWare network to utilize TCP/IP. NetWare/IP allows you to rely on an existing DNS server, if your network has one already. It matters not if the DNS server is running on a Unix host, Windows NT server, or even another NetWare server. As long as your NetWare server adding NetWare/IP can reach the name server over your TCP/IP network, your NetWare/IP server will function properly.

This brings you to a decision. Your NetWare server can be either a DNS client or a DNS server. Obviously, the setup and configuration are a bit different for the two options. Rather than flip a coin, I suggest you rely on an existing DNS server if possible. Why? Because it's up and running, and your existing TCP/IP network is happy and functional. This indicates that you should configure the NetWare/IP server as a DNS client first, then for a DNS server if necessary. However, we're not doing it the logical way, because little of NetWare/IP is as logical as the rest of NetWare.

Why must you configure the DNS server software first? So your DNS client configuration will be able to verify itself with the server. That's not the official word, but it's all I can figure out.

If you have an external DNS name server, it will already be up and running before you start. In that case, configure the DNS client information, and skip the DNS server setup. After all, you can't configure what you don't control, can you?

You'll see that you skip back and forth between the NWIPCFG and UNICON programs. The configuration functions seem almost randomly distributed between the two systems. Don't try to figure out the logic of what function is configured where, because you'll keep chasing your tail and falling down.

If you skipped out of Novell's installation routine, welcome back. I told you it was a problem.

First UNICON Shot

Go to the server console and type **LOAD UNICON**. If you aren't the regular network administrator, go get the password, because you'll need it. Although you can log in with a supervisor-equivalent name, I suggest installing system utilities as the Admin user to avoid any future inconsistencies about file ownership and rights. There are so many critical functions available through UNICON that this safety precaution is wise.

Figure 3.6 is a shot of the login screen for UNICON. The bottom status line is informational only, since none of this information down there can be changed from this screen.

The main UNICON menu will become familiar, believe me. We'll take a tour of the choices offered here in the next chapter, when we talk more

FIGURE 3.6

Proving yourself to UNICON

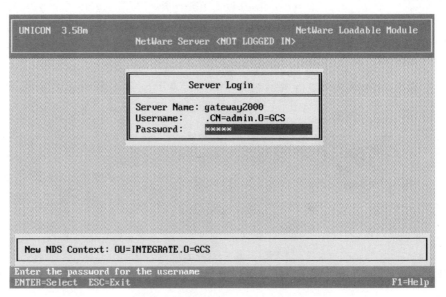

about DNS server setup. For now, you just need to take care of the necessities for NetWare/IP installation.

From the main menu, choose the Manage Services option. Pressing Insert pops open the Available Services window, with a highlight bar on the first listed service. Choosing one of the services that isn't running loads and starts the software if all configuration details are correct. You might notice that DSS is not on this list. This is because that software is managed through the NetWare/IP configuration file. Does that make sense to you? I didn't think so. But pick NetWare/IP anyway.

Services included with NetWare/IP are the DNS Server, DSS Server, NetWare/IP Server, NetWare-to-Unix Print Gateway, and the XConsole Server (vt100 terminal support to configure the NetWare server over TCP/IP). The NetWare/IP server depends on the DSS server and either a NetWare DNS name server or an external name server referenced in the configuration files.

Pick DNS Server. You'll see three more choices: Administer DNS, Initialize DNS Master Database, and Save DNS Master to Text Files. In Chapter 4, we'll look into the capabilities provided by the first choice. Now we're interested in Initialize DNS Master Database. Although well hidden, this is an important step. Until the database is configured with IP address and domain information and initialized, nothing works, particularly the NetWare/IP server. You are given a chance to configure DNS for specific subnetworks if you wish, and to replace existing databases with newer ones. Go ahead and select the Initialize the DNS Master Database option. Figure 3.7 shows the DNS name setup for my lab network.

What have you done? Configured and initialized the master DNS database, that's what. Now we can continue.

F I G U R E 3.7

My DNS database setup

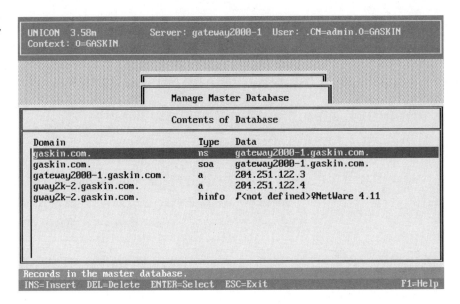

Your DSS Configuration

You might think you should exit UNICON and typing LOAD NWIPCFG at the server console prompt to configure the NetWare/IP server, but you would be wrong. I learned the hard way. From UNICON's Manage Services submenu (the Running Services list), you must choose NetWare/IP to configure your DSS server first, then your NetWare/IP server.

After you choose to manage NetWare/IP and get to the NetWare/IP Administration menu, bypass Configure NetWare/IP Server and Delete NetWare/IP Server Configuration to pick Configure Primary DSS. The opening window asks you to name the NetWare/IP domain. The default will be your DNS domain; that will be wrong. Add **nwip** to the beginning to differentiate between the two. My DNS domain gaskin.com had to be changed to nwip.gaskin.com before the NetWare/IP server would load. Luckily, no children were within earshot as I figured this out. Figure 3.8 shows the correct configuration information for my network.

Two other fields in the Primary DSS Configuration window are Primary DSS Host Name and IPX Network Number. The help screen for

FIGURE 3.8

Don't forget the *nwip*.

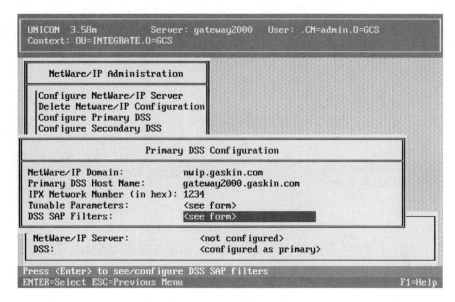

```
UNICON  3.58m              Server: gateway2000   User: .CN=admin.O=GCS
Context: OU=INTEGRATE.O=GCS


    ┌────────────────────────────────┐
    │  NetWare/IP Administration      │
    ├────────────────────────────────┤
    │  Configure NetWare/IP Server    │
    │  Delete Netware/IP Configuration│
    │  Configure Primary DSS          │
    │  Configure Secondary DSS        │
    └─────┬──────────────────────────────────────────────────┐
          │          Primary DSS Configuration                 │
          ├────────────────────────────────────────────────────┤
      NetWare/IP Domain:           nwip.gaskin.com
      Primary DSS Host Name:       gateway2000.gaskin.com
      IPX Network Number (in hex): 1234
      Tunable Parameters:          <see form>
      DSS SAP Filters:             <see form>
          └──────────────────────────────────────────────────────┐
        NetWare/IP Server:               <not configured>          │
        DSS:                             <configured as primary>   │
                                                                   │
Press <Enter> to see/configure DSS SAP filters
ENTER=Select ESC=Previous Menu                              F1=Help
```

the Primary DSS Host Name field says this name must be "fully quali-fied" as if it meant the NDS fully qualified name. That won't work, because in this case Novell wants the DNS qualified name (for example, gateway2000.gaskin.com)—another potential hang-up poorly explained. The IPX Network Number field must contain a unique IPX network number for your new virtual network segment supporting NetWare/IP.

The other choices here allow you to synchronize server times and set up DSS SAP filters. We'll go into a bit more detail about these in Chapter 4.

Your NetWare/IP Server Configuration

Now, back to the Configure NetWare/IP Server menu option on the NetWare/IP Administration menu. Choose it to set the name of the NetWare/IP domain (again), the preferred DSSs (IP address or host name of one to five DSS systems), and contact retry numbers and inter-vals between attempts.

The Slow Link Customizations setting allows time padding for slow remote connections. The setting to make this server a gateway between your NetWare/IP clients and NetWare IPX clients (the Forward IPX Infor-mation to DSS? field) is also here, but the default is No. Since most networks are a mixture of both protocols, at least two of your NetWare/IP servers should forward information so each side can see network resources on the other side. Multiple gateways automatically load balance requests. Take a look at Figure 3.9 for a blueprint.

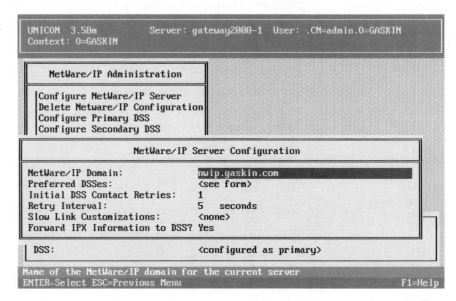

The second option on the NetWare/IP Administration menu is Delete NetWare/IP Configuration. Don't be embarrassed if you must use this choice at least once or twice to start over. I did.

Once your configuration is done, you may return to the UNICON main menu (press Escape until you get there) and start NetWare/IP. Now, finally, it should work. Your only sign of success is a lack of failure messages and, on the server console, a message saying "NetWare/IP Server is initialized and functional." Whew.

Return for DNS Client

No, you're not quite finished yet. Back up and load the NWIPCFG program so you can configure the DNS client software. You must fill in the

DNS domain name, the name server IP address, and any other name server addresses you wish. Does this look like some of the information detailed for the TCP/IP support on the server? Yes, it does.

This screen offers more than just the DNS client setup. Notice the status information at the bottom of Figure 3.10. Notice that the DNS domain is gaskin.com, while the NetWare/IP domain is nwip.gaskin.com. The difference means your NetWare/IP system works or doesn't work. Remember that the NetWare/IP configuration needs a NetWare/IP domain name that is the same as your DNS domain name, except with *nwip* added to the front.

Yes, you must configure the DNS client settings, even if the same server does all the NetWare/IP configuration. That's the situation in the lab here, and you see that the IP address for the DNS name server is that of the Gateway2000 server.

Must you have the DNS server configured before the DNS client? Yes, you must. If you have an external DNS name server that is already up and running, then you can skip the DNS server setup and go right to the client setup. See Chapter 4 for more details about DNS name servers.

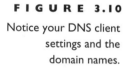

FIGURE 3.10

Notice your DNS client settings and the domain names.

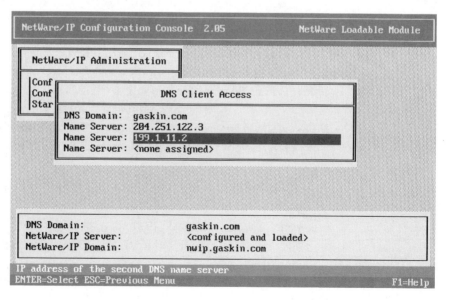

Cleanup consists of rebooting the server, and crossing your fingers while all the NLMs scroll by. Once the server is up and running, start the DNS server, the DSS server, and the NetWare/IP server software—in that order. If you don't believe me, try starting them in some random order. Maybe you'll get lucky, but I never have.

Configuring NetWare/IP Clients

You may think you're finished, but we forgot one little detail: the client. Oops. At least the client setup is amazingly quick and easy.

NetWare 4.11 needs to use Client32 for all "fancy" client tricks, such as the IPX/IP Gateway and, more important now, NetWare/IP client software. If you chose to install the client setup files on your server during installation, you are a smart administrator. If you are adding new clients, you can use the Novell CD-ROM disk itself, or you may choose to make the set of diskettes if you have more time than CD-ROM client drives.

The default directory on the server is \PUBLIC\CLIENT with subdirectories for WIN31, WIN95, and WINNT. Pick your poison.

Screens and screens of lawyer talk will appear, all of which you must agree to before continuing. In other words, agree or stop your installation.

I have to take credit for some of this verbiage on your screen, because of a review I did in *Information Week* concerning the Microsoft File and Printer Services for NetWare. In that review, I pointed out that using a NetWare client to communicate with anything but a NetWare server was a license violation. This time, Microsoft said "oops," and Novell's lawyers got to put pages of legalese on the client installation screens.

To enable NetWare/IP, you must also choose TCP/IP support for your clients. Provide the IP addresses for the client and router, along with your subnetwork mask, domain name, NetWare/IP domain name, and address of your name server(s). If you have installed Novell's pretty decent DHCP server software on a server, it will configure these IP parameters for you. Instead of providing this information for each client, you can merely provide the IP address of an existing DHCP server at each Net-Ware/IP client.

Does this all work? Absolutely, and your clients may not know the difference. Is this a huge advantage in networking? Again, as I've said before, this is the longest and most troublesome method for TCP/IP support at your NetWare clients. However, even the longest road has travelers, and even NetWare/IP has its fans.

Wrap

Now you have all TCP/IP network transport traffic between your Novell network clients and servers. This is not always necessary, of course, in the real world. It is necessary in the world of "checkboxes for vendor features" when large (nay, huge) network customers are looking for software.

If the world continues the move toward TCP/IP for everything up to and including elevators and elephant collars, your NetWare network is ready. If the Internet does take over civilization as we know it, not only will your network need to be completely TCP/IP, but you will be as well. I hope you get a cool domain name for your IP tracking collar.

Coming up next are some more details about a topic touched upon here: DNS setup.

CHAPTER

4

Your DNS Setup

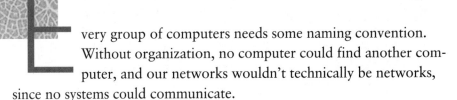

very group of computers needs some naming convention. Without organization, no computer could find another computer, and our networks wouldn't technically be networks, since no systems could communicate.

DNS (Domain Name Service) works across the global Internet to facilitate communication between systems near and far from each other. Normally invisible to users, DNS is used by applications to locate systems across the network using the TCP/IP protocol components (described in Chapter 1).

Your IntranetWare network, whether connecting to the Internet or creating a private intranet, will almost certainly need DNS. A completely NetWare network, using NDS, could function quite well without DNS, and many large networks work that way today. However, if that were the case for your network, you would have no reason to read about Proxy Servers, IPX/IP Gateways, and VPNs. The fact that you're reading this book tells me you need to know at least a little bit about DNS and how your network will use DNS to find and connect to systems within and outside your company.

DNS History and Overview

DNS was developed primarily by Paul Mockapetris in the middle 1980s while he was at the USC/Information Services Institute. You may read all about it in RFC 1034 and RFC 1035 if you wish.

In Paul's own words (and I've had the pleasure to meet Paul, and he's a pleasant fellow), "the DNS database follows a very simple model: a name space tree (called a hierarchy) with data items attached to its leaves and interior nodes." Once again we see a name space with top levels, supporting middle levels supporting lower levels, and finally end nodes, which are generally computers.

Does this sound familiar? It should, because it's the same concept used by NDS in IntranetWare. Replace Root with the DNS root, and organizations and organizational units with network names, and the two systems will look remarkably alike.

Both systems are distributed databases, with many thousands of systems (in the case of DNS on the Internet) sharing the name server load. Both systems use the same methods to discover needed information by querying the nearest servers, and letting those servers query servers farther upstream when necessary. Domain names in DNS are ordered lists of names, starting at the node and ending at the root node. Since each root node is unique, names unique within a domain are automatically unique across the entire Internet. Does that still sound like your NDS tree? Yes, it does.

One of the biggest differences between NDS and DNS (keep your abbreviations straight, now) is that NDS controls all network objects, including users, disk volumes, printers, and even directory pointers. DNS tracks hosts, which in Internet parlance generally means any network computer. DNS doesn't worry about the users; those problems belong to the computer systems themselves.

Domain Names

There are seven primary domain root names in the Internet today, which are far too few. The domain names as of the middle of 1997 are:

com	Commercial organizations, such as novell.com (Novell, Inc.)
edu	Educational organizations, such as berkeley.edu (U.C. Berkeley)
gov	Government organizations, such as nasa.gov (NASA, the National Aeronautics and Space Administration)
mil	Military organizations, such as army.mil (U.S. Army)

net	Networking organizations, such as nsf.net (NSFNET)
org	Nonprofit organizations, such as eff.org (Electronic Frontier Foundation)
int	International organizations, such as nato.int (NATO, the North Atlantic Treaty Organization)

I know Novell agrees with this listing, because it's the same one, in the same order, as the Novell writers use in their DNS examples in their Border-Manager documentation. Early domain names were heavily slanted toward the gov (for example, whitehouse.gov for the White House) and edu domains, since the Internet was developed by government groups and university researchers.

The most critical for many people is the first domain listed, the com domain. Gaskin.com is mine, novell.com is Novell's, and sybex.com is the Sybex domain. Trademark attorneys are getting involved in domain name issues, which is why many groups are advocating more commercial domains. After all, trademark law allows businesses in non-overlapping industries, such as pianos and computers, to have similar trademarks. "Keyboard maker for the stars" could apply to both industries, and neither group would get confused. But which deserves the domain name of "keyboard.com," since there can be only one?

One of these days, the domains will expand, causing growing pains for everyone involved. However, there's no other way to accommodate trademark law and the expanding commercial use of the Internet. The following domains have the best chance of being added sometime in 1998:

firm	Businesses, much like com
store	Companies offering products for sale
web	Web-devoted companies, vendors, and suppliers
arts	Cultural groups, expanding the org domain quite a bit
rec	Recreational and leisure entertainment sites

| info | Sources providing information services of some kind |
| nom | Personal and individual domains, taking *nom* from *nomenclature* (although that doesn't sound either personal or individual to me) |

Under these recommendations, my domain might be gaskin.firm, and the ground-breaking amazon.com online bookstore might be amazon.store. Critics of this plan charge there is still not acceptable protection for trademark holders, since so few new options are presented. Wouldn't large companies that also sell directly to the public need multiple listings? Gateway2000, the huge mail-order computer vendor that graciously supplied two of the systems used during this book's preparation, would likely need gway2k.firm and gway2k.store to go along with the gway2k.com that it already has in order to protect its name integrity.

This list is considerably smaller than some; hundreds of new domain options have been argued about lately. For now, your company will almost assuredly want to be part of the com domain, and your ISP can tell you if your favorite names are already taken. Be sure to provide them with a list of potential names, because the com domain is crowded.

Domain names are technically the label of a DNS tree, rooted by the company domain name. There are thousands of computers within the sun.com and novell.com domains. Each official domain name starts with the node name and continues through the domain name. If I headed a large, prosperous company, I might have a computer named host3.r&d .engineering.gaskin.com (but I don't). From the outside, however, any messages from that system would look like they came for gaskin.com, hiding the internal complexity from outsiders.

Domains within Domains

To make life more confusing, people refer to the "domain" within domains all the time. Inside mythical gaskin.com could be the engineering, marketing, sales, and production domains, each with multiple subordinate networks. Each domain usually, but not always, has its own name server, to make name queries quick for local systems. The administrative zone, or group of domains, will usually also have its own name server, to provide information for the entire company.

At the top of each domain in the Internet sits a name server, each referring to a single system at the very top. Not long ago, that single system was a Pentium 75 PC. DNS is fast, compact, and reliable, making it possible to run the world on a single PC now considered underpowered by even your least-technical users.

Just like NDS, DNS has replica servers and backup name servers and the like. Cache servers at the top of a subdomain can hold information requested by some network users, figuring that same information will be needed soon again. Large networks may even have a DNS cache read-only server, if the load is high enough. After all, without a reliable name service, your TCP/IP network isn't much good.

This should give you some understanding for the role IPX and NCP play in keeping your NetWare and IntranetWare network simple and uncomplicated. Administering DNS systems takes time, work, and much sweat when things go wrong. If you're thinking that sounds just like your own NetWare administration job when the going gets tough, you should realize you have more in common with a TCP/IP network administrator than you might think. However, addressing woes and address configuration are not problems facing IntranetWare network managers.

Using an IntranetWare Server for DNS

We saw in Chapter 3 that NetWare/IP needs a DNS server to maintain compliance with the TCP/IP method of operation. The primary NetWare use of the DNS server is to find a special DSS (Domain SAP Server) software server to provide information normally part of the IPX broadcast function.

NetWare/IP doesn't use the full range of DNS name services. When a NetWare/IP client needs network resources, it queries the DNS name server listed in the client configuration files only for the address of the DSS. The DSS name services pertain only to IPX information, and are of no use to traditional TCP/IP clients needing name services.

The IntranetWare DNS name server can be used as a full DNS name server for a mixed network, but it's a stretch. Even Novell employees hesitate when asked if this is a good idea. The honest ones will tell you that a mixed TCP/IP and IPX network is better off using a Unix host for a DNS server, particularly when that system is in place before you start adding IntranetWare BorderManager.

Using an existing DNS server for NetWare/IP clients requires little: Add an NS (name server identification) record for each DSS server in the NetWare/IP domain. Using a NetWare server running DNS server software requires that you add both the NS and A (host address) records for each DSS server and an SOA (start of authority) record for the DNS domain.

This may all sound like Internet addressing gibberish, but the UNICON console utility handles this stuff for you without too much stress.

Checking Your DNS Server

Since NetWare/IP installation and configuration, including DNS server setup, was covered back in Chapter 3, we won't go through all those gory details once again. You do need to verify a couple of items, however, especially if you aren't using NetWare/IP on your network.

Unfortunately, you need to install NetWare/IP to get the UNICON utility and other support files necessary. The good part of this bad news is that you don't need to install NetWare/IP on the client, or even get all the server parts configured exactly right. But you will need to mess around with NetWare/IP, at least until IntranetWare becomes a bit more modular. I expect that by the next release of IntranetWare, individual Internet service and software server modules will be separated a bit more, rather than grouped under NetWare/IP.

You won't need to configure or start the DSS server software just to get the DNS software loaded. In fact, the opposite is true, if you remember the "Lucky 13" list back in Chapter 3. You needed to start DNS before you started DSS or NetWare/IP. So, starting DNS but not the other modules for NetWare/IP won't cause a problem.

IntranetWare and UNICON offer both DNS client and DNS server software. If you have an existing DNS server on your network, you may wish to copy the information and make your NetWare server a client of your existing network. If you have no existing DNS server, then, by necessity, your IntranetWare server will do the name server honors as well for your NetWare/IP clients and servers. If you have no existing DNS server on your network, why are you adding all the IntranetWare Internet, intranet, and extranet features to your network?

Managing with UNICON

Once you have NetWare/IP installed, you can start UNICON by typing **LOAD UNICON** from the server console. The main menu looks like this:

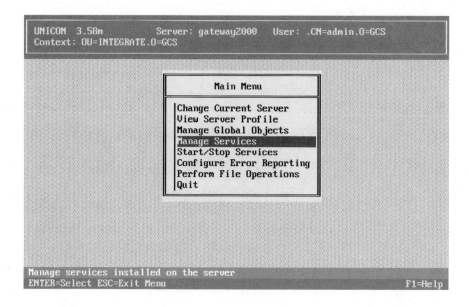

Let's go over what these options do, with some details about the DNS-related choices.

Change Current Server   You may manage remote servers through the first menu choice. This becomes a handy trick when you're working on large or dispersed networks.

View Server Profile   The window displayed by this option is read-only, but provides plenty of helpful information. This window shows the server IP name (same as the server's NDS name if you're consistent… hint . hint), IP address, and subnet mask. NetWare Information, when chosen, pops open a subwindow showing the operating system version, current NDS context, and NDS tree. Again, these are read-only, but at least the information is gathered in one place.

Other subwindows of View Server Profile show installed products and their versions, server time zone, and the time between server synchronization with three configuration files handling the integration of NetWare and NFS users allowed on the server. DNS client configuration is shown here as well, listing the domain name (gaskin.com) and the name server's IP address. Up to three name servers may be listed, if you have that many.

Manage Global Objects   The next choice on the UNICON main menu allows you to set many of the server details that are displayed by the View Server Profile option. The subwindow allows you to set the synchronization interval, enable DNS client access, and set the domain name and the name server addresses. The other manageable objects are hosts, giving you a front end to the \ETC\HOSTS file on the server.

Each configured host in the local domain is listed after you press Enter twice on the Hosts option. You can add more hosts by pressing Insert, or delete a host by highlighting a name and pressing Delete. Host information gathered here includes the host name and primary IP address, which are the only mandatory fields. Optional fields include physical address, aliases, other IP addresses, machine type, operating system, and NDS object.

Manage Services As we saw in Chapter 3, the Manage Services option lets you pick what you would like to manage from the list of Running Services. Under the DNS service, you'll find the Administer DNS, Initialize DNS Master Database, and Save DNS Master to Text Files choices.

When you choose Administer DNS, another menu appears offering Manage Master Database, Manage Replica Databases, Link to Existing DNS Hierarchy, Query Remote Name Server, and Disable DNS Service. Here you can verify NetWare/IP works with existing DNS systems, or you can just receive information from external name servers.

When you pick Manage Master Database, you find yet another menu offering Manage Data, Delegate Subzone Authority, and Delegate Subzone by IP Authority. You can choose from the Master Zone and Subzones list that appears, as shown in Figure 4.1. If you're counting, the DNS Resource Record Information screen, where you can actually describe record names and types, is the seventh level from the top. Each DOS ASCII window that opens blocks the ones behind it. I'll never complain about cascaded menus on the Windows 95 interface again (well, at least not soon).

FIGURE 4.1

Picking your zone

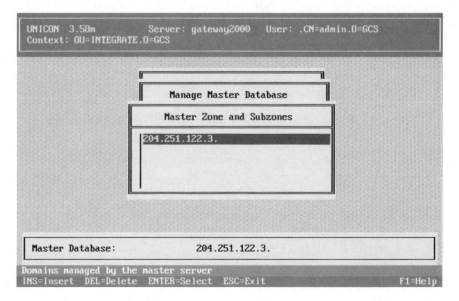

Subzones can be parceled and assigned to others to manage. This is particularly useful with geographically split networks; the site administrator can work under the remote supervision of a central administrator. Remember, this entire menu tree can be reached only after providing a supervisor password.

The Initialize DNS Master Database choice is the one we used in Chapter 3 for our NetWare/IP setup. And as I said there, this is a crucial choice, because until the database is configured and initialized, nothing works. You can configure DNS for specific subnetworks and replace existing databases with other databases. Check back in Chapter 3 to see the DNS name setup for my lab network, in Figure 3.7. In real life, you may have several NS (name server identification) entries, for backup name server support. You may also have many A (host address) listings, for hosts (servers) in the domain, or at least your server's domain (sometimes called *zone*, especially by Microsoft in the Windows NT help files for DNS).

Start/Stop Services   Choosing this option opens a window labeled Running Services, and pressing Insert pops open the Available Services window with a highlight bar on the first listed service. Choosing one of the services that is not already running loads and starts the software (if all the configuration details are correct).

Configure Error Reporting   This option lets you display, save, or clear the audit log, and clear the product kernel (often called the *P-kernel*) log. Both of these logs have their own screen in the switchable NetWare server console screen rotation, and the audit log can be saved for future reference. Error logging levels and SNMP alert levels are set in this menu as well. Each log screen can show a range of information levels, from none to verbose (although Novell calls it "informational"). The default size for the audit log file is 10,240 bytes but may range up to 262KB before the new information overwrites the old. SNMP alert levels range from none to verbose as well, although the SNMP trap and alert destinations are set back in the INETCFG utility (which we used for NetWare/IP setup in Chapter 3), confusingly enough.

Perform File Operations   This option allows you to set file access permissions and copy files using FTP. Do you need an /etc/hosts file from one of your Unix systems? This utility will copy it for you. A configuration file editor is included, although it's the normal NetWare server EDIT utility, a poor text editor with limited functionality and a proprietary command structure.

Checking Your DNS Client

Checking the status of your DNS client isn't too difficult. Figure 3.10 back in Chapter 3 shows the DNS client software up and running properly. Merely using another TCP/IP station to ping the server doesn't verify DNS software is active, because the pinging station will be the one needing address information for the target of the ping.

As I mentioned before, if you have NetWare/IP and wish to use NetWare/IP clients for Internet access, you need an Internet-connected DNS server. Your IntranetWare DNS server can function in this role, but if you have an existing name server, use it instead.

Checking Your DSS Server

The DSS server options are several layers down from the UNICON main menu's Manage Services choice. Pick NetWare/IP Services from the Manage Services list, choose NetWare/IP, then Configure Primary DSS.

Along with the Primary DSS Host Name and IPX Network Number options, which we covered in Chapter 3, are options labeled Tunable Parameters and DSS SAP Filters. The first option configures synchronization times between primary and secondary DSS servers, and the DSS and NetWare/IP servers. You may set more synchronization timer ticks for nodes on different IP networks or subnetworks, to allow for router and transmission delay. Secondary DSSs may be configured on other NetWare servers. SAP filters control how much information is exchanged between servers, to control network traffic.

If you're curious, you can back up to the NetWare/IP Administration menu and choose Browse DSS Database. Quite a bit of DSS SAP and RIP information is available under this menu option. You can save the databases to text files, and set the number of hops and ticks between DSS servers and networks. However, little of this information will help anyone except a serious network expert; this is not the place to look for initial configuration help.

Using Windows NT Software for a DNS Name Server

This sounds like a good idea, but it won't really work as well as you think. Sorry if you were misled by the heading. You're better off using a Unix server for a DNS server, or a third-party software application written for an NT server, than trying to make the default Windows NT software function as your sole name server.

Windows NT books recommend that you set the NT DNS server software to be a caching-only server. Local clients should be pointed to that server address so their queries will be faster, since many network clients query for the same IP addresses. Caching addresses used earlier helps both previous clients and those with new queries. After all, if you can query a local system rather than a name server at another location, such as at your ISP, the time saved may be your own.

Until Windows NT 4.0, Microsoft didn't supply a DNS server for NT, except in the optional Windows NT Resource Kit. Other companies have filled that gap, and you can find a variety of third-party DNS servers for NT today. In most cases, they ship along with Web and/or e-mail server software, since each is dependent on DNS.

Microsoft disparages the static nature of DNS, and offers an improvement (their words, not mine). Adding DNS to the WINS (Windows Internet

Name Service) support software makes it look like Microsoft is making some huge step into Internet naming, because of the WINS acronym. However, closer examination will show that WINS is really a step backward for Internet naming, because it is used by Microsoft to map NetBIOS names to IP addresses. Those NT network users who know a WINS name for a station but need the IP address are well served by WINS, but no one else is.

Rumors are (don't you love computer buzz?) that Microsoft will drop WINS in the next NT version, Windows NT 5.0. That would actually be a step forward for Microsoft, and lessen the hypocrisy of claiming to "run" on TCP/IP when in reality the default network protocol is NetBEUI on top of IP packets.

Microsoft's DNS server is easy to start, mainly because all of the network configuration is done during initial TCP/IP setup of the NT system. From the Control Panel, choose Network then Services. If Microsoft DNS Server is not listed as one of the running services, click on the Add command button, choose Microsoft DNS Server from the pick list, and click on OK. Little else will be necessary to start the service.

Configuring the service is a bit different. After installing DNS, you will notice that DNS Manager appears in the Administrative Tools folder under Programs. Starting DNS Manager will allow you to add new servers by right-clicking on the Server List icon on the left frame of the application. The "zone" name the dialog box refers to is the domain name for your network.

The management options are limited, although Microsoft includes a good help file with DNS Manager. Again, if you have an existing network name server, use it rather than the Microsoft NT name server software. However, if you have no Unix name server and must make a choice, the NT software is more complete than the IntranetWare software, and is better able to support heterogeneous client populations.

Wrap

If you get the idea that neither IntranetWare or Windows NT make a great name server, you are exactly right. Microsoft is better than Novell in this area, but not by a whole lot.

If you're buying BorderManager strictly for the IPX/IP Gateway and other ways of connecting NetWare clients to the Internet, you can use your ISP's DNS name server. If your company already connects to the Internet in other departments, you will be able to use their name server, or make your IntranetWare or Windows NT name server a backup copy of their server. Then you'll get all the access you need without fighting your way through DNS hassles.

In the next chapter, we'll turn to another aspect of your intranet setup: the clients.

CHAPTER

5

IntranetWare Client Improvement

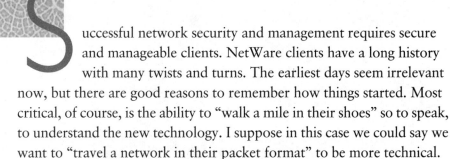

Successful network security and management requires secure and manageable clients. NetWare clients have a long history with many twists and turns. The earliest days seem irrelevant now, but there are good reasons to remember how things started. Most critical, of course, is the ability to "walk a mile in their shoes" so to speak, to understand the new technology. I suppose in this case we could say we want to "travel a network in their packet format" to be more technical.

Novell has always been the leader in networking by providing the longest list of supported clients. NetWare was the first file server that supported the Apple Macintosh. Before that, Novell connected such strange machines as the TI PC, the Victor 9000, and the DEC Rainbow to the early S-Net NetWare server.

This "welcome all comers" attitude continues today. Novell still supports more clients than any other LAN operating system, ranging from DOS PCs (yes, they're still around) through Unix hosts, all flavors of Windows clients, OS/2, and of course, the Macintosh.

Why is this important when discussing Internet and intranet security and management? Because you can't secure a client you can't manage. Since Novell connects to the most clients of all the competitors, Novell security and directory products have a head start over all the "also-rans."

NetWare Client History and Overview

In the beginning, there was no "client" software as we think of client software today. These days, the client software is frequently tied to some remote server or other network service, such as browser or e-mail client software. Now that 32-bit desktop software handles multiple protocols at once, the notion of being restricted to a single protocol boggles the mind.

The Way It Was

Just let me say <geezer mode on> that in the old days, the clients were tied not only to the network protocol, but also to the individual network interface card, and we liked it like that <geezer mode off>. No, I'm not kidding. A diskette (360KB 5¼-inch floppy, no less) came packed with drivers for each Novell-approved network card. Those files, and those files only, could coerce that network card to communicate with a Net-Ware server. (Okay, you're right, we didn't really like it like that.)

Imagine the hassle if you lost your network files for a particular interface card. Need to change something about that client? Too bad. Your disk crashed, and you need the files to restore and reconnect to the server? Cross your fingers and hope that the backup diskettes (yes, client stations used diskettes for backup) held the proper files. If not, the easiest way to deal with the problem was to order another interface card of the same kind for the next computer, and copy the floppy that came in the box. That was certainly better than trying to generate a new shell for the client, using the old Novell drivers and slow computers and floppy disks.

Client upgrades have consistently moved from more specific (unique disk with each interface card) to more general (most interface card drivers included within Windows 95). Both ODI (Open Datalink Interface), from Novell and partners, and NDIS (Network Device Interface Specification), from Microsoft and partners, separate the transport layer software from the application support software within the network client software.

The 90s Style Client

Life in the client software world has progressed to where we are with Windows 95/NT clients in 1997: Quick utilities embedded in the operating system support any card we desire, simply and easily. That is, if it all works. Automated procedures are wonderful until something the procedure designers didn't imagine happens. Then you scramble around checking here and there, hoping to find the setting that causes the client to "perform sub-optimally" (translation: crap out).

Including network services into the operating system makes sense today. A computer that is not attached to a network through an interface card, to the Internet, or to a commercial service through the Internet is an anomaly rather than the norm. After all, Macintosh and all Unix clients have included networking in the basic operating system since the beginning.

Of course, weaving the network software into the operating system means it's more complicated to troubleshoot and fix a problem with the network. How can you tell if the network or the operating system is at fault? Who can you blame?

If you use the Microsoft NetWare client software, included with Windows 95/NT, then it's easy to assign blame: Microsoft. One can make the easy joke here, and imply that one can blame Microsoft for almost anything wrong with all computer hardware and software, but that would be another long book. In fact, it's another whole company: IBM for I Blame Microsoft.

Don't start feeling good if you think running Microsoft's NetWare client will narrow the field of possible troublemakers. IntranetWare and BorderManager don't allow the use of the Microsoft client. Why not? Because Microsoft, eager to blunt the advantage Novell has with NDS, keeps releasing client software that either ignores or poorly supports NDS. Another example of political, not technical, problems causing customers grief.

Is NDS support critical for your network clients? Only if you want any shred of support, management, or security. In other words, no NDS support, no BorderManager. You can't have a comprehensive, single login security and directory service without an intelligent client. Novell's Client32 provides that intelligence.

IntranetWare Client Features

Let's focus on the Windows 95 client for now, and the equivalent Windows 97 (or 98 or 99…) operating system upgrade. Microsoft's operating system goals are murky, with NT and 95 overlapping in many areas, but the majority of Microsoft's explanations indicate Windows 95 is the expected mass-market client. Most new PC systems ship with Windows 95 as of this writing, with NT available on high-end machines or at extra cost.

Microsoft's stated goals of supporting the same software on Windows NT and 95 have fallen far behind reality. Novell, and other network operating system vendors, are forced to make separate 95 and NT clients. The early work went into 95, but NT client improvements came quickly when NT 4.0 became available.

One huge advantage of Windows 95 is intelligent filename support. No longer limited to the 8.3 DOS filename straightjacket, Windows 95 allows long filenames including spaces. NetWare versions as far back as NetWare 3.0 support those longer filenames through the use of either the OS/2 name space for older versions and the LONG name space with IntranetWare.

WARNING Verify that your tape backup software supports these name spaces, or you'll get a surprise when you restore a file with a long name that suddenly truncates to a short name.

The other main features of Client32 include:

- Support for Ethernet and Token Ring topologies

- Concurrent IPX and TCP/IP protocol support

- Performance enhancements such as client-side caching, Packet Burst, and LIP (Large Internet Packets)

- Security options, including packet signatures and RSA encryption

- Management through SNMP (Simple Network Management Protocol) agents in the client

- NetWare network resources available through Windows Explorer and Network Neighborhood

- Mobile connections

- Automatic reconnections to lost network resources

- Plug-and-Play support

- Connecting to multiple NDS trees

- Single GUI login for all NDS resources

Anything missing in here? The marketing people may think I left some of the features out. However, I don't believe a new client rates a national holiday, and this list offers plenty of advantages; it's not necessary to make up some more features.

Marketing hype aside, Novell has reworked its initial poor Windows 95 client and now ships an excellent client with IntranetWare. NAL (Novell Application Launcher) comes with the client, but it is really an extra little utility for managers. NAL presents applications to users in a taskbar, which can be configured by group, operating system, or individual user. Running software from the server and controlling it with NAL ensure that productivity is not lost, because updates and other changes take a trip to every client.

Client32 Installation and Configuration

It would be great to tell you that Client32's installation is simple, clean, automatic, and foolproof. Unfortunately, nothing concerning Windows 95 is simple, clean, automatic, or foolproof. Novell has made some strides, however, and there are fewer problems than there used to be.

"Fewer" doesn't mean none, unfortunately. Windows of all flavors have so many possible configuration settings that no application, even Microsoft-written programs, work every time. Since a network client digs more deeply into the client operating system than a typical application, be prepared for some installation hassles.

Picking Your Installation Source

IntranetWare provides a variety of sources for your installation. The main IntranetWare CD-ROM will install client software from the INSTALL.BAT in the root directory. If you prefer, you can create a set of diskettes, especially if you're interested in boosting your overtime hours. The Windows NT client didn't make it on the disk, but the other operating systems are represented.

Today, most PCs running Windows 95 have a CD-ROM drive, so you can rely on the faster CD-ROM rather than the slow floppy drive. If your systems don't have a CD-ROM drive, the cost of a single drive that runs from the parallel port will save enough time to make it worth the purchase price.

The most logical place for the client update files are on the server. IntranetWare offers a chance to copy the client files to the server during installation. You should take advantage of that opportunity.

How can you connect to the server to reach the new client software? Even old NETX clients will connect to an IntranetWare server through Bindery Services. If your workstations use the same network interface card, a floppy diskette can hold enough boot files to get you connected to the server.

If any station has the slightest trouble running the client installation across the network, stop and copy the NetWare directory that holds the client files from the server to the workstation. Missing a single *.DLL file will cause no end of client frustration, so don't just cross your fingers and hit the "skip this file" option during the installation process. Wouldn't you rather do it right than have this station's user catch you as you're leaving for a big date, and demand that you spend two hours fixing the system?

Storing CD-ROM Files on the Client

Copy the *.CAB files from the Windows 95 CD-ROM \WIN95 directory to the client hard disk. The smart route is to create a \MASTERS directory, with the NetWare and Windows 95 stored in appropriate subdirectories. Yes, it takes about 50 extra megabytes, but if you don't have that much space on the client PC, you have no reason for installing Windows 95 in the first place.

Once the NetWare and Windows files are local, you may configure and reconfigure all night (a horrible thought, but it happens) without swapping CD-ROMs. You will need to tell Windows 95 to look in the local directories rather than on drive D:, but Windows 95 will actually remember the path from one installation to the next.

You may believe that Microsoft's NETSETUP program will do the trick for you, but it won't. Novell's Client32 doesn't support network-based Windows 95 executables. Since executables now include DLL files, everything needs to be resident on the client.

You may also believe that Novell's MSBATCH program will upgrade a Windows 3.1 machine to Windows 95. After all, that's what the literature says. Don't believe that, either. The method of storing the CD-ROM files on the local system, along with several other tricks required in a full upgrade, will always work better than MSBATCH.

Much of the upgrade information credit belongs to reader Daniel Foo Shih Chieh from Singapore. He and I corresponded after he bought my *Complete Guide to NetWare 4.1*, mostly about upgrading large numbers of PCs to Windows 95 and Client32. After weeks of trial and effort, Daniel came to the conclusion the local storage method was the best of a bad set of options. I agree, which is why I pass this on to you.

New with Client32 are three full screens of "legalese" that appear when you're installing the client software. You should read all three pages before deciding whether you accept the terms or not (yeah, right). If you don't accept the terms, the installation program stops.

Client Installation Options

Figure 5.1 shows the Additional Options dialog box for the Client32 installation process. Remember I mentioned NetWare/IP had a choice on the client installation screen? Here it is, but it doesn't become an active checkbox until after you check the TCP/IP box. Notice the last checkbox is for the IPX/IP Gateway, which works perfectly well with Windows 95. (See Chapter 6 for IPX/IP Gateway details.)

FIGURE 5.1

Installation options for the Windows 95 client

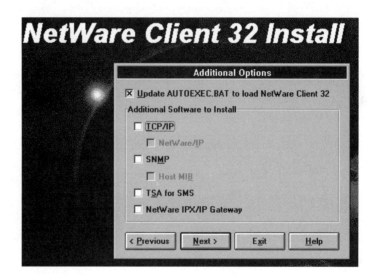

You may be slightly startled to see Novell's first installation comment: "Removing Existing Client" or something equally scary. Is that a good idea? Too late, it's gone. That's why I recommend you follow my advice, and copy the installation files for both Windows 95 and IntranetWare to the local hard disk. At least, if the installation bombs (which it will all too often), you will be able to restart the process quickly.

Client Configuration

After installation, you may start looking for the NET.CFG program. Sorry, that's gone, and all those details are now controlled by the Windows 95 Network Control Panel. In fact, you have even more options to consider than you ever had in NET.CFG.

You may have noticed the inclusion of "client-side caching" in the list of new features for Client32. What does this mean? Some of your local system RAM will be dedicated to caching network drive information, just as a NetWare server uses RAM to cache drive information. The speed increase is useful, since the overhead of Windows 95 and Client32 has resulted in some folks feeling communications are slower than before.

Using local RAM for caching is always a delicate option, and the defaults for the Client32 software, at least the early versions, took more RAM than most users felt they wanted to dedicate to the cache. Figure 5.2 shows the screen where this cache level can be changed. The setting of 1, as shown in the figure, provides some caching, since I want to get all the speed for my client that I can, without taking 60 percent of my free RAM, as some users have reported losing to the cache.

FIGURE 5.2

Balancing cache versus RAM

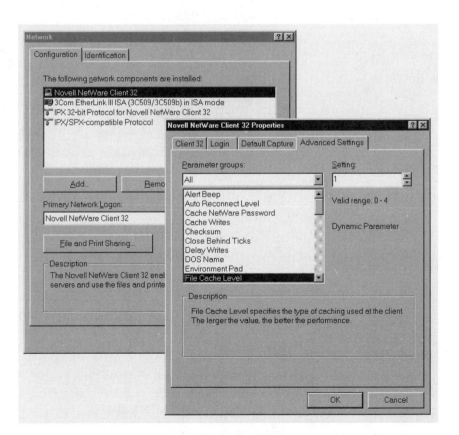

Notice all the other options you have to choose from? You will rarely, if ever, feel the need to change any of those settings. But it's just so good to know that curious users, tinkering with their Control Panel, can change some setting deep within Client32 that you won't be able to find for hours! Thank you, Microsoft and Novell.

Client Management and Control

You have a wide variety of client management and control tools available for your network administrative tasks. These range from utilities that will do the maintenance for you automatically, to the NDS controls that govern every client.

Automated Maintenance Tools

Since so much can go wrong with modern network client software, vendors have actually started trying to help. Far too much of this help is still vaporware, but at least the marketing literature is getting more and more specific about what is coming.

SNMP Support

As mentioned earlier, Client32 includes SNMP client software, called Network Management Instrumentation (NMI) Agents by Novell. Client SNMP software used to just be called *agents*, but name inflation has struck.

While small networks never use any type of SNMP system, all the major management products use at least parts of the SNMP tool set to manage clients. Novell's NMS (NetWare Management System), HP's OpenView, and SunNet Manager can all manage Client32 stations using SNMP. However, only large companies with multivendor networks tend to buy the HP and Sun products. Various NDS-based LAN management packages won't use SNMP, even for the Client32 stations on the network.

What's my suggestion? Don't enable any of the SNMP support options unless you already have an SNMP management console up and running. Doing so will just add to client overhead for no purpose.

Automatic Client Update

More typical network problems concern the constant upgrades by various software vendors. Does a company with a large network ever go a week without receiving an upgrade for at least one of its supported packages? Probably not.

ACU (Automatic Client Update) works through both the login scripts and from the NAL (Novell Application Launcher). Groups of Client32 users can be addressed with particular updates, or you can specify the update down to the particular user. IntranetWare will check the client's versions of the various modules within Client32, and update the client software automatically. At least, that's the plan (and it often works that way, too).

Miscellaneous Tools

Client32 includes such goodies as high-resolution time-stamp services, process and thread synchronization services, sophisticated event exposure, remote control, and configuration management. Some of these fancy tools are used by current management systems, while some are not. Plug-and-Play support is included, and most new PCs have Plug-and-Play support in their BIOS now.

NWAdmin Control

NetWare Administrator, often called NWAdmin, requires Client32 on both Windows 95 and NT. It's fully graphical now, and almost every detail concerning NetWare clients and servers can be controlled from NWAdmin. While you or I may not call a Windows 95 station running Client32 and NWAdmin an indication of Novell's superior management and maintenance tools, the Novell literature certainly does.

The good thing about the increased power of NWAdmin is that Novell has allowed third parties to plug in their own programs to the NWAdmin framework. This also means those companies must utilize NDS, so Novell wins on both counts. But the advantages to network managers are real, and systems are easier to manage when all the tools are in one place.

NDS Controls

Speaking of NDS, here we are at a section describing some of the advantages of NDS client control and security. BorderManager will build upon what IntranetWare already provides, which is quite a bit in most cases.

NDS controls every aspect of what IntranetWare clients can see and where they can go on the network. Some of the client options for Intranet-Ware clients include:

- List NDS server and NDS trees

- Browse the NDS tree and file systems of NDS servers

- Log in and out of the NDS service from within Windows 95/NT

- Redirect output to NDS-controlled system printers

- Change the NDS context and NDS tree

- Set their own NDS passwords, subject to limits set by the administrator

- Log in to IntranetWare from Windows 95 without using DOS

These features are made available from within NDS, meaning that they can be taken away via NDS. Although these features control the company's network, NDS doesn't have any control over Internet access.

Or does it? One of the important security features of BorderManager and Novell's Proxy Server is the ability to control what IntranetWare clients can see, read, and utilize on the Internet or even within your own intranet.

There are three ways used by firewalls and proxy servers to control networks. Let's cover them quickly (the details are in Chapter 9):

- **Packet filters:** Use router technology to monitor and filter information coming into and leaving a network. Unknown packets are blocked, for security against outsiders. Each packet from a known source is checked against the access controls set up by the network administrator.

- **Circuit-level proxies:** Control the connection between applications and the Internet or intranet at the Session layer of the network. The most common use is to compare the user request for a protocol service, such as FTP, HTTP, Telnet, and Gopher, against that user's authorizations to use that particular service.

- **Application-level proxies:** Relay all the data from Internet or intranet sources to the user application. During that relay, examine the traffic packet contents and apply authorization rules concerning time of day, source address, and need for encryption.

Is there anything left out of this list? Can you see where every network client can be controlled, monitored, and restricted as necessary? Can you see how outsiders will be kept on the outside?

Traditional firewall technology has relied on the Unix operating system and TCP/IP. There's something inherently bizarre about building your firewall on an operating system and protocol freely available all over the Internet and the computer business in general. True, dedicated firewalls can chop out parts of Unix that are less secure, since the system won't be used for development and resource sharing. But you're still starting with a known quantity in the Unix operating system and the publicly defined TCP/IP protocol suite.

Security for Network Clients

Novell critics charge that the IPX protocol, being nonstandard, is "worse" than TCP/IP. It seems to me that the only safe protocol would be a proprietary protocol. Critics also complain that relying on IPX for security is at odds with the IntranetWare move of making TCP/IP a network transport option between NetWare clients and servers. It seems to me, again, that critics are being unreasonable. They don't like using proprietary IPX for security, but then complain about NetWare's lack of security when clients use TCP/IP for transport?

Let's take a quick look at how IntranetWare with BorderManager provides better protection for your network than any other firewall/client system on the market today. Critics, take note: We're calling your bluff right here.

The primary method of control in any NetWare 4.0 or higher network (including IntranetWare, of course) is NDS. More than just a "directory," NDS provides a complete directory, authentication, and security service. Nothing happens on a NetWare network without the approval of NDS.

TCP/IP fans may complain that NDS doesn't support native TCP/IP clients with its control. Well, that depends. If you're speaking of NetWare/IP clients, NDS is absolutely in control. No NetWare/IP client can communicate with any NDS-secured resource without authentication.

If you're speaking of a separate TCP/IP client or server, such as a Sun SPARCstation in your intranet, the answer is that NDS doesn't control that system's security—yet. Novell has made arrangements to license NDS technology to all the major computer networking system players that matter (except Microsoft, whose developers still contend that their next version will have a better directory than NDS, except that the directory keeps getting pushed back to the "next" next version). Someday soon, SPARCstations will take their security cues from NDS, as will Unisys and HP and SCO and the rest of the Unix group.

Today, however, NDS can't control, limit, or block the activities of a Unix client or host on your network. That's why BorderManager includes many security pieces, as we just discussed, that do control non-NetWare clients. So you Unix bigots will need to find something else to complain about, because BorderManager has answered all your complaints.

IPX NetWare Clients

How does BorderManager work to control clients? Let's expand on what was discussed a bit earlier.

IPX clients are automatically included within the purview of NDS, because they are automatically NetWare clients. Other systems can use IPX for network transport services, but the only systems that they will connect with are other NetWare networks.

When the IPX clients reach out to the Internet, they must use the IPX/IP Gateway. This server-based software converts the IPX network packets into TCP/IP packets for the trip through the Internet. When the packets are answered, the reply packets are converted from TCP/IP to IPX at the gateway. Using IPX, the packets are routed to the proper NetWare client, awaiting their arrival. This is all described and illustrated in greater detail in Chapter 6, but here's the short, security-oriented version.

Novell uses the WinSock version 1.1 standard software at the client to support TCP/IP-based applications at the IPX-based client. The WinSock standard describes a software layer between the application on top and the network protocol software and hardware details on the bottom. This isolates applications from TCP/IP protocol stacks.

By *spoofing* the TCP/IP WinSock software hooks, Novell's special WINSOCK.DLL and WSOCK32.DLL programs tell the TCP/IP application all is well. Then the WinSock files transport the application packets over IPX to the IPX/IP Gateway server. At the gateway server, the application packets are moved to TCP/IP packets, with a port number attached to use for NetWare client identification later. Hosts on the far side of the IPX/IP Gateway accept the port numbers without problem, and use them in their reply packets.

Returning packets undergo just the opposite operation. Using the port number for client identification, the TCP/IP packet is replaced by an IPX packet for transport within the NetWare network. The client-based application receives the response through the WinSock layer, never knowing (or caring) that IPX was used for part of the journey.

One of the easiest security options employed by experts is to hide the valuable object. In this case, the valuable object is the NetWare client and other network resources. Hackers and outsiders of all kinds may want to get their hands on these objects, but the IPX/IP Gateway server eliminates that possibility completely.

How? Hackers across the Internet are forced to use TCP/IP for their nefarious deeds, since the Internet supports only TCP/IP packets. But is there any shred of TCP/IP within your network? Nope. All the TCP/IP packets stop at the IPX/IP Gateway server, no matter what.

Your NetWare network resources are safe in two ways: outsiders can't see them, and even if they could, they can't reach them. Valuables that can't be seen or touched are pretty darn safe.

TCP/IP NetWare Clients

The critics are now yelling that the previous example is unfair. Some critics are never happy, are they?

What about the TCP/IP-based NetWare clients? What about other TCP/IP resources within your local network, such as TCP/IP printers and print servers? Aren't those visible through the IPX/IP Gateway server?

The critics have the right idea, but the wrong detail. No part of your local IPX network can be seen through the IPX/IP Gateway server from the Internet, because all TCP/IP packets hit a red brick wall at the gateway. The critics correct idea is that other, non-NetWare clients and hosts, such as TCP/IP-based systems, must have another connection to the network besides the IPX/IP Gateway.

Mixed protocol networks tend to have two internal networks and an "external" internal network, sometimes called a *lobby* network—like the lobby to your offices. One internal network will be all IPX, and the connecting point will be the IPX/IP Gateway server. No traffic leaves the IPX network to the Internet except through the IPX/IP Gateway server, and the control and security is absolute.

On the other side of the IPX/IP Gateway server is the small, external lobby network. This will connect just a few systems, such as the e-mail server, the IPX/IP Gateway server, your Web server, and the like. Also on this network will be the router used to reach the Internet.

The TCP/IP internal network will also connect to the lobby network. But just as your office building allows outsiders in the lobby but not into the office proper without authorization, so will the internal TCP/IP network have security between the internal and lobby network. The security may be as lax as a router with some packet-filtering capabilities or some software on the Unix host acting as a router between the two networks.

However, if the last two examples are the norm in your company, you have a serious security problem. Neither of these configurations is enough to protect your network. This is a good excuse to add NetWare Border-Manager to the TCP/IP side of the house.

Using a "hide the resources" approach, similar to the IPX/IP Gateway, the IP/IP Gateway (or NAT) hides your internal TCP/IP network resources by translating the IP addresses for the internal systems when they communicate outside your own network. This works a bit like an alias used by a celebrity registering at a hotel. If the celebrity's real name was used, everyone would want access, just like your internal network resources would draw attention. By hiding behind a false name, the celebrity can avoid crowds, just like your TCP/IP network can hide by using different IP addresses when communicating outside your network. You'll find details about the IP/IP Gateway in Chapter 7.

If you prefer, you can use the Proxy Server software to provide controls on outsiders coming in and insiders going out. Earlier in this chapter, we examined the options for controlling insiders through packet filters, circuit-level proxies, and application-level proxies. These control options are available through BorderManager, even on non-NetWare clients running TCP/IP. We'll see all the details later, in Chapter 9, so just take my word for it right now.

Wrap

This chapter showed some details about how and why the Intranet-Ware clients are critical to BorderManager. Client improvements are wonderful advances, and Novell is to be commended for making Client32 as strong as it is. Since Microsoft wasn't able to deliver a decent NetWare client with Windows 95 or NT, Novell had to step up and do so. Regardless of which company is to blame, slow client software delivery makes life rough on the customers.

On one hand, there are fewer ways to check what is happening with client software, since there are no more NET.CFG files and the like. On the other hand, the Network utility within Control Panel for Windows 95 and NT offers a wide range of control settings and is easier to work with than text files.

Does all this graphic client stuff slow down performance? Critics say Client32 is slower than VLM clients. That may be true. As a network manager, do you care more about an eight percent performance decrease or clients that are easier to install, configure, and maintain? There's no free lunch, and more complex clients will always be slower than smaller, simpler clients. But our desktop systems are getting more complex, so our clients must be complex enough to support those systems. The complexity and cost always spiral upward when we're speaking of computers.

CHAPTER

6

IPX/IP Gateways

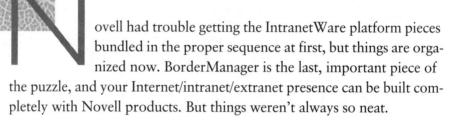 ovell had trouble getting the IntranetWare platform pieces bundled in the proper sequence at first, but things are organized now. BorderManager is the last, important piece of the puzzle, and your Internet/intranet/extranet presence can be built completely with Novell products. But things weren't always so neat.

First, Novell released the Internet Publisher, using a third-party IPX/IP gateway, licensed Web server software, and a few pieces of its own to bind this motley group together. Internet Publisher lasted just a few months before Novell released its own products, in better versions, to obsolete the bundle of third-party options it shipped at first.

The critical part of Novell's Inter/intra/extranet strategy, at least for your humble narrator, is the IPX/IP Gateway. Until the 60 million NetWare clients had an easy way to use TCP/IP network resources, Novell couldn't stake any serious claim to being an Internet-involved company. The fact that Novell let a dozen companies into the market before releasing its own product speaks more to management indecision than technical details, I believe.

For those of you who are interested in how this gateway business got started, I'll begin this chapter with a bit of background material. Then, we'll switch out of "Novell mode" and take a look at some third-party IPX/IP gateway products, so you will know what other options are available. Finally, back in Novell-mode, we'll go through the IPX/IP Gateway installation and configuration procedures.

IPX/IP Gateway History and Overview

The history of generic IPX/IP gateways is not that old, as you can imagine. First we had to have IPX, then we had to have people rushing to get attached to TCP/IP networks, before anyone could make money selling a gateway.

Once the consumer market noticed, in early 1994, that the Web might turn into a big deal, the rush to connect NetWare clients to TCP/IP networks (mostly the Internet) began. A few companies had already organized "NetWare client-to-other" types of gateways, mainly to facilitate communications with Unix hosts for access to run internal applications.

What goes into such a gateway? The goal is easy to state: Convert IPX packets to TCP/IP packets, so these packets can traverse the Internet. Remember, only TCP/IP packets are allowed on the Internet. That doesn't sound too hard, does it? I guess you're not a programmer.

What's the Problem?

There are two critical points for an IPX/IP gateway. The first is at the client, where TCP/IP-based applications expect to find a TCP/IP protocol stack. The second point is at the server, where many NetWare clients may wish to peruse the Internet at once, and somehow the gateway must track which returning packets go to which NetWare client.

Before we solve these technical details, some of you may be wondering if it just wouldn't be easier to add a TCP/IP protocol stack to each NetWare client and be done with it. After all, don't Windows for Workgroups, Windows 95, and Windows NT ship with TCP/IP installed? What's the problem?

The problem is extra administrative overhead. IP addressing can be painful and time-consuming, especially for those used to NetWare rather than TCP/IP. Even in shops with a long history with TCP/IP, tracking individual IP addresses for each workstation is a pain.

What about DHCP (Dynamic Host Configuration Protocol), you ask? Good question, and I'm glad you're paying attention.

As I mentioned back in Chapter 1, even automatic IP addressing doesn't eliminate the problems with TCP/IP on the desktop. Cost is a component, whether you're setting up Windows 3.1 workstations that don't have TCP/IP as part of their feature set, or you're adding more functionality than is provided by the included TCP/IP (many find the "free" components inadequate).

Because of the way IP addressing works, allowing an extra 1000 or more PCs into the TCP/IP group requires subnetwork creation and existing network reconfiguration. The time spent upgrading the routing tables and other components of your network to accommodate another 1000 IP addresses is not trivial.

Thus was the impetus behind IPX-to-IP gateways. If there could be some easy way to coordinate many PCs through just a few IP addresses, the network manager's job would be a lot less difficult. Controlling those 1000 PCs would be much easier if there were some single administration points where access control could be used. Sounds like a good job for WinSock, the WINdows SOCKets specification that started in 1991 and eventually made the IPX/IP gateway market viable.

WinSock Development

You saw the short version of the WinSock story in Chapter 5, but here's a more technical and detailed account. After all, no WinSock—no IPX/IP Gateway from Novell (or anyone else).

Well, that may not be exactly true. The technology used to create an IPX/IP gateway could be done without WinSock, but it would be much more complex. We could ignore a decade of modular programming, and write IPX/IP translation software for each network interface card that NetWare and IntranetWare support. Yes, we would need a different version for each and every different network interface card.

WinSock started when members of the TCP/IP community had one of their favorite arguments in favor of their "TCP/IP everywhere" philosophy thrown back in their faces. "If you guys make such open and standard software," said a critic, setting them up for the kill, "why don't applications from Company A work with a protocol stack from Company B?"

Oops. The "open and standard" argument worked in favor of the TCP/IP community when speaking of any TCP/IP client communicating with any TCP/IP host, but not when speaking of the TCP/IP clients themselves. In other words, each company's TCP/IP applications, such as Telnet, FTP, and e-mail, worked only with their own protocol stack. The "open" application developers violated "standard" rules by tying their own applications directly to their own network software.

You can't really blame them too much. After all, this is all happening in the late 1980s, and the pain of trying to jam TCP/IP into the small-memory and single-tasking DOS software was considerable. With the growing emergence of Microsoft Windows, however, their excuses were wearing thin.

So Martin Hall (now with Stardust Technologies, a WinSock compliance testing company) organized a BOF (Birds of a Feather) meeting at the 1991 InterOp conference. Thirty companies, all competitors, met and discussed this problem. Microsoft representatives were there from the beginning, as they should have been. Novell representatives were also there, of course, mainly because of the LAN WorkPlace TCP/IP software products they gained when they bought Excelan in 1989.

WinSock was proposed as layer of "mayonnaise" between the meat of the client application code and the bread of the network transport layer. Using WinSock rules, the application developers were supposed to write their applications using generic network services (such as "get file name") rather than specific function calls for a particular version network transport software.

And that is exactly what has happened. Each TCP/IP vendor provides a WinSock layer of software on top of the network transport software and below the application software. Yes, this is slightly slower, because each application function must make a call to WinSock, which then makes a call to the network transport software. The tiny speed loss is well worth the advantage of application independence from the network layer.

The first version of the WinSock specifications was released in January 1993. The first shipping version of a WinSock product was ready later that year, with the version number of 1.1.

WinSock Spoofing

Each TCP/IP protocol stack vendor developed its own WinSock software in the form of the WINSOCK.DLL program for Windows 3.1. This file was generally placed in the \WINDOWS directory.

WINSOCK.DLL files are tied to the TCP/IP software underneath them. The specification calls for only a common, standard interface on the application side, so all applications can use any WinSock.

Notice in the previous paragraph that I said the WINSOCK.DLL files are tied to the *TCP/IP* software underneath them. That is what the specification calls for: TCP/IP network transport software. This makes sense, since all the developers who attended the BOF meeting wrote TCP/IP protocol stacks and applications.

Figure 6.1 is a high-level diagram of where the WinSock software fits in a client machine. Notice that the TCP/IP protocol stack is still proprietary and unique to each vendor.

FIGURE 6.1

Adding layers for platform independence

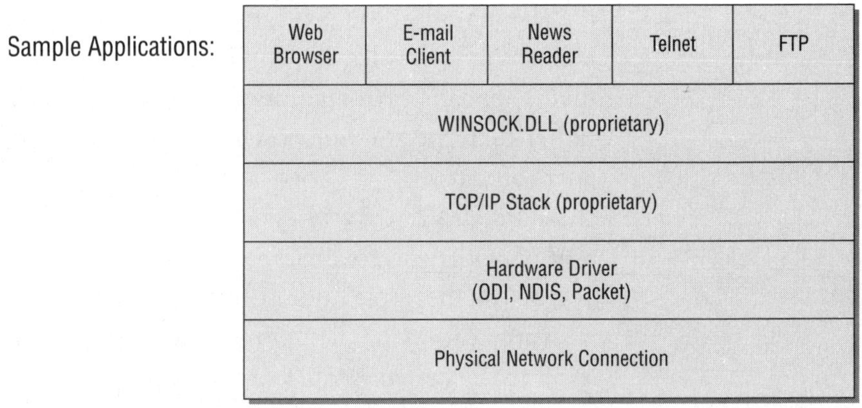

Sample Applications:

Web Browser	E-mail Client	News Reader	Telnet	FTP
WINSOCK.DLL (proprietary)				
TCP/IP Stack (proprietary)				
Hardware Driver (ODI, NDIS, Packet)				
Physical Network Connection				

Brian Walker is a senior communications programmer/analyst as MCS, a vendor of NetWare-to-Internet gateway products (among other things). I've had the pleasure to meet the nice folks at MCS after reviewing their products and mentioning them in other books. Brian took some time one day to sketch out the working aspects of programming with WinSock. Much of the information you're reading here is based on that lesson.

The Client and Server WinSock Pieces

Companies interested in providing TCP/IP access to IPX clients came up with a clever idea: Use the specified WinSock API, but split the WinSock into two pieces. The client WinSock piece speaks IPX/SPX, since that's the standard protocol NetWare clients have available. The server WinSock piece speaks IPX/SPX at the top, to communicate with the client, and TCP/IP at the bottom, to communicate with the gateway server host software.

The gateway server software can reside on a variety of different platforms. NetWare servers are a good place, of course, since they already speak IPX/SPX and have a good TCP/IP protocol stack available. Windows NT stations are popular for the same reasons, and some companies make turnkey hardware/software units that sit on the network. The trick is that the bottom part of the client WinSock software runs on this server, hidden within the gateway server software. Figure 6.2 illustrates this setup.

This process is distributed computing, although no one really calls it by that name. The PC client software must satisfy all application function calls for the network, then transport those calls across a NetWare IPX network to the TCP/IP protocol stack of the Internet gateway.

FIGURE 6.2

Splitting WinSock

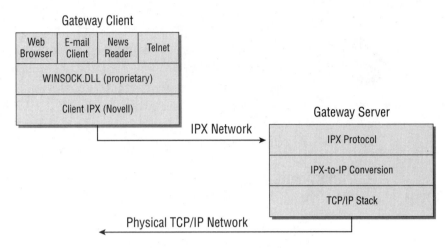

Dividing WinSock Components Across a Network

Vendors have three components to arrange in traditional WinSock:

- **Socket routines:** Berkeley Socket APIs, including connect, bind, accept, close the socket, get Internet address, and send and receive packets.

- **Database routines:** Get host name and address, get server name and port, and get protocol name and number.

- **Microsoft Windows-specific extensions:** Start up, clean up, and provide the protocol, server, and host names and information to the application.

How do you split these components across a network? Obviously, the Windows-specific extensions will stay in the PC client software. The IPX/SPX stack used by NetWare clients must be converted to TCP/IP in the gateway, and may handle the socket and database routines locally (at the client) or remotely (at the gateway). This choice is often dictated by how much control the NetWare-to-Internet gateway vendor has over the TCP/IP stack. Some gateway vendors control their own gateway, including the protocol stack in the gateway. Other gateway vendors use existing machines (such as NetWare servers or Unix hosts) as gateways, and must rely on the TCP/IP stack resident in the gateway host.

Locally converted functions place less stress on the gateway; remotely converted functions place less strain on the client. The good news is that even the slowest NetWare-to-Internet gateway product will perform faster than any WAN connection of T1 speeds (1.544Mbps) or less. Only when the other side of the IPX-to-TCP/IP conversion runs at near-Ethernet rates of 10Mbps does any performance variation appear.

The entire NetWare-to-Internet gateway market hinges on this ability to spoof TCP/IP inside the client WinSock software. All Web and Internet applications, such as browsers, e-mail clients, and the like, rely on WinSock and TCP/IP. The fact that the software vendors have modified WinSock and moved the TCP/IP protocol stack is unknown to the applications.

What Should and Shouldn't Be Part of the Network Operating System?

When it debuted, NIAS (Novell Internet Access Server) was the internal name given to the IPX/IP Gateway that somehow got written all over the documentation and installation routines. This seems like another example of executive indecision, or perhaps the old story of the right hand not knowing what the left hand (or any other part of the body, for that matter) was doing.

Part of the problem comes from trying to define what should and shouldn't be part of the network operating system. Is the ability to go from IPX to IP worth extra money, or is that a sign of a good network operating system? Different folks have different ideas on this, as you can imagine. I lean toward the idea that the capability to connect to networks outside the network operating system is a valid extra-cost feature. By the time Novell folks decided it wasn't an extra feature (and when the Internet craze started, that was the only way they could really go), other companies had filled in those gaps.

Of course, Microsoft regularly lets other companies define new feature areas for Windows. New companies develop new applications, like Web browsers (Netscape), and Microsoft decides they are a good idea (Internet Explorer). Novell developers may have just been doing the same thing; they didn't let me in on their product development plans.

Novell's plans for the IPX/IP Gateway get even more confused with Border-Manager. Now, the IPX-to-IP translation function is lumped together with the IP-to-IP address translation into the Novell IP Gateway product. You have the option to configure IPX-to-IP or IP-to-IP addressing inside the Novell IP Gateway product.

Will this change drastically when the next version (code name Moab) of the network operating system ships? Probably. Not only must Novell executives make their decisions based on technical product issues, but they must always consider the PR battle with Microsoft. If the Redmondians include IPX-to-IP services in Windows NT 5.0, Novell may need to counter by moving some or all of the Novell IP Gateway product into the base network operating system. If Microsoft bundles its entire proxy server product line into Windows NT 5.0, Novell may be forced to push all of BorderManager into IntranetWare 2 (or whatever it will be called).

The other option for Novell is to keep BorderManager separate, as it has done with ManageWise and GroupWise. Novell may release the IP gateway products with the network operating system, but keep the proxy server, firewall, and VPN components separate. This plan continues the product segmentation somewhat as it is now. This also makes room for any Novonyx (the company formed by Novell and Netscape) products to sell separately and resist the push into the basic network operating system package.

I'm hoping that Novell can keep the NetWare/IntranetWare operating system fairly clean, and offer BorderManager and other products separately. Some people forget that millions of customers need local networking only, not fancy Internet connections, Web servers, and circuit-level packet filtering. Adding these features into NetWare/IntranetWare will raise the price painfully high for small network owners. By keeping the operating system price low, and properly packaging enhanced services such as BorderManager, Novell can offer economical options to small and large customers.

Third-Party IPX/IP Gateway Products

Novell was late entering the NetWare-to-Internet gateway market, and that vacuum was filled by nearly a dozen vendors. Some vendors rely on the NetWare server for the gateway host, some use Unix hosts, some use NT hosts, and some use all three. Another popular method is to build a stand-alone hardware and software turnkey box that plugs into the network, relying on none of the aforementioned hosts.

Besides the "whole truth" aspect of providing information about non-Novell products, there is another reason to let you know what else is out there: Novell's IPX/IP Gateway doesn't solve the problems of everyone in this market.

First of all, the Novell product works on only IntranetWare or NetWare 4.*x* servers. Why? The IPX/IP Gateway uses NDS for authentication and NWAdmin for management. These are specific to NetWare 4.*x* servers. There are many NetWare 3.*x* servers out in the field, chugging right along. Those customers are forced to either upgrade (Novell's hope) or turn to third-party products for an IPX-to-IP gateway.

Also, some customers don't wish to use their NetWare server as a gateway, no matter how secure the gateway product. The idea of placing their NetWare server on the Internet gives them the willies, and they don't want to do that. If it makes them uncomfortable, that's their business, and they deserve other options. Since Novell won't get that business no matter what, I might as well help those customers.

This doesn't mean that BorderManager is worthless if you choose a non-NetWare gateway server host. Many of the advantages of BorderManager have nothing to do with the IPX/IP Gateway portion. Even more exciting, many of the control features of BorderManager still work with a third-party gateway in use.

NOV*IX (Firefox–FTP Software)

Let's start with the first product on the market: NOV*IX from Firefox. Now a part of FTP Software, Inc., Firefox started in England, making NetWare-to-OSI (Open Systems Interconnection) gateways. Yes, OSI had enough customers in Europe to make this a profitable product.

From there, expanding into TCP/IP gateways was a snap (hey, I didn't have to do the programming). By using its own TCP/IP protocol stack in a NetWare file server (Novell didn't provide one with NetWare 286, when Firefox first started), Firefox provided some features still unmatched by other gateway vendors. Most important among those features is the ability to pool IP addresses and specify particular addresses for particular users. In other words, the Firefox product can function as a DHCP server for the gateway users. Some security applications demand specific IP addresses for authentication, and NOV*IX satisfies that requirement.

Novell heavily recommended NOV*IX to its customer base. For several years, it appeared that Firefox would become a Novell subsidiary, but it didn't happen. The two companies were always close, however, and Firefox developers didn't pursue gateway servers on other platforms while they were working with Novell.

Now that Novell has its own gateway, the gentleman's agreement between Firefox and Novell has ended. Firefox is free to offer its gateway on other platforms, and now has one running on Windows NT.

Firefox provided versions with no client software, some client utilities, and full application suites. Since the company has teamed up with FTP, it is integrating FTP's suite of TCP/IP client applications, offering a single source for your gateway and application software. You can get more information from the FTP Web site: http://www.ftp.com.

Inetix (MCS)

Firefox/FTP now has two options for your NetWare IPX-to-TCP/IP gateway, but MCS has always had many options. While Inetix does not have a lot of client options or applications, it does offer the widest range of server platforms available.

The MCS developers have taken the same server software and compiled it for NetWare servers (3.*x* and 4.*x*), Windows NT, and just about every flavor of Unix. If you have one of the major Unix machines, MCS has a product for you.

Companies with multiple gateways over a variety of platforms can use the same client software for all gateways, easing administration. The only application that comes with Inetix is a graphical FTP utility, preloaded with sites containing popular Internet software. For more information about these gateway products, visit the MCS Web site: http://www.mcsdallas.com.

Instant Internet (Bay Networks)

Another merger saw Bay Networks (itself the merger of Synoptics and Wellfleet) buy up Performance Technology, Inc., in 1996. The most important Performance Technology product for Bay Networks was the Instant Internet turnkey gateway/router.

A true turnkey solution, Instant Internet ships as one hardware box shaped like a small PC system, but without a monitor or keyboard. Software is preloaded, and management happens across the network via a graphical application.

The first Instant Internet came with a 28.8Kbps modem for Internet connection and a 10Base-T Ethernet connection. New models offer dual network connections, internal ISDN routers, load balancing between systems, and impressive management and user control. The Web sites to go to for more information about these products are http://www.perftech.com and http://www.baynetworks.com.

CyberJunction (Frontier Technologies)

This is an interesting case: Long before FTP Software bought Firefox, Frontier Technologies was the first well-known TCP/IP application vendor to get into the gateway business. The developers maintain it makes sense to offer gateways, and they can help their customers by offering PC-loaded software or a gateway option running on a Windows NT server.

The fact that the company also has a complete intranet software package called Intranet Genie, also running on the Windows NT platform, should tell you it has a strong product list.

SuperTCP Suite was one of the strong players in the desktop PC market when Frontier Technologies started its gateway development program. Until FTP bought Firefox, Frontier Technologies remained the only desktop player also in the gateway business. My guess is that this trend will continue, and all major desktop TCP/IP application suite vendors will either develop a gateway option or partner with one of the gateway vendors. The Frontier Technologies Web site is http://www.frontiertech.com.

IPeXchange (Cisco)

Here is an example of another merger, or more accurately buy-out, since Cisco is huge and Internet Junction was tiny when purchased. Originally software that ran on NetWare, Windows NT, and a few Unix platforms, Internet Junction morphed into a turnkey hardware solution similar to Instant Internet. Cisco certainly has the expertise to develop, sell, and service small routers, and IPeXchange is a solid product option in this market.

Continuing the Internet Junction tradition, Cisco still supports the software-only solution for both NetWare 3.*x* and 4.*x* servers and Windows NT. All have information available on their Web server, but the software versions can be downloaded for a trial run. Go to http://www.cisco.com. (I can't figure out how to download the hardware router, however.)

IWare Connect (Quarterdeck)

Yet another merger story, InternetWare (sometimes referred to as IWare) was a small startup company in the IPX-to-IP gateway market when it was purchased by Quarterdeck. This turned out well, since Quarterdeck added its strong InternetSuite of applications to the product, making a nice, all-in-one Inter/intra/extranet connection product.

IWare Connect runs on any NetWare 3.*x* or 4.*x* server equipped with Novell's TCP/IP protocol stack. IWare Connect doesn't have the IP address flexibility of NOV*IX, but it does have excellent user monitoring and management features. The Quarterdeck Web site is http://www.quarterdeck.com.

NetRoad FireWALL (Ukiah Software)

A fairly new entrant into the IPX-to-IP gateway business, NetRoad Fire-WALL from Ukiah Software is really a firewall security product that includes an IPX/IP gateway. Of course, using nothing but IPX inside your local network makes your network resources effectively invisible from the Internet. But Ukiah also includes some traditional IP-to-IP protection. If you want just the IPX/IP gateway, ask about the NetRoad FireWARE product. This works with NetWare 4.*x* and 3.*x*.

The unusual part of the product is that most IP firewalls don't use a NetWare 4.*x* server as the host, but Ukiah's product does. The company also offers a news server application, NetRoad NewsServer, that runs under NetWare. Visit the Web site for more information: http://www.ukiahsoft.com.

Netra (Sun)

Believe it or not, even the venerable Sun includes IPX-to-IP gateway software for its server. The marketing people soft-peddle this product a bit, probably in deference to their own PC-based Sun PC/NFS product, but it is in their catalog. Pricing tends to be steep, since the Netra box is not a cheap solution, and the gateway software costs extra. However, Sun probably powers more Internet communication than any other company, so you do get fair value for your money. The Sun Web site is at http://www.sun.com.

LANlink (FEL Computing)

FEL Computing is a small company that got into the market by making DECnet connections, and LANlink is aimed at ISPs and resellers more than the end-user market. This hardware/software system supports dial-up, ISDN, and frame relay connections. Networks supported go beyond Novell to include Banyan VINES and any MS-NET network, such as LAN Manager or Windows NT Advanced Server. For more information, check out the Web site: http://www.tic.net.

WebRamp IPX Gateway (Ramp Networks)

Another new, all-in-one box comes from Ramp Networks. Called WebRamp, this futuristic-looking box includes eight 10Base-T LAN ports as part of the box, along with an ISDN plug. A free Internet browser is the only client software included besides the installation and management utilities.

Small offices and home offices (the SOHO market) often need a few computers tied together, and WebRamp saves the cost of a small network hub. Several other WebRamp products offer IP-to-IP routing, with the 10Base-T hub included. Although the routers support up to 253 connections, the IPX gateway box is limited to 50 simultaneous sessions. The Ramp Networks Web site is http://www.rampnet.com.

IPX/IP Gateway Installation and Server Configuration

Now that we've done the honorable thing and investigated the competition, let's get back to Novell.

There are two ways to install your IPX/IP Gateway: one applies to the IntranetWare version, and the other is for the new version that came with BorderManager. Let's start with the original.

Setup for the IntranetWare Version

The IPX/IP Gateway is on CD Number 3 in your IntranetWare set, and you may need to install the gateway software from there. As I write this, however, an upgraded IPX/IP Gateway is part of BorderManager, meaning you should upgrade your gateway software. You don't have to upgrade, of course, but I think you should. Several of the management tools we'll be examining in later chapters count on the newest version of the IPX/IP

Gateway server and client software. Besides, newer is always better, right? If you heed my advice, you can skip to the next section for details on installing the BorderManager version. But if you're stubborn and want to stick with your IntranetWare version, continue reading here for installation instructions.

Standard operating procedure says you should put the CD into the file server CD-ROM drive, and upgrade that server. You may certainly copy the CD contents to a server hard disk, and install it from there, if that is your normal mode of operation. You may also mount the BorderManager CD as a volume, even if your CD-ROM drive runs from an IDE or EIDE controller. That's assuming your already have IntranetWare, of course, or at least NetWare 4.11.

Go ahead and type **LOAD INSTALL** at the server console. The standard screen will appear. Choose Products. The IPX/IP Gateway product should be listed, although you may see NIAS (for Novell Internet Access Server) instead (Novell engineers promised they wouldn't mess that up again, but since they messed it up last time, we can't be sure).

The product installation screen will appear. Soon you will be asked about installing some previously configured routing information, as in Figure 6.3. What? You probably have no idea what this is about.

As the caption to the figure says, just say No; that is, unless you are installing a preconfigured set of routing tables. If you have gotten clever enough to preconfigure and preload routing information from a previous installation, why are you reading this now? In other words, this is useful to a small set of NetWare customers, and your company probably isn't one of them. But it is a nice touch, if you are working for one of those few companies that can take advantage of this feature.

If you're installing from the NetWare 4.11 or IntranetWare CD-ROM, the license material from your main NetWare software will apply. Provide any license disk requested if you want to continue.

Boring file copy screens will appear, as the files from the CD are copied to a temporary working area on the server disk. This will go fairly quickly, but the files are in condensed mode here. The actual expansion

FIGURE 6.3

Just say No

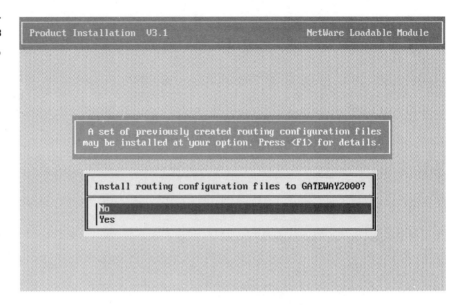

and placement of files in the proper directories will take longer, depending on the amount of horsepower and memory your server has. Go get a drink and come back.

Once you return, you'll have the pleasure of pressing the Enter key, because the installation will be finished. You may peruse the installation log file if you wish; it's not necessary, but it is the default. After you exit past the log file view option, you will be asked to down and restart the server. After all, those new NLMs and other system files must be used to start the gateway.

The LOAD IPXIPGW command will be added to your AUTOEXEC .NCF file during installation. IntranetWare uses the INETCFG utility to enable the IPX/IP Gateway. Go to INETCFG and choose Protocols, then TCP/IP. Near the bottom of the screen is the IPX/IP Gateway Configuration field, currently disabled. Highlight that field, press Enter, and choose Enabled. Save your work, just like all smart computer people.

BorderManager's Gateway Arrangements

Nothing is constant except change, right? And Novell, greasing the skids for NetWare over Native/IP in the Moab product, is changing the gateways for us.

Why change this gateway stuff? Because the BorderManager Proxy Server can handle more than just NetWare clients, that's why. By working on the idea that any client must go through an IP gateway of some kind, Novell engineers ensure that any client, regardless of operating system or hardware platform, can be controlled with the Proxy Server.

Starting with BorderManager (at least at this writing), all gateways will fall under the heading of "NetWare IP Gateway" in some form or another. This makes more sense when you remember that the IP-to-IP address translation gateway comes under this heading as well. However, it just confuses things for us right now when speaking of the IPX/IP Gateway.

When you install BorderManager and the NIAS bundle (there's that name again), all the gateway software will be loaded on the server. Unlike the IntranetWare IPX/IP Gateway, the BorderManager IPX/IP Gateway is activated through NWAdmin. There are just two steps to complete before you can activate the gateway:

- NWAdmin must be used at least once before adding the gateway installation snap-ins. If your network is an active network, you will have used NWAdmin plenty of times. If your network is brand new, execute NWAdmin once; at least expand and contract some of the containers and check the details of a user or two. That will be enough to tell the operating system that the program has been used, and to create the NWADMIN.INI file for later snap-ins.

- You must run \PUBLIC\BSSNAP\W95\SETUP.EXE from the Windows 95 workstation used as your management station. The BSSNAP subdirectory is installed during the IPX/IP Gateway installation process (although the installation screens didn't tell you that). SETUP .EXE adds some extra command buttons to NWAdmin for the server acting as host for the IPX/IP Gateway.

Following gateway installation, and after the server is rebooted, the IPX/IP Gateway should be active on the host server. One of your console screens is labeled Novell IP Gateway Access Status, but that screen is blank. You'll have details on that screen soon, after our next steps:

1. From your Windows 95 management station (the one that just ran the SETUP program to snap in the new command buttons), start NWAdmin. Then double-click on the server object running the gateway software.

2. Toward the end of the list of command buttons for that server, you will see a few new buttons. Click on the first new button, labeled Border Services Setup. (If Novell engineers get around to changing the label to BorderManager Setup for a later version, choose that instead.)

Wow, look, you must make a decision right away. The first time you click on the Setup command button, the dialog box shown in Figure 6.4 appears, forcing hard thought.

Which answer is "right" for you now? That depends. If your network is already connected to the Internet, choose Yes to block outgoing and incoming Internet traffic. Why? Because you have no controls set for your users yet, and anyone on your network can connect to the Internet without any restrictions. This is a bad choice for companies adding Internet access

FIGURE 6.4

Security choice necessary

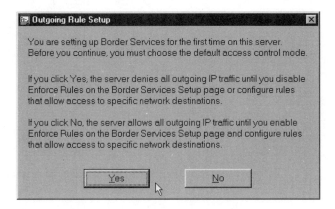

for groups that have no training in Internet use, and no explanation of your company's rules and regulations concerning Internet access. If your network is not yet connected to the Internet, you may choose No. Since no one can get out and make any mistakes or accidentally transfer your sales plans to a newsgroup, you have time to train and threaten your network users to behave themselves before Internet access is available.

Although you may choose No so that you don't restrict Internet use, I suggest you choose Yes and block everything. Why? Novell follows a smart security plan here. When introducing a new communication channel, it's better to block all access except for those users specifically allowed to communicate. This is the safest method to choose, and the one I recommend. Block all except those you specifically train and trust by clicking on the Yes command button.

3. Click on Yes (my suggestion) or No. Passing this decision point, you see the Border Services Setup window. This is a new window, and came into NWAdmin from the SETUP program you ran earlier. (Notice there are a few more command buttons down the right side that you haven't seen before; you'll see what they are in later chapters.)

4. Now you must configure the IP address of the server hosting the gateway. Yes, you set that during TCP/IP installation, but you may have multiple IP addresses if you have multiple interface cards. Here, you set the single IP address used for each of the new services in the Enabled Services list. Double-click in the Configured IP Address section under IP Address.

Figure 6.5 shows the Configure IP Address dialog box open, with the IP address used for this server. You've seen this IP address before in other examples.

FIGURE 6.5

Setting your IPX/IP
Gateway address

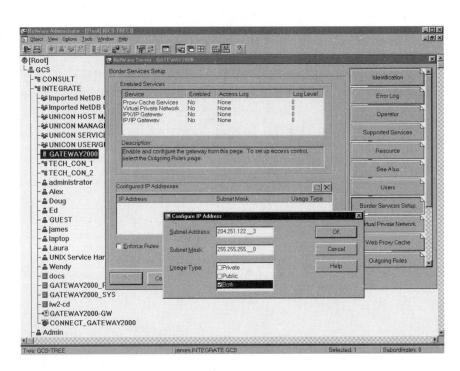

 WARNING   In case you're new to networking, please don't use this IP address shown in Figure 6.5. That's *my* IP address, not yours. If you use it, your gateway will not work, and people in your company will come and yell at you for being stupid. If I find out, I'll send you a mean e-mail message.

5. The Subnet Mask will be 255.255.255.0 on your network unless you have segmented your Class C network or have a small IP address allocation from your ISP. If your ISP or network managers give you a different subnet mask, such as 255.255.255.192, be sure to use that address without fail.

6. Usage Type, the last field in the Configure IP Address dialog box, refers to the type of network using the IPX/IP Gateway service. If your network is strictly an intranet with no Internet connection,

choose Private. If your network connects to the Internet, or will be used for internal and external networking, choose Both. It's better to choose Both than just Public (in my opinion).

All that's left now is to actually enable the IPX/IP Gateway. No, we don't need to go to the server console. That's the old way, and being modern, with-it network administrators, we want to do things the new way.

7. Double-click on the IPX/IP Gateway field in the Enabled Services section of the Border Services Setup window.

Yet another dialog box opens (chatty program, isn't it?) with some more choices, as shown in Figure 6.6. The last field in this dialog box, Port, won't need your attention unless your IP network administrators have changed the default values for things they shouldn't have changed. In other words, don't change the Port field value.

FIGURE 6.6

Activating your IPX/IP Gateway

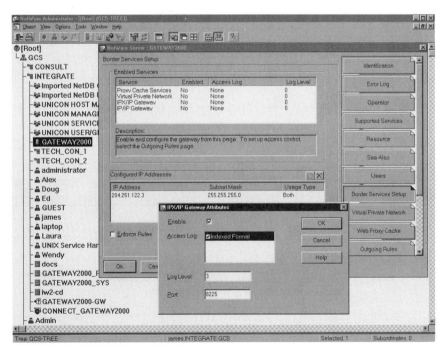

8. Check the box for Enable to activate the IPX/IP Gateway.

9. The second field in this dialog box allows you to enable the Access Log. Some logs have several choices for the log file format, but not this gateway service log. When you check the Indexed Format box, you've made your only possible choice.

10. The Log Level setting ranges from 0 to 3, but it doesn't tell you that. Lower numbers provide less information. You might start at 3 to get the most information possible at the beginning for help with any troubleshooting needs, then lower the setting later.

11. Click on OK here, then the OK command button in the main setup window, and your choices will be activated.

Your server will beep and start the IPX/IP Gateway process. Your gateway is now ready for clients, if your clients are ready for the gateway.

The IPX/IP Gateway Client

Once again, we need to discuss two types of the IPX/IP Gateway: the one that ships with IntranetWare and the one that ships with Border-Manager. Your four-CD-ROM set of the complete IntranetWare operating system includes the IPX/IP Gateway client. With IntranetWare, there is a feeling that this is a different client altogether, which isn't really true. With BorderManager, at least, you feel the gateway client is the same basic client with a few added goodies. And that, in fact, is what it is.

Installing the IntranetWare Gateway Client

When you install the IntranetWare Windows 95 client (which is our focus here, since the gateway aims to serve 32-bit clients) from the NetWare CD, you choose the IPX/IP Gateway client support in the Windows 95 Control

Panel's Network utility. From the Network Control Panel, click on the Add command button, select Protocol, and click on Add again. The IPX/IP Gateway client will appear in the next dialog box.

Files will be copied, and CDs will churn. If you do this often, you should have learned to copy all the Windows 95 CAB extension files to each workstation. Sure, they take up about 34MB, but if a station is that tight on disk space, it has no business running Windows 95 anyway.

Figure 6.7 shows how I have my system configured. See the Copying Files dialog box at the top right of the figure? Notice I can copy files from C:\MASTERS\WIN95 as well as from D:\WIN95 on the CD-ROM. If I choose the one for the CD-ROM, then I must find that CD and load it into the system. Few CD-ROM drives run as fast as hard drives. I like the shortcut of keeping the Windows 95 files close at hand.

The second file source choice in Figure 6.7 is the subdirectory on the BorderManager CD-ROM for the English files for Windows 95. Using this method, I open the CD-ROM drive once to start, and again only after I'm finished.

After rebooting, a new dialog box pops up before Windows 95 loads. This dialog box has two fields with radio buttons, asking if you wish to Enable the IPX/IP Gateway (button 1) or Disable the Gateway (button 2). When you click on the first button to enable the gateway, Novell renames any WINSOCK.DLL programs in the \WINDOWS directory to WINSOCK.N01, then N02, and so on. The real WINSOCK.DLL for

FIGURE 6.7

Cheating just a bit

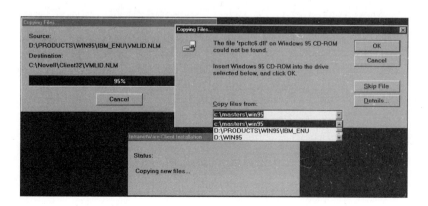

your gateway will be copied to the \NOVELL\CLIENT32 directory. You may copy this file to your WINDOWS directory if you wish. Your path statements may find another leftover WinSock file or two on your hard disk. E-mail applications often have WinSock files stuck in their own directories, so check carefully.

> WinSock applications are supposed to be compatible across all WinSock implementations, but that doesn't always happen. Novell's installation routine renames any existing WINSOCK.DLL file in the \WINDOWS directory to WINSOCK.N01, so you can reclaim your old version without much trouble.

A new folder named IPX Gateway will appear in the Novell folder of your Programs folder. This includes two programs:

- Switcher, which opens the dialog box asking if you want to enable or disable the IPX/IP Gateway, just as you saw the first time you rebooted after installation.

- WinPing, which is the Novell utility that pings other IP hosts through the IPX/IP Gateway for test purposes. If a user is having trouble, but you can use WinPing to go through the gateway, then your search can narrow down to that user's system.

Installing the BorderManager Gateway Client

BorderManager changes the rules slightly for the IPX/IP Gateway functions. If you use the INSTALL.BAT program on the BorderManager client CD-ROM, you will have a chance to check whether you wish the IPX/IP Gateway function to be copied to the client. Your other option is to use the Windows 95 Network Control Panel.

Using **INSTALL.BAT**

If you use the INSTALL.BAT program and choose the Typical (rather than the Custom) installation method, the IPX/IP Gateway will be installed to the client automatically. It won't be enabled until you reboot the system, but it will be loaded and waiting. If you choose the Custom option, you may avoid installing the Windows 95 dialer utilities and save the disk space.

Figure 6.8 shows what Novell believes is your choice for the Typical installation. Notice the cursor arrow pointing to the Description box on the upper right. Notice that the Novell IP Gateway is highlighted on the left, but the description looks exactly like that of the IPX/IP Gateway of days gone by.

After you click on the Install command button, files are copied. First, however, Novell gleefully informs you that the installation routine is "Removing existing client." I hate that, and wish I could get over that nagging fear every time I see that little note.

FIGURE 6.8

The default options

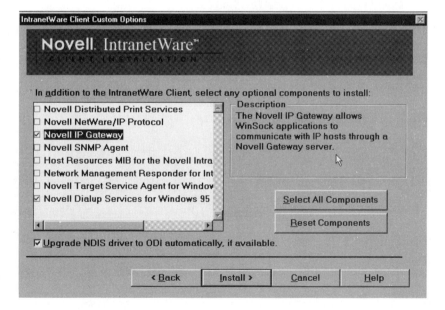

Using the Windows 95 Network Control Panel

Working from the Windows 95 Network Control Panel makes some sense, especially if you and your group are used to the Microsoft installation and configuration routines. The trick to remember is that you must specifically add the Novell IP Gateway support during Windows 95 configuration by choosing Add, then Services, then the option. The BorderManager installation, by default, installs the IPX/IP Gateway.

Figure 6.9 takes a look at the long and tortuous route through the Control Panel to add the IPX/IP Gateway. Notice the highlighted line is called Novell IP Gateway, as mentioned earlier. The dialog box in the upper right of Figure 6.9 shows that we are looking at a network service now, rather than a protocol difference.

FIGURE 6.9

Fighting through the Windows 95 Network Control Panel

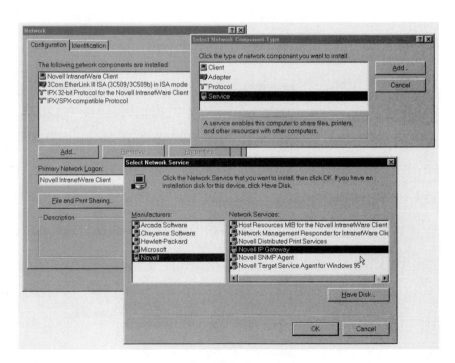

Choosing any of the options in Figure 6.9 starts the file copy and configuration process. Make sure you have a book to read if you wind up doing many of these in a row.

Configuring the Client

After saving the configuration and rebooting, the Gateway dialog box will appear the first time the system is restarted. This time, however, you have three radio button choices; Enable Gateway for IP-to-IP is added. Choose that option only if you're using the IP/IP Gateway for address translation, as we'll discuss in Chapter 7. Figure 6.10 shows the new, expanded dialog box.

Notice that the dialog box informs you that the gateway is already enabled for IPX to IP. Nothing really bad would happen if you chose this option again, but providing this information is a nice touch.

Neither client installation option requires you to add much information at all. You will need to specify the IPX/IP Gateway server, so the client software will go through a particular gateway if it's available. Many clients can share one gateway, so this choice will help your network arrangements. Every NetWare user going through the gateway will use the IP address of the gateway, so no more IP address configuration is necessary.

F I G U R E   6.10

New Gateway options

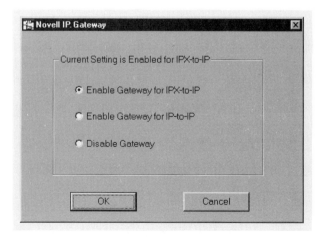

IPX/IP Gateway Security

Everyone has heard the stories of pornography run rampant across the Internet. Everyone has read about hackers deleting entire disks worth of information for no apparent reason. It's common knowledge that half your employees with Internet access will waste half their day surfing. Everyone "knows" that viruses on the Internet are worse than everywhere else, and if one gets onto your network, it will infect every computer and other electronic device within minutes.

As usual, the "conventional wisdom" that everyone knows is wrong. Not completely off base, but wrong enough, and some people believe the crazy stories whispered over water coolers.

Pornography is available on the Internet. Pornography is also available at the corner convenience store, depending on your definition of pornography.

Here's an important point: Never talk about "dirty pictures" on the Internet, because you will get into an argument with someone who disputes your version of what is dirty. Refer to pornography, obscenity, indecency, or just plain bad taste as "inappropriate" material for the business environment. People may argue about what is dirty, but they will readily admit any material falling into the various descriptions is definitely inappropriate for the business day.

There are hackers on the Internet. There are car thieves on the streets. Reasonable precautions are necessary in both cases.

Any resource as attractive as the Internet wastes more company time than committee meetings. Wasting time isn't new, of course, but computers make it easier to waste time while appearing busy. The Internet is so full of valuable information most companies allow users to explore and research topics on the Internet. But while the companies officially encourage use of the Internet, the managers often feel the employees see that permission as license to play. Every corporate executive interviewed by a major nontechnical newspaper or magazine lists "employee productivity" as an Internet concern. These executives roundly curse employee loafing, while visiting with other executives during "conferences" at golf resorts at four-star hotels. Isn't irony wonderful?

With Internet access comes Internet files, and sometimes with those files come viruses. The Internet is not filled with viruses, especially when you download from respectable support or business sites. If your employees make a habit of downloading from "Ratzo's Rack O'Files" you will have trouble. The precautions you have in place already (you do have some precautions in place, right?) will help, and a change or two will upgrade your virus protection to cover the new Internet source as a checkpoint.

The IPX/IP Gateway from Novell, and the products from every third-party listed earlier in this chapter, have options to control access to Internet or TCP/IP-based resources. We will discuss this quickly, because frankly, the Proxy Server (the subject of Chapter 8) offers much better protection than the gateways. Besides, this is a book about BorderManager, not IPX/IP gateways.

Blocking TCP/IP Hosts

The title here was originally "Blocking Nonproductive Internet Resources," but your network may need to go much farther. Every company intranet contains servers (hosts) with information restricted to a small group, such as the payroll database in accounting. Extranets bring up a new range of full, limited, and restricted access hosts. Blocking user access on the user side to known restricted hosts adds a double-whammy to internal host security rejecting unauthorized users. Double the protection, double the peace of mind for you and your bosses.

Traditional TCP/IP host-access control is pretty coarse. Every gateway vendor listed, including Novell, has a way to deny access to specific Internet resources. There are two options available in most cases:

- Block all connections not specifically allowed.

- Allow all connections not specifically blocked.

The first option is much more restrictive than the second. Typically, this is used in only intranet and extranet situations. After all, what good is the Web if you must get permission to follow links to every new host?

The second option works for those managers determined to block access to every "dirty" Web and FTP server on the Internet. This is a never-ending task, however, and results quickly in frustration.

Do you wonder why Novell made a deal to include Cyber Patrol in BorderManager? To provide users with weekly updates of "CyberNOT" sites for the Cyber Patrol software. But this software works on the Proxy Server, not the IPX/IP Gateway. See Appendix A for information about installing and using Cyber Patrol.

Are these two sides of the same coin? Yes, as a matter of fact, they are. This makes it easy for vendors to devise a simple database with "yes" and "no" fields. Some go so far as to allow the flexibility to allow different levels of access to different groups of users. Novell goes as far as anyone in this area, using the power of NDS to control access to network resources.

Figure 6.11 shows new NWAdmin windows provided to control host access for all gateway clients. The command button to open this screen is a new one labeled Outgoing Rules. It's a bit misleading, since you can control some incoming traffic as well, but the "Rules" part shows the intention.

Look at the foreground window, where the arrow cursor is pointing to the Add command button. What are we adding? It's a restriction to the host name of "host.inappropriate.com" as listed in the Source Details field above the Add button. The Source List, in the bottom-left corner of the foreground window, already lists an entire Class C network blocked by NDS. No hosts on that network can be reached by anyone using this gateway.

The middle window, with Action in the upper-left corner, has two radio button options: Allow or Deny. The Deny button is active, meaning any host or network listed will not be available to all gateway users. Farther down the left side of the middle window you can see an area labeled Access

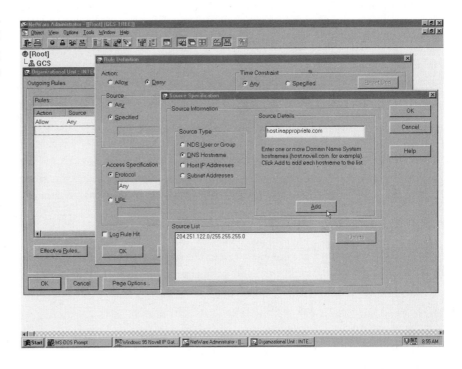

FIGURE 6.11

Denying specified
hosts and networks

Specification. Currently, the Protocol radio button is active, meaning all
protocols are blocked by the gateway. If you want, you can specify only
HTTP to block Web access, or more typically, specify FTP to stop file
downloads. Minimum control for some companies just blocks FTP access
for everyone except network managers and other trustworthy folks.

Just under the Access Specifications area is a checkbox labeled Log
Rule Hits. This instructs the gateway to track the NDS username of all
who attempt to access a restricted resource.

Is this the best log file you have available with BorderManager? Not at
all. The Proxy Server has much better ways to track and monitor
employees, as you'll learn in Chapter 9.

Random Monitoring and Your Users

Even though the IPX/IP Gateway isn't the best place to monitor, this is a good spot in the book to stress the importance of log files and user monitoring.

Let this be a second warning (the first one is in Chapter 1): Inform each user that any and all electronic transactions are monitored on a random basis. If possible, put up a notice saying "Log file now active" when each person fires up his or her LAN connection or starts using the gateway. After all, employees who believe someone is watching tend to be much more honest than employees who believe otherwise.

Inform your employees that all electronic (computer) transactions belong to the company, not to the individual. Put this in writing if possible. If you fire or reprimand someone later for inappropriate network use, that employee shouldn't be able to cry about never knowing the rules. Tell them the rules up front.

More Virus Protection Needed

Viruses aren't as prevalent as some scaremongers would have you believe, but they are a problem. You must take action in two areas to protect your company against infestation: restrict file downloads and check for viruses.

Limiting File Downloads

You should limit the number of users who may download files from any network resource. This is tough to enforce, and getting tougher. It used to be simple to block FTP access through the gateway, and declare your job done. Today, it's still easy to block FTP access at the gateway, but that won't stop the downloading. More files are being transferred with HTTP within Web browsers today than with FTP client software.

There's no easy answer to blocking HTTP downloads. Users routinely download applets, plug-ins, cookies, and other software bits during Web access. To block all HTTP traffic means no Web client. To allow HTTP access means some files you don't want on your network will get there.

Checking for Viruses

The next step is to check for viruses at the client and at the server. This probably means you'll need to upgrade your virus-protection software to cover one side or the other. Sorry about that; if your boss balks, pull out one of those inaccurate but scary *New York Times* articles about viruses eating their way across company hard disks.

Even e-mail is a source of viruses now. Many people, including me, have had trouble with macro viruses within Microsoft Word. Thank you, Microsoft, for allowing viruses to now infect non-application files such as Word documents. Check out www.mimesweeper.integralis.com for information about MIMEsweeper, the first e-mail virus checker on the market. There are other virus packages that do this, but MIMEsweeper was first.

Firewalls and proxy servers of all kinds are increasing their virus protection. Look for application-level filters that scan each and every packet that comes onto the network for virus signatures to become readily available soon. Scanning each packet slows down traffic, so investigate your options before buying the first virus gateway you see.

Yes, more virus protection is needed when connecting to the Internet or an extranet. If your current budget doesn't include a virus upgrade, you're not finished. Doors both allow exit and entrance. While your network gateway clients are going out to the Internet, make sure nothing is coming back in through that open door.

Wrap

This chapter pretty well wraps up the task of bringing Intranet-Ware into the present, and showing some details about how and why the IntranetWare applications are critical to BorderManager. You may feel this stuff has all been review, and, in a sense, it has been. If you or your bosses need some help understanding how NetWare became IntranetWare and how that leads into BorderManager, I hope this and the preceding chapters help.

Of course, the last-minute changes to the IPX Gateway procedures make it hard for us to tell which parts of IntranetWare are completely separate from BorderManager. The trend for operating systems to include all manner of utilities that used to be separate will continue, and Novell will be faced with tough choices in explaining the differences between the products. But that's why all those marketing folks make those big salaries, right?

We haven't had the time or space to provide complete details in all IntranetWare and NetWare areas. If you are new to NetWare, you may want to pick up a solid, complete reference book. May I suggest *The Complete Guide to NetWare 4.11/IntranetWare*? It's written every bit as well as this, and the author is a nice guy. I promise.

PART

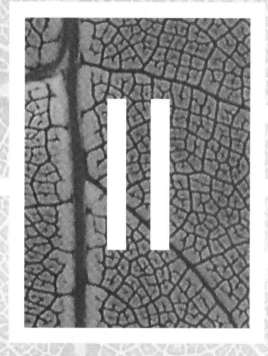

II

IMPROVING SECURITY AND
PERFORMANCE WITH
BORDERMANAGER

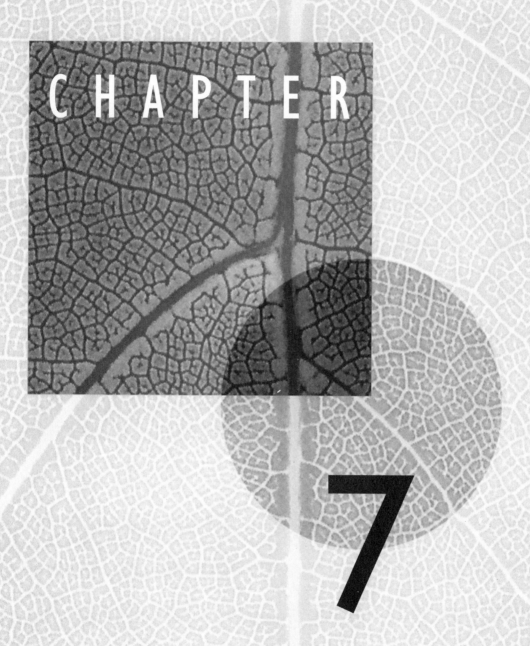

CHAPTER

7

Network Address Translation
or the IP/IP Gateway

NAT (Network Address Translation), or the IP/IP Gateway (as it is sometimes called in the documentation), may seem like a strange idea. If you're familiar with NetWare but new to the Internet, that feeling is perfectly logical. As mentioned before, Internet addressing isn't nearly as neat as NetWare addressing.

TCP/IP addresses, or more technically, IP addresses, are set for each client by the network administrator. The setting may be done by a configuration file on the client or be supplied by a DHCP (Dynamic Host Configuration Protocol) server on the network. Either way, some person or some thing must set the address.

NetWare takes the network segment number set at the file server and combines that with the unique network interface card number set by the card vendor. This works great for Ethernet and Token Ring, which are about all the varieties in common use today.

The good part of this scheme is the network manager (that's you) doesn't need to mess with any addressing. The bad part is that the numbers on your network aren't unique in the world. Oh, sure, the network interface card numbers are unique, but every Novell network uses network number 1 as the first segment, and random numbers are offered for all subsequent segments. There is no central clearinghouse for network segment numbers, so there is no guarantee that the numbers aren't duplicated all over the place.

Yes, friends, the IP addresses used on the Internet, or any public shared network, must be unique. Multiple IP addresses on the Internet cause all sorts of problems, none of which are easy to resolve.

For a variety of reasons, many network addresses used within companies or departments aren't unique. These systems need help, and Novell's NAT provides that help.

Why Use NAT?

The quick answer to this question is because people are lazy creatures, unwilling to take responsibility for their earlier mistakes. In today's world of networking, however, this answer is not the correct one.

Here are the two best reasons to use NAT:

- Internal IP addresses don't match the Internet, or other departments.

- NAT provides an extra layer of security.

Both are excellent reasons. I don't care which reason moves you, or if you have another reason to use NAT that I never considered. No doubt, somewhere in the world of NetWare, there's a network manager named Nat who thinks it would be above and beyond cool to use NAT. More power to him, I say.

Speaking rationally, the first reason listed was the original reason for NAT technology. We'll get to those details in just a bit.

The second reason was a happenstance that turned out well for all concerned. After all, if your routers and Web servers used one IP network address, hackers assumed all your computers were on the same network. Nope, not even close. There's no reason to coordinate your private and public network addresses, and many reasons you shouldn't.

Does This Sound Like Your Network?

Way back when, someone else installed the first Unix system in Engineering, long before you joined the company. The Internet wasn't a big deal, so no one realized that the IP address of 1.0.0.1 that came on the

Unix box wasn't a perfectly good number to use. Then the next Unix box used the IP address of 1.0.0.2, then 1.0.0.3, and your network grew. Grew typically, but grew haphazardly. Perhaps we should agree that "typically" for networks usually means "haphazardly," and this is no exception.

Your numbering system, as you no doubt have figured out, is a problem. Two out of every three other users of that Unix system also used the default network address, meaning that there are literally hundreds or thousands of networks starting with the address of 1.0.0.1. And none of them are legal on the Internet.

So what are your choices? Renumber each and every device on your network running TCP/IP. Replace the existing IP addresses with official IP addresses assigned by your ISP, using numbers assigned to them by the IANA (Internet Assigned Numbers Authority). This way, your network will be legal for use on the Internet.

"But that's a bad choice," you say? You don't want to go to each and every machine, reconfiguring control files scattered all over the operating system? I don't blame you—NAT to the rescue.

How about this problem: Your management declares the company will pay for overtime and enough manpower to renumber the network the way it should be, but your ISP representatives say that they don't have enough contiguous network numbers to handle the systems you have. Or, they may have enough numbers, but weaving together seven Class C networks is more trouble than you can handle.

Here's another example: I bet your company has merged with another company in the last few years. Even if you both had legitimate IP network addresses, they weren't the same. Or, rather than merging with another company, perhaps several departments want to link to the new corporate backbone, but they have competing addresses. How can you handle this problem? NAT is the solution once more.

Run the NAT software on your Proxy Server system or IPX/IP Gateway host. You want to make sure all network connections to the outside world go through the NAT software.

If you have come here directly from the table of contents hoping to use NAT to solve all your problems, take a deep breath and think again. Yes, NAT acts somewhat like a proxy server by adding some security and traffic control. However, BorderManager includes a much better Proxy Server than NAT, with lots of extra features and controls. If you want some security and management, use the Proxy Server and do it properly, rather than patching together a mediocre solution relying entirely on NAT. See Chapters 8 and 9 for details about the Proxy Server and its security.

Private Network Addresses and Internet Connections

As the Internet began to resemble the Network That Ate New York, growing by leaps and bounds, the problem of companies with non-unique addresses grew larger. You would guess that with more companies wanting to connect to the Internet, a proportional number of them would be "address-challenged." Even if the proportion of companies with address problems remained the same, the numerical number of companies between a rock and a bad IP address grew constantly.

Besides companies who accidentally found themselves full of illegal IP addresses (non-unique and therefore not allowed on the Internet), some companies changed internal addresses to numbers not allowed on the Internet—on purpose, really.

Why would anyone do this? For easy internal routing and network design, that's why. If you've tried to cram 500 users into four different Class C addresses and make sense of the subnet masks and router setup, you will understand. When your existing mess of incompatible network addresses demand renumbering for the entire network, Internet-legal address blocks large enough for every system are few and far between. "Help," you cry, "help help!"

The IANA set aside three blocks of IP addresses for private networks. These fall into the following ranges:

- 10.0.0.0 to 10.255.255.255

- 172.16.0.0 to 172.31.255.255

- 192.168.0.0 to 192.168.255.255

These addresses are for use in private networks *only*, and they are not allowed on the Internet. Routers on major Internet backbones have router table entries to ignore these addresses, but not all ISPs implement this restriction. Therefore, don't even try to use any of these addresses for any public networks, or for any clients that may ever reach the Internet.

The Class A address, 10.0.0.0, makes network division and routing a snap. There are nearly millions of available addresses within this address space, so your network can grow and grow and never be restricted. Dividing buildings, departments, and existing networks is simple, since each major network division can have its own Class B address, and each small departmental network within that division can have its own Class C address. Does accounting on the third floor really need 256 addresses for the 12 PCs connected to the departmental server running accounting software? Who cares? You have networks to burn. Life, and routing, is much easier.

Thus you see the advantage of a private network address. But when you want to connect to the Internet, guess what? That's right, address translation is now mandatory for all public networks. NAT to the rescue once more

NAT Installation and Configuration

There's no special installation procedure for the NAT components; the NAT pieces get swept up in the installation of TCP/IP and the IPX/IP Gateway (or NIAS), which we did in Chapters 3 and 6. Don't waste your time going to the console and trying to LOAD INSTALL and look for the "Install NAT" option, because you won't find it. So, with the installation taken care of, we can turn to the configuration part.

Back to NIASCFG

You're forced to use NIASCFG to configure NAT, although you'll really wind up in INETCFG. There's no advantage to going straight to INETCFG, however, and Novell shows signs of phasing out INETCFG before long in favor or NIASCFG. Either way, you're back in the C-Worthy interface, time-warped back to 1986-style control programs.

The following steps take you to your main NAT decision:

1. From your server console or remotely, type **LOAD NIASCFG** at the colon prompt.

2. Follow the breadcrumbs to Configure NIAS ➤ Protocols and Routing ➤ Bindings.

3. Highlight the LAN or WAN connection linking you to the Internet and press Enter. This screen should show the IP address for your server, or at least this TCP/IP-enabled segment of this server.

4. Cursor on down to the last option on the screen, Expert TCP/IP Bind Options, and press Enter. Your screen should look much like Figure 7.1. The network interface on your system is probably named differently than mine, but everything else should be the same.

5. Guess what you do next? You're right, press Enter on the Network Address Translation field. After all, you're being directed to Select to View or Modify, and you certainly want to Modify. The next screen is somewhat sparse, listing only the network interface name and the status. Since you haven't done anything yet, the Status field is now Disabled. This is what you would expect, since address translation is turned off by default.

6. Press Enter, and you have a surprise.

F I G U R E 7.1

Getting ready
for your NAT

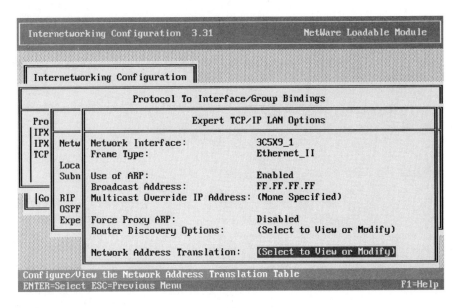

```
Internetworking Configuration  3.31                NetWare Loadable Module

  ┌ Internetworking Configuration ┐
  │                               │
  │         Protocol To Interface/Group Bindings         │
 ┌───┐ ┌──────────────────────────────────────────────────┐
 │Pro│ │              Expert TCP/IP LAN Options            │
 │IPX│ ├──────────────────────────────────────────────────┤
 │IPX│ │Netw│ Network Interface:        3C5X9_1            │
 │TCP│ │    │ Frame Type:               Ethernet_II        │
 │   │ │Loca│                                              │
 │   │ │Subn│ Use of ARP:               Enabled            │
 │   │ │    │ Broadcast Address:        FF.FF.FF.FF         │
 │ Go│ │ RIP│ Multicast Override IP Address: (None Specified)│
 │   │ │OSPF│                                              │
 │   │ │Expe│ Force Proxy ARP:          Disabled           │
 │   │ │    │ Router Discovery Options: (Select to View or Modify)│
 │   │ │    │                                              │
 │   │ │    │ Network Address Translation: [(Select to View or Modify)]│
 └───┘ └──────────────────────────────────────────────────┘
 Configure/View the Network Address Translation Table
 ENTER=Select ESC=Previous Menu                             F1=Help
```

Your choice is not what you expect. You expect to see Enabled, but instead you see this list:

Disabled

Dynamic Only

Static and Dynamic

Static Only

Hmm.... Perhaps you should stop and examine the choices, rather than blindly guessing and hoping you don't mutate network security into a welcome mat. Lucky for you, the next section covers exactly this subject.

Dynamic, Static, or Both?

These choices aren't difficult, and the wrong choice won't shred your security profiles. However, there are guidelines for your choices.

Dynamic Only

Dynamic Only mode converts all outgoing, private IP addresses to the same address as your NAT server. In other words, any IP address on your private network going to the Internet will appear to be the same IP address as the Local IP Address field back on the Binding TCP/IP to a LAN Interface screen. You passed that screen three Escape key presses ago.

The address mapping performed by the Dynamic Only choice works much like the IPX/IP Gateway covered in Chapter 6. Remember that each outgoing packet is assigned the same IP address as the gateway server, and port numbers are assigned to differentiate each user.

NAT works much the same way, although there's no need for any protocol conversion. After all, the stations using the NAT gateway already run TCP/IP as their primary protocol. Their only problem is their addresses don't fit into a numbering scheme approved for use on the Internet.

Because of the lack of protocol conversion, the NAT assignments work much more quickly than the IPX/IP Gateway and put little strain on the server. In fact, you can run 5000 TCP connections, 5000 UDP connections, and 5000 ICMP connections, all mapping at once in the server. I don't know why you would configure such a single point of failure for up to 15,000 users, but you could if you like to live on the edge.

The only incoming packets allowed past the NAT software filters are those packets with the correct IP address (your NAT server) and the correct port number currently used by one of your internal stations going out to the Internet. Packets to the wrong address, or the correct address with the wrong port number, are dropped. Period. This sounds like a firewall, doesn't it?

Static Only

Static Only allows you to map exactly the public addresses for your private network nodes. This works great for e-mail, FTP, and Web servers that need to be accessible to the outside world.

The NAT software allows public network packets addressed with your configured static addresses through, but all other public packets are stopped. Even if an outsider discovered the private address of a workstation on your network, the NAT software would not allow packets for that station through the barrier. Only IP addresses in the static address table are allowed to have visitors from outside.

Port numbers don't enter into the Static Only NAT choice. Each local address will be mapped, one private address to one public address, with no port numbers needed for stations to share a single IP address.

Static and Dynamic

The Static and Dynamic choice, not surprisingly, offers both the options just described. A table is built, matching some of your private addresses to specific public addresses. Incoming packets addressed to those IP numbers are allowed through. All other private addresses are mapped to the NAT server address, and a port number is appended. Returning packets with the correct port number are passed through the NAT software. Packets that don't match either a defined static address or an active port number are dropped.

Figure 7.2 shows the Network Address Translation Table, which is used to map private addresses to public addresses. Pressing Insert from this screen pops open a window that asks for the public address first, then the private address. Pressing Escape from that window enters the address pair into the table.

According to this table, 199.1.11.65 will appear on the Internet as 204.251.122.13. No one outside your private network will know the difference. If you want to consider this an Internet disguise, like plastic glasses, a fake nose, and a mustache, go ahead, but people may laugh at you.

The good news is that you can change your mind about Static Only or Static and Dynamic without reentering your address pair table. The same addresses appear no matter whether you choose just Static or add the Dynamic option. Being persistent, the table even reappears after you disable NAT, or set the status to Dynamic Only.

FIGURE 7.2

Building your NAT table

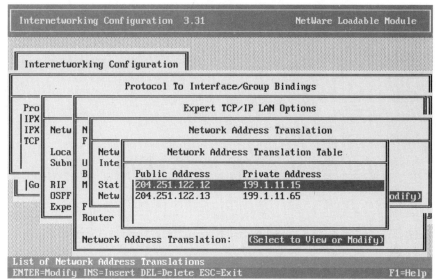

WARNING

Security alert: There is no authentication performed on the user starting NIASCFG and changing your address table. Keep the server console behind locked doors and guard your RCONSOLE password carefully.

In case you're wondering, the private IP address can be for any TCP/IP-enabled system on your network. NAT doesn't care if the addresses belong to Macintosh systems, Sun boxes, RS 6000s, or even Windows NT stations running Microsoft's (mediocre) native TCP/IP. Feel free to list all IP addresses you want, and don't feel limited to only NetWare clients.

Client Changes

You're dreading this, aren't you? You hate going from client to client to reconfigure some setting, and you hate trying to design and test some type of automatic updating procedure. Boy, oh boy, are you dreading this.

Happy news! There is no client configuration whatsoever required for NAT services! Really, I'm not lying. Much like the BorderManager Proxy

Server, NAT's work is based on the addresses and protocols of the packets whizzing by, not on any NDS parameters that depend on NetWare clients.

Don't touch a client to modify any parameter to accommodate address translation. Just verify the NAT software is running on your Proxy Server or on your other host between your private network and the Internet.

Intranet and Extranet Uses

The descriptions of address translation services may have made you assume that this technology was helpful for only Internet connections. However, this is not true.

Any time two networks must communicate, but have serious IP addressing problems, NAT can help. Do you have a corporate backbone with corporate Web servers? Great. Now you merge with another company, and none of their IP addresses match yours. Or you add a WAN link to a division formerly stranded, who developed their own IP addressing scheme, ignoring all your carefully worded memos about the corporate TCP/IP addressing guidelines.

You can gripe and complain, or you can set up a NAT server or two inside your corporate network. Nothing says you must connect to the Internet for NAT to work. Did you see anything in the figures that said, "Internet only"? Neither did I.

Older NetWare servers, too small and slow for general file and print service, can become excellent NAT servers. Remember, there is little server overhead in address translation, and dynamic addressing is quick and easy to configure. An old 486/50 running BorderManager's two-user license, and with only the NAT software activated, will support hundreds or even thousands of internal network clients.

Wrap

Address translation for networks used to be a major big deal, and it saved the corporate hides of many customers. Today, the technology is well advanced and accepted. If it wasn't, it wouldn't be in NetWare, would it?

Since BorderManager includes an excellent Proxy Server (coverage for this begins in the next chapter) and other security controls, don't configure the NAT software and think you've done all you need for your network's security. Use NAT as one piece of your security puzzle, not the entire door, lock, and deadbolt.

CHAPTER

8

The Proxy Server

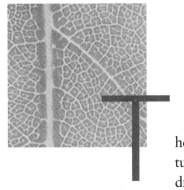

The BorderManager Proxy Server includes all sorts of new features and capabilities. In fact, these features finish Novell's drive to become a complete Internet provider, able to supply all the pieces any company needs to safely go into the Internet business.

Well, that does sound a bit grandiose, doesn't it? I guess I've been reading too much marketing literature again. However, the Proxy Server portion of BorderManager does have a long list of necessary Internet technology. And the good part is that you already have all the management and platform tools that you need to support these new features.

Proxy Server History and Overview

There's no real history of BorderManager's Proxy Server, unless you count the user authentication and access control features within NDS. That's a bit of a stretch, but we can draw a direct link between the control features used by NDS for the last several years and the control features offered by early firewall and proxy server vendors. Of course, you can also say that the features in BorderManager Proxy Server and other firewall products make sense for user control, so every product will look somewhat the same. After all, competing spreadsheets look alike, as do competing word processors.

Early Firewalls

TCP/IP was developed by a consensus of users, programmers, and commercial vendors. All open standards have one serious security problem: Open standards development means information is widely available. TCP/IP is to security what politicians are to verbal honesty. You can say TCP/IP is secure, but the record speaks otherwise.

As the Internet moved from a few connections between cooperating universities and research labs toward the global network it is today, security became increasingly more important. It's one thing to trust professional peers in a small network environment, but quite another to trust people half a world away who have no interest in research.

How could TCP/IP be made more secure? There was no easy way, so the next step was to look at the intersection of the local network and the Internet. Adding security intelligence to the routers at the borders of your network meant a single outsider checkpoint controlled access, rather than adding security to each and every host on the network. Of course, adding security to all hosts was necessary anyway, but the choke point of access to your local network was a great place to start with your security.

And so it came to be that the firewall became a necessary part of life. Old-timers talk about walking to school barefoot, leaving their front door unlocked at home, and connecting to the Internet without a firewall. Hand them some Geritol and be kind.

The first firewalls were built into Unix hosts that also acted as network routers. Remember the problem with TCP/IP being so open that the bad folks knew all the tricks? The same can be said, and emphasized, for the various Unix operating systems. Unix firewalls are like building a brick wall on soft sand: Your foundation will betray you.

Does this mean no good firewalls can be built on a Unix foundation? No, not at all, but you have your work cut out for you. Making some version or another of Unix secure for your firewall application takes quite a bit of work. Firewalls and proxy servers often work best on Unix systems dedicated to the routing and protection of remote-connection traffic.

Advantages of Proxy Servers

A proxy is a firewall mechanism that hides the internal IP addresses from outsiders. The official definition of *proxy* is one who is authorized to take the place of another, and that fits the use of proxy IP addresses by fire-walls. By substituting the IP address of all internal clients with the address of the proxy server or other address, security is enhanced.

As the proxy idea became more important and critical to network security, some vendors began separating the firewall and proxy software. Generally, however, the proxy services are included with a more comprehensive firewall package.

Hiding your internal network addresses is an excellent security technique, and one of the big advantages of several BorderManager options. Thieves have a harder time stealing your car when it's locked in your garage than they do when you leave it on the street. The same principle supports hidden networks, making them more safe by keeping them out of sight.

The other big advantage of proxy servers comes from the fact that every client who wants Internet access must pass through the proxy server, giving you an excellent management point. This allows the application-, circuit-, and packet-level utilities to control user access to external resources and to monitor user activity. (These filters and controls are covered in the next chapter.)

True, a firewall can add those same functions without needing to change the IP address. However, more protocols and functions on a firewall mean more opportunities for a security breach. IP spoofing is one of the more insidious hacker techniques used today, where a good address from inside the network is copied and used to penetrate the firewall. If the firewall and network clients have completely different IP addresses, IP address spoofing becomes nearly impossible.

WARNING   Never say something is absolutely impossible in the computer world. I try to avoid that blanket statement when talking to you, and you should take the same care when talking to your managers. After all, nontechnical people don't understand that virtually anything in the computer world is possible if you have enough time and money to throw at the project. We understand that, and should protect the unknowing by denying that the impossible is possible under certain conditions.

Are all computer systems in your company absolutely safe when protected by the BorderManager Proxy Server? Only if they are disconnected from the network, unplugged from the AC outlet in the wall, and hidden from all other employees. In other words, no.

Employees will cause more security problems than malevolent hackers seeking thrills and files to delete. Sometimes these problems will be caused intentionally, but more often they're caused by mistakes, misunderstandings, or just pure stupidity.

Fortunately, the Proxy Server is well equipped to track activity by users and report problems. Whether a user breaches security parameters on purpose or by accident matters less at the time than whether security held or was actually breached. Timely tracking through the NWAdmin utility makes handling these problems easier than ever before.

Why Novell's Proxy Server Runs So Fast

The first reason Novell's Proxy Server runs so fast is that it runs on a NetWare server. Microsoft folks can complain all they want, but the fact that Novell servers provide files faster than Microsoft NT servers is well known. In fact, the higher the load, the larger Novell's performance lead.

After all, what is a Web server but a specific type of file server? HTML pages, forms, and Java applets are nothing more than files sent to your computer from the Web server. If those files come across the Internet, you may think speed at the server isn't important, but it is. You can't service the next customer request until the current file is processed, so the faster the files go, the better.

Novell bypassed the CERN (Council European for Research Nuclear, when loosely translated) caching algorithms and settled on a combination of Harvest and Squid algorithms. Formed by research into the next generation of caching technology, Harvest/Squid technology promises tremendous Internet performance improvements. The ICP (Internet Core Protocol) papers sent to the Internet powers-that-be are based on the work in this area.

What Is Harvest/Squid?

What a funny name, right? Where did this come from, and why would Novell put so much time and effort into something with such a funny name?

Let's start at the beginning, and take a look at the Harvest project. Originally funded by ARPA, the full title is The Harvest Information Discovery and Access System. ARPA funding ended in August 1996, but Harvest lives on for a variety of reasons and through the work of loyal supporters.

I'll quote from the group's home page, so you'll get the words exactly from the source:

> "Harvest is an integrated set of tools to gather, extract, organize, search, cache, and replicate relevant information across the Internet. With modest effort, users can tailor Harvest to digest information in many different formats from many different machines, and offer custom search services on the web."

Who likes Harvest besides Novell? Netscape's Catalog Server is based on the Harvest design. Expert developers are expanding the technology, and discuss their work in the Usenet newsgroup comp.infosystems.harvest.

Squid grew out of the Harvest research. The Squid proponents describe their software this way:

> "Squid is a high-performance proxy caching server for web clients, supporting FTP, gopher, and HTTP data objects. Unlike traditional caching software, Squid handles all requests in a single, non-blocking, I/O-driven process. Squid keeps meta data and especially hot objects cached in RAM, caches DNS lookups, supports non-blocking DNS lookups, and implements negative caching of failed requests. Squid supports SSL, extensive access controls, and full request logging. By using the lightweight Internet Cache Protocol, Squid caches can be arranged in a hierarchy or mesh for additional bandwidth savings."

NetWare fans will notice a few kindred thoughts in the Squid paragraph. Notice the part about keeping meta data cached in RAM? Doesn't that sound like Novell's directory cache strategy to speed file access?

Notice the last line, about arranging caches in a hierarchy. That will become important soon.

As far as I can tell, Novell is the only company mashing Harvest and Squid technologies together into Harvest/Squid. If BorderManager takes off, however, look for lots of copycats to check these technologies out themselves.

If you're curious about the evolution of these processes, check out the Harvest and Squid Web sites. The Harvest URL is http://harvest.cs.colorado.edu/. The Squid site is http://squid.nlanr.net/, and there you can read about Squid enthusiasts keeping the faith alive, just like the Harvest group. One last interesting note is that both these technologies are developed and implemented on Unix platforms, yet Novell quickly rewrote them for the NetWare server as NLMs. Hmm... perhaps NetWare and Unix are getting closer together, at least on a functional level, than we thought. It certainly seems like the NetWare platform still has some life supporting new applications after all.

Web Client Acceleration (Standard Proxy Cache)

The Web client acceleration cache method takes Novell's proven file-caching technology and adds other Web servers to the cache, not just an individual NetWare file server. By using RAM to hold the most recently viewed Web files, performance jumps for the next client who accesses those same Web pages, or when the same client returns to an earlier page.

Web clients have a cache like this built in as well, but there is a limit to how many Web pages a client can keep on disk. Some companies may wish to disable the client Web cache and depend on BorderManager caching. Why? Personal Web caches help only one person, but the BorderManager cache helps the entire network. Besides, personal cache pages are more likely to become outdated. The disk cache will keep an old file for quite a while, meaning a user may see an old version of some Web pages. If a particular Web server is a popular one for your clients, the Border-Manager cache will have the most recent Web page in RAM cache, and not display a disk cache that's two weeks old.

Who Needs Web Client Acceleration?

Client acceleration is the easiest use of cache server technology, especially for small installations, such as single sites with multiple clients. A single server can be your IPX/IP Gateway, firewall, and Proxy Server for security and access control, and it can cache Internet data used by clients. Routing many clients through one Proxy Server doesn't slow anyone down; in fact, the effect is just the opposite. Many users through one Proxy Cache Server tend to duplicate Web server targets, meaning the cache will be able to serve more users more quickly than your Internet connection, which may not have all the bandwidth you would like. Intranets with just a few corporate servers see considerable speed improvements, since many clients go to the same server.

Check your Web client users for traffic patterns. If your users visit a limited number of Web servers during the work day, the BorderManager cache will speed their download times considerably. Power users (and computer support people) may hit scores of Web sites during an online session, but other network users often refer to the same Web servers supporting their job function time after time. These repeat users will see the greatest performance increase.

This method also offers improved control over client access to the Internet. Access controls in the Proxy Server work with NDS for Intranet-Ware clients, and by IP address for non-IntranetWare clients. Logs track exceptions to the rules.

Remember, the BorderManager Proxy Server supports more than just NetWare and IntranetWare clients. Almost all systems running Web client software have a way to specify a proxy server for Internet access.

Every Web-enabled client on your network can have better performance through the BorderManager Proxy Server.

WARNING   Since Novell has developed a variety of new caching schemes, some of the terminology is new. You may see other companies selling proxy servers refer to some of these same features with different names, or use the same names to describe different features. There's no way to set a standard name for all these features until the market settles down a bit, and a consensus for terms is reached. What's my point? Check the feature details when comparing other products, not just the feature names.

The Client Acceleration Arrangement

The client acceleration cache method is the simplest to set up and diagram. Figure 8.1 shows the most basic configuration for general Web client acceleration to all available Web servers.

FIGURE 8.1

Caching the entire Internet

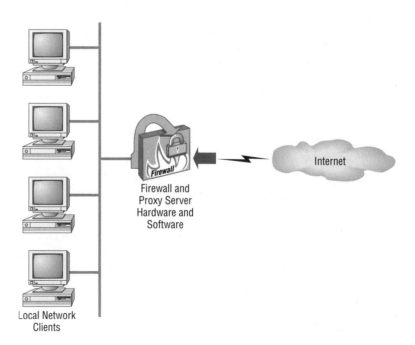

Firewall and Proxy Server Hardware and Software

Internet

Local Network Clients

In this configuration, all clients must go through the firewall and Proxy Server to reach the Internet. For clarity of this example, Figure 8.1 shows the server connected directly to the Internet, which may not be the case. However, each client must go through the Proxy Server to reach the Internet, regardless of where the actual ISP connection exists.

Why does this work so well? If your computer support department has trouble with Windows workstations and new network drivers (and who doesn't?), you may regularly connect to microsoft.com, novell.com, and the sites of several companies supplying driver software or the actual hardware. Each time one person requests a Web page, that page will be cached on the Proxy Server. The next person to request that page will download the page from the Proxy Server, over the local network, rather than from the actual server across the Internet. Bingo, fast screen updates.

Configuring Client Acceleration

You noticed in Chapter 6, when we set up the IPX/IP Gateway, that the BorderManager Proxy Server was enabled through NWAdmin rather than at the server console. This practice continues for all the configuration details for the BorderManager components.

After starting the NWAdmin program, double-click on the server object hosting the Proxy Server. The primary dialog box for that server appears, usually displaying the Identification page information unless you have changed the defaults. Find the Web Proxy Cache command button, toward the bottom of the command button list, and click on that.

The dialog box shown in Figure 8.2 appears, and it should be enabled, since we started the Proxy Cache in Chapter 6. Notice the arrow cursor is in the upper left of the screen, pointing to the checked box for Enable HTTP Proxy. The HTTP Listening Port number is provided automatically with the standard default. You should never need to change the 8080 port number unless your network has been extensively customized.

We'll get to the next checkbox in the upper left, Enable HTTP Accelerator, in the next section. Don't worry about that yet; you'll have plenty of time for various worries later. The same goes for the HTTP Accelerator List in the middle of the dialog box.

FIGURE 8.2

The Web Proxy Cache
dialog box

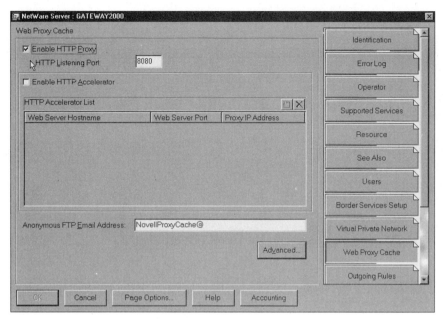

The Anonymous FTP Email Address field shows the default answer and can be changed without a problem. Before you change it, however, make sure you understand why the anonymous e-mail address is required.

Anonymous FTP

Anonymous FTP servers ask for a username and password. This looks like security, but it really isn't, because the username is "anonymous," and the password is your e-mail address. No verification is done, so any e-mail address will work as long as there is an "@" in the middle of the address. Addresses such as james@gaskin.com work, of course, but so do bill_c@whitehouse.gov or fooled@you.

FTP servers can be set up to authenticate the names and addresses, but then they wouldn't be anonymous FTP servers, would they? The Anonymous FTP Email Address field supplies the address of NovellProxyCache at whatever domain you have listed for your BorderManager server. This little detail makes FTP transfers within Web server sessions invisible to the user. The remote server is satisfied by the address of NovellProxyCache @gaskin.com, for example, and the remote Web master knows a cached network made a copy of the Web page. If the Web master has any sense, he or she will realize that more than one person has the ability to see what was downloaded, even though only a single address hit those Web pages.

Advanced Settings

You may be wondering about the Advanced command button sitting below the Anonymous FTP Email Address, as well you should. This opens a dialog box that provides a variety of settings for the Proxy Cache itself. Take a gander at Figure 8.3 to see what I mean.

This is the only page you may need to configure in the Advanced settings. And frankly, you won't need to configure these unless things change drastically, or you have lots of clients needing cache support and you want to increase the storage room for more cached pages. What do I

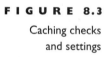

FIGURE 8.3

Caching checks
and settings

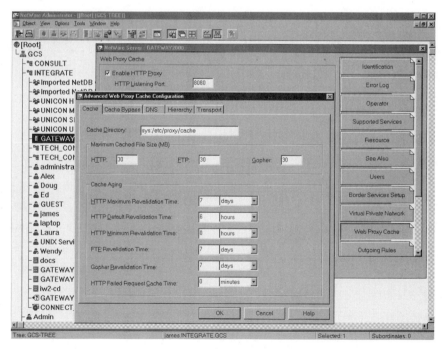

mean by "change drastically"? This might be adding lots of extra users, running low on server disk space, or getting twice as much RAM for that server (hold your breath for that one).

Let's take a look at what these settings do and if you would want to change the default settings:

- **Cache Directory:** Storage location for the cached files that overflow RAM on the cache server. Do not change the default unless you plan to unload PROXY.NLM before changing the file, then reload PROXY.NLM after changing the default. The only reason for changing this is to add more cache space than the SYS volume can hold.

- **Maximum Cached File Size (MB):** Maximum file cache size for the various sorts of files. Settings for HTTP, FTP, and Gopher files are independent of each other. You might change these sizes to add more or less space for the usage level of your cache server.

- **HTTP Maximum Revalidation Time:** Maximum time cached HTTP data is kept before validating with the source. Yes, cached files are checked to verify they haven't changed and the source is still available. This setting overrides the Time to Expire value set on the host Web server if this value is greater.

- **HTTP Default Revalidation Time:** Default time cached HTTP data is kept before validating with the source. This is used if the source Web server doesn't specify a Time to Expire value.

- **HTTP Minimum Revalidation Time:** Minimum time cached HTTP data is kept by the cache server. The source server's No Cache and Must Revalidate settings override this setting.

- **FTP Revalidation Time:** Time FTP retrieved data is kept before revalidating with the source FTP server.

- **Gopher Revalidation Time:** Gopher data time before revalidation. Gopher and FTP servers change far less often than Web servers.

■ **HTTP Failed Request Cache Time:** Time the failure of a cached item revalidation is displayed. It's better to let the items that can't be revalidated just be deleted from the cache.

As you can see, cached pages can be regularly checked against their source servers to make sure the information is still valid. This overcomes one of the most critical complaints about proxy cache servers: that they display old data. After all, fast-changing data servers may change more often than you think, and your revalidation settings may be too slow.

Fear not, friends, for BorderManager has already solved that problem for you. Notice the second tab on the Advanced Web Proxy Cache Configuration dialog box (Figure 8.3), which says Cache Bypass. That tab opens a dialog box that lets you list URLs and certain patterns that should never be cached. This forces the Web clients to go to the source server every time.

Where would you use this? It's appropriate for news-oriented servers, pricing servers, stock market sites, weather map displays, and other quickly changeable information servers, such as one that shows the current number of Congresspeople under indictment this month.

You may list HTTP (Web), FTP, and Gopher servers and my bank account as no-cache sites in this dialog box. If you put too many sites in this list, performance will suffer. You can also list patterns, such as /cgi-bin/ to exclude program query pages, for the caching algorithm to skip.

Web Server Acceleration (Turbo-Charging HTTP)

How can you turbo-charge access to your own Web servers? It's simple, and there are a variety of reasons beyond performance that make this move a smart one.

Heavily loaded Web servers benefit from offloading repetitive page queries to the proxy server. Novell developers claim their Proxy Server, running on a 200MHz Pentium Pro machine with 128MB of RAM and 16GB hard disk, can handle about 250 *million* hits every 24 hours. Yes, more than 10 million hits per hour (10,416,000), or 173,611 hits per minute. Novell guesses that only half the hits will be satisfied by the Proxy Server cache, meaning half the queries will continue on to the source Web server. That still means that the Proxy Server cache software can successfully answer about 86,805 queries per minute. That's 1446 fulfilled requests per second.

Please reread the description of the cache server hardware in the previous paragraph. Is this some super Sun multiprocessor server costing hundreds of thousands of dollars? No. Admittedly, 128MB of RAM and 16GB of hard disk space put this box into the realm of heavy-duty servers, but these are not unusual features any more. Even better, the majority of PC hardware vendors can supply this system, making the cost competitive. It may be expensive, yes, but not outrageous. Besides, the way Microsoft's Windows 95 is going, in two years you may need to buy 128MB of RAM and 16GB of disk space just to run Windows 95 and the Microsoft Office Suite at acceptable performance levels.

Who Needs Web Server Acceleration?

Performance is the biggest reason to front your Web servers with a Proxy Server or two, but there are other reasons. Let's take a look at a few:

- Increased capacity. More hits means more Web clients can be supported by the same amount of Web server hardware. Adding a Proxy Server costs money, but not as much as a stout non-NetWare Web server.

- Increased security. Using Proxy Server as the entry into your Web site enables you to hide the actual IP addresses of your Web servers. The Proxy Server also keeps the Web servers from connecting directly to the Internet (you can see this in Figure 8.4, coming up soon). Your Web servers can be in a completely different subnetwork from your Proxy Cache Server, and no one from the outside can easily see your Web server addresses.

- The ability to offload simple queries from a processing Web server. Web servers responding to Web clients by calculating, searching, or formatting queries can't handle as many "simple" queries. Using a Proxy Server to front a commerce server, for instance, allows catalog queries and simple page downloads to come from the cache server rather than the commerce server. Everyone wins, since the simple page requests will be handled quickly, and the processing time on the commerce server won't be interrupted for nonprocessing queries.

- Again, performance. The numbers mentioned at the beginning of the Web server acceleration section are just the estimated number of hits the cache server would fulfill under heavy-load conditions. Double those numbers for the number of queries processed in one way or another. In other words, the cache server component of Border-Manager can handle nearly 3000 queries per second.

The Web Server Acceleration Arrangement

Figure 8.4 shows a typical arrangement of a Proxy Cache Server fronting a series of Web servers. For a more complicated drawing, we could include a firewall between the Proxy Cache Server and the Web servers, or show multiple Proxy Cache Servers supporting the Web servers. But I bet this simpler diagram will give you the necessary details.

Do these Proxy Cache Servers work well in intranets as well as on the Internet? Absolutely. One way a cache server saves you, the network administrator, time and trouble is through access controls. Moving the access controls to the cache server means a single management point can control access to multiple Web servers. Why configure security on six Web servers when you can define the same security controls on a single Proxy Cache Server?

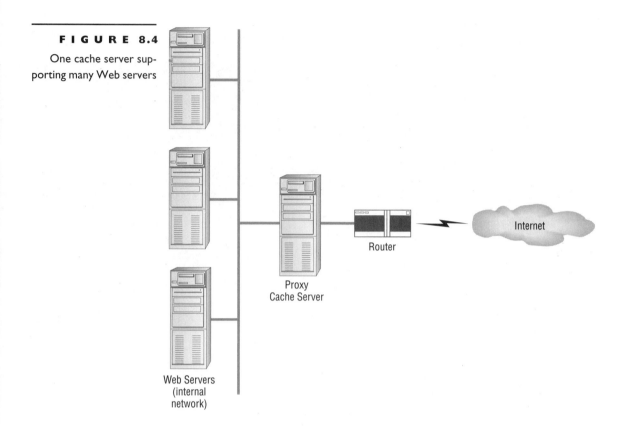

FIGURE 8.4

One cache server supporting many Web servers

Configuring Web Server Acceleration

Figure 8.5 shows how to configure the Proxy Cache Server. This is the same NWAdmin dialog box (shown earlier in Figure 8.2) that appears when you double-click on the server that hosts the Proxy Server, and then click on the Web Proxy Cache button.

The difference between Figures 8.2 and 8.5 is that the Enable HTTP Accelerator List checkbox is checked in Figure 8.5. Notice that the formerly empty box under the Accelerator checkbox now has two server names listed. The foreground dialog box is what appears when you click on the Add icon (the icon beside the X for delete) on the same line as the HTTP Accelerator List.

FIGURE 8.5

Speeding Web
host response

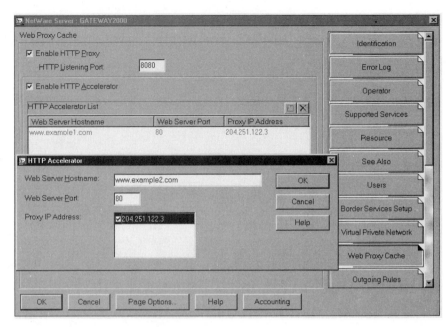

When the HTTP Accelerator dialog box opens, there is no Web Server Hostname or Proxy IP Address listed, but the Web Server Port field has a default of 80 filled in. Type the name of your Web server in the proper spot, as well as the IP address of your Proxy Server. In my case, that IP address is 204.251.122.3, and the number was provided automatically. It's rare for any port numbers other that 80 or 8080 to be used for public Web servers, but you can set any port number you wish.

You can see in Figure 8.5 that this single Proxy Cache Server will support two Web servers (www.example1.com and www.example2.com). Limits aren't listed, but you can certainly support a large handful of servers, as my testing showed. However, remember that the idea of the Proxy Cache Server is to offload processing from the Web servers themselves, so make sure your Proxy Cache Server is stout enough for the job. In other words, put in twice the amount of RAM you think you need.

After you click on the OK command buttons in the dialog boxes to save your settings, your server will beep a time or two as the Proxy Server adds these servers to the list. If you want to see your success, change the server console screen to the Novell Internet Proxy Server screen, by pressing Control and Escape and choosing it from the pop-up menu. Each successful accelerated Web server will have an entry on the screen saying something like "Initialized HTTP Reverse Proxy for www.example1.com:80 at TCP/IP address 204.251.122.3:80." Your server names and addresses will vary, as will your mileage.

Network Acceleration (Hierarchical Caching)

A result of technology outlined in the ICP (Internet Core Protocol), hierarchical caching, or network acceleration, is an advanced technique that benefits large sets of clients, Web servers, and proxy installations. This isn't a casual two- or three-server feature, but you may find this more helpful than you realize. The stronger presence your company has on the Internet, or more developed intranet you have, the more value you will find with network acceleration.

What we have here is an increased capability to communicate, with a series of Proxy Servers working together. Organized into peer, parent, or cascade relationships, this grouping of cache servers works to provide Web pages from within their collective cache if the hits are not served by departmental cache servers. In other words, network acceleration provides a second-layer-cache network of intelligent, communicating cache servers. If client HTTP requests are not satisfied by the first-level cache on departmental cache servers, the request is processed by the second layer of cache servers before being routed directly to the source server.

Peer servers are other proxy servers that respond to ICP requests, but those requests don't obligate the second server to start searching on behalf of the requesting system. If the peer server has the cached information, that's great, but the requesting server must decide to send it farther along.

A parent server takes on more obligation when a cache is requested (parents everywhere are already overlooked, and now parent servers feel responsible if they don't answer a child server's request). If the parent server does not have the information in cache, it will initiate the search for that information up the line on the Internet.

A cascade server does not have ICP software loaded, but Novell can fool it into allowing a search of its cache material anyway. How Border-Manager does it isn't terribly important (it has to do with UDP requests and tricking the server into providing the information), but it opens up the possibility of more caches on more servers.

Who Needs Network Acceleration?

The ability to coordinate Proxy Cache Servers into a mesh network extends the network server acceleration into an entirely new area. You may consider the network server acceleration a simple way to organize cache servers to increase Web client performance for single sets of Web servers; network acceleration improves performance for entire Internet and intranet networks.

Am I saying that a few well-placed cache servers would help the entire Internet? Yes, but I'm quoting the National Laboratory for Applied Network Research, who calls the current Internet method inefficient today. After all, when your Web client software connects to a Web server, you are setting up a one-to-one connection across the entire Internet.

Popular information requests particularly show the mistake in having a single, client-to-server connection for every Internet file transaction. If you take a look at the popular measurement of any activity, 80 percent of the people want 20 percent of what's on the Internet. In other words, a few servers are overloaded, while most others are practically unused.

A 1993 report showed that a few well-placed cache servers would lower FTP traffic by 44 percent. Since downloading a file with FTP is much more efficient than downloading most Web pages, cache servers for the Web would likely have an even greater impact.

Let's focus on the value provided by network acceleration for your company. Check these ideas and see if they apply:

- Multiple networks. Every network connection point is a potential performance drain. This multiplies tenfold when discussing large numbers of LANs and WANs within a single company. Proxy Cache Servers as the connecting point between your network and the company backbone or WAN will improve performance for all Web-derived information.

- Slow Internet links. Proxy Cache Servers help two ways with slow links. First, slow links delay response, so increasing response speed to all queries helps alleviate the slow link problem. Second, if a peer cache server has the information and your request goes there instead of to the Internet, you save time.

- LAN to WAN congestion. The speed differences between LANs and WANs make each connection a bottleneck. Bypassing the Internet delays for some requests will improve performance.

Again, this is not for small installations. Big companies often demand the most improvement of system speed and reduced bandwidth usage. Network acceleration from BorderManager does both.

The Network Acceleration Arrangement

Figure 8.6 shows a fairly involved network acceleration design. Notice the speed differences between the lower-level peer cache servers and the parent-level peer cache servers. Do all your remote sites have the same speed connections to the corporate WAN backbone?

Let's say someone in Austin wants a new press release from Corel about a WordPerfect upgrade. He looks for corel.com, and the site pages are not on his personal Web client cache. Of course, if someone else on the local Austin network had connected to the Corel home page earlier, the local server would have the information cached. No such luck, so a decision must be made by the cache software.

FIGURE 8.6

Intranet network
acceleration

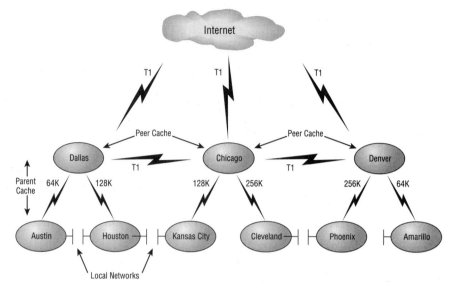

If there were no network acceleration, the request for corel.com would be passed up the line through the Internet to the physical site supporting the Corel Web server. Depending on the number of hops between the client and the Corel server and the Internet traffic at the time, response may range from acceptable to dismal.

Network acceleration software sends a request from the Austin Proxy Cache Server up to the Dallas server. No luck. Then the Dallas server sends the query over to Chicago via the T1 connection between the two sites. Bingo—someone there checked out www.corel.com recently, and the page is sent back down to Austin and the requesting client.

Does this travelogue seem longer than necessary? Well, it does seem roundabout, but that's only because we don't know how many hops would be made between the Austin client and the actual Corel server. Yet the connection between Dallas and Denver is just as fast as the one between Dallas and the Internet. Unless the Corel server resides at the ISP in Dallas, the query will then go from the ISP to the Internet. If the query is answered successfully in Chicago, there is only one extra hop past Dallas. On the Internet, there may be a dozen or more extra hops.

Notice that the parent-level peer-to-peer cache between Dallas, Chicago, and Denver will be updated by each client query in any of the six child cities. This means that the larger host cities will see even better performance than they would without the parent-to-child cache arrangement.

Configuring Network Acceleration

As with the other Proxy Server configurations, for network acceleration, go to NWAdmin and double-click on the server object hosting the Proxy Cache Server. When the server dialog box opens, click on the Web Proxy Cache command button. Next, click on the Advanced command button toward the bottom right of the dialog box, beside the row of command buttons—you remember, the command button you didn't select to change the maximum disk cache sizes described earlier in the chapter. Go ahead, flip back to Figure 8.3 and take a look; I'll wait.

Now that you're at the Advanced Web Proxy Cache Configuration dialog box, click on the Hierarchy tab to define your network accelerator. The major portion of the dialog box is gray until you check the Enable ICP box. Then the Neighbors List section snaps from gray to white, indicating that the neighbors are ready and willing to become involved (well, at least, you can start putting in the information about the neighboring Proxy Cache Servers), and the ICP Listening Port and ICP Neighbor Timeout fields suddenly become active.

For those who think that the Proxy Server uses some proprietary software and keeps Novell out of the mainstream, prepare to be surprised. Any other Squid-based proxy server can become neighbors or parents for an IntranetWare BorderManager server. Be sure to get permission before listing some other company's cache server as a resource for your servers; a move polite, courteous, and designed to keep you out of unfriendly legal entanglements. Your own cache servers are fair game, of course, even those in other departments, when set up for internal caching.

The port number of 3130 is the default for ICP (that does stand for Internet Cache Protocol, and the port number is supported by all vendors following that protocol specification), so don't change that.

The ICP Neighbor Timeout is a different story. This specifies the time this cache server will wait for information from a neighboring cache server before passing the request on to the next listed neighbor or the Internet. The default, as you can see in Figure 8.7, is 2 seconds. You may certainly lower that value if neighboring servers are connected via fat pipes of bandwidth. In other words, if the neighboring servers respond quickly, set the time to 1 second, a testament to how quickly the Intranet-Ware Proxy Cache Server can respond. Or, set it to 2 or 3 seconds, which is still quicker than going to the source server across the Internet.

If your connection to the neighboring servers isn't all that fast, you may lengthen the amount of time for waiting to hear about local cache. But if you set the time delay too long, your clients will whine and moan about how slow Internet access is all of the sudden. They won't stop whining until you improve the connection speed or lower the waiting time, or they discover how to bypass your Proxy Server by changing their

FIGURE 8.7

First stage of network acceleration setup

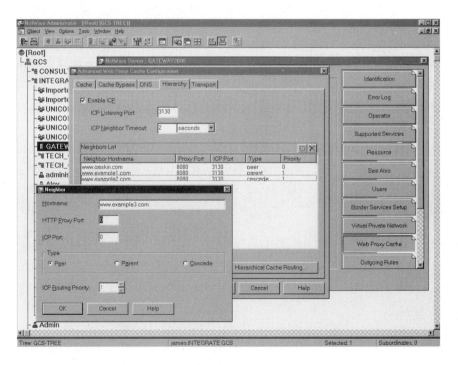

own browser configuration. Better you let a few more connections hit the Internet than lower the performance so far that every client hates you.

The Neighbors List box in Figure 8.7 contains three server names (these are made up, so don't try to connect to them). The same Add and Delete icons as you've seen for the other NWAdmin lists appear across from the list title.

Adding Neighbors

When you click on the Add icon for the Neighbors List, you see the Neighbor dialog box, as shown in the bottom-left corner of Figure 8.7. Adding new neighbor names is fairly simple, as you can tell. Add the name, the port numbers, and choose whether the neighbor server is a peer, a parent, or a cascade server. Remember the differences:

- **Peer:** Provides material from its own cache, but won't search for requested cache items it doesn't have.

- **Parent:** Provides material from its own cache, and will search for requested cache items. Once retrieved, the parent cache system and the requesting server both have the material in cache.

- **Cascade:** Doesn't have the cache server software, but will respond to cache requests if material is available in its cache.

The ICP Routing Priority setting becomes active only for parent and cascade servers. The default priority is 1, and higher numbers bump the priority a bit. If you have only one or two servers listed, the default setting for each is fine. If you have a large network of cache servers connected over a local network, feel free to raise the priority on a couple of them with the most RAM cache space. Remote servers, or those located across WAN links, are less helpful in this situation. (I told you that network acceleration isn't a feature that tons of people can use.)

Advanced ICP Cache Routing Settings

Notice the large command button beneath the Neighbors List section of the Hierarchy tab. Click on that, and you'll open the Advanced ICP Cache

Routing dialog box. Here we are, already confused and overwhelmed, and we just now hit the Advanced stuff. Hang on, and take a look at Figure 8.8.

There are two major parts of the Advanced dialog box, as you can see in Figure 8.8, as well as a checkbox. The checkbox, labeled Treat a URL's Home Site as a Peer Cache, asks for some other Web servers that can be used as cache servers. Similar to the Cascade option for specific Web servers in the Neighbor dialog box, the domain names listed here can be searched for the answer to the cache request. Although the Web servers are not configured as cache servers, they will respond to cache requests under certain conditions. Domains listed will be checked.

The top window in the dialog box, labeled Local Domains, offers a space to list the other domains to check for the requested cache information. If the checkbox has a check, just the home server for the domain will be checked.

FIGURE 8.8

Domains and pattern exclusions

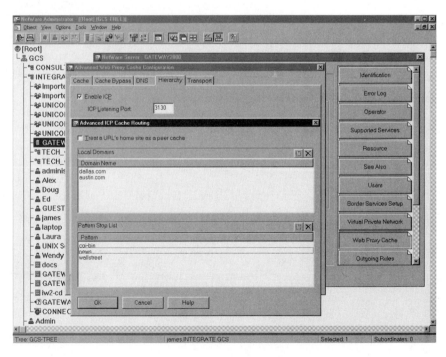

Every good search routine has a way to exclude certain patterns from your search. In this case, certain text patterns found in the URL should not be answered by cache servers; they should go directly to the source. Sometimes, you can dictate the source. For example, in the bottom section of Figure 8.8, the last name in the list is "wallstreet." If you were looking for information from the *Wall Street Journal*, you most likely would want the update directly from the *Journal*. A cache server may respond more quickly, but getting yesterday's news isn't all that helpful. Sometimes, you want the news archives, but more often, you want fresh, hot news, straight from the oven.

Of course, other Web servers provide news as well. (One of my favorites is run by c|net, and is called news.com.) However, many companies provide news on their servers, and you want that news fresh as well. That's why I didn't just say to bypass news.com, and let it go. That doesn't ensure fresh news from novell.com/news, antiques.com/news, nasa.org/news, and barbershop.com/news. With the second entry shown in the Pattern Stop List in Figure 8.8, any of these sites with the text "news" in the URL will be contacted directly, rather than letting a cache server provide old information. Or, in this case, old news.

The first entry shown in the figure is "cgi-bin." URLs with this address almost always refer back to a database running on the Web server or associated system. In other words, the URL is asking you a question that will churn through a database before providing you with an answer. Since these questions require interaction in almost all cases, you want to hit the original server rather than a copy in cache.

Specifying Proxy Servers for Clients

Current Web client software versions come with support for proxy servers built into the basic product. You don't need to add any NetWare client software to any Web client to enable them to reference a proxy server.

IntranetWare clients using NDS are automatically contained in the database used to control access to remote resources through the Border-Manager Proxy Server. Using the IPX/IP Gateway makes this connection absolute, especially when the gateway doubles as the Proxy Server, but is not necessary. The WinSock software installed as part of the IPX/IP Gateway client software handles the connection through NDS, and the Proxy Server controls user access to resources through NDS as well.

There are more browsers out in the world today than just Netscape and Internet Explorer, but the process is similar for every browser. Let's take a look at the two most popular browsers, covering the majority of the market, and then you can apply what you've learned to all other browsers.

Both Netscape and Microsoft allow you to set addresses that will bypass the proxy server. This is similar to the settings Novell allows on the Proxy Cache Server itself to bypass constantly changing hosts or local connections. In fact, Microsoft's Internet Explorer includes a checkbox to bypass the proxy server for all intranet addresses.

Configuring Netscape

As you discovered when you installed your IPX/IP Gateway client files (in Chapter 6), you have a copy of Netscape branded by Novell. Unfortunately, the branding doesn't go so far as to configure the Proxy Server address when you install the software, but that's asking quite a bit. Software may think it's intelligent today, but you and I both know intelligence is relative. Right now, most software is not as intelligent as those stupid cousins your family always makes fun of during reunions.

Since the software is slightly lacking in configuration intelligence, you'll need to supply the brains. This isn't difficult, although I'm not sure you want to trust the users to do it themselves. This is certainly a job that the newest network tech can perform, however, or even an intern who is hanging around.

After starting Netscape, follow this path to get to the Manual Proxy Configuration screen: Options ➤ Network Preferences ➤ Proxies ➤ Manual Proxy Configuration ➤ View. This will pop open the dialog box you see in Figure 8.9.

FIGURE 8.9

Proxy settings and options

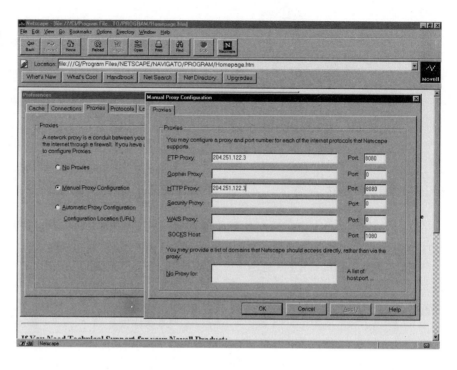

FIGURE 8.9

Proxy settings and options

The dialog box in the foreground opens when you click on the View command button in the Preferences dialog box in the background. Netscape's default is set for no proxy server.

Notice in the Manual Proxy Configuration dialog box that Netscape offers you ways to connect through multiple different proxy servers if you wish. Notice also that each protocol has an option for a different port number.

If you're wondering about all these ports and why we keep talking about ports when there aren't any ships around, check out RFC 1700. This paper deals with assigned, available, and reserved port numbers. It will also cure insomnia without drugs, as will most of the RFCs you read.

HTTP Proxy, field number three, is the most critical. HTTP is an inefficient protocol, often requiring dozens of reconnections to download a single page. Using the BorderManager Proxy Cache Server for HTTP saves more user time and bandwidth than any other option.

You may put the IP address or host name of your Proxy Server. I prefer to put the IP address, just so the DNS lookup step is bypassed. This can save a tiny bit of time, and also gives you a chance to connect even if your DNS server is having problems.

The default port number for HTTP is 8080, and that should work for your network as well. If you didn't set up the Proxy Server yourself, verify with the setup person that 8080 is the port number to use.

Field number one, FTP Proxy, has been set up just as a test. You'll see in just a bit that FTP statistics are cached, and sometimes you will have enough FTP traffic to make it worthwhile.

When I configured the FTP Proxy, I tried port number 21, the traditional port for FTP services. No such luck. Netscape or the Proxy Server kicked out that port number because of a security violation. FTP is subject to hacker attack, and either Netscape or BorderManager may block port 21 for that reason. Fortunately, 8080 works fine and is cached through the Proxy Cache Server without a problem.

NOTE   Notice in the Proxy tab of Netscape's Preferences dialog box that there is an option for Automatic Proxy Configuration. Netscape allows you to configure the proxy details for all users, store that file on a central server, and download this file to all users with a single click. Unfortunately, the proxy file configuration details lean toward Java scripting and vary widely depending on the host server. We don't have the time here to cover all the possible configurations. If you're interested, check out Netscape's help file.

Configuring Internet Explorer

Microsoft's Internet Explorer, of course, comes loaded with Windows 95/ NT. If you thought Microsoft people hated Novell more than anyone, then you haven't seen what they say about Netscape.

Regardless of competition, Novell supports Internet Explorer, just as the BorderManager Proxy Cache Server supports all Web client software. The steps for configuring the Proxy Server location in Internet Explorer are quite similar to those for Netscape, although the names of items are different. From the menu of Internet Explorer, choose View ➤ Options ➤ Connection. (Why Microsoft didn't call this Proxy or Network I have no idea, but it is often easier for a camel to pass through the eye of a needle than to fathom the thinking of Microsoft.)

All the same protocols are supported in Internet Explorer as in Netscape except for WAIS (Wide Area Information Services), which is a bit of a surprise. Microsoft does include a nice checkbox that sets all protocols to use the same proxy server, so you need to fill in only one field. There is no mention of any way to download a proxy configuration file from a central server.

Proxy Server Console Displays

All configuration for the Proxy Server happens through NWAdmin, after TCP/IP and other network details have been configured through UNICON and NIASCFG. For your entertainment, however, an abundance of Proxy Server information is available on the server console.

The reason I say it's for your entertainment is because you can't really change much from the server console. NWAdmin configuration dictates what is shown on the server console screens. Also, as you'll see later in the chapter, NWAdmin provides some of the more popular displays in full-color, GUI format.

Still, the displays on your server console have value in showing how active the Proxy Server is, and getting a quick idea of some settings. These screens are also safer displays for management, since the managers can see something is happening but can't accidentally change any settings.

Novell Internet Proxy Console

This screen has the most information, and actually allows you to perform some cache maintenance. You won't need to fix anything often, but you can.

Figure 8.10 shows the Novell Internet Proxy Console screen in all its glorious black and white. This time, the lack of color in screen shots doesn't hinder your enjoyment one bit.

We're not going to churn through each of these choices, because some aren't all that helpful. There are a few, however, that I have found either useful or interesting. Sometimes the information is both useful and interesting—always a happy circumstance.

Feel free to check out some of the other settings, especially when you need to look busy but don't want to really work. It's easy to choose option 7, nod your head wisely, scratch some notes onto a legal pad, then choose 8 and compare the results to 7. Is this useful? Not particularly, but it's a good way to be left alone for a few minutes. After all, if those screens weren't important, they wouldn't be there, would they?

FIGURE 8.10

Eighteen semi-helpful choices

```
Novell Internet Proxy Console

1. Configure Error Injector
2. Ignore no cache requests from browsers
3. Cache operations.
4. Display current activity
5. Display DNS statistics
6. Display cache statistics
7. Display HTTP server statistics
8. Display HTTP Client statistics
9. Display Connection statistics
10. Write DNS cache entries to file
11. Read DNS cache entries from file and resolve
12. Get a list of most referenced origin hosts
13. Get a list of origin hosts with most bytes received originating at host
14. Get a list of origin hosts with most bytes received from host
15. Get a list of origin hosts with most cache bytes transmitted
16. Display FTP statistics.
17. Display GOPHER statistics.
18. Display memory usage statistics.

Enter option:
```

Browser Setting Impact

If you choose 2 and press Enter, the line will change to "Do not ignore no cache requests from browsers." While somewhat overwhelmed with double negatives, the intent here is to respect client browser settings to bypass the cache. The default is to ignore the browser setting and cache everything. (Personally, I think the default should be to respect the browser settings, but they didn't ask me.)

Proxy Server Activity

Most people want to know how busy their Proxy Server is at any one time. For this, go to option 4, Display Current Activity. You'll see the information in Figure 8.11.

I ran a Windows NT server/workstation to generate the numbers that show up in Figure 8.11. This system has its own TCP/IP stack, and doesn't use the IPX/IP Gateway. I do have Internet Explorer configured to use the Proxy Cache Server, however, showing that any system can be forced through the Proxy Server after simple configuration.

FIGURE 8.11

Real time, more or less

```
Current Activity
Connections in use: 32
Idle client persistent client connections: 0
Idle server persistent connections: 20
Pending DNS TCP Lookups: 0
Total DNS TCP Lookups: 0
Pending DNS UDP Lookups: 0
Total DNS UDP Lookups: 51
Requests being serviced by the cache: 4
Cache updates in progress: 0
Threads waiting on cache hash lock: 0  Highest ever waiting: 0
Cache writes in progress: 4  Cache reads in progress: 0
Active HTTP client fill requests: 4
Total HTTP client fill requests: 336 (1 this second)
Number of HTTP client requests in retry mode: 0
Active HTTP server requests: 30
Total HTTP server requests: 406 (1 this second)
Number of cache nodes: 2796  Hot: 132  Cold: 2664
Hot cache hits: 23  Cold cache hits: 60  Cache misses: 283

Press a key to return to the menu (press S to switch to log screen)
```

The numbers in Figure 8.11 update just like all console screens, once every second. Does this mean you're not getting the freshest information? Actually, only people in the computer business are crazy enough to complain that a one-second resolution isn't good enough for current information. No wonder people make fun of us and call us names.

Let's see what could be helpful on this listing. "Connections in use" doesn't mean IntranetWare connections; it means TCP/IP and HTTP connections. Most browsers today are getting smarter, and they can manage four or more connections while you see only a single Web page. No wonder the Internet is slowing down.

"Idle server persistent connections" drops to zero when no one is going through the Proxy Server. During this screen shot, I was the only one using the connection, so five sets of four connections each from Internet Explorer must have been waiting for a few seconds for a response.

Skip down past the middle to "Total HTTP client fill requests" that shows 336, but one this second. The Proxy Server hadn't been up for long when I took this screen shot, but it does capture quite a bit of information quickly.

The last line sums up the story of a single-user cache waste: only a few (23) hot cache hits (in RAM), with 60 cold cache hits (from disk). You get your best value from a cache server when there are lots of people going to similar network resources through your cache server. This and the line above it, reading "Number of cache nodes: 2796 Hot: 132 Cold: 2664," amplify that story even more.

DNS Statistics

Option 5 on the Novell Internet Proxy Console screen, Display DNS Statistics, can also be useful. Check out Figure 8.12 for an example.

Notice the last two lines, showing the configured name servers and their status. 204.251.122.3 is the Gateway2000 server acting as IntranetWare server, IPX/IP Gateway, Proxy Server, and NetWare/IP server, which is why it's configured as a DNS name server. Busy machine, right?

F I G U R E 8.12

DNS details and
name servers

```
DNS Statistics

Number of DNS Get Host Calls: 407
Number of DNS Lookup hits: 387
Number of DNS Lookup negative cache hits: 1
Number of DNS Lookup misses: 19
Number of DNS Lookup Errors: 0
Number of DNS TCP Requests: 0
Number of DNS TCP Replies: 0
Number of DNS TCP Replies Aborted: 0
Number of DNS UDP Requests: 55
Number of DNS UDP Requests Send Done: 55
Number of DNS UDP Replies: 37
Number of DNS UDP Timeout Packets: 18
Number of Connect To Host Calls: 358
Number of Connect To Host Calls in progress: 0
Number of Connect To Host Calls That Failed: 2
Number of Connect To Host Calls That Succedded: 356
DNS Name Server(s) Status:
        204.251.122.  3 is UP
        199.  1. 11.  2 is UP

Press a key to return to the menu (press S to switch to log screen)
```

It's only a 120MHz Pentium with 32MB of RAM, and it's doing well, thank you.

The next two lines from the bottom, "Number of Connect to Host Calls That Succeeded" (minus the beta spelling error) and "Number of Connect to Host Calls That Failed" show that the Web still isn't 100 percent reliable. Don't tell your management that the Proxy Server will make the Web more accessible, because it won't. However, although there are many reasons why your clients won't be able to reach a Web site now and then, the Proxy Server will rarely, if ever, be one of those reasons.

Origin Hosts Lists

One great tool, and possibly the one you will use most often to impress nontechnical folks, is option 12 on the Novell Internet Proxy Console screen, followed by 13 through 15, which give many of the same details. Check the results out in Figure 8.13.

These sites are ranked in order, as you can see, with the most hits first (okay, the most "Times Referenced" first).

```
Enter number of hosts: 16
                    Host Name                   Times Referenced
                www.pdavidson.com                      93
                 www.techweb.com                       68
                 techweb.cmp.com                        44
                 www.novell.com                        38
                  www.news.com                         31
                 www.boston.com                        29
                www.filemine.com                       25
                  www.aifp.com                         21
                www.mediainfo.com                      18
               www.realmedia.com                       14
                  www.cnet.com                         10
               www.rtvf.nwu.edu                        10
                www.infoweek.com                        2
             gateway2000.gaskin.com                     1
               ad.doubleclick.net                       1
             omnibus-eye.rtvf.nwu.edu                    1

     Total hosts returned: 16

        Try again (y/n): n
```

Options 13, 14, and 15 show similar information but use bytes and cache bytes for the ranking rather than hits. In my case, the order was similar, but not exact, for each of these options.

Be careful when checking these pages. As you can see on the top line of Figure 8.13, you choose how many site listings to display. You would think that if you put in 22, or any number past one screen full, that the program would stop the listing and let you press a key to display the next page. Not in this version, friends. Don't pick more than 21 unless you want to start missing the top entries. The corresponding screen in NWAdmin is more flexible, however, so stay tuned.

Memory Statistics

The last Novell Internet Proxy Console option, number 18, will be interesting to all of you with memory constraints on your server, which is just about everyone. Nobody feels they have enough memory if the server has been running more than a week or two. Adding all the BorderManager features onto a multipurpose IntranetWare server will make you even more paranoid about memory. So, let's choose option 18 and see what it says. Figure 8.14 does the honors.

FIGURE 8.14

Where your RAM went

```
Proxy Memory Usage Statistics

Request Blocks:                   75,264 bytes
Connection Blocks:                25,744 bytes
DNS Cache:                        97,136 bytes
Object Cache Tables:             541,184 bytes
Object Cache Nodes:               72,544 bytes
Object Cache URI Strings:          2,256 bytes
Object Cache Other Allocs:             0 bytes
Skip List Nodes:                  42,944 bytes
ICP Client and Server:                 0 bytes
FTP Client:                       56,800 bytes
FTP Other Allocs:                      0 bytes
Gopher Client:                         0 bytes
Send ECBs:                         3,600 bytes
Send Fragments:                    2,432 bytes
Global Config Blocks:              1,488 bytes
Proxy Log:                             0 bytes
User Names:                          128 bytes
Console Screen:                    8,192 bytes
Debug Allocs:                          0 bytes

Total Allocated Memory:          929,712 bytes

Press a key to return to the menu (press S to switch to log screen)
```

You shouldn't be surprised that Novell can use a cache effectively, and it does so here. Total memory for the cache in the system displayed in Figure 8.12 is less than 1MB, a fairly small amount for the benefit. Truthfully, I don't have a lab with 50 people surfing wildly through the Internet all day long, so I can't say exactly how much RAM that type of cache would need. I can say that three machines did quite a bit of touring around, and all in less than 1MB of RAM.

Again, you can't change any of these settings here. This RAM listed supports the 64 cache directories on the server, full of more than 3000 files taking nearly 26MB of disk space. As far as I can tell, the object cache tables, taking 541,184 bytes according to Figure 8.14, track those 3025 files in the cache directories. Check your system; you'll find a ton of strange directories created without your knowledge under SYS:\ETC\ PROXY\CACHE. In my case, those 3025 files are scattered around 66 directories. If you don't want the cache on SYS:, you can change the location. Refer back to Figure 8.3 to see your chance to change the value for the Cache Directory field, although you can also set limits on the size of the cache.

Cache Operations

The last interesting option on the Novell Internet Proxy Console screen is number 3, Cache Operations. After typing 3 and pressing Enter, the Proxy Cache Operations screen appears. It's pretty dull, so I won't take a screen shot. Here are the three choices, exactly as they appear:

```
Proxy Cache Operations

1. Check cache entries (takes a while if cache is big)

2. Perform LRU refill

3. Chill the whole cache

Enter option (ESC to exit):
```

Number 1, if the option to scan the cache is enabled, checks each and every site and Web page listed to see if they are still current. Novell's warning that it "takes a while" is an understatement.

Number 2, referring to the least recently used (LRU) blocks, pulls Novell storage management system into play. Choosing the second option tags which disk blocks in the cache are old enough to move from the high-availability hard disk to another storage medium. This isn't a particularly good idea, because you don't want to reclaim cached files at a later date. Caching is good for performance, but bad for long-term reliability. When you revisit a site, you want to know that the site is current. That's the whole idea of the first Proxy Cache Operations option, remember?

The last option is to stop adding to the cache and leave it alone. "Chill" is a particularly hip way to say that, and I hope this doesn't get changed by some Novell vice president with cold feet.

NetWare Proxy Cache Configuration Console

What looks like a wonderful configuration program, PROXYCFG, turns out to be less than exciting. Again, too ugly for a real screen shot, here's what you see on your console screen when you switch to PROXYCFG:

```
NetWare Proxy Cache Configuration Console

1. Display Object Cache Configuration.

   2. Display DNS/Miscellaneous Configuration.

   3. Display TCP Configuration.

   4. Display ICP Configuration.

   5. Display FTP/Gopher Configuration.

   6. Display HTTP Configuration.

Enter Option:
```

Notice the "bait and switch" tactic of offering a screen name indicating configuration of some type, then starting each of your six options with the word "Display." Worse, little of this is interesting.

The only information display I found to be worthwhile was option 3, the TCP configuration. One of the system capacities that I can't find a way to set anywhere is the maximum number of connections. I figured this would be in the many hundreds, since each client generates many Web connections, as we saw earlier.

I was wrong. The maximum connections number is 50,000. How many hundreds of client systems can go through this Proxy Server before we get to 50,000 active connections? I'm guessing "hundreds" doesn't cover the number; we should talk "thousands." Remember that number

(50,000 active connections) when you look at proxy server software for Unix and Windows NT systems. You won't see anywhere near that capacity for anywhere near the price of BorderManager—I guarantee you.

Novell Internet Proxy Server

If you wondered about the last line in Figures 8.11, 8.12, and 8.14, which says "press S to switch to the log screen," here is where you will discover what it means. I'm afraid the anticipation will be more exciting than the result.

The information on the Novell Internet Proxy Server screen (what the console line calls the "log screen") consists of your number of cache directories (64), and that the directories are configured to have 64 (even though I still don't know where that 64 number comes from). The next lines tell the DNS names and IP addresses bound to the server. We've seen that IP address all over the place, haven't we? There is no reason to go to a special console screen to discover that address.

There is a decent listing of configured services, although you can view and modify the services inside NWAdmin. RCONSOLE does start quicker than NWAdmin in most cases, however, so these screens will give you information slightly sooner than when you go through NWAdmin.

Proxy Server NWAdmin Displays

After complaining that the console server screens were full of obtuse and uninteresting information, now I'm going to complain that the NWAdmin screens don't show enough. The good news is that the NWAdmin screens will likely add more and more features over time, while our desire for Gopher statistics will likely wither.

Viewing BorderManager Services

Open NWAdmin and click on the Tools menu item. You should see, after installing the BorderManager snap-ins, a new tool labeled Border Services, or this may be BorderManager in your copy. Either way, it's new and promises lots of fun details in graphic format. Don't be confused if you don't see the BorderManager or Border Services label at first. You must highlight a server hosting some of these services before the menu item will become active.

Figure 8.15 shows everything opened and displayed from the Border Services option. The top dialog box, in the background, shows the three BorderManager services (how's that for base covering?), all in one screen.

When you double-click on Proxy Cache, the second dialog box opens. That's the one in the middle, which shows recent cached sites. The early version doesn't seem to sort the listings in any way, but that type of cosmetic cleanup often is taken care of during the final polish or in a patch.

FIGURE 8.15

Graphical overload or helpful information?

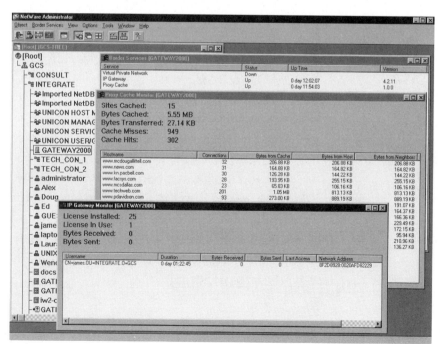

I expect that you will be able to sort the contents of the window by clicking on the column heading you would like to see them ordered by.

The last dialog box, in the foreground, appears when you double-click on IP Gateway in the top dialog box. Current users are listed, although I'm the only one working, once again.

Notice the username is the complete authorized NDS name. Since users from anywhere in your intranet could use a common IPX/IP Gateway, this is a nice touch. Just listing "laura" or "alex" wouldn't give enough information to track down a user in case of a problem.

Bytes Received and Bytes Sent make me look lazy, don't they? Another case of no activity on a lab network. The same lack of activity appears for Last Access.

The last entry, Network Address, takes the final step toward tracking the current users of the gateway. Since you have the option to block users by NDS name or network address, Novell is smart to provide the network address so conveniently here.

Now that we know where we're going, let's take a look at the log files generated by various BorderManager modules. You didn't know about the log files? Neither did I, until I accidentally right-clicked on the Proxy Cache entry in the dialog box that lists information about the three services. Out popped a floating menu, listing several log choices.

Of course, had I been clever, I would have noticed the main menu items changed when the new BorderManager window opened. That should have been my first clue. What was my second clue? All the choices listed in the pop-up menu were also available as active buttons. No matter where you look, these options are waiting for you. And since you're reading about it here, you don't need to admit that it was an accident that lead you to these features. I guess I didn't really have to admit it either, but I'm a firm believer in "poking around" in new software, especially when the manuals are incomplete or incomprehensible, so I discover many things accidentally.

Proxy Cache Server Information

Since this is the Proxy Server section of the book, let's look at the Proxy Cache information. Double-clicking on the Proxy Cache listing in the main Border Services dialog box opens the Monitor Realtime Activity dialog box. This lists the host sites cached, the number of connections, the bytes to and from, and the bytes from any neighboring systems. If you think that sounds amazingly similar to the middle dialog box shown in Figure 8.15, you are exactly right. Tell your boss you deserve a prize for cleverness above and beyond the call of duty, and that you clearly exceed the definitions of your job description.

Now that you've been properly recognized for your brilliance, let's take a look at what else is lurking under the covers of the Proxy Cache listing. Highlight Proxy Cache and right-click, and a menu appears holding these active choices:

Monitor Realtime Activity

View Common Log

View Extended Log

View Audit Log

Border Services

Let's try our luck with the second option, View Common Log.

A Look at a Common Log

Clicking on the View Common Log menu item will generally display a message that the log file is so long that it won't fit into the display area, and will be truncated to the last 32k. Since even 32k is quite a bit for our purposes, let me excerpt a snip of continuous log:

```
204.251.122.4 - - [Thu, 05 Jun 1997 21:19:07 GMT] GET http:/
/www.comicbook.com:80/gifs/comics/aulogo.gif CACHE_MISS 3591

204.251.122.4 - - [Thu, 05 Jun 1997 21:19:44 GMT] GET http:/
/www.tv.com:80/news CACHE_MISS 227
```

```
204.251.122.4 - - [Thu, 05 Jun 1997 21:19:46 GMT] GET http:/
/www.cnet.com:80/Content/Tv/Tvcom/news CACHE_MISS 1429

204.251.122.4 - - [Thu, 05 Jun 1997 21:19:48 GMT] GET

204.251.122.4 - - [Thu, 05 Jun 1997 21:19:49 GMT] GET http:/
/www.cnet.com:80/Images/404.gif CACHE_MISS 2458

204.251.122.4 - - [Thu, 05 Jun 1997 21:20:22 GMT] GET http:/
/www.comicbook.com:80/news.html CACHE_MISS 53

204.251.122.4 - - [Thu, 05 Jun 1997 21:20:27 GMT] GET http:/
/www.hollywoodnetwork.com:80/news CACHE_MISS 207

204.251.122.4 - - [Thu, 05 Jun 1997 21:20:36 GMT] GET http:/
/www.hollywoodnetwork.com:80/news.html CACHE_MISS 207

204.251.122.4 - - [Thu, 05 Jun 1997 21:20:39 GMT] GET http:/
/www.hollywoodnetwork.com:80/news.htm CACHE_MISS 207

204.251.122.4 - - [Thu, 05 Jun 1997 21:53:19 GMT] GET http:/
/www.novell.com:80/manuals CACHE_MISS 159

204.251.122.4 - - [Thu, 05 Jun 1997 21:53:21 GMT] GET http:/
/www.novell.com:80/manuals/ CACHE_MISS 3087

204.251.122.4 - - [Thu, 05 Jun 1997 21:53:37 GMT] GET http:/
/occam.provo.novell.com:80/docs/toc.pubs_server.html
CACHE_MISS 2726

204.251.122.4 - - [Thu, 05 Jun 1997 21:53:39 GMT] GET http:/
/occam.provo.novell.com:80/docs/art/line.gif CACHE_MISS 65
```

Okay, you get the idea. The IP address is the Windows NT system on my network, proving once again that an IP system that's not part of NDS can still use the Proxy Cache Server. The time and date part is simple enough, as is the GET command. The full URL is given, and a report of whether there is a cache hit or cache miss for that object.

In the example above, it appears someone was busy checking out some inappropriate Web sites during work hours. Not obscene, but few company managers would believe that comicbook.com, tv.com, and hollywoodnetwork.com are vital workday resources.

Lest you believe the Proxy Cache is worthless, since there are no cache hits in the above section, let me show you a section down a bit in the log:

```
204.251.122.4 - - [Thu, 05 Jun 1997 21:54:04 GMT] GET http://
occam.provo.novell.com:80/docs/art/webmstr.gif CACHE_MISS 1797

204.251.122.4 - - [Thu, 05 Jun 1997 21:54:13 GMT] GET http://
occam.provo.novell.com/docs/art/cdleft.gif CACHE_HIT 23180

204.251.122.4 - - [Thu, 05 Jun 1997 21:54:13 GMT] GET http://
occam.provo.novell.com/docs/art/butnfdbk.gif CACHE_HIT 1206

204.251.122.4 - - [Thu, 05 Jun 1997 21:54:13 GMT] GET http://
occam.provo.novell.com/docs/art/butninfo.gif CACHE_HIT 1216

204.251.122.4 - - [Thu, 05 Jun 1997 21:54:13 GMT] GET http://
occam.provo.novell.com/docs/art/manhome.gif CACHE_HIT 2019

204.251.122.4 - - [Thu, 05 Jun 1997 21:54:13 GMT] GET http://
occam.provo.novell.com/docs/art/butnofpk.gif CACHE_HIT 1201

204.251.122.4 - - [Thu, 05 Jun 1997 21:54:23 GMT] GET http://
occam.provo.novell.com:80/docs/tociware.html CACHE_MISS 2405

204.251.122.4 - - [Thu, 05 Jun 1997 21:54:26 GMT] GET http://
occam.provo.novell.com:80/docs/art/lgoiware.gif CACHE_MISS
4522
```

Notice that reading the Novell manuals online (a nice feature from Novell, if you're not familiar with this section of that company's Web site) provides plenty of cache misses. This is expected, since I'm reading the manual for the first time. Also notice, however, that many of the repeated images, such as cdleft.gif, are provided from cache. Since many graphic images take much longer to load than a section of manual text, my performance in this section was increased considerably. Not every image was in the cache already, but plenty were, and that helped speed through the manual.

If you prefer your log files unvarnished and in raw ASCII format, check out the SYS:\ETC directory of the server running the Proxy Cache. You'll find all the log files right there, in glorious, unformatted, black-and-white ASCII.

Activating Logs

To activate the various logs, go to NWAdmin, double-click on the server object hosting BorderManager, then click on the Border Services (or BorderManager) Setup command button. Double-click on the Proxy Cache Services item in the Enabled Services list at the top of the dialog box.

Pick your log option, or, if you have trouble making decisions, pick all three. Whoopee, more log files than you'll ever remember to delete now and then, because there is currently no size limit setting.

Choose HTTPD Common Format, Extended Format, and/or Indexed Format. The Log Level runs from 0 to 3, but why put 0 if you're going to start the silly thing? A Log Level of 255 works during beta to give complete logging for diagnostic purposes, and may still work on the software you have. If you do set the level at 255, be sure and check the log file size on a regular basis. There is no sense getting a rude surprise in a month, after a log file eats your spare disk space.

Wrap

This is a big chapter, full of fun and interesting stuff. Okay, "stuff" may be a bit flippant, because many of the core pieces of BorderManager are described in this chapter.

Are the features covered in this chapter used by every network? No, not at all. You and your management must decide what is best for your network. My job here is to make your choices easier, and help guide you through the different options.

Your Proxy Cache Server is the only piece of BorderManager that has effective competition from companies such as Microsoft. The Redmondians dismiss all the security components of BorderManager, because they have no competing products. Don't let marketing gamesmanship confuse your management. After all, what's at stake is your entire network. I bet your boss believes your files deserve more protection than a few marketing brochures full of promises. Your boss might prefer a product available today, with all the strength necessary to protect and improve your network. That's what this chapter (and the next one) is all about.

CHAPTER

9

Firewall Services

Although you know better now, many people (including managers reading nontechnical scare stories) believe that network "security" means blocking hackers. You know that's only one small part of your security job, but it is an important part. Besides, you need to be able to reassure your bosses traveling down their one-track management mind.

For this discussion of security features, we're assuming no individual remote clients need access to your internal network. Put simply, no one has access to enter your network through the Internet connection. The exception will be allowing a limited amount of traffic to reach an internal Web server. We will discuss ways to keep that Web server on the outside, however, allowing you to tighten the inbound security even more.

Of course, many readers do need to allow wandering employees onto the local network, whether you call it a fancy intranet with eye-popping Web pages, or just your plain ol' NetWare network server holding some files and e-mail. We will cover that in some detail in Chapter 11, when we discuss NetWare Connect. (Yes, that solid, proven product has been included in this big BorderManager package.)

Why IP Filtering at the Router Isn't Enough Anymore

Here is some help to get you over your first big hurdle with your managers: Why do they need to approve a firewall, when your router has IP filtering built in?

This isn't as dumb a question as you may think. After all, it's up to you to educate your management about the subtleties of networking, or take care of things for them so they never need to worry about it. Sometime or another, you or someone else said, "IP filtering at the router takes care of our security needs." That may have been two or three years ago, but management remembers. This is especially true when you ask for more money in the same area.

Yes, IP filtering at your router worked (marginally) acceptably two or three years ago. The world has changed. Your car's door lock works fine, but you also have an alarm and an insurance policy to guard against theft. Your network deserves every bit as much protection as your Buick.

One of the most popular attack methods today is to "spoof" IP addresses. An outsider discovers one of your valid internal network addresses and tacks it onto the packets coming from outside. This equates to stealing your card key for your office door. If the only protection is your IP filtering (or single card key check), then your security is breached, and your sensitive information is hung from the flagpole.

Before IP spoofing became prevalent, you may have been protected by your IP filtering router (but not as well as management thinks you were). Now that everyone in Hacker 101 knows this trick, you must take the next step. That step is a combination firewall and proxy server, both of which are provided by BorderManager.

Firewall Design Options

There are almost as many places to position your firewall and proxy server as there are network designs. As you might expect, however, a few standard positions for firewalls have stood the test of time, and are a good way to start with your designs.

Let's take a look at simple network designs and get progressively more complicated. That's probably how your network grew, anyway, as more people jumped on and other departments started hooking up to yours. You looked up one day, and bam, your simple, clean network was complex and convoluted.

Single Connection, IPX Internal Network

With a single internal network and single Internet contact point, life is relatively simple. There is one security checkpoint, and all traffic must pass through this checkpoint. The flip side of this neat arrangement appears when your system isn't configured safely enough, and your entire network is exposed. After all, if there's only one gate, there's only one place for the lock.

Much depends on the makeup of your internal network. If your network clients are all NetWare clients running IPX/SPX and reaching the Internet through an IPX–to–IP gateway, your security is already extremely solid. The only network devices running TCP/IP, and thus vulnerable to outside hackers, are the IPX–to–IP gateway and the router connecting you to your ISP. In many cases, both functions are inside the same box. Take a look at Figure 9.1 for a basic drawing of this design.

FIGURE 9.1

Single connection, IPX internal network

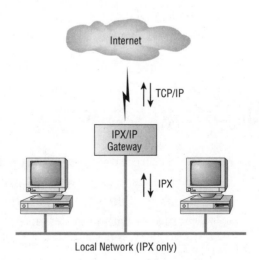

Examples of this method are all over the place. The best example, of course, is the IPX/IP Gateway included with IntranetWare. The MPR (Multi-Protocol Router) software included with BorderManager utilizes many communications boards to connect your NetWare server to your ISP. This means your single IntranetWare server can act as a router, gateway, and firewall if you wish.

Other good examples were covered back in Chapter 6: stand-alone boxes such as Instant Internet, WebRamp, Netra, IPeXchange, and LANlink; other NetWare-based gateways, such as NOV*IX, Inetix, and IWare; and gateways running on NT or Unix, such as Inetix (again) and CyberJunction. Paranoids can use a gateway not utilizing NetWare, to keep their server away from the Internet. Those who prefer using a NetWare server because they are used to managing NetWare will have just as good security, even though at least the one gateway NetWare server will be on the Internet and have a public IP address.

Internal Network Protected, TCP/IP Network

Today, however, few networks are completely IPX any more. Many companies are using TCP/IP to connect to internal network resources to utilize Web client and server software within the company—you know, that whole intranet idea. Relying on the IPX/IP Gateway to protect that network is inadequate, since outside hackers will have many internal targets running TCP/IP.

Here's where we step up into the world of real firewalls and proxy servers. You need features of both, which is why BorderManager includes both. Here we also introduce the idea of an internal network separated by a lobby network with a dual-homed firewall. Well, that's what some vendors call their products. Let's take a look at Figure 9.2, and see a standard protection design.

Could you condense this network design a bit, if you wanted? Certainly. The Proxy Server and Web server software will run on the same box if you wish. You may also use the MPR software on that server to

FIGURE 9.2

Lobby exposed, internal
network protected

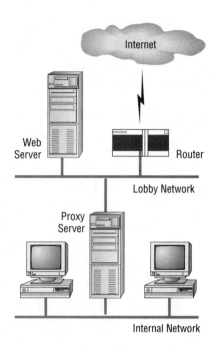

make the connection to the Internet. Then you will have the same physical design as in Figure 9.2, but all the protocol locations will be different.

More Internal Networks

Imagine that the lobby network connected more than one internal network. Would your design be so different if there were three internal networks and three Proxy Servers, all connecting to one lobby network? The Proxy Server software could easily run on one of the departmental network servers. Performance wouldn't be a problem, and security would still remain strong.

You can also expand this network design. Most companies now have many departmental networks that connect to a backbone network. Sometimes the servers are all on the backbone network, so they are all equally available to users in all departments.

Some features of the traditional internal backbone can overlay and complement the design in Figure 9.2. What if the lobby network was a third network, between the internal backbone and the Internet? All servers are protected, all users have access, and security remains strong.

Although only the Web server is labeled, companies usually put their e-mail server in the lobby network. This makes it simple for mail to be delivered and easy for insiders to get that mail. It also makes it easy for remote network clients to connect to the e-mail server over the Internet.

Intranet Web servers can remain on the internal network, safe from outsiders. Assuming you were using the IntranetWare IPX/IP Gateway or a similar system to support existing IPX clients, this design still works. All you must do is use the Proxy Server in Figure 9.2 as the IPX/IP Gateway. IPX packets will go to the gateway, get converted from IPX to TCP/IP, and then go back inside to your Web server, rather than out through the other network connection to the Internet.

I like the designs using dual-homed servers and lobby networks. Using your protective devices as the conduit for all connections between the inside and the outside makes details such as address translation work wonderfully. Higher protection comes at the cost of an extra network hub and network interface card for a few server/routers, which sounds like a bargain to me.

Configuring Firewall Hacker Controls

While BorderManager tends to lump inbound and outbound packet control into the same configuration processes, many users' first fear is that of malevolent hackers terrorizing their network. To soothe those fears, let's take a look first at ways to block outside packets from reaching your internal network.

Blocking All Access

BorderManager opts for full security during the initial startup configuration. When started, all access in and out of your Proxy Server is blocked. Changes must be made to the configuration to allow packets in and out of your network.

This is the best choice. After all, you're never more liable to make mistakes than when you first get the Proxy Server installed and running. The whole idea of packet filtering and blocking may be new to you, and you haven't had time to read the documentation, this book, or other supporting material bringing you up to speed on security. Hence, when you turn on the Proxy Server, it is in "locked down and secure" mode.

Be prepared for this setting and the consequences. If your network clients already have access to the Internet when you start the Proxy Server, they will suddenly lose that access. This is the safest way to run your network, but will cause the users to yell at you, or at least send impolite e-mail to you and your boss. If you have clients that are allowed to connect to the Internet, begin your configuration after work hours. This way, you won't close the network connection and disrupt authorized business. Plus, your overtime pay will fatten your pay check (ha ha ha).

Setting Filters for Internal Web Servers

Setting filters looks a bit complicated when you first get into the configuration screens, but you'll get the hang of it. Our goal is simple: We want to stop packets at the router (Proxy Server) unless they have authorized destination address data. This indicates the packet is a response packet to a query from an internal client. We also want to stop the router from adding information to its Routing Information Table, hiding internal routes and addresses from other routers.

Take a deep breath and head to your server console or RCONSOLE program. Yes, once again we must wrestle with the C-Worthy interface. It may be old and clunky, but it is also a pain to use.

Enabling Filter Support

Start by enabling filter support on each protocol you want to block. This essentially means you must enable filter support for TCP/IP. The documentation says you enable filtering through NIASCFG, but you really do it under INETCFG. Your path is Protocols ➤ TCP/IP ➤ Filter Support, which is found at the bottom of the TCP/IP Protocol Configuration screen within INETCFG. If you start with NIASCFG, add the Protocols and Networking choice in the main NIASCFG menu to your path.

Getting Filter Information

Now we go to where the real work is performed: FILTCFG. There are five choices in the opening menu, four of which configure protocol filters (AppleTalk, IPX, Source Route Bridge, and TCP/IP) and one that saves filters to a text file. Here are the steps:

1. To experience the joy of yet another C-Worthy interface program, type **LOAD FILTCFG** at the console prompt. Highlight Configure TCP/IP Filters and press Enter. Ack! More choices and strange names!

2. Ignore the options for outgoing RIP and EGP filters and skip to the last menu choice. Pick Packet Forwarding Filters and press Enter.

You get to Figure 9.3, where you see that the Packet Forwarding Filters are now enabled, and that your action is to Deny Packets in Filter List, yet Permit Packets Not in Filter List. Does that look too permissive to you? Ah, yes, but look at the last two lines. For the Filters field, there is a List of Denied Packets. Well, that sounds better, doesn't it. For Exceptions, there is a corresponding List of Packets Always Permitted. Have we covered all our bases?

It looks good so far, but we haven't yet seen which filters on which server interface are denied or always permitted. For that information, we drill down one more layer.

FIGURE 9.3

Barring hackers with filters

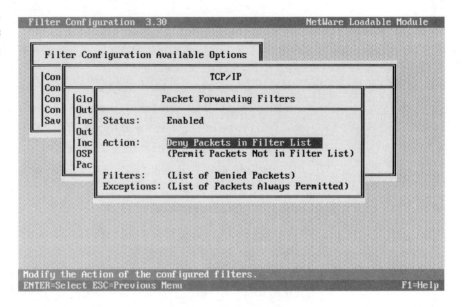

FIGURE 9.3

Barring hackers with filters

3. Press either Enter or the Insert key to open the Packets Denied screen, displayed below the long-winded The Highlighted Filter Will Not Forward The Following TCP/IP Packets window.

If you press the Tab key, the Packets Denied window will expand, and the other window (I'm not typing that again) will disappear. Press Tab once more to return things to the way they are in Figure 9.4.

Notice what we're doing here. In the Packets Denied window, I've highlighted the <All Interfaces> entry. The top window now shows that any protocol packet from any source to any destination in the network is blocked. What can come in? Nothing. If you go back to the screen shown in Figure 9.3 and highlight the bottom field, Exceptions, and press Insert, you will see a window exactly like this allowing you to list packets you want to allow through your Proxy Server firewall router, and so on. We'll get there in just a minute.

Notice that the top window in Figure 9.4 shows that any IP packet from any interface, all circuits, and any address, will *not* be forwarded.

FIGURE 9.4

Details for
barring hackers

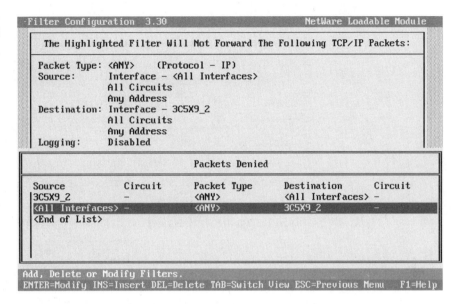

The destination is just as limiting. All circuits, for any address on the network, will not accept those IP packets. That sets a pretty solid standard: No packets from any source are allowed to any address on the inside of this network.

Configuring Filters

So far you have pretty much the same effect as before you turned the filters on at all. Why would you do such a thing? Because you can log packets attempting to get into your network, if you wish. You can also turn on the filters to allow internal clients out, but keep outsiders on the outside.

What if you want to make a mail server, or Web server, on the internal network available to outsiders? This is a common occurrence, especially when you don't let the world into your Web server, but just a limited number of customers and mobile users. Can you open the door just a little, without getting into danger of letting hackers run wild? Of course.

One of the advantages of filters with so many options (and you've seen just the beginning of these options) is the ability to specify particular protocols and port numbers and let them through the firewall. That's exactly what you must do to allow outsiders to access your Web server sitting on the inside of the firewall and Proxy Server.

Go back to your console and the FILTCFG screen showing the Packet Forwarding Filters (Figure 9.3). Change the highlighted field from Deny Packets in Filter List to Permit Packets in Filter List.

You need to specify some protocols that are necessary for Web server communication, but keep the rest out. You must make a new filter definition for each protocol. Press Enter on the Filters field, and then press Insert to open the Define Filters window, shown in Figure 9.5.

Notice where the highlight cursor is in Figure 9.5—in the Packet Type field. There is a list of over 50 protocol names predefined for you, filling in the foundation protocol and port number for you automatically. Press Insert with the cursor in the same place as it is in Figure 9.5, and you'll see more protocols than you ever knew were important.

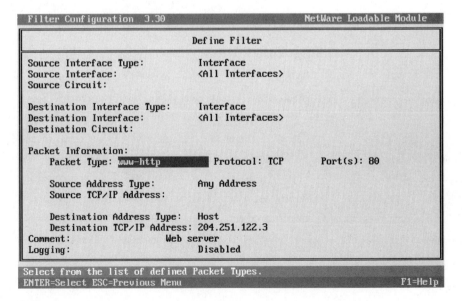

FIGURE 9.5

Specifying protocol filters

I have already filled in the host address in Figure 9.5, which must be done by hand. I also filled in the Comment field, but don't be surprised if the system fills that in for you now and then. When you're finished with the filter definition, press Escape and save the filter.

Take a look at Figure 9.6 for an example of blocking protocols. The list of three protocols in the Packets Permitted window required three trips through the Define Filter screen.

In the Packets Permitted window, you can see that I've allowed SMTP (Simple Mail Transport Protocol) for e-mail communications with the Web server. Most Web servers today have a button to initialize an e-mail address display or a form to fill in. If your e-mail server is outside the firewall, you may not need this setting. The second permission is for TCP, the front half of TCP/IP. Finally, the highlighted permission is for HTTP, descriptively named here www-http so there's no confusion on your part.

Notice the information in the top window, where the protocol details are spelled out. You can see that I am allowing connection over HTTP using port 80 (the default HTTP port) through the firewall *only* if it is connecting to my Web server at 204.251.122.3. You have the choice to

FIGURE 9.6

Web stuff in, and other stuff still blocked

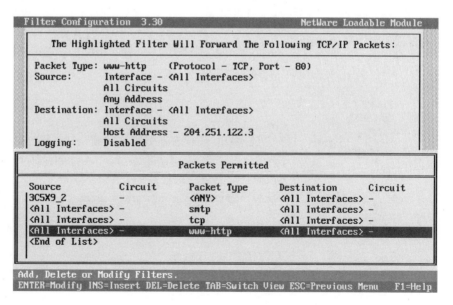

allow connections to all addresses (bad idea in this case) or to a particular network address (which is okay if you have a special network configured for outsiders). When you pick a particular host for access, as I did, you must supply the IP address for that host.

If you are really serious about security, you should start logging the connections when you first configure the Web server and the path through the firewall. This slows the server down a bit, but does allow you to verify who is checking out your Web server while not making formal HTTP connections to the server.

To allow outgoing traffic, do the same thing as above while switching the Source and Destination values. For the Source, list all interfaces and the Web server address. For the Destination, put only the interface connection used by the server to reach the Internet. Allow all circuits, and any network address, so response packets from your Web server will reach their destinations.

Is this a smart way to run your network, advertising an internal Web server on the Internet? Well, let's just say it's a matter of preference. Many companies do configure their network this way, even though I still prefer putting all public systems out in a lobby network. There are times this configuration makes sense, but if you have a choice, put the server outside. This is especially important if you expect lots of traffic on that server, because the Proxy Server and firewall will become a bottleneck if traffic rates zoom.

WARNING If you have one server doing triple duty, such as acting as a DSS (Domain SAP Server) or NetWare/IP as well as your Proxy Server and firewall, these filter definitions will cause you trouble. Blocking filters like this short-circuits the DSS. There is a limit to how many jobs one server can handle, if only because those jobs are at cross purposes.

BorderManager Filters and Controls

Let's take a look at a little table to help explain packet-filtering firewalls, circuit-level gateways, application-level gateways, and stateful inspection firewalls. The first three are the topics addressed for the remainder of this chapter. Stateful inspection firewalls are the newest level, and are not fully implemented in most products. These advanced devices carefully match incoming packets with an outgoing packet address, and require more intelligence than the other options. Some of the BorderManager features are the result of this technology.

Each filter works at different layers of the OSI protocol model. Remember that diagram back in the first chapter (see, it wasn't just padding to make that chapter run longer)? Table 9.1 shows the OSI model, along with Internet protocols and applications, all matched with the appropriate security filter.

TABLE 9.1

The OSI Model and Internet Protocols Matched with Security Filters

OSI Model Layer	Internet Protocols	Firewalls
Application	HTTP, FTP, DNS, NFS, Ping, SMTP, Telnet	Application-level gateway, stateful inspection firewall
Presentation		
Session	TCP	Circuit-level gateway
Transport	TCP	
Network	IP	Packet-filtering firewall
Data-Link		
Physical		

See why the basic packet-filtering firewall won't do the job anymore? More and more popular applications (Web browsers) are running far above the Network layer. Clever programming in the upper layers will fool the lower layers every time. The only way packet filtering can check authorized versus non-authorized packets is by the IP address. In other words, IP address spoofing will fool a packet-filtering firewall every single time.

Firewall and Proxy Server locations make no difference in how the various filters function. Obviously, placing your security device in the wrong place on the network makes it easier to bypass. All traffic forced through the firewall and Proxy Server can be checked against any or all of the tests in Table 9.1.

Since all these various controls are new with BorderManager, Novell hasn't yet had time to mash them all into nice programs labeled "Packet Filters," "Circuit-Level Gateways," and "Application-Level Gateways," as in the table here. We'll go back and visit FILTCFG for the packet filtering and some circuit-level action, then move onwards and upwards to NWAdmin for the application-level controls.

If you look at this the right way, you can almost make a case for splitting these filters into various control programs. Lower-level stuff will be set once, at the server and/or gateway, using server controls such as FILTCFG. Higher-level controls, such as ways to allow or deny groups of users to network resources, are found in NWAdmin, where other user controls are located. So maybe the current configuration of BorderManager makes more sense than it appears at first glance.

Packet Filtering

Let's take a closer look at packet filtering. In truth, the earlier section concerning access to internal Web servers was really about packet filtering as well. I just didn't call it that, so you would have a clear, hacker-protection scheme chapter heading ("Configuring Firewall Hacker Controls") to show your paranoid bosses.

There are two things I want to show you right now: how to block FTP packets for everyone on your network, and how to keep your internal network topology a secret.

Blocking FTP

Is blocking FTP a good idea? Only if you want to cut down the number of stolen software programs and viruses on your network. If users can copy all the files they want, you'll have plenty of both.

"But wait," you wail plaintively, "technical support folks need FTP for downloading drivers and the like from vendor sites." True. You may need to set up another path to the Internet just for your MIS department and trusted users. This is more trouble, but better than trusting some of your users to virus-check file downloads before running the programs.

Here are the steps for blocking FTP:

1. Go back to FILTCFG, through Configure TCP/IP and Packet Forwarding Filters, and verify that your Status field is Enabled (Figure 9.3).

2. Set your Action field to Deny Packets in Filter List.

3. Press Enter on the Filters field, and then press Insert to open the Define Filters window (Figure 9.5).

4. Define your Source Interface Type and Source Interface. This will be the interface connecting your server to the Internet.

5. Set the Destination Interface and Type to All Interfaces, since you want to control all connections your server has on your local network side.

6. Highlight Packet Type and press Insert to open the Defined TCP/IP Packet Types list.

7. Scroll down to FTP (or press F and then scroll) and hit Enter. The system will automatically fill in the Protocol and Port(s) fields for you.

8. For the Source Address Type, choose Network, then specify your (most likely) Class C address, using 0 (zero) for the last number. This goads the system into supplying the standard subnet mask of 255.255.255.0 for you automatically.

9. For Destination Address Type, you don't need to be nearly as picky, because you want to exclude everyone and deny them all (refer to the Action field on the first screen). Pick Any Address, which means you won't need to enter a particular IP address in the next field. Make a comment if you want, then hit Escape and save the filter.

The result should look amazingly like Figure 9.7, except showing your network address rather than mine.

F I G U R E 9.7

Shutting down FTP

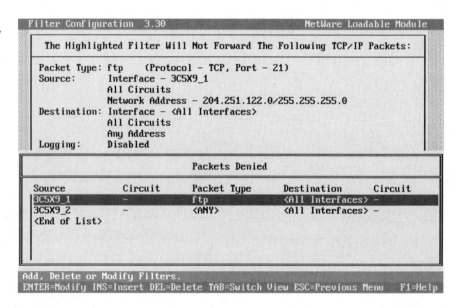

```
Filter Configuration  3.30                        NetWare Loadable Module

   The Highlighted Filter Will Not Forward The Following TCP/IP Packets:

  Packet Type: ftp      (Protocol - TCP, Port - 21)
  Source:       Interface - 3C5X9_1
                All Circuits
                Network Address - 204.251.122.0/255.255.255.0
  Destination: Interface - <All Interfaces>
                All Circuits
                Any Address
  Logging:      Disabled

                            Packets Denied

  Source          Circuit      Packet Type     Destination       Circuit
  3C5X9_1         -            ftp             <All Interfaces>  -
  3C5X9_2         -            <ANY>           <All Interfaces>  -
  <End of List>



Add, Delete or Modify Filters.
ENTER=Modify INS=Insert DEL=Delete TAB=Switch View ESC=Previous Menu   F1=Help
```

Hiding Routes

Now for a another example of hiding as a security mechanism. You already know that address spoofing is a problem, and here's another way to help block address spoofing using the packet filters:

1. You're still in FILTCFG, but back up to the main menu and choose Outgoing RIP Filters this time.

The Status is Enabled, of course, and the Action is to Permit Routes in Filter List. However, we're going to be somewhat clever here. Hang on.

2. Set the Action to Permit Routes in Filter List, even though you think that's backwards, because you're trying to hide things, not permit them. Just be patient.

3. On the Filters field, press Insert twice, and leave the Filtered Route on All Routes setting, which is the default. Back out with the Escape key, saving the filter.

4. Back on the Outgoing RIP Filters screen, move down to the last field, Exceptions. Press Insert twice yet again, and yet again accept All Routes as the value for the Filtered Route.

5. In the Do Not Advertise Route To field, put in the interface used to communicate with the Internet. Check out Figure 9.8 for a guide.

What are we saying here? That we will *not* advertise *all* routes. That's a bit obtuse, if you look at it the wrong way, but it does work. We set up the filter to actively make sure we're not telling the world about the interior makeup and addresses of our local network. This is worth checking out for your own network.

FIGURE 9.8

Hiding in plain sight

```
Filter Configuration  3.30                        NetWare Loadable Module

  The Highlighted Filter Will Not Advertise The Following TCP/IP RIP Routes:

  Filtered Route: All Routes

  Do Not Advertise Route To:
                    Interface - 3C5X9_1
                    All Circuits
  Comment:          <none>
  Logging:          Disabled


                    Exceptions: Routes Always Denied

  Route                     Destination            Circuit
  All Routes                3C5X9_1                  -
  <End of List>




Add, Delete or Modify Exceptions to Filters
ENTER=Modify INS=Insert DEL=Delete TAB=Switch View ESC=Previous Menu   F1=Help
```

Circuit- and Application-Level Filtering

Yes, Table 9.1 showed that circuit-level and application-level filtering are really two different things, and happen at two separate protocol levels. Realistically, however, they tend to overlap. Novell engineers put both functions within NWAdmin, which I think is a good idea. So, I'll cover them both in the same place.

What are the differences, technically speaking? Circuit-level services include the IPX/IP and IP/IP Gateway. NDS gets involved to verify that a NetWare client is authorized to make use of the appropriate gateway, and what the limitations are on that use. More circuit-level control happens as users access sessions based on protocols, such as an FTP session.

Application-level services fall primarily into Web access and control, especially filtering all the various URL sites. While the application-level services work with the circuit level to determine if a user has the authority to use an application, the packet-level filter steps in and sorts out the access details for that user. It's common for companies to allow Web access all the time but limit newsgroup access until after work hours, for instance. Using the Cyber Patrol software sample included with BorderManager, your management can get even more stingy, and block all the sports, television, and other general entertainment Web sites during the work day.

Does this sound like the various control services all work together in some strange, hard to fathom manner? They are all mashed together, but they aren't that difficult to understand. Don't worry about the details of how you control access; focus on the access controls necessary to keep your users happy and productive. Does it matter if the hate speech Web servers are blocked by a packet-, circuit-, or application-level filter? Not at all.

The good part of all this mess is that you are now finished (at least for a while) with the C-Worthy interface, and back in graphics land with NWAdmin—much nicer, much easier to handle, and the continuing focus of NetWare engineer development efforts. Let's roll up our sleeves, pump up those muscles, and start clickin' the mouse.

How Access Controls Work

Working with various application-, circuit-, and packet-level filters, Novell has developed a set of access controls consisting of access rules and control lists. There are a series of steps needed to create each rule, and the rules are additive. If you understand the concept of inherited rights in NetWare, you can handle these rules. If you don't understand the concept of inherited rights and the use of the IRF (Inherited Rights Filter) in NDS, you can still handle these access rules. Just ask someone else in the group to manage file and server access rights until you read up on inherited rights, okay?

Novell documentation calls access controls by all sorts of different names, and this is no worse than what happens with anyone else in the business. I suppose if I dug up the official names according to Internet security documentation, those names would look strange and inconsistent as well. Even if I can't name these rules exactly, let's see if I can explain them to you.

Here's the first, and most critical design guide for your access controls: What is not explicitly allowed is denied. This is a good rule to remember, whether you're controlling co-workers or raising your children. Not that either group will listen, but saying "What is not explicitly allowed is denied" out loud while waving your finger at your disappearing offspring, off to do what they want to do no matter what you say, is good for a laugh.

When first activated, BorderManager blocks all activity. You took care of the first part of allowing access back in FILTCFG, when you enabled or disabled the filtering. If you didn't read my warning earlier, let me repeat myself: When you start BorderManager, all traffic through your network will stop until you either set up rules allowing communication or disable the filters in FILTCFG. Until I realized what was going on, there was plenty of yelling and cursing in the lab. Since I work alone for the most part, this wasn't a problem. Your boss may not look kindly on you cursing a file server in a voice that carries throughout the entire department, however, so take care.

Access control rules start from the server object, and move up through the container holding the server object, organizational unit, organization, and to the root of your NDS tree. The sum total of all rules for a user object up through this chain forms the control list, detailing authorization. Rules are defined as follows:

- **Action:** Allow or deny access.

- **Source:** NDS users or groups, DNS host names, IP addresses, IP subnets, or <Any>, applying to all users.

- **Access Specification:** The destination or service that is allowed or denied. Allowable entries include any protocol, destination address, or URL.

- **Destination:** DNS host names, IP addresses, or subnet addresses. You must separately allow the use of the appropriate protocol used to reach these destinations.

- **Time Constraint:** A 24-hour grid allowing you to tailor access based on time of day.

Users must match an Allow listing in the access control list in order to use the network. All the pieces of the rule, not just the destination or time and so on, must match in order for the user to be authenticated—no match, no surf.

Here's an example: The CONSULT organizational unit is allowed to use HTTP. However, all network users are denied the use of the FTP protocol, as a safeguard against importing viruses into the company. The Programmers group, part of the CONSULT organizational unit, is allowed to use FTP because the members of this group are responsible users (this is just an example, so play along) and they need to download patches and code updates on a regular basis.

The question: What time will the blue train reach Cleveland? No, sorry, wrong question. Can user LAURA use FTP?

- **All users:** FTP denied

- **Programmers includes:** LAURA, ALEX, NATALIE

- **Consultants includes:** MSMITH, NICHOLAS, BRADLEY

- **Programmers:** FTP allowed

Yes, Laura can use FTP because she's a member of the Programmers group, and specifically allowed to do so. Can MSMITH use FTP? Nope, she's a consultant, and they're even less trustworthy than the programmers.

Rules-Based Behavior for Robots

The best example I can give for rules-based behavior comes from Isaac Asimov's "Three Laws of Robotics" from his 1950 classic short story collection, *I, Robot*. No, robots weren't a big deal in 1950, but the time setting started in 2057 and went forward, and the rules were from the *Handbook of Robotics, 56th Edition*, 2058 AD. Here are the three rules:

1. A robot may not injure a human being, or, through inaction, allow a human being to come to harm.

2. A robot must obey the orders given it by human beings except where such orders would conflict with the First Law.

3. A robot must protect its own existence as long as such protection does not conflict with the First or Second Law.

Unfortunately, your IntranetWare server isn't as smart as Robbie, the robot in the first story. However, Dr. Asimov certainly sets the standards for dependent rules. See how Rule 2 refers to Rule 1? Then Rule 3 refers to both of the previous rules? Your BorderManager access controls work in a similar fashion.

Specifying Sources

Assuming you have NWAdmin running, we can get rolling. Highlight a server, server container, organizational unit, or organization to begin.

When you installed BorderManager, a few more command buttons appeared in NWAdmin, as you discovered before. What you want now is the one labeled Outgoing Rules, so find it and click on it. For my example, I'm using the organizational unit called CONSULT.

You can create access rules for all the NDS objects you would expect. In other words, users, user containers, servers, server containers, organizational units, and organizations. As you'll soon see, you may also specify IP hosts, networks, and DNS host names, even if none of them connect to a NetWare server.

Let's get started looking at some nice, graphical screens. Figure 9.9, albeit crowded, shows some of the address source information necessary to build a new access control rule. Notice the Source Specification dialog box in the foreground, on the bottom left of the screen. I moved things around so you could see the foreground dialog box, the Source specifications that called this dialog box from the Rule Definition dialog box behind it, and the Organizational Unit information in the background. At the bottom of the background dialog box, you can see that the Outgoing Rules command button is depressed.

FIGURE 9.9

Allowing access a variety of ways

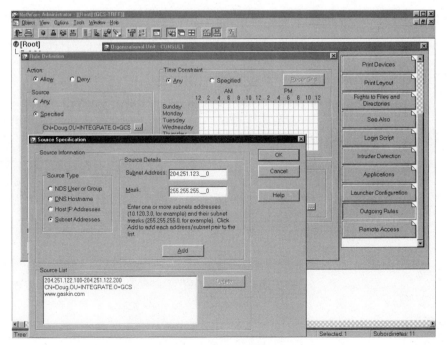

There are four ways to identify the Source Type for the rule, according to the foreground dialog box in Figure 9.9:

- **NDS User or Group:** This was the first one I tried, and you can see in the Source List at the bottom of the dialog box that I chose user DOUG as my guinea pig for this example. Notice as well that DOUG is in another organizational unit, but no one cares; this is perfectly allowable. If you choose the NDS User or Group radio button, the standard Select Object dialog appears, allowing you full view of everyone in the NDS database (at least virtually). Point and click and save, and you're finished.

As you would expect, if you click on the Any radio button in the Rule Definition dialog box (the middle one in Figure 9.9), then the rule applies to any and all users on your network. We're going into some detail here for illustration purposes, but many rules use the Any designation. A rule saying "Any" user is blocked from connecting to news servers would stop all users on your network from reading and replying to newsgroups.

- **DNS Hostname:** Notice in the Source List that I have put www.gaskin .com as one of the addresses. This was simple: A blank field was presented, and I typed in the host name, and that's that. By being part of the gaskin.com domain, all hosts in that domain will fall under this rule as well. If you want to exclude individual systems in the domain from this source list, you must identify them individually.

- **Host IP Addresses:** You can see the results of this choice as the first item in the Source List. It's simple to specify a range of IP addresses, since the Source Details fields show a start and end address. If you want a single IP address in your rule, put in the starting address only.

- **Subnet Addresses:** The source address format being defined in Figure 9.9 is a full subnet. Check out the Source Details fields in Figure 9.9, and you'll see I'm specifying an entire Class C address in one fell swoop. If you put a 0 (zero) as the last byte in the Subnet Address field, the system automatically puts in the proper subnet mask.

Just under the Source Details fields is a small text area describing the source type of the active radio button. Think of this as a help field, placed directly under the fields waiting for input.

After typing in the source address, regardless of type, you must click on the Add command button just under the help text box. You can add as many source addresses as you wish; the system will just keep adding them to the box.

Just above the Source Specification dialog box in the foreground of Figure 9.9 you can see a text field. In Figure 9.9, the contents start with a full NDS qualified name for a user, CN=Doug.OU=INTEGRATE. O=GCS. To save space in the Rule Definition dialog box, all the names are listed in that field as a string of text. Clicking on the field-display box (the one with three dots) beside the text will display all the specified addresses. They are arranged in alphabetical order, with numeric entries first.

In the upper-left corner of the Rules Definition dialog box, notice that the Allow radio button is clicked, meaning that the rule being created will allow access for the source addresses. Whatever you do with all these source addresses, they will have access to something all the rest of the network can't see.

There's a lot of verbiage here, but source specifications aren't that difficult. Unlike with regular NetWare, however, you can include non-NetWare clients by their IP addresses or DNS host names. That's a new twist, and one that gives you complete control over your network.

Specifying Protocol and Destinations

The next step in rule creation is to set the protocol and destination for the list of users you just defined. We'll be focusing on the Rule Definition dialog box that was in the middle of Figure 9.9; now it is the only dialog box in Figure 9.10.

Before we look at the protocol and destinations for the rule, notice the results of our earlier handiwork. In the Source section in the upper-left corner, you see a text field containing the address that was being entered

FIGURE 9.10

Protocol access choice

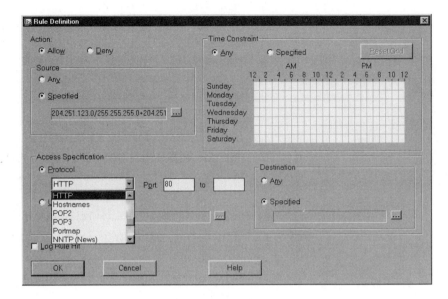

back In Figure 9.9. Those are the network clients, and the only network clients, that this rule will affect.

Specifying Access   Now let's look at the Access Specification section. There are two radio buttons: Protocol and URL (the URL button is hidden by the drop-down list of protocols). This display changes depending on your choice of protocol or URL. If you choose Protocol, as I have, the Destination section of the dialog box, on the right under the time grid, is active. We'll get there shortly. If you choose URL, then the rule applies to that URL, and the protocol is automatically set to HTTP.

All the protocols you would expect are in the drop-down list. Besides what you can see in Figure 9.10, FTP, FTP Data, Time, Whois, Finger, Login, shell, printer, Kerberos, Gopher, name, SMTP, and others are listed. You can pretty well block or allow access to any destination you wish using all the major protocols.

Notice the Port fields next to the Protocol list. When you pick a protocol, the default port number is entered automatically in the first Port field. If you want a range of port numbers, such as 1024–65535, to control all TCP open ports, put the top end of the range in the second Port field.

If you choose URL instead, click on the list box at the end of the text field to open the URL Specification dialog box. It's pretty dull, so I won't clutter the page with a picture. If you click on the Add icon, the system fills in the "http://" section of the address, and waits for you to put "www .novell.com" or whatever other URL your heart desires. Clicking on OK in this URL dialog box lists all the addresses into the text field labeled URL. Again, they are listed alphabetically in the text field.

Specifying Destination   Once you choose your protocol, you may move to the right and work on the Destination box. The first radio button is Any, and if you choose that, the rule covers any and all destinations that are reached via the chosen protocol. If you picked HTTP and the Any button, all network users would be able to use the Web.

For a more specific example, you may create a rule to allow all users to use the POP3 (Post Office Protocol version 3) to access mailhost.gaskin .com. That designation would force all users listed in the rule to use only the mailhost.gaskin.com e-mail server, but no other. Remember, that which is not allowed is denied. Allowing POP3 access to one server also has the effect of locking out all other DNS hosts reached using the POP3 protocol.

The dialog box called by clicking on the list button at the end of the Specified field looks exactly like the Source Specification dialog box in Figure 9.9, with one exception: No NDS addresses are allowed, because the destination is the Internet.

As of yet, the Internet hasn't seen the wisdom of using NDS to track all the millions of Internet hosts. Novell engineers are talking to the Internet folks, but they have no real chance of convincing the Internet to go with NDS. That's why the Destination Specification dialog box doesn't list NDS addresses.

Logging User Attempts   Just under the Protocol drop-down list is a checkbox for Log Rule Hit. Yes, it's there, just hiding. If you put a check in that box, user attempts to connect to destinations and services listed in the rule will be written to the log file. Check the file by selecting the BorderManager entry in the Tools menu.

Specifying Time

The upper-right corner of the Rule Definition dialog box is filled with the standard NWAdmin time grid. There are improvements in this grid, however. You can specify a variety of times, rather than single blocks of on or off times.

If you click on the Any radio button, then the rule you are creating applies all the time, day and night. If you click on the Specified radio button, you can select which times the rule is effective.

Is this valuable, or just here because it's possible? I vote for valuable. I mentioned before that some companies allow newsgroup access after work hours; here's how you set those hours for your access rule. Keeping people off the Internet between 2:00 a.m. and 5:00 a.m. will reserve all your bandwidth for bulk file transfers, system backups, and even backups across the Internet. You probably won't have many people in the office at 2:00 a.m., but you never know. Many companies block system access during the wee hours of the morning to ensure tape backups don't encounter any more open files than necessary.

Rule Summation

Yes, there's a lot of stuff to remember about rules, if you look at the entire rule-making process as one big job. But if you break up the process by each component, as I've done here, rule making shouldn't seem any more difficult than any other network management task.

Figure 9.11 shows the Outgoing Rules page inside NWAdmin, now that I've completed several rules. Notice I am setting rules for the CONSULT organization, not the entire network.

FIGURE 9.11

Rules to live by

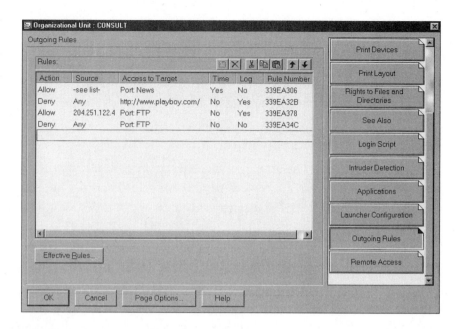

Quick icon explanations are in order. The first icon on the upper right of the Rules dialog box adds a new rule, and the X deletes the highlighted rule. Editing tools are next, allowing you to cut, paste, and put various rules into the clipboard. This feature helps you move rules from one container to another, which is a handy trick at times. The up and down arrows move the highlighted rule up or down the rule list.

The first rule says to allow a list of users (double-click on the rule to open the Definition page again) to use the News protocol during certain times, but not log the results. The Rule Number listed at the end is a unique ID to track this rule through the various log files you'll see here and there.

The second rule says to deny all network users access to www.playboy .com, and log any attempts to reach that URL. (Yes, every Internet book uses Playboy as the "bad" example; it's written into the book contract.)

The third rule says to allow a specific IP address to use FTP, but log when this happens. This goes along with the last rule, denying FTP to all network users. These two rules block FTP for everyone, but allow one specific and trustworthy Windows NT workstation to use FTP. However, the NT user isn't trustworthy enough for me not to want a log hit every time FTP is used.

As with any NetWare management process, the higher in the NDS hierarchy you set the rule, the more users are controlled by the rule. You can narrow the scope down to a single station, as I've shown you in Figure 9.11, but that's a lot of extra time and trouble.

Do you think that the Effective Rules command button provides anything fancy? I doesn't—just a read-only screen of what you see here.

Wrap

Security matters a great deal to your network, and you will sleep better if security is tight rather than just convenient for you. Overtime will go down if fewer viruses get onto your network, and you can block your managers from trying to show off and reconfiguring their own systems.

Firewalls are not perfect, because they are installed by people and must control people. There are more people with keys to your computer room than you realize, and some may be tempted to help your "fix" the security access rules for their own benefit.

Stay vigilant, stay focused, and keep some scare articles from the nontechnical press around to build your credibility. It is possible for some idiot executive to cancel the purchase order for your BorderManager firewall on one day while yelling at you to get the network on the Internet the next. Pull out those scary articles, shake your head, and say how you hope the company insurance covers loss of data (it probably doesn't). Then mention how executives are particularly good targets for hackers (we don't know if it's true, but your boss doesn't realize that). Put "VP" in their name fields, so hackers will be drawn to them. Then come back in a week and see if they feel differently about the continuing need for security controls.

CHAPTER

10

Virtual Private Networking

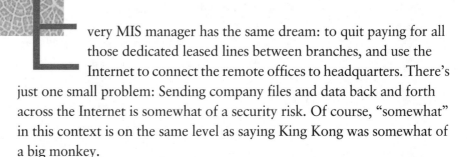

Every MIS manager has the same dream: to quit paying for all those dedicated leased lines between branches, and use the Internet to connect the remote offices to headquarters. There's just one small problem: Sending company files and data back and forth across the Internet is somewhat of a security risk. Of course, "somewhat" in this context is on the same level as saying King Kong was somewhat of a big monkey.

Can anyone with more than three functioning synapses truthfully suggest that you route all your private traffic across the tremendously public Internet? No, not really. Still, the cost savings would be enormous, wouldn't they?

That they would, and that they are. Not only can you dream of disconnecting your expensive dedicated leased lines, you can pull the plug yourself. Just make sure that you don't unplug the circuit to your ISP, because you're going to need that one.

Turn the Internet into Your Private Network Backbone

Those of you who are very familiar with NetWare may say, "Hey, this is nothing but IP tunneling." You aren't quite correct, but you are on the right track. There are two main differences between IP tunneling and VPNs (virtual private networks):

- Traffic is encrypted over the VPN.

- VPNs handle more traffic with less network load due to the power of the MPR (Multi-Protocol Router) software.

Some Caveats

Of the two advantages of VPN over IP tunneling, the encryption is by far the most important. Take this information to your managers, and show them how Novell does the VPN encryption and decryption. If they can't understand, or still don't feel comfortable, don't continue down the VPN road. Keep those dedicated circuits to your remote sites, and don't bring this up again.

The ability to package IPX packets within UDP packets for a trip across TCP/IP networks was developed for IP Tunnel. This product worked, but didn't become as popular as you might expect. Part of the problem was timing. IP Tunnel came out with NetWare 3.11, back in 1989, and the Internet wasn't a big deal at the time. Companies interested in TCP/IP networks rarely used NetWare, and vice versa. Actually, SNA Tunnel would have been a much more popular product at that time, but since IBM developers hold all the SNA technology close to their vest, that wasn't possible. Now, SNA over IP is the big deal. My, how times change.

There's another detail you should relate to your management before starting a VPN: Traffic across the Internet is sometimes congested and prone to delays. This is not the case all the time, of course, but it happens now and then. Users running interactive programs across the VPN will experience more delays than when using dedicated links between the same sites, assuming the line speeds are the same.

If you have 56Kbps dedicated lines but T1 connections to the Internet, your VPN performance will likely outperform the dedicated lines. Just remember to compensate for Internet traffic fluctuations and the packet security overhead before speaking to management. Don't brag about how you're going to "turbo-charge" remote connections before you test and verify.

One last note: No encryption algorithm is 100 percent safe and secure. The chances of someone capturing data zooming back and forth across your VPN are slim, and the chances the interceptors can read the information are slimmer still. However, in the security business, there's no such concept as absolutely secure when computers are concerned. There is always the possibility that someone will leak the encryption details to your competitor, for instance. But although I'm obligated to tell you that your encrypted data has an extremely tiny chance of being snatched and viewed, it's unlikely. A more likely scenario is that the insider in a position to give away your secrets will skip the encryption hassle and just sell your competitors the information they want. Computers and security algorithms are marvels of safety and security compared to people.

Some Prerequisites

You may be able to guess all the prerequisites for your VPN installation, but let's go over them just to be sure. Some are obvious, but some are less apparent.

- Install BorderManager on all master and slave servers.

- Each master and slave server must be connected to the Internet.

- Decide on your master VPN server.

- Verify that MPR software is loaded on each VPN server.

- Update NWAdmin with the BorderManager snap-in.

- Write down all the IP addresses to use in your network setup.

- Prepare your encrypted keys.

Are all these steps necessary before you start building your VPN? Can't you just "wing it," as everyone else does when installing some NetWare modules?

Sure, you can (and might), but think a bit first. This project has a high profile and involves at least one remote site. No matter what you promised your management, at least a few of the managers and executives believe you will slice the telecom budget from the size of a redwood to the size of a red ant. You can't, but when you say the magic words "reduced cost," most managers quit listening to the rest of the details.

You will be better served by preparing for VPN installation in an organized way. There are many steps you can take before the actual installation that will help the installation flow smoothly. So, let's take the time to look at each of the prerequisites in a bit more detail.

Master and Slave Servers with BorderManager

Yes, every master and slave server must have BorderManager installed, configured, and running. Some believe only the master server needs to be so equipped, but that's not the case. Install, configure, test, and verify BorderManager on all involved servers before starting your VPN project.

Master and Slave Server Internet Connections

Sorry if this seems insulting, but it's easy to overlook one server somewhere that isn't really connected to the Internet. This is especially true if you're upgrading an internal WAN configuration. Turn off all WAN links for your test, or dial in to your ISP from home and ping all the servers. If you can't reach each and every server from an independent Internet connection because of lack of Internet access or a firewall configuration, you can't make an effective VPN.

Since you will test each and every server involved, there's no reason to explain how to install TCP/IP in this chapter. If you've skipped to this chapter because VPN is the reason behind your BorderManager purchase, backtrack just a bit before your start. Skim over Chapter 3 and make sure that all the TCP/IP and NetWare details are under control.

Master VPN Server

While any IntranetWare- and BorderManager-equipped server can become your master server, pick one close at hand. Yes, you can remotely manage and control VPN servers, but there are times when nothing but threatening a server with dismemberment will make it behave. Long-distance threats don't carry much weight, so pick a server you can physically intimidate.

The best choice is to place your master server where the largest and most experienced technical staff resides. This isn't to say departmental technical support specialists can't become VPN experts, because they can. Realistically, however, the more brains you have to focus on a problem, the higher your chances of success. HQ has the most brains, at least in the technical department. (We'll let Scott Adams and Dilbert continue to prove that HQ somehow acts as a black hole for executive intelligence, sucking it into another dimension and leaving us with the golf-playing, glad-handing shells of overpaid executives.)

A third important indication for your master VPN is which server will have the most connections. Since all roads lead to HQ (this idea was started in the days when HQ was in Rome), the HQ server tends to get the most traffic.

MPR Software Verification

You can install pieces of BorderManager and IntranetWare on a server, without installing everything by default. Verify that MPR software is loaded on all the servers participating in this project. It wouldn't hurt to verify that all the routers are running, even if they aren't doing any actual routing. Check to see that dynamic routing for both IPX and IP is enabled.

NWAdmin Update

You can't manage BorderManager until the controlling NWAdmin stations have run the BorderManager snap-in found in \PUBLIC\BSSNAP\W95. You might as well get your administration programs up to date before starting this new project. If you don't, you won't get far, because you won't be able to configure many of the VPN details.

IP Address Recording

Your VPN will need a private IP address never seen on the Internet. This is used to designate the server network interfaces connecting to the VPN links. Put all the addresses in a table before starting installation, and save that table. You may even take the radical step of updating the table when and if things change.

Encrypted Keys

The installation steps always say to generate the encrypted keys during the process. Since you are more clever than most, and have all your addresses defined before you start, feel free to generate your keys and send them to your remote sites.

Configuring Your Servers for VPN

VPN is new, and controls for remote server configuration have yet to be included. Since you're starting at the server console, however, you can easily use RCONSOLE to reach any server on your network.

Once again, Novell engineers seem intent on making NIASCFG the primary management utility. All directions start from NIASCFG, even though the first real choice starts up VPNCFG. Oh well, make the engineers happy for a change and start NIASCFG and choose the Configure NIAS option, which is listed first.

Now you're facing the Select Component to Configure screen, aren't you? You have three choices:

Remote Access

Protocols and Routing

Virtual Private Network

This isn't too difficult of a choice, is it? Highlight the last choice and press the Enter key. Then guess what appears? Yep, the VPN Server Configuration screen is next. The only window on this screen is titled VPN Server Configuration (descriptive but redundant).

All snide comments aside, here are the options on the main VPN screen:

Master Server Configuration

Slave Server Configuration

Update VPN Filters

Display VPN Server Configuration

Remove VPN Server Configuration

It's pretty clear that you're in the right place for a chapter on virtual private networking, isn't it? There are a few other things we can deduce from this menu:

- The master and slave configuration information is much the same. That would make sense, because they will share the virtual network, meaning most of the IP addresses would be in common.

- Some filters are involved. We've been through the filters a fair bit (in Chapter 9), and you've seen that there are plenty of filters that can help you hide VPN traffic from the Internet. I doubt that you'll want to announce your virtual network IP address, since there's no reason for it to be a legal Internet address.

- It must not be too hard to configure a VPN server, because if you make a mistake, you should just remove the entire configuration and start over.

As you read in Chapter 3, I went through many mistakes with the NetWare/IP server installation. However, I must say that no matter how poorly I configured the NetWare/IP server, it was quick and easy to clear it all out and start from scratch. It looks like, even if I'm no smarter than in the NetWare/IP chapter, I can still manage to get a VPN server configured.

Isn't it nice to start a project so full of confidence? I believe positive thoughts send electromagnetic signals that are received by the computer. So I start positive, and the computer understands I'm confident and well prepared. What it doesn't know won't hurt it. If only I could feel the electromagnetic signals when Windows is about to crash again, life would be good.

Master Server Configuration

Let's go ahead and start with the master server setup:

1. When you press Enter on the first menu choice in the VPN Server Configuration screen, you must start making choices. First, a word of warning from Novell. A Note window opens, in purple no less, saying:

   ```
   A VPN can have only one master server. Make sure this
   server is the only master server on your VPN.
   ```

2. You must confirm your understanding of this statement by actually moving to the next menu choice in the small Confirm window. The default is to Return to the Main Menu, which returns you from whence you came. Only by moving the cursor to the Continue choice can you, well, continue.

Now we're getting to some action here. Since I'm tired of typing all the menu items, I thought I would give you a screen shot this time. Take a look at Figure 10.1, and match these menu choices with the prerequisites I listed earlier (and you probably ignored).

FIGURE 10.1

Primary master server setup screen

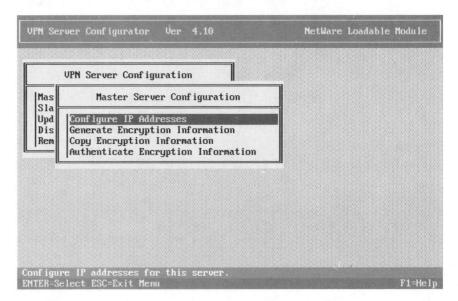

The IP addresses hold no big surprises, since you must define the network you already have and the virtual network you are creating over the Internet. Let's do these in order, so the encryption software will have some addresses to use when churning the encryption file.

3. First enter the public IP address for this server. It doesn't say "this server," but that's what it means. The help screen goes so far as to mention this must be the same IP address configured for initial TCP/IP support through NIASCFG. So, you ask, why doesn't this screen pick up that IP address and fill it in automatically? The only answer I have is that particular interface refinement will come later.

4. The next field is the subnet mask that goes along with the IP address for the server. Novell continues to insist on listing these in hexadecimal in the manual and help screens (FF.FF.FF.0 rather than 255.255.255.0). Ignore that and use the decimal numbers whenever possible. Believe me, you won't run into many other companies that list your subnet masks in hex. Yes, this subnet mask is the same as configured earlier for initial TCP/IP support. In most cases, the number will be 255.255.255.0. If the number is different, be quite careful when typing the subnet mask. A wrong number means no network connection.

Let's take a look at what we've done so far, and show you what's coming. All the details are in Figure 10.2.

So far, the IP address has been the real address and subnet mask for your server. That's the last "real" address you're going to see for just a bit. Notice the cursor is sitting on the field for VPN Tunnel IP Address. The answer, Not Configured, is clear enough. That's what every field on this screen had when we started.

FIGURE 10.2

Listing addresses once again

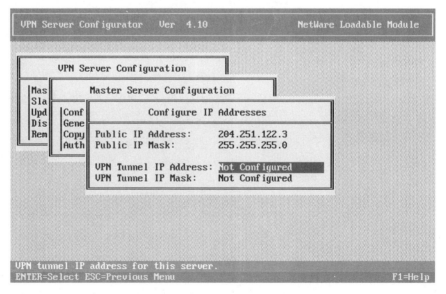

5. Let's make up an IP address. The IP address for your VPN tunnel will never get out to the Internet, so any IP address you fancy will be fine, as long as it's not a reserved address.

If you go brain-dead and put in an address of 127.0.0.1 because that address seems vaguely familiar, the screen will flash "Stupid Stupid Stupid" at you. Why? Because that's the reserved address for the local machine, often called the *localhost*. It looks familiar because every TCP/IP host has that number in the configuration file.

Pick something obviously not reserved, but not something so oddball you'll never recognize it when you see it again. How about a Class B address that closely matches your Class C address? This assumes your network is a full Class C and you have control over all 254 addresses. If your ISP gave you a CIDR (Classless Internet Domain Routing, a way to conserve scarce IP addresses on new networks) address, you can play the same tricks.

How about the VPN tunnel address of 204.251.1.2 for your master server? See where that number came from? Good. Novell suggests you make your master server ".1" and your first slave server ".2," but I have a small problem with those choices. I prefer always listing the network router as the .1 address. Even though there isn't a separate network router on the phantom (excuse me, virtual) network, I hate to break that habit.

6. After putting in 204.255.1.2 for the VPN tunnel address, remember you must provide the subnet mask. Once again, 255.255.255.0 works perfectly well, thank you.

7. The system will ask "Save IP Addresses?" politely, and you should politely press Enter for Yes, the default. More blinking, and a few filter update messages, and you return to the previous menu.

Unless, of course, you don't have your filters set up properly. In my case, I forgot to check my filters. Did I put that in the prerequisites? No wonder I missed it.

What happened and how did I fix it? The message is displayed in Figure 10.3. I'm just sorry you can't see the purple color here; it's so demanding.

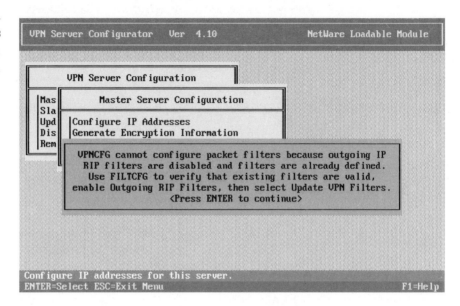

Novell has a pretty good error message here, don't you think? It's clear, precise, helpful, and spells out exactly what I must do. Excuse me while I go follow directions.

If you're lucky and cross your fingers, the system will set the filters for you. If not, now you know how to fix them.

Once your filters are set correctly (as in Enabled rather than Disabled), a series of updates flash on the screen. Filters are checked, filters are configured, filters are saved, and everyone is happy. The last message stays on the screen to tell you, "VPN packet filters were successfully added." Nice to see the good news, rather than guess that things went well because no error message showed itself.

Configuring Encryption

Next stop on our tour is to Generate Encryption Information, back on the Master Server Configuration menu. When you choose that item, all you get is a window labeled Enter Random Seed. My first inclination was to say "petunia," and that would actually work. What *random seed* means in this context is a string of characters used as a start for all the security encryption algorithms used to protect your connections across the Internet.

There are two major encryption heavyweights, and BorderManager uses them both:

- The RSA (Rivest, Shamir, and Adleman, the three inventors of the security algorithm) public key encryption system, used for both encryption and authentication

- The Diffie-Hellman system, named for Whitfield Diffie and Martin Hellman, who wrote a paper on public key cryptography two years before RSA was released

RSA is more widely used, mainly because of its use in PGP (Pretty Good Privacy, used mostly for personal e-mail). RSA codes are the result of multiplying two prime numbers, and can be broken with enough time and computer horsepower spent attacking the security algorithm itself. Diffie-Hellman has no point to attack the algorithm, and is considered more secure. Of course, it also requires more overhead. The combination of the two methods is stronger than Fort Knox ever considered necessary.

Following my seed joke, I decided to use the random seed of "Petunia seeds make nice flowers." The beta software limited the seed to 80 characters, while later versions offered up to 256 characters for the random seed. The U.S. Government (at this writing) still considers encryption programs in the same category as weapons, and limits exports of powerful examples. The overseas version of BorderManager may need to cut the seed length down to stay within the legal limits.

Of course, you can't see what you're typing in the field. All keystrokes are written as asterisks. Since there's no reason to generate that same key pair again, don't worry about it. If you lose this key pair or feel your security has been breached, generate a new key pair immediately.

More messages flash by, informing you that the RSA key pair is being generated, and the Diffie-Hellman parameters are being applied and parametized (don't you love the way the computer biz fractures language?) as necessary. Suddenly, a distinctly NetWare message appears, telling you that VPN details within NDS are being added and updated. This being NetWare, NDS controls your virtual network just as well as your real network. Pretty soon, you'll get to close these ugly C-Worthy interface screens and move to NWAdmin.

Look, another message. An NLM, VPMASTER, was successfully loaded also. Things are rolling now.

Finally, your success message, again in purple, tells you that the encryption information was generated successfully. More than that, the VPN server type was successfully updated in Directory Services. It seems that you're all set, so press Enter.

Copying the Encryption Key

There are two menu choices you can't read in the background window in Figure 10.3. The third and fourth lines on that menu are:

Copy Encryption Information

Authenticate Encryption Information

After all, the secure keys are in pairs, so the slave servers and their administrators must have access to the public part of the master server's VPN encryption key. So, press Enter on the Copy menu item.

The goal for this menu is to copy a file named MINFO.VPN to a floppy disk or to a hard disk available to the other administrators. Since I don't need to mail the floppy anywhere, I decided to try to save the file to my local server. Although the Copy window offered A:\ for the start of the path name, I changed that to SYS:\KEY\. Yes, that's a new directory, and I wanted to see if NetWare would create the directory as well as put the key there.

No problem for me, but if the system balks for you, just create the directory first. The directory was created and the file, MINFO.VPN, was quickly copied where I specified. In case you're curious what a key file looks like, here is mine:

1

0

GATEWAY2000

94

```
30 5c 30 0d 06 09 2a 86 48 86 f7 0d 01 01 01 05 00 03 4b
00 30 48 02 41 00 cf 81 6c dc e9 59 8c d6 d8 d2 7d bc 20
10 84 af 53 ec aa 05 2a 78 c0 9d 6b 35 fc f8 93 dc 15 5b
d0 6b fb 2c 7c ff 1f 49 f0 62 c8 e1 21 1d 75 03 eb 6c 90
aa dd d2 6d 95 65 b9 4d ea 38 9d bb d5 02 03 01 00 01
```

154

```
30 81 97 06 09 2a 86 48 86 f7 0d 01 03 01 30 81 89 02 41 00
8d 38 7b e4 f1 c0 d5 21 04 b8 9d c2 57 fd 14 08 60 17 3d b6
17 27 1a e3 da d5 3d f0 45 09 19 a7 61 4c a6 80 83 3d 3d f4
ee 48 f9 43 d6 82 c7 95 0b 3f c7 2a a8 a0 bf 84 d9 fc 66 87
67 43 b4 95 02 40 6a 2e af 15 39 da 15 cb b5 6b 2e 89 81 a9
77 0e 52 db 1d a0 b3 63 8c 3d 08 91 c2 4d 78 c8 f4 69 6f 35
70 4e ed 91 4d 6e 08 d5 c9 11 e3 67 44 91 3e da 21 44 4f 08
7f c8 91 26 9c b2 8c f0 08 31 02 02 01 f8
```

Believe it or not, that's the result of providing "Petunia seeds make nice flowers" in the earlier random seed field. The only thing legible is the name of the server, GATEWAY2000. All the rest of the file means something only to the encryption software. Yes, spaces were included in the key, since

I typed spaces in the random seed. The longer the message, the more secure the encryption, in case you're wondering.

A success message appears, thoughtfully telling you that the file is copied to the location you requested. There was no message about creating a directory on my server, but the directory and file were where I asked them to be.

Authenticating Encryption

One last step, and we can leave the master server configuration process. You must authenticate your encryption information. While you may trust a login script modification and leave without testing it, encryption failures have a much higher negative consequence. So, let's check things.

Pressing Enter to authenticate pops open an odd window. Take a look at Figure 10.4 and see if you can figure out what they want here.

This Message Digest for Authentication shown in Figure 10.4 is your only way to authenticate slave server encryption. As you'll see in a bit, when you create a slave server, this number must match what the slave server shows, or you will need to go back and start all over. So keep this

FIGURE 10.4

Write this down—it's important.

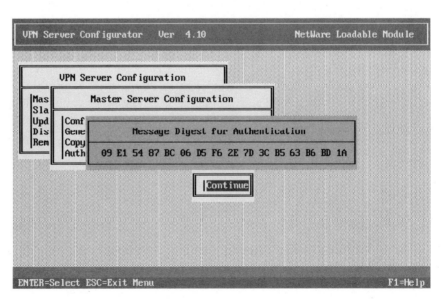

number in a nice safe place, but not so safe you can't find it again when you need it. No, don't write down *my* message digest; write down yours.

That's it for the master server. You should do this only once, since, as the warning message said, there can be only one master server. You might need to repeat the slave server configuration a number of times, so let's get started.

Slave Server Configuration

Okay, boys and girls, hang on, because this is going to go by quickly. How quickly? The slave server configuration is exactly like the master server configuration.

Well, almost exactly. See if you can tell where the few tiny differences are. Hey, we haven't had any tests in here, like those "CNE" test books full of answers divorced from real-world problems. So count yourself lucky, and see if you can spot the changes.

From the VPN Server Configuration menu on the server that will be used as the slave, choose (guess what) the Slave Server Configuration option. No, this isn't the difference. Obviously, it's too obvious.

You will see the Slave Server Configuration menu, which looks amazingly similar to the Master Server Configuration menu in Figure 10.1 (you will believe cloning has spread from Scottish sheep to computer programs). Choose Configure IP Addresses, and let's keep rolling.

Here we go with the same screen as Figure 10.2. Obviously, you must list the IP address of the server, which depends on the individual server. Back in the earlier figure, I hadn't yet filled in the VPN Tunnel IP Address field, but I put in the address of 204.251.1.2 because I like to leave the .1 address for the router. Here, put 204.251.1.3. The mask will be 255.255.255.0, just as it was before.

WARNING A forceful reminder: Each VPN server, master, and slave must be on the same subnet.

Oh, you clever reader, you noticed the first change. Good for you.

Save the IP addresses, and the same NetWare housekeeping messages will flash on and off the screen. So far, so good. See, there's nothing to this, is there?

Configuring Encryption

Here we are again under the exact same subheading as for master slave configuration. So, let's do the same thing. Choose Generate Encryption Information from the menu.

You will need to provide the location for the MINFO.VPN file you created earlier. The system assumes that the file is on the floppy. If the file is on the network instead, just put in the path; the system will happily read it wherever.

Look, another change. Instead of generating a new key pair, the slave server authenticates the file from the master server. Take a gander at Figure 10.5 to see how this differs from the master configuration.

FIGURE 10.5

Yes, it matches.

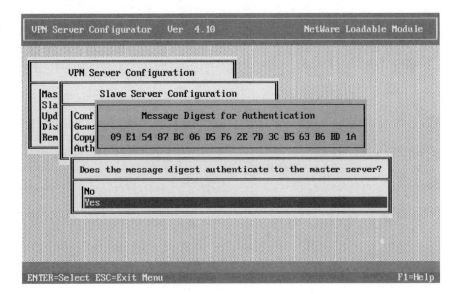

The message does authenticate, and the pair matches. Don't bother to look back and see if they match, because they do. I checked, I rechecked, and Marilyn the Wonder Editor checked. They match.

Since they match, go ahead and press the Enter key while the cursor overlays Yes and be done with this section. Messages about successfully saving Diffie-Hellman parameters and the RSA public key file will force you to press Enter to clear them.

Oh, another random seed request. This time, I put in "My petunias are growing nicely" as a way to tie together the earlier random seed pun. See, those books on writing structure are paying off, aren't they?

Another flash message talks about generating something, but goes by so quickly that it's tough to read. I suppose if it were important, I would need to press Enter to get past it. Obviously, the success screen saying all is well, and the server type is now installed in Directory Services, is important, because I do need to press Enter to get past that one.

Back to the menu, where you may want to copy the encryption information. This file is named SINFO.VPN; the *S* designates slave rather than master server. You can put this on a floppy or in the same SYS:\KEY directory as the master file.

Here's the slave server key file. Notice there is more personal information than for the master server, and the slave server part of the key is half as long as the master server file.

```
1

0

GATEWAY2K-2

1

205.112.12.7

255.255.255.0

0.0.0.0

0.0.0.0
```

```
204.251.1.3

255.255.255.0

64

57 01 3d 91 93 39 c9 d9 f2 65 1c 90 58 dd b0 19 6e c6 97 c2
1e a6 11 32 e4 26 4f 61 e6 7d 5b 63 a4 f9 93 a2 53 0a ce ff
de 1c 59 90 21 ca 07 6d a7 fa 9b 4c b9 7d 6a 22 e0 e8 28 38
88 fc b0 a5
```

You can see that the key file identifies the slave server and the slave server address right at the front. The address for this slave server, 205.112.12.7, shows that the server is on a completely different network from the master server. That's what you would expect to find, since these servers are in different locations.

Notice, however, that the VPN network address (204.251.1.3) is the same subnet as the master server. This shouldn't be a surprise, since I told you that was necessary. We're making a virtual network of these separate servers, and to be one network, the addresses must all be for the same network.

Of course, you'll need to make some name adjustments when you configure the second slave server, and generate a different SINFO.VPN file that still has the same name. Develop a naming system, such as SINFO-3.VPN for your third slave server, and put all these VPN files in the same directory. Then copy them all to a floppy just for safekeeping.

A Look at the Other Options

Back at the Slave Server Configuration menu, you may be curious and try the Authenticate Encryption Information menu choice. The result will look exactly like Figure 10.4, except for one minor detail: The digest is different. Why is it different? Because the random seed I typed was different, that's why. Each slave server must have its own key, so the master server will know messages are from an authorized slave, and not some slave-wannabe hacker computer.

Press Enter or Escape as necessary to return to the main VPN Server Configuration menu. The third option, Update VPN Filters, is of little use at this time. After all, if your server filters didn't work, they would have stopped the installation procedure. I know that from experience. But the filter updates are necessary when a slave changes keys, or some new network management adds a new restriction.

Does the Display VPN Server Configuration option provide any valuable information? I think so. Take a look at Figure 10.6 and see if this information isn't reassuring. Don't you feel better knowing this slave server is all configured, exactly the way you want it?

Yes, the server name and IP address are the same for this slave server as for the master server. Proud of yourself, eagle eye? I use the same server for all configuration details to make it easier to get screen shots and control the environment.

There's one tiny difference between the information for the slave server versus that for the master server. For the master, there is a RSA Private Key field, just under the RSA Public Key field. This is because the master server tracks the RSA details, which takes some of the security load off the individual slave servers and puts NDS to work supporting these key management chores.

FIGURE 10.6

Read only, but helpful

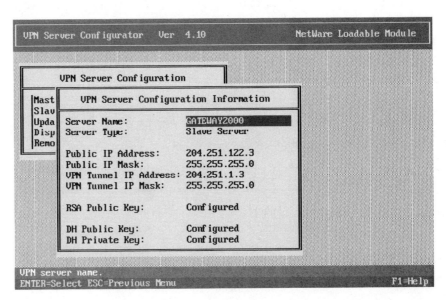

The last menu choice lets you remove your VPN configuration. Now that you realize how little there is to creating a new VPN configuration, you shouldn't hesitate to blow away the current configuration if necessary. The only potential problems will appear in large WANs where some servers may be on older software versions. Since this VPN software is all brand new, feel free to play with the stuff, particularly if you and another site can find the time to experiment.

Using NWAdmin on Your VPN

Finally, you can close the C-Worthy interface screens and move to NWAdmin. You have added the \PUBLIC\BSSNAP\W95\SETUP snapins to your NWAdmin program, haven't you? I thought so. If you just skipped here from the table of contents, be sure to run the aforementioned SETUP.EXE program on your Windows 95 management station before going farther. Well, to be honest, you can't go farther until you load the program, so hop to it. When you're ready, you can proceed as follows:

1. Open NWAdmin, double-click on the VPN master server object, and click on the command button that says Virtual Private Network. Now you can actually see something. Before going through all those console configuration commands, the VPN couldn't be seen through NWAdmin.

2. Here is where you add the slave servers to the official VPN network member list. Click on the little Add icon at the top right of the VPN Members box in the Virtual Private Network dialog box.

3. Rather than server names and locations, you are asked to supply the SINFO.VPN file. Remember, all the server and location information comes from that file. If you put the file on a floppy, feed that floppy now. If the file is on the network, the system will happily pick up that file that way. Figure 10.7 shows the process of adding a new slave server to the network.

FIGURE 10.7

Adding slave servers

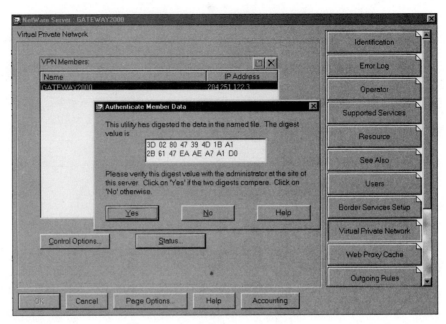

All this talk in the dialog about "digesting" the digest information is making me hungry. Doesn't this seem slightly cannibalistic to you? Never mind about that now (why yes, we always put carrots in the guest hot tubs), because you must verify the digest number with someone at the remote site. If these keys don't match, you won't get a connection. After all, these are security keys, and you've gone to a lot of trouble to make unique keys to share among your central site and others in the new virtual network.

4. You have the option to build static routes between master and slave servers by choosing the slave servers through their IP addresses. There's not a lot of advantage to this, but it's possible. If you want to add the static route, highlight the slave server, click on the Add icon, and choose whether it's a network or a host (choose network). Type the IP network address, and let the system add the subnet mask automatically. If the mask is wrong (unlikely), correct it. Click on OK, and you're finished.

5. Notice the Control Options command button back in the Virtual Private Network dialog box (Figure 10.7)? Click on that, so you can dictate connection details.

Anytime there are remote connections, you have some choices to make concerning the amount of keep-alive packets and other connection traffic details. In this case, you have five choices to make, none of them particularly difficult. Check Figure 10.8 for your five easy choices.

FIGURE 10.8

The default choices work fine.

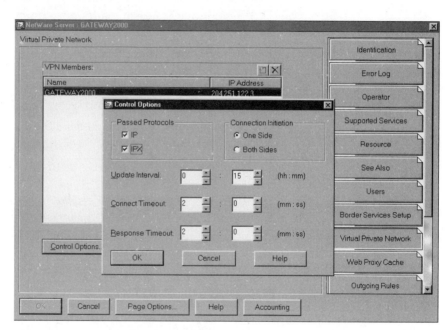

Here are the connection choices in the Control Options dialog box:

- **Passed Protocols:** Which protocols are encrypted and passed along across the Internet. Both IPX and IP are enabled by default, but choose only IPX if your NetWare clients are still using IPX to communicate with their NetWare servers.

- **Connection Initiation:** Specifies which systems starts communications. While you may think that having both servers try to establish the connection to each other would supply some fault tolerance to the connection, it doesn't work quite that way. If both servers try to establish the connection, the initiation sequences get in the way of the response sequences, and the two servers argue about which is supposed to lead (and you thought people were petty). Setting only one system to establish connections works reliably and the connections are made more quickly than if both servers try to take charge.

- **Update Interval:** Defines how often the master and slave servers send topology and encryption information. The default is 15 minutes, but you may set it longer if you wish. Topologies don't change that often, and any encryption changes should be followed by a forced update of VPN filters. On the other hand, no changes mean small packets, so it's best to leave it at 15 minutes.

- **Connect Timeout:** Sets the time the master server tries to connect to a slave server during a synchronization update. A good time for this is 2 minutes, which is also the default. If the server is busy or the Internet is heavily loaded, many seconds at a time may be necessary for the connection sequence exchange. But Internet traffic flows change greatly minute by minute, so a 2-minute window works fine.

- **Response Timeout:** The flip side of the connect timeout. The same problems a server will have in receiving a synchronization packet can happen on the server side while waiting for the response.

See, nothing here was too taxing, was it? Unless you have some unusual circumstances, leave the defaults. Novell engineers have done this more than you and I put together, and they chose the defaults. (Of course, we're assuming that they chose the defaults based on personal experience rather than by throwing darts at a board, but give them a chance either way.)

For a fun time, click on the Status command button beside the Control Options button. Don't get caught admiring your handiwork for too long, however. I'm sure you have plenty of other work waiting.

Firewall Considerations

There are a few firewall considerations for your VPN. Check your firewall to verify that all routes not allowed are denied. You don't want the IP address of the VPN tunnel network to inadvertently get sent through the firewall. It's not likely to happen, but check it anyway.

The next most important consideration is to keep the firewall's IP address from being sent through the tunnel. If the firewall address does get out onto the VPN network, all traffic from your remote sites will start using the encrypted tunnel. This is fine in most cases, but public addresses must be kept public.

Sorry, but you'll need to go back to FILTCFG for any changes necessary to your BorderManager configuration. Load FILTCFG ➤ Configure TCP/IP Filters ➤ Outgoing RIP Filters, and see what it says.

The outgoing RIP filters should already be enabled. I saw that the VPN software is somewhat adamant on that point earlier, as it gave me an error message in purple prose (okay, prose with a purple background).

If your filters are in Permit Mode, check the list of Routes Always Denied for the firewall address. Enter your firewall address there to make sure it won't get out onto your VPN network.

Save, confirm, exit, cross your fingers, and let the system do whatever reinitializing it may feel is necessary. Once things return to normal, your network should be doubly secure.

Wrap

Large companies with existing WAN infrastructures will be slow to utilize VPN, because they have a working solution already. Yes, their solution is more expensive, but most network managers are so busy that changing something that works comes after fighting fires.

Small and medium-sized companies, however, don't have the investment in WAN infrastructure that precludes them from testing a VPN. Cost savings tend to be more important, especially in the small companies, encouraging a search for cost-effective options. A VPN works perfectly well with just two sites, and it offers a chance for shared computing not available at this price from any other vendor.

PART

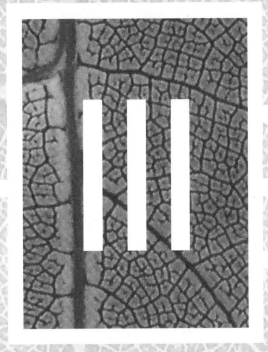

III

PROVIDING CONTENT
WITH BORDERMANAGER

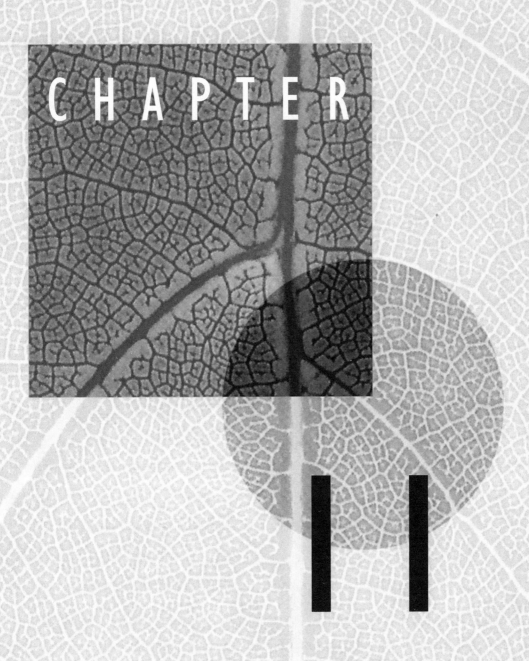

CHAPTER

11

Remote Client Support
with NetWare Connect

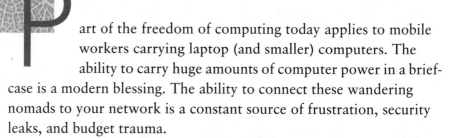

Part of the freedom of computing today applies to mobile workers carrying laptop (and smaller) computers. The ability to carry huge amounts of computer power in a briefcase is a modern blessing. The ability to connect these wandering nomads to your network is a constant source of frustration, security leaks, and budget trauma.

Maybe I shouldn't be quite so negative. After all, you may be skimming through this in a bookstore before taking a job with a company running IntranetWare and BorderManager, and trying to see if you can get up to speed quickly. Reading too many negative statements may send you screaming into the night, looking for a security job patrolling empty warehouses, far from computers. But I bet not.

Here's the positive side: If you've had experience dealing with NetWare Connect in earlier versions, you can handle the job with IntranetWare and BorderManager. If you're familiar with the pros and cons of remote control versus remote-node computing, you can get through this unbloodied and unbowed. If you can handle all the various modem configuration and telephone line connection details, you are a genius and worthy of respect from all people.

Although NetWare Connect provides many features, here we're going to concentrate on supporting outside users getting safely into your network. Dialing out using NetWare Connect should be discouraged, since you have other options with BorderManager, and those other options include some control and security management. If possible, gather all desktop modems from your network shortly after BorderManager and the other network components are installed. Your life will be happier when you deal with fewer modems and more network connections (at least, my life is happier that way).

Remote Communications History and Overview

Remote communications and LANs have had a long and disharmonious relationship. Back in the early days of LANs, the middle 1980s, the only deal-killing disadvantage of a LAN over a Unix-based multi-user system was remote access. When I spent time in Sales and Sales Support (not exactly a condition of parole, but close), a customer demanding to call into the system from home almost always went with a multi-user system.

All those BBS (bulletin board service) systems we dialed in to in the early and mid 1980s were essentially multi-user systems. Our intelligent PCs (wow, blazing 8080 chips!) acted like dumb terminals when connected to the BBS. Yes, exactly the same way a terminal (or a PC running terminal software) acted when connected to a remote Unix system.

Therein lies the difference between the LAN and the Unix system: where the actual program processing happens. I know this is basic stuff, but with all the talk of client/server computing, it's helpful to go back to the source to help understand some of the compromises we're stuck with today.

The Shift in Processing Power

LANs used the processing power of the PC to run programs, and the LAN server provided shared files and printers. As the LAN operating system got smarter (and NetWare got smarter first), the individual programs running on the PC could coordinate file access. Multiple users could access the same files on a record level, so files could be shared while individual record contents were protected. This technological leap forward allowed thousands of multi-user business applications to migrate to NetWare. Programs written in Business Basic and COBOL became popular vertical and horizontal applications for NetWare, especially in accounting.

Putting the processing power in the PC at the end of the LAN cable helped performance, but made life difficult for remote users. After all, LAN cables stretch only so far.

Multi-user systems were originally tied to the central processing unit via serial cables. The communication used between terminals (even if a PC was involved, the terminal emulation software lobotomized it back down to dumb terminal level) was the same for both local and remote terminal connections. A null-modem cable was used between the terminal and system, or a modem was attached to the system, waiting for a call from a terminal.

You may remember that modem speeds at the time were pretty dismal. But speed doesn't matter as much when you're sending only text to the screen. The fancy systems used ASCII graphics, with stars and dashes for boxes and the like.

Aha, you say, if the performance was slow anyway, a remote caller from another office or home could get acceptable performance even with those slow modems. That's exactly right. Remote warehouses often called into the main system, for instance, because the serial cable reach wasn't all that far. Once you put a modem on the system, the remote terminal can be anywhere in the world that has a telephone connection.

Internet sites used Ethernet cabling for local connections, even though they used TCP/IP rather than a LAN operating system. Terminal servers evolved to connect groups of terminal (or modem) ports anywhere on the network cable.

Remote Internet connections were based on Telnet, the remote-connection protocol. Once terminal users made a connection to their own system, they could connect anywhere else on the Internet they had a login. Dialing in from home or remote sites was simple, as long as you knew some telephone numbers for modems attached to systems or terminal servers.

Today, remote users are getting militant and demanding. The term is "global roaming," and users demand network access from anywhere with a telephone connection back to the company. Voice mail and e-mail aren't enough for the mobile professional of today; full access to data of all kinds is demanded. When you say "no," they whine and go complain to your boss's boss, and you have to support them anyway. Worse, your boss's boss probably won't approve nearly enough money to support them directly, so you'll be scratching and fighting to make the system usable.

Remote Node versus Remote Control

While the Unix, Internet, and multi-user fans were all happy and telecommuting in 1985, PC users were left out of that game. Sure, they had color monitors and personal hard disks by then (10MB in the XT, remember), but communicating from the road was impossible. Two options developed for remote PC communication: remote node and remote control.

Remote-Node Computing

Remote node owes quite a bit to the Unix host and terminal server philosophy. A user dials in to a modem, attached somehow to the network, and runs the regular LAN operating system over this link. In essence, the telephone link becomes a really, really long LAN cable.

The problem appeared immediately: performance. Modems were blazing up to 2400 baud (long time since you saw that phrase, right?), but even the doubling of speed offered by new technology didn't make for a snappy connection. All the PC LAN software was written for PCs attached to the file server via Ethernet or ARCnet connections. Oh yes, there was also that new Token Ring stuff, just out from IBM.

Even ARCnet, slow as it was, looked like warp drive compared to a modem connection. Remote-node computing was technically possible, but practically impossible, throughout the 1980s and even into the early 1990s.

A faster modem helped, as did ISDN. I did a test of remote-node computing in late 1993, focusing on ISDN connections. With a 64Kbps ISDN network connection, remote-node computing was possible. Using Windows 3.1 remotely was about as fast as a local network with lots of traffic and an overworked server. It was aggravating at times, but possible.

The early 1990s saw the beginnings of the ISP market, as companies started selling access to banks of modems and terminal servers to the general public. A few of the early systems, including my ISP (OnRamp Technologies), allowed only full remote-network connections rather than terminal access into the system. The procedure was simple: You connected over the telephone using PPP (Point-to-Point Protocol), you were assigned an IP address during connection, and you were on the Internet.

PPP replaced SLIP (Serial Line Internet Protocol). PPP is able to support multiple protocols over a single connection. SLIP, as you can guess by the name, was limited to IP connections only. PPP is still the de facto standard for dial-in Internet connections, as you'll see as we get a little farther in the chapter.

Speed remains the problem of remote-node computing. No matter how fast the analog modems get, and how widespread ISDN support is, no remote option is as fast as your LAN connection.

Remote-Control Technology

The heyday for remote control was in the middle and late 1980s, as people with LANs realized that remote connections were impossible to make, or impossible to live with once made. Clever software companies developed a way to connect remote computers into the network, but have the LAN computer do all the processing.

pcANYWHERE and Carbon Copy are the two names I remember from the beginning of this market. I don't recall who was first, but these two battled each other relentlessly and advanced the technology with each release.

Taking a hint from the Unix and multi-user vendors, remote-control products just send screen information and leave all the processing power on the network. Unlike Unix systems, however, remote-control systems need a PC to run the processing. The more power the host PC has (that's the PC on the network), the better. All the remote PC must do is display images echoed from the host PC.

The advantage of remote control is speed. The processing is done where the programs and data live, so there's no delay while you copy program and data files across a slow modem link. The disadvantage is cost. Two complete PCs are being used to support one user.

Which Is Better?

The best choice depends, like so much of life, on what you're trying to do. Not many companies today run all their business with character-based applications on Unix hosts, so remote terminals don't offer much help.

One could assume from that statement that the "fat client" PC applications demand remote control and two PCs for each connection. But the rise of Web clients and other Internet technology is blurring those lines. Remote Web client users are accustomed to the response of a modem to a remote host, since that's how they surf the Web from home.

Rather than argue about which option is better, BorderManager includes support for remote node and remote control. You pick what you want, and install the appropriate software. Just be prepared to hear, "It's too slow" or, "It costs too much," no matter which option you install.

Remote Access Services Installation and Configuration

More than with some of the other services we've looked at, remote access needs some preparation. There are several areas that will be just about impossible to configure without specific information. So, before we get to the installation and configuration steps, let's make sure you're ready.

Gather Your Tools and Information

Your first consideration is that modems are involved, and modems are squirrely devices. It is wonderful if your company uses a single brand of modem for all users. Several modem lines have the breadth necessary to support modem racks for incoming calls, as well as desktop, portable, and PC Card modems for laptop computer slots. Companies with intelligent, proactive management will set a modem standard for the company and buy modems from only that one manufacturer.

Since this is the real world, however, big companies usually have at least one of every modem made in the last six years. Don't feel bad if this is your situation, because no company has been able to absolutely control what types of modems are purchased by every department. Modems are cheap enough that many department managers and employees can buy whatever modem they want without permission from MIS or the computer support department.

Get a sample of all the modems you can before starting to install and configure remote-client access services. The more information you can supply during installation, the fewer frustrating support calls you will have from traveling executives who are furious because their off-brand modem won't connect to your network access modems.

Gather the manuals and specifications on all modems you have, which is an easy task if you buy them just for this project. Gathering manuals for modems bought more than two months ago is hopeless; give up now. You don't get overtime pay for fruitless searches (as if you get overtime pay for anything, right?).

One more impossible task: Find all the documentation for WAN devices stuck inside the NetWare server. You'll need to coordinate any setting changes between the hardware and system software, and guessing at jumper settings won't do it.

Server-Side Installation

Because the BorderManager remote-access procedures are based on the old NetWare Connect, the majority of the configuration happens through the server console. This means, once again, we're relegated to the digital dungeon of the C-Worthy interface.

Maybe I should write a horror movie with the C-Worthy interface as the evil computer spirit that sucks the creative life force from network managers. Nah, nobody would believe it. If network managers had any creative life force, they would learn to lie and transfer to the marketing department for shorter hours and longer paychecks.

Interface bashing aside (for now), head once again to your server console or start RCONSOLE on your workstation. Load the NIASCFG utility, then stop and verify that the modem plugged into the server is turned on. Go back to NIASCFG and choose Configure NIAS by pressing Enter.

Press Enter again on the first choice of the Select Component to Configure screen, which is conveniently labeled Remote Access. If you get some odd message about time not being synchronized on the network, just try to cancel. Instead of canceling, you will get to what you want: the login screen for NDS. This is serious, because you're extending the NDS schema, and only an administrator can do so. Figure 11.1 shows the warning screen.

The NWCSU.NLM referred to at the start of the message in the login screen (Figure 11.1) is a part of NWCCON, the NetWare Connect Control utility called by NIASCFG. (See, I told you that Novell is starting to combine all these menus into just a few major front ends, rather than a large handful of utility control programs.) But you don't need to be concerned with this now. Just put your password in the field and keep going.

A nice touch, and one I haven't seen from a console screen before, is an option to read instructions before starting. When you say Yes, seven screens of configuration instructions appear. Unfortunately, there's no way listed to print the information, unless you cheat. Cheat? Yes, cheat. Go to the SYS:\SYSTEM directory of the server you are working on, and

FIGURE 11.1

Warning before entering secure territory

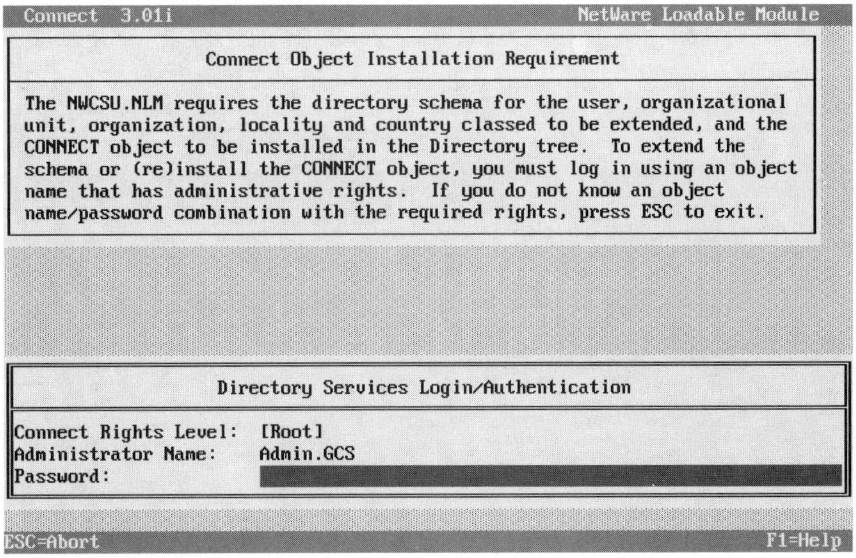

```
Connect 3.01i                                    NetWare Loadable Module
┌──────────────────────────────────────────────────────────────────────┐
│                  Connect Object Installation Requirement               │
│ ┌────────────────────────────────────────────────────────────────────┐│
│ │The NWCSU.NLM requires the directory schema for the user, organizational││
│ │unit, organization, locality and country classed to be extended, and the││
│ │CONNECT object to be installed in the Directory tree.  To extend the  ││
│ │schema or (re)install the CONNECT object, you must log in using an object││
│ │name that has administrative rights.  If you do not know an object    ││
│ │name/password combination with the required rights, press ESC to exit.││
│ └────────────────────────────────────────────────────────────────────┘│
│                                                                        │
│ ┌────────────────────────────────────────────────────────────────────┐│
│ │                  Directory Services Login/Authentication             ││
│ │Connect Rights Level:   [Root]                                        ││
│ │Administrator Name:     Admin.GCS                                     ││
│ │Password:                                                             ││
│ └────────────────────────────────────────────────────────────────────┘│
│ ESC=Abort                                                    F1=Help   │
└──────────────────────────────────────────────────────────────────────┘
```

print the NWCINST.TXT file. That's where the installation instruction screens come from. Be sure no one is around if you read or print the instructions—you have your reputation to protect. The operative phrase when someone is watching is, "Damn the manuals, and full speed ahead."

The instructions let you in on the secret you probably already figured out: The streamlined installation method can be stopped or bypassed if you wish. All these steps and screens can be reached through the NWCCON or NIASCFG utility.

The nice touches just pile up on each other, as you'll see when you exit the configuration and setup instructions. A new screen, shown in Figure 11.2, appears. If you press F8 to "view an overview of the configuration process," you will once again see the configuration instructions. One can only hope these friendly screens multiply across the entire system.

FIGURE 11.2

Friendly screens abound

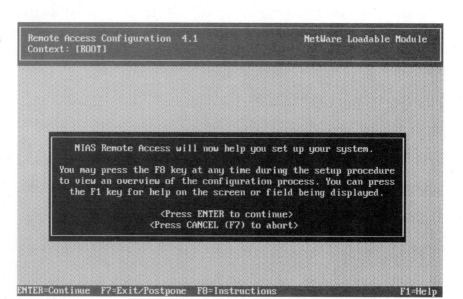

Am I worried about books like this one not being necessary if the software help screens get really good? Not one bit, because the screens only help you do what you have already decided to do. Knowing what to do and when to do it is an entirely different matter, as is the ability to reference other options to achieve similar goals through different means. Manuals and product online help rarely give coherent instructions for the task at hand, much less do they have the time or ability to address critical but non-task-oriented questions.

Adapter and Modem Choices

The next screen asks if you have any synchronous adapters, such as X.25 (yes, people still use that). I'm assuming that you have a modem or two attached to the server for this exercise, so I'm bypassing this screen. If you are going to use higher-speed devices, you should be looking at other options for across the Internet rather than dialing in to the server. However, the default answer for this screen is to configure synchronous adapters. Regardless, I'm forging ahead to configure an attached analog, asynchronous modem.

If you have no AIO (asynchronous input output) ports defined, you now have the chance to define one or more. I'm betting you don't have any ports defined, since you're just starting your async adventure.

An even two dozen options for serial adapters are presented. If you have more than one modem, it makes sense to add a serial adapter rather than rely on the server's modem port. With a serial adapter, much of the interrupt processing is handled by the adapter, and then passed on to the server. While you may think this sounds as if it delays remote-connection speed, it actually speeds the connections. The server processor won't be interrupted by every change in the remote conversation and housekeeping packet to keep the line clear, open, and stable. Only real communication packets get off the serial adapter board to the server. A server-connected modem is fine for occasional use, but regular use, or use by more than one person at a time, cries out for the processing power of an intelligent serial adapter rather than a communications port alone.

Here we see another problem with remote communications direct to the server: speed. Here's the connection information displayed on the server console when I told the system to configure one of the server's serial ports for a modem:

```
GATEWAY2000:LOAD AIOCOMX PORT=3F8 INT=4 NAME=COMX1

Loading module AIOCOMX.NLM

 Novell AIO Serial COM Port Driver (v2.13, 12 Jan 1995)

 Version 2.13  January 13, 1995

 Copyright 1994 Novell, Inc. All rights reserved.

 For AIOCOMX Driver Load Information, Enter 'LOAD AIOCOMX ?'

 Installed I/O Address 0x3F8 (Interrupt Number 4) as Board 0,
 Port 0

 16550 device detected - FIFOs enabled

 Driver rated at 19200bps (RXT=4/TXQ=16)
```

See the last line: "Driver rated at 19200bps" and some other information? Maximum speed for server-attached modems is 19.2Kbps. Would you stand for such a slow modem at home when you connect to the Internet? No, of course not. With remote connections off the server's serial port, faster speeds used to be impossible. Third-party serial adapters supported much higher speeds, which was another good reason to use extra equipment if you were doing this on a big scale. Now Novell allows you to bump up the serial adapter speed with this SET command:

```
parameter maxrate=115200
```

Back on the serial adapter choice screen, the message window says, "The requested driver was loaded successfully." Smile to yourself and press Enter to continue.

As things stand, I have one AIO port available. If you are using a third-party serial adapter board, there will be a configuration program from the board manufacturer to activate the two, four, eight, or more ports on the board. For our purposes here, however, I'm accepting my single AIO port and going on by saying "No" to the question, "Do you need to load more AIO drivers?"

The port setup screen flashes briefly, and then you are asked to verify that the modems attached to the newly activated ports are active. A flashing red-and-black warning screen repeats the request by blinking, "Make sure all modems are turned on" over and over. Check once more to verify that your modem is connected and active, and press Enter.

Modems are squirrely, as I mentioned before. Detecting modems is not an exact science, no matter what modem manufacturers and Microsoft's Plug and Play (or Plug and Pray) utilities tell you. Figure 11.3 displays what the modem-discovery utility has found, and offers you a chance to try again in case of failure.

The "Modem checking is complete" line blinks on and off. Unfortunately, I can't show that blinking effect with the figure here in this book.

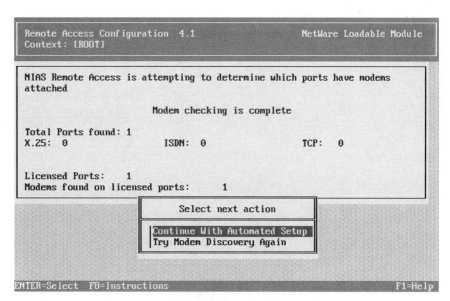

FIGURE 11.3

Success, believe it or not

If you want to make this a multimedia presentation, cover the line with your pencil, then move the pencil on and off the line to approximate blinking. Don't let anyone else see you do this, or you'll have quite a bit of explaining to do.

This nice NIAS Remote Access utility will attempt to determine the modem type automatically if you say "Yes" on the next screen. There are only about 50 choices listed in the MODEM.INF file in the SYS:SYSTEM\ CONNECT subdirectory, so your chances aren't great. The system didn't determine my modem was made by MultiTech, so I went to the next screen of modem types.

Scores (maybe hundreds) of modems are listed in this file. You can zero in on your modem style quickly by typing the first few letters of the manufacturer's name. I chose the MultiTech MultiModem II MT1432 (I know it's old, but it still works great) from the list and pressed Enter.

Remote Service Choices

Now that the modem for the activated COM port is chosen, you must determine which services should be allowed over that modem. Hence the information in Figure 11.4.

FIGURE 11.4

Remote service options

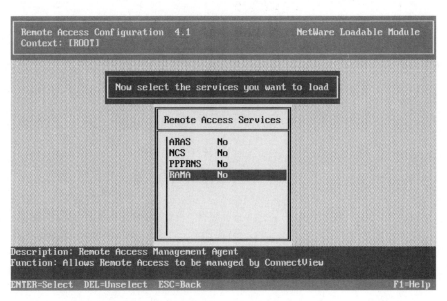

You have four options:

- **ARAS:** AppleTalk Remote Access Service, for Macintosh clients to connect as remote AppleTalk nodes.

- **NCS:** NASI (Novell Application Services Interface) Connection Service, for remote-control stations dialing in and LAN users dialing out through the configured modem controlled by the server. NCS manages the connection between a remote client and the local client being controlled remotely. If you allow outside clients to run remote-control sessions to LAN workstations, you must initialize the outgoing system as well. Don't let the users know that they have this option; see my tirade a bit later in the chapter.

- **PPPRNS:** PPP (Point-to-Point Protocol) Remote Node Service, for DOS, Windows, and Unix systems to become remote nodes on the network. We will look at the Windows systems trying to be remote NetWare nodes, which is the most popular option. Remote Unix or TCP/IP clients have other options for remote connections to the network.

- **RAMA:** With apologies to Arthur C. Clarke, RAMA (Remote Access Management Agent) starts the NCMA.NLM utility for remote access to be managed by SNMP consoles, ManageWise, or BorderManager's ConnectView software. The management agent is useful, but not as interesting as Clarke's *Rendezvous with Rama* (a story in which Rama is a huge but empty alien spaceship).

Let's go with PPPRNS, since PPP is the standard dial-up protocol used to connect to ISPs. Using PPP as a transport for IPX makes sense, because you utilize the easy links to ISPs and thus to the Internet, yet can send IPX traffic. To hackers, IPX data embedded within TCP/IP packets will look more like gibberish than data, so your information is relatively safe. This is not guaranteed, unbreakable encryption, but a reasonable amount of security via the "out of sight, out of mind" method.

Choosing PPPRNS opens a new screen asking which protocols to configure for the service. When you choose IPX, you must give a network number. You must provide a unique network number not duplicated anywhere else in your network. Since there's no registry, you won't know if your network address duplicates anyone else's IPX network number, but you don't need to care about that. Just pick a hexadecimal number with one to eight digits.

A virtual LAN segment is created using this network number. Having a separate segment adds to security controls (keeping people on the inside under control) and makes it easier to eliminate IPX housekeeping broadcasts. Bandwidth is limited, so you don't want to send server-configuration updates to remote nodes struggling to work under a severe lack of bandwidth.

This is the last step in our quick remote server soiree. When you save the IPX network number, settings are changed and the system reinitializes. You may get some stray messages about services dropping during the reconfiguration, but you're way too smart to be doing this type of work during the day when users need the system. The fact that a network segment may bump off some users won't bother you, will it?

Port Configuration

Next is not part of the automated installation procedure, unfortunately, but it should be. Although the COM port is set and expecting a modem to be there, we haven't actually configured the port itself.

Enabling the Modem Port

To begin the configuration, back up in the menu structure until you return to the main NIAS menu, then choose Protocols and Routing. Yes, you have just opened the standard INETCFG menu, and it even declares itself Internetworking Configuration, as you can see on the top left of the banner at the top of the screen. But remember, Novell is pushing NIASCFG, not all these submenus, so humor them and start with NIAS.

If you check Boards, the first menu choice on the INETCFG main menu, you should see that your COMX1 "board" is listed there and enabled. It will have some strange name under the Driver column heading, such as WHSMAIO. Don't worry about this name, because the system adds it and you don't need to change it. If your board isn't listed on this screen, choose the WHSMAIO driver, assign a board name, port address, and interrupt, and make appropriate comments.

The change you must make is through the second INETCFG menu option, Network Interfaces. Here you see COMX1 again, this time listed under the heading of Board Name. It will not belong to a group, nor will it be configured. That's what you must change, so highlight that line and press Enter.

A new window opens. This one is labeled Select a Medium. Since we activated only PPPRNS during the earlier configuration, that's the only medium that will appear (makes your choice easy, doesn't it?). Figure 11.5 shows the configuration screen that appeared after I selected my medium.

FIGURE 11.5

Enabling the modem port for routing

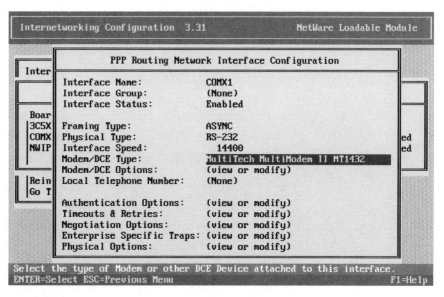

There are quite a few fields on this configuration screen. You should try everything with the defaults at first, of course, but you may find that you need to change one or two of these values. Let's go down the list from the top:

- **Interface Name:** That's the COMX1 port, the only modem connected to the server.

- **Interface Group:** Not surprisingly, this is a group of individual interfaces bound loosely together. You may use 1 to 17 characters to describe the group of ports bound neatly together via software. Why do this? Because many PPP calls and destinations allow selection by group rather than individual port. Most managers would prefer to call all the ports on an intelligent serial adapter by one name, allowing any available port on a board to accept the call. If you allow but a single telephone number to more than one person, Murphy's Law will guarantee that you get busy signals at least 60 percent of the time. A group of modems serving a group of mobile users will be much more effective in reducing user frustration.

- **Interface Status:** Enabled or disabled.

- **Framing Type:** Async only in this case, since we configured async during setup.

- **Physical Type:** RS-232 is the default and our value, since we configured the server's serial port during setup. Other options include V.35 for high-speed connections, as well as X.21, RS-422, and RS-423.

- **Interface Speed:** The default for async is 9600bps, but you can choose a faster setting. This is an improvement, since server connections used to be limited to 9600bps. Sync devices typically use an external clock timed with the carrier, and the default is external time when you configure sync devices.

- **Modem/DCE Type:** Hundreds of options, listing tons of available modems and support for ISDN external devices treated like modems, such as the 3Com Impact IQ ISDN.

- **Modem/DCE Options:** Primarily a place to add initialization strings for the attached modem after the standard script has been performed. Modems smarter than the average bear can have special features turned on by listing the initialization codes here.

- **Local Telephone Number:** The inbound number used when running BACP (Bandwidth Allocation Control Protocol). Remote peers use this number when they wish to establish a new member link. This does not apply to our purposes here, but was once a smart way to coordinate some server operations before the Internet became a conduit for all connections.

- **Authentication Options:** Assorted verification and security authentication options, including the use of more or less restrictive authentication protocols. A database file of authorized incoming users may be listed in this screen.

- **Timeouts & Retries:** Connection timeouts, keep-alive packet times, and the number of retries before actions are taken.

- **Negotiation Options:** Includes details such as the MRU (maximum receive unit) sizes for maximum, minimum, and optimal packet sizes, along with PPP header and data compression.

- **Enterprise Specific Traps:** Settings for companies using SNMP consoles to manage anything and everything, including modem connection details. Ignore this unless you have serious network management software in place. All the settings are disabled by default.

- **Physical Options:** Details such as the number of packets in the queue (100 is the default) and whether to simulate modem indicators (DSR, DCD, CTS, and so on). Your equipment manual will have these details if they are necessary. (See why I said to gather the manuals before you started all this?)

Things get complicated quickly when you start talking modem support, don't they? The screen in Figure 11.5 hides three pick lists and six complicated submenus. Now you can understand why everyone had such trouble configuring NetWare Connect in the past. And here you are trying to configure the same information quickly, so you can get back to the "serious" stuff.

The discouraging part of all this so far is you're not quite through configuring this port. There is another entire menu you haven't seen, so let's look at it now.

Configuring the Modem Port

Back out of INETCFG to return to the NIASCFG screen named Select Component to Configure. Now, having added a modem to the server, you have something to configure, so highlight Remote Access and press Enter. Ah, look, a new menu has appeared.

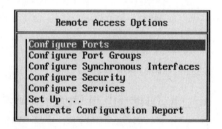

Fortunately, the questions hiding behind these menu options have more to do with security and the PPP settings than with the modem. Maybe it's just me, but networks are much easier to deal with than modems. I'm certainly glad to be out of the modem quagmire.

The first option, Configure Ports, seems like a good place to start, so let's go. The Port Configuration screen that appears next doesn't cover anything important except the port name, the description (being a typical network manager, I didn't put anything there so it will be more exciting trying to retrace my steps in six months), and the status, listed as Available. You need to choose the <Additional Parameters...> option at the bottom of this screen to reveal more details. Figure 11.6 shows those details, as well as the screen we went through to get here (in the bottom window).

FIGURE 11.6

Port and modem details

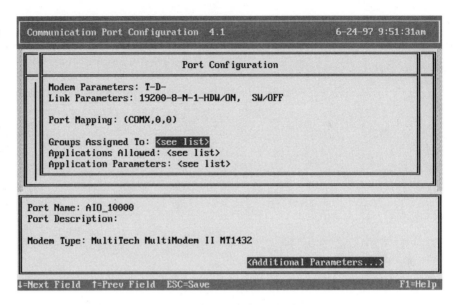

Unfortunately, there are some modem details in this screen. Here are brief descriptions of the modem-related and other fields on this screen:

- **Modem Parameters:** Sets the dial type (tone), whether this is a leased line or not (not, in this example), and any modem initialization string you wish to add.

- **Link Parameters:** Sets the data rates, data bits, parity, stop bits, and flow control. The field values are as you would expect, since the system takes the speed closest to the modem speed set earlier (19,200) and applies default modem parameters of 8 bits, no parity, 1 stop bit, and flow control handled by hardware rather than software. If you wish to argue with the flow control default, your choices include all off, all on, and hardware off and software on.

- **Port Mapping:** Read only, meaning that you can't change the mapping here.

- **Groups Assigned To:** Those port groups we ignored earlier. If you wish to include this port in one of those groups, here is one more chance to do so. Press Insert and pick your group.

- **Applications Allowed and Application Parameters:** Allow you to restrict the applications running over this port. However, using client security controls provides better security than these restrictions, and in a place you'll actually remember to check when there's a problem. It's one thing to make things exciting by not filling in the description fields, but entirely another to set binding restrictions deep within one of the rarely used console utilities. Avoid this potential mistake when possible, and leave these two options set to their defaults of any application and no blocking keywords.

When you're finished here, press Escape to get back to the Remote Access Options menu. For now, let's skip the Configure Port Groups and Configure Synchronous Interfaces choices. If you have a synchronous interface adapter, there are complicated instructions that vary wildly based on the type of adapter and manufacturer, so read your adapter's documentation.

Don't you hate it when books tell you to read the manuals? If the manuals were any good, you wouldn't have bought the book, would you? I hate it too, but the instructions for synchronous interface adapters vary too widely to cover here, really. I'm telling you the truth. Honest.

Configuring Security

Now we get to the Configure Security choice on the Remote Access Options menu. You're probably sick of hearing me talk about the importance of security, but don't grab your barf bag; there's no big speech here (because I'm holding off till the next section).

As you can see in the Configure Security menu that appears when you choose the option of the same name, there are a variety of port, service, and user restrictions available in this screen. Here, take a look.

```
┌─────────────────────────────────────────────────┐
│              Configure Security                  │
├─────────────────────────────────────────────────┤
│ Restrict Ports by User                           │
│ Restrict Service by User                         │
│ Restrict Service by Port                         │
│ Set Global Parameters                            │
│ Set User Parameters                              │
│ Set User Remote Client Password                  │
│ Set Remote Client Password Restrictions          │
└─────────────────────────────────────────────────┘
```

In all these fields, an entry of –1 means no limit. Why Novell designers didn't use zero like most other companies, I don't know. Perhaps they were worried about the difficulty of telling the number *0* from the letter O. More likely, this is a holdover from a bad choice years ago when they first developed NetWare Connect.

Let's go over the choices here:

- **Restrict Ports by User:** The default is to allow all users access to all ports.

- **Restrict Service by User:** The same as the first option, since all services are allowed to all users.

- **Restrict Service by Port:** Yes, all services are available on all ports. See a trend here?

- **Set Global Parameters:** Covers such details as disconnect times for idle connections and dial-back configuration (if allowed). You may limit dialing out to specific numbers if you wish, which is the least you can do. The most you can do is disable dial-out altogether, which we'll cover shortly.

- **Set User Parameters:** Gives you the opportunity to change the global parameters by user. If you don't have enough work already, feel free to make individual exceptions for users all over the place. I guarantee that your free time will evaporate when you start managing on a user-by-user basis. On the other hand, it's extremely career-limiting to tell the VP that you don't allow certain applications to the user community at large, so they're out of luck as well. If you must make exceptions (and you must now and then), be sure to write down the exceptions in the detailed service log you keep. Stop laughing; you should keep track of all server and user changes, you know.

- **Set User Remote Client Password:** Allows you to set a case-sensitive (yes, CASE-SENSITIVE) password for users. This password is not nearly as secure as a NetWare password into NDS. Don't give remote users the same NDS and remote password; they're smart enough to remember two passwords if they're smart enough to travel.

- **Set Remote Client Password Restrictions:** Sets the minimum password length (default of none), maximum invalid login attempts (none again, a really stupid setting), and offers a way to stretch passwords up to 16 characters instead of just 8. My advice is to enable long passwords, cut the invalid login attempts down to 3, and force a minimum password length of at least 6 characters. In other words, this is one screen where I change every default. I disagree strongly with this lack of security consciousness in this installation section for NetWare Connect. I see this section going against the trend of blocking access until permitted, the way the Proxy Server and firewall security settings are used.

Setting Up Dial-in Only Port Usage

Now that you've survived the security configuration, go back to the Remote Access Options menu. The next choice, Configure Services, pops open a pick list of remote-access services, and allows some changes to some parameters. It's better to use the configuration screen covered earlier in this chapter (Figure 11.5) for such changes.

The penultimate choice on the Remote Access Options menu, Set Up, sounds interesting, doesn't it? The underlying settings are actually pretty dull and redundant, except for the third option on the System Setup Options menu, as shown here.

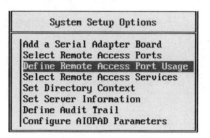

When you highlight the third option, the status line at the bottom of the screen says, "Restrict ports to dial-in or dial-out use only." When you choose the Define Remote Access Port Usage option, a new pick list, entitled Port Usage Options, appears. There are three choices: Dial-in Only, Dial-out Only, or both.

For the sake of security and user control, set this to Dial-in Only, the first choice in the pick list. Why? You have a variety of ways to get out from your network, all of which offer more control, management, audit tracking, and security than NetWare Connect. This is the least secure method of allowing client access to the rest of the world. Don't do it (my apologies to Nike).

Yeah, yeah, you're tired of hearing about security, and probably think I'm more paranoid than average. Fortunately, I'm not nearly as paranoid as some, or you would have to wade through plenty of distressing anecdotal stories about hackers dialing in through a forgotten desktop modem and sucking the entire worth of the company out of the bank accounts. And if I didn't have any distressing anecdotes, I would make them up. Lucky for you, I'm only moderately paranoid. Some believe the skill of a LAN administrator is directly proportional to the level of paranoia. Unfortunately, the esteem of the administrator's co-workers is inversely proportional to that administrators level of paranoia.

After you choose Dial-in Only, a pick list will appear, and it will be empty. Press the Insert key to open a list of available ports, and pick all ports (and Peter picked a peck of pickled peppers). Save that information, so all outgoing calls will be blocked.

No Dialing Out Allowed

Yes, NetWare Connect allows network clients to use modems connected to the server to dial out. You should disarm this feature, confiscate modems on desktops, and inform your users that no modem connections are allowed from their desks.

Is this harsh? Not really. After all, what do users need desktop modems for today? CompuServe and AOL (America Online) can be reached across the Internet, and you have provided Internet access to all authorized users. E-mail services should forward all company mail to the company e-mail server. Fax modems aren't necessary, because you can use e-mail for many transactions that previously required fax. If your company still needs fax access, and many do, there are dozens (or scores, or maybe hundreds) of third-party fax gateways.

There, all your user objections about losing their modems are answered. Of course, you may feel the urge to explain why modems are no longer allowed at the desktop. When challenged (or as justification), trot out this list:

- Desktop equipment cost. Modems are cheap today (relatively) but even $100 dollars extra per desktop adds up quickly. Some computers, especially laptops, come with modems installed. Laptops should keep their modems, for connections while traveling, but desktop systems should be ordered without the modems.

- Wiring cost. Every extra telephone connection to a desktop costs money. Many wiring companies charge a flat rate per cable connection, and that cost starts at about $100 and goes up quickly. Buildings with poor layouts or historical designations may require special handling and/or equipment, running the cost to hundreds and hundreds of dollars per connection. Ouch.

- Phone equipment cost. Large companies use special-purpose computers disguised as telephone systems. Like your computer, the telephone system can add extra ports for extra dollars. More telephone connections for modems mean more extra dollars. Digital phone switches require special analog ports to support modems, which cost even more extra dollars.

- Lack of security and control. We spent many pages so far, with more to come, examining security and control functions within BorderManager. Guess what? Desktop modems bypass all those security and control points in NDS, your IPX/IP Gateway, and your Proxy Server. Firewall software can't stop outsiders coming in through a modem port to a desktop system. If security really is important to your boss, then desktop modems threaten that security. Play the security card whenever possible; it makes you look like a concerned employee rather than a conniving manager working to protect your department budget.

Do you see anything good coming from users playing with desktop modems? I didn't think so. What you see is lots of extra expense and a total lack of management, control, and security. In other words, avoid desktop modems at all costs. Heck, avoid them for all the *extra* costs incurred, if nothing else.

Finishing Up Server Configuration

Back on the Remote Access Options menu, you are offered a chance to Generate Configuration Report to the screen or to a disk file. This is a handy option to use, especially if you're forced to make security or service exceptions for individual users.

You will come back to some of these port configuration screens now and then, especially as you are setting up these services. Don't feel like a failure if remote access doesn't work the first time or three. In fact, look at it just the opposite. If you get remote things working within two days of starting, you're eligible for an award for Remote Management Efficiency. The award plaque comes COD, but it's worth it.

Remote Access Client Configuration

None of the server hassle we've been through will help much if you can't get a client ready to connect. Here's where we do the messy client stuff. After all, Novell can control what your server configuration encompasses, but only Microsoft holds the magic keys to the Windows client configuration treasure chest.

Client software is copied to the server when the NetWare Connect services are installed. Check under the SYS:\SYSTEM directory for such subdirectories as CONNECT and REMOTE for clues as to where to start.

The easiest place may be your own portable PC. All the major laptops bought since early 1997 have Windows 95 installed, whether you want it or not. I'm still not sure if the extra features are worth the extra hassle over Windows 3.1, but then I've actually seen GUIs that work (Solaris, UnixWare, AIX, and so on).

So, let's look at how we can make Windows 95 into a remote-node NetWare package. It's possible, believe it or not, but can be painful depending on your Windows 95 and modem situation.

I'm taking your word that you have Windows 95 Dial-Up Networking loaded and going on your remote system. You wouldn't lie to me, would you? If you don't have it going, check your Windows help file to get your modem and Dial-Up Networking started. If you're not sure if Dial-Up Networking is already running, check the My Computer icon on your desktop. Don't start looking all over Control Panel and cursing Microsoft (as I did), because it's not there.

Remote Node Setup

To begin, double-click on the Make New Connection icon in the Dial-Up Networking folder. This opens the dialog box to describe a new icon and service, so give the new icon an appropriate name and get started. As you can see in Figure 11.7, I named mine LAN test.

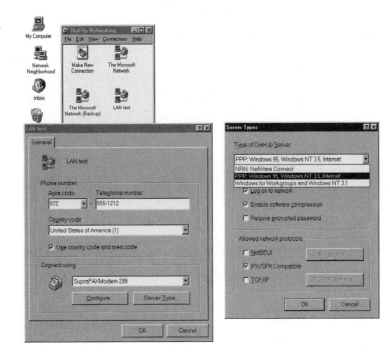

You can see all the setup information I put in the General tab, the one
to the lower left in Figure 11.7. The telephone number, with area code,
is necessary, and the SupraFAXModem 28.8 is the only modem I have
attached to this Windows 95 station. I used the directory information
number of 555-1212 not because I have an unlisted number, but just on
the off chance you work for a telemarketing firm. Enough of my dinners
are interrupted already, thank you.

The second dialog box in Figure 11.7, labeled Server Types, appears
when you click on the command button labeled Server Type in the General
tab. (I tell you, those Microsoft engineers are getting smarter every day.)

Here, there are several choices you must make. Since Windows 95
remote networking hopes you are dialing in to a Windows NT network, the
default details all lean toward Microsoft. We must "un-lean" those details.

Disable Require Encrypted Password at the top of the Server Types
dialog box, as well as NetBEUI in the Allowed Network Protocols portion at the bottom. Since I'm using only IPX, I disabled TCP/IP as well. If

you are using TCP/IP, then disable Log in to the Network, because you won't be logging in to the NetWare operating system as much as connecting to the TCP/IP network at large. I found the best success using the PPP, Windows 95, Windows NT 3.51, Internet connection choice from the Type of Dial-Up Service pick list.

Using TCP/IP requires setting the TCP/IP details, of course. You should know all about unique IP addresses and subnet masks by now, so I won't go into details. Besides, I suggested you use this only for IPX and rely on other methods to connect over TCP/IP. If you're going to ignore my advice like that, don't expect me to provide all the gory details.

Making the Connection

After you save the Dial-Up Networking setup information, connecting to the network isn't all that difficult. Ready? Double-click on the new icon you created, and stand back.

The modem will click and buzz, lights will flash, and you will get a login prompt. Log in as you normally do, and all the typical stuff will happen (slowly, but it will happen).

Figure 11.8 shows the dialog box that opens during the dialing process and connection. Yes, 14.4Kbps is slower than you will likely use for connections, and it is slow. It isn't as deadly slow as I expected, however. Novell has added some packet compression and other tricks to speed things along. Nonetheless, your newest, fastest modem won't make you forget Ethernet.

If you click on the No Details command button, the bottom part of the screen disappears. All you're left with is the icon, connection speed, duration, and command buttons. Although there are not many details on the screen for you, that's okay—other places show more information.

One of the NIASCFG screens we didn't talk about before shows all sorts of connection details. From the opening NIASCFG menu, choose View Status for NIAS. You are given two choices in the Select Component to View Status menu that appears: Remote Access, and Protocols and Routing. If you choose the second option, you can see all sorts of dull statistics about how many IPX packets have been sent and received, how

FIGURE 11.8

Connected at last

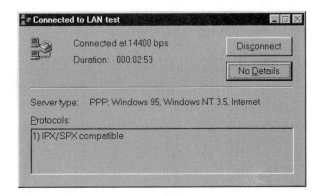

many circuits you have active, and the status of cryptic networks you didn't know you had. Ignore those for now, and try the first option, Remote Access.

The Status Options menu has four options, two of which you want to see. The last two, Display Alerts and Display Audit Trail, are not as important for us now. The second, Display Service Status, offers quite a few details about your PPPRNS service, but only when you drill down to the second screen showing all the statistics. Bytes sent and received are near the top of the list, along with a variety of error packet types you hope stay at zero.

Your first option, Display Port Status, opens to a two-part screen listing the active ports first. Figure 11.9 shows my meager little server chugging along with only a single port listed, but this screen does give useful information.

The bottom portion of the screen shows the port details and, more important, who is connected. Figure 11.9 shows that I am connected (what a surprise), my username (which should be different from my local name, just so I can bypass the search drives on the server and refer to my remote client machine), and my allowed connection time.

So there you have the server and client sides of remote-node connections. If you ask me (and you did, kind of, when you bought this book), I am still nervous about hanging modems directly onto the server. Even multi-port serial cards, although they are an improvement, give me pause.

FIGURE 11.9

Remote information
for each port

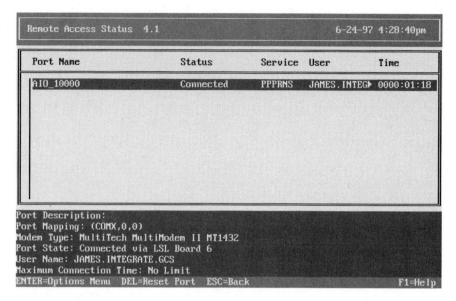

The server doesn't offer enough real-time management and automatic hung-modem clearing support. Modems hang constantly, and third-party products dedicated to remote-access technology do a better job than Novell at controlling those modems.

If you run things as I have here, however, the situation can be bearable. It's better to call from home over a slow modem than go to the office at 3:14 a.m. to see why the tape backup system blew up. Workers from home also like the easy method of transferring files—they can use a regular mapped drive. This is simple and effective, and there's no learning curve.

Management and Security Details

Since we just finished watching packets go by (or at least tracking who was sending packets where), let's see what happens when you start ConnectView, the GUI management program for NetWare Connect. Yes, this is another management program that will no doubt get folded into NWAdmin for the next release.

Using ConnectView

Check your SYS:\PUBLIC\CVIEW directory for Disk1 and Disk2 subdirectories, which are installed during the remote services installation. Running the SETUP program in the Disk1 directory loads the software and adds, unfortunately, a Btrieve connection to the workstation in question. The BREQUEST.EXE file will be loaded automatically, so be prepared. You may also find the CVIEW directory on the CD-ROM, if you prefer to look there. Setup will make a new folder and pack in some new programs for you.

Take a gander at Figure 11.10, and you'll see why I believe this will become a toolbar within NWAdmin before too long. Notice the multiple, overlapping windows on the screen, and the active icons across the toolbar.

Until the two administration programs do merge, ConnectView is its own program and shows the heritage of years of general NetWare support, rather than being written specifically for NDS. But even if you've never seen ConnectView before, you can get around inside it with no problem if you've spent even a few minutes using NWAdmin. Notice the background window in the upper left of the display area. This hierarchical display looks amazingly like NWAdmin, doesn't it?

In Figure 11.10, the one port connected on my server is in use, although the background status window has yet to catch up by polling the server. The foreground window, Port Connections, shows some interesting stuff. Of course, a pie chart with a single item isn't particularly impressive, but at least it does show there is a working connection.

The bottom-left side of that display window shows that the AIO_10000 port, the only active port, is in use for a dial-in connection. The lower-right side shows all the modem details I set up on the server console. The fact that the information is read-only should clue you in to the fact that you're still stuck with the server console utilities for a bit longer.

FIGURE 11.10

Connection control and monitoring

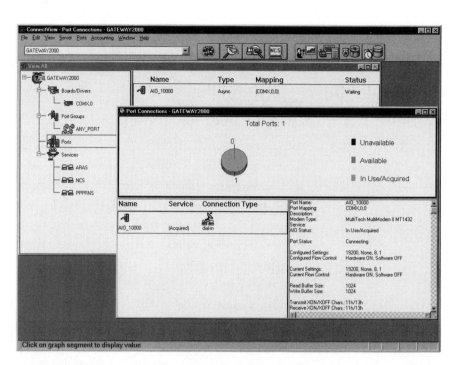

There are quite a few more things you can do with ConnectView, but I'm not really in favor of charging accounting for remote services running this program alongside ManageWise. Don't get mad if you really want to run trend analysis on your remote connection data, but that's wandering just a bit too far afield for my tastes and this book's topic. It is nice to know that controls exist in a GUI presentation, rather than suffer along with all the C-Worthy interface utilities forever.

Using NWAdmin

To show how close ConnectView and NWAdmin are getting, take a look at Figure 11.11. Yes, these new NWAdmin command buttons for remote access control showed up after the remote services installation. Isn't it nice that Novell provides little surprises throughout your workday?

FIGURE 11.11

First remote
process screen

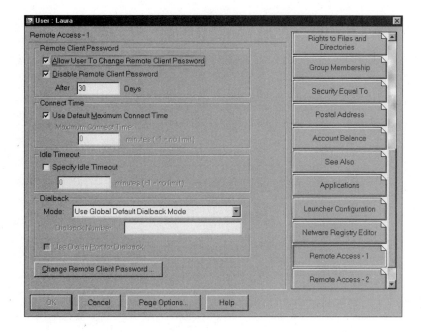

Now do you see why I skipped some of these very settings in the earlier discussion about the server console utilities? You have a chance to exercise your mouse with the two Remote Access windows in NWAdmin, rather than typing.

Notice the title in the upper-left corner of the dialog box in Figure 11.11 says it belongs to user Laura. Yes, working on one user at a time leads to eventual network breakdown and antisocial behavior. Yes, you can set these same controls on any container, allowing control over all users in one fell swoop. Yes, Laura is my daughter, and I need to get her name in the book.

Figure 11.12 shows what may be the more interesting of the two Remote Access windows. Here we have Macintosh support through ARAS (Apple-Talk Remote Access Services) and parameters for IP configuration. There is more here than you want to get hooked into, believe me. Novell provides no client software for remote Macintosh systems, relying on Apple's ARAS for all client support.

FIGURE 11.12

Second remote
process screen

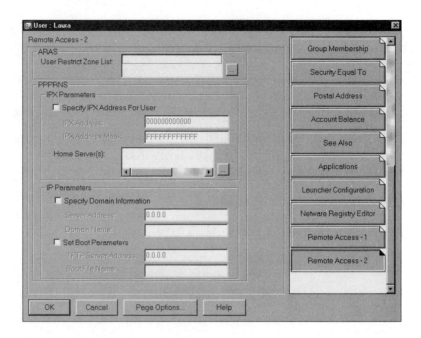

The bottom section of the dialog box, labeled IP Parameters, has two sections. In case you can't read the grayed-out field names, here's what the checkboxes specify:

- **Specify Domain Information:** The domain name, user, and IP address access for remote IP clients.

- **Set Boot Parameters:** Works especially well for those few stations requiring some version of BootP or DHCP. The TFTP (Trivial File Transfer Program) address should list the BootP or DHCP server address. If you have any choice, avoid dynamically assigning IP addresses when connecting to your new server.

Are these valuable screens? I assure you they're easier to use than another grab bag of Novell server utilities. Will you use them regularly, even if you use the NetWare Connect services? Probably not, but at least you now know where they are if a problem appears.

Third-Party Options

Novell developers were a bit late coming to the dial-in support product area, leaving a vacuum in their product catalog. You know what happens to a vacuum, don't you? No, not that it gets put in the hall closet; it gets filled by others. That is not only a law of nature, but the primary method for small companies to break into product areas controlled by large companies.

Many products made for remote TCP/IP connections have added IPX and SPX protocol support. Check the buyer's guides for "communications servers," and you'll find more than you ever believed possible.

Do you want some company names? 3Com, Xylogics, Systech, Cubix, Shiva, Microdyne, Ascend, Bay Networks, Multi-Tech, Digi International (Digiboard), NDC Communications, Attachmate, Brooktrout, and RAD Data Communications are a good place to start. Platforms supporting products from these companies include NetWare, Window NT, Unix, and stand-alone boxes.

Don't forget software for management and control, because these third-party vendors certainly didn't. Almost every product option has better control and management than NetWare Connect. Sorry, but that's the truth.

Try an end run around the remote-access problem by providing the necessary information through other means. Many companies are beginning to use Web servers to provide mobile professionals with access to critical information. The Web server may be on the public Internet like your "regular" Web server, or it can be hidden by not advertising the name. If your remote users have Internet access, even dial-in access to AOL or CompuServe, they will be able to reach your Web server.

Wrap

Remote access can be a royal pain. Try to work your way out of supporting large numbers of remote users dialing directly into NetWare servers. If you must support dial-up users, get some hardware and software so you can keep NetWare focused on file serving. If remote support is important, it's worth dedicating a server to properly support your non-resident clients. Adding intelligent serial ports with their own processing power to support NetWare Connect provides a much more reliable solution than just plugging a couple of modems into the server's serial ports.

Can you support a few traveling clients without a problem? No, because modems always bring problems, but the problems will be relatively easy to work out. Can you overload your remote support server, yet believe it will run forever? Boy, are you going to be surprised soon.

Avoid remote-control functions that call in through the firewall to control LAN-attached workstations. Look into third-party options to help support NetWare's rather weak remote-node support.

Make arrangements with ISPs who cover employee's regular travel destinations, so access to the Internet won't be a problem. Use e-mail, the FTP server, or the Web server to make life a bit easier for those not in the office physically. Remember, travelers need access to information, not file servers. Making information available on FTP or Web servers may solve their problems and avoid banks of modems altogether.

CHAPTER

12

The Web Server

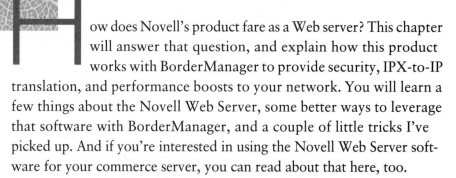

ow does Novell's product fare as a Web server? This chapter will answer that question, and explain how this product works with BorderManager to provide security, IPX-to-IP translation, and performance boosts to your network. You will learn a few things about the Novell Web Server, some better ways to leverage that software with BorderManager, and a couple of little tricks I've picked up. And if you're interested in using the Novell Web Server software for your commerce server, you can read about that here, too.

Your boss will learn quite a bit more about the capabilities of NetWare to provide a solid Web server, especially when you repackage some of this information for reports and new budget requests. After all, your boss hasn't been keeping up with the technical details—that's your job. It's up to you to provide those details, so your network can expand in the direction you're most able to support. In other words, use NetWare for as many pieces as possible, since you're so familiar with the various new Novell products in the Internet and intranet market space.

This chapter will not be about Web server design, programming with HTML, or Web image manipulation. I am not a programmer, and will not publicly claim I have any talent for Web server design and implementation. I can, however, show you some things about networking these various pieces together into a manageable, secure, and high-performance network.

If you want information about the Web content part of the equation, such as HTML programming and Web page design, there are plenty of good books devoted to that subject. You should find these books at the same fine bookstore you purchased this book. If you're still reading this standing in the middle of the bookstore shelves, the Web books are behind you and to the right.

What Is a Web Server?

Novell describes a Web server like this:

"A Web server is an application running on a computer that serves or publishes files electronically. Files or pages are stored on a Web server. Client applications (called browsers) connect to the Web server over networks or communication links and make requests to view these files or pages."

I've already mentioned, in earlier chapters, the connection between the duties of a Web server and those of a traditional file server. Actually, a NetWare file server has more to handle than a Web server. Add printing and security tasks to the job functions of a Web server, and that Web server is still doing less than a NetWare file server. The file server performs all these functions, plus stays synchronized with the network and NDS, as well as compresses files at night and decompresses those files when someone wants them. Whew.

Initially, Web servers were Unix machines running strange software. Today, almost every computer in your company, from a 386 PC running Windows 3.1 to the mainframe, can be a Web server. You have more options than ever. Unfortunately, having more options makes the decision harder rather than easier. Let's see if we can get over one of the first hurdles you're likely to encounter.

Novell's Web Server or Windows NT?

Well, really now, which do you think I'm going to recommend? I admitted I'm not a programmer; I'm a network consultant. I've also made jokes at Microsoft's expense, showing a startling disregard for the beauty of Microsoft's marketing by focusing on the performance of Microsoft products.

My suggestion for your Web servers (drum roll, please): the Novell Web Server.

I hope you're not startled by this selection. I also realize that this may not be a popular suggestion at your company, because Microsoft has done such an excellent job of promoting Windows NT as the first choice in Web servers.

Novell Web Server Features

Let me point out a few of the fun features of the Novell Web Server that put it ahead of the competition:

- Runs on NetWare servers. You know them, you have them, and you can manage them. Why add another server operating system (Windows NT) that's not as reliable, scalable, manageable, or efficient as NetWare?

- Integrates with NDS. You have, with NDS, the best directory and security system available for LANs. Although NT workstations and servers are being folded into NDS, IIS (Internet Information Server, Microsoft's Web server software) isn't. Why give up security when you're inviting more users into your network resources?

- Indexes with QuickFinder. Novell uses the indexing technology originally perfected in WordPerfect and puts it on the Web server. More than 20 file formats are supported, including all the typical formats used by office productivity programs such as word processors, spreadsheets, and presentation programs. Web managers can add customizable search forms, and developers can call QuickFinder from their own applications using NetBasic and the QuickFinder API (Application Programming Interface).

- Supports virtual server directories. Web pages can reside anywhere on your NetWare network, not just on the Web server. Do you have hundreds of old contracts you want to search on your intranet Web server? Use QuickFinder and point to the NetWare server still holding those contract files, and success is yours. There's no limit to the number of virtual directories, and all are controlled via NDS.

- Allows multihoming. One hardware server can support a number of (apparently) different Web servers. Let's say I wanted to publish a separate Web site for each of my books. On one physical server, I could support both BorderManager.gaskin.com and Complete-guide.gaskin.com to publicize this book and my *Complete Guide to NetWare 4.11/IntranetWare*. Your company could use the same technique for your intranet, running finance.you.com and marketing.you.com on the same physical server as sales.you.com and hr.you.com. "Reduce hardware costs while increasing secure access" sounds like a good bullet point for your budget proposal.

- Supports Oracle integration. If your company uses Oracle 7 or 8, here's good news: the Novell Web Server supports easy links from the server to any machine running the Oracle software. Dynamic Web database pages are just a few lines of code away.

- Supports SSL (Secure Sockets Layer), versions 2.0 and 3.0. Combined with NDS, SSL public key/private key encryption technology secures and encrypts the entire communication stream between the browser and server.

- Provides quick connections. Everyone says they're fast, of course, but Novell has demonstrated 700 cps (connections per second) on a 128-user network. That's a lot of hits, folks.

The Novell Web Server and Your NetWare Network

Since Novell includes the Web server software as part of IntranetWare, feel free to fire up one or two for your intranet. The Web server doesn't cost extra, and it is efficient enough that you don't need to dedicate a system to provide Web services. Start one up on a lightly loaded server with some extra disk space and plenty of RAM. Here's a Novell Web Server checklist showing how it fits within your network:

✓ Run the IPX/IP Gateway on the same system running the Web server software.

✓ A Netscape license for each NetWare users is included with the IntranetWare package.

✓ You have a working Web server for no extra money, and little extra work.

✓ The Web server sits on the very platform holding all your important information, making it simple and secure to grant access via NDS to all appropriate users.

Can you do most of the above with Windows NT IIS? Sure, but it will cost you extra money for the IPX/IP Gateway. Then there's the fact that NDS can no longer control access. Also, Internet Explorer is included only in Windows 95 and NT, so you'll need to download and install Internet Explorer for every workstation on your network. Oops, you can't install Internet Explorer on Macintosh or Unix systems, can you? Well, it looks like you'll end up with a mixed bag of Netscape and Internet Explorer client software if you have a multiprotocol network.

Breaking the Microsoft Spell

Do those who support Windows NT have a good case to make? Sure they do, and feel free to check out Microsoft's Web site to read the company's marketing information. Can you keep Windows NT out of your network completely? Probably not, because your VPs or CIO will go to a fancy Microsoft seminar, get lunch, get goodies, and shake hands with Microsoft executives. When they come back, they will demand that you convert the entire company to Microsoft products.

The only way to break the Microsoft spell holding the executive entranced is to ask for a tenfold increase in your budget to accommodate the new software, hardware, and management costs such a change will entail. When actual money gets mentioned, the trance is broken, but not until at least one Windows NT server has wormed its way onto your network.

Perhaps you should employ the philosophy basketball teams use when they play the Chicago Bulls and Michael Jordan: Acknowledge you can't stop him, but try to keep him from killing you. Windows NT and Microsoft's IIS will get into your network, if they haven't already, and you can't stop this. Just don't surrender NetWare to NT until you understand all the consequences.

Web Server Installation and Configuration

Before we begin the actual Novell Web Server setup, let's be clear on what we're setting up. Remember, the word *server* in most of our examples doesn't mean the physical computer, but the software running on a computer. Sometimes, the server software isn't even running on a box recognizable as a computer, but it really is. Examples include the stand-alone IPX/IP gateways, routers, and ATM machines at the bank.

It stands to reason, following this line of thought, that the Web server software will run on a NetWare server. In fact, the Web server will be one of many server processes actually running on the NetWare server at that time. After all, the file and print services count as servers, as do the directory service software and the remote-console software that I recommend regularly. All those utilities or programs are actually servers of one type or another. You may not think of them that way, but they fall within the definition of a server software process in every computer dictionary I've seen.

The Web server software is easier to install than most of the other software we've discussed in this book. Here are the prerequisites:

■ NetWare 4.11 or IntranetWare operating system

■ 24MB of RAM and at least 8MB of disk space

■ Windows 3.1, 95, or NT workstation for the Web Manager utility

■ TCP/IP installed and configured on the soon-to-be Web server

You and I already have all these things, because we've been working through some of these exact issues. Aren't you glad you paid attention earlier?

Installing the Web Server Software

Now that all your prerequisites are under control, you can install the Web server software itself. The installation procedure is the same as with any other NetWare product, so go to the console (or start RCONSOLE on your workstation) and type **LOAD INSTALL.**

Up pops the familiar installation utility you've seen several times before. Choose Product Options ➤ View/Configure/Remove Installed Products, and take a look at what's loaded on this server already.

Why not just pick Choose an Item or Product Listed Above and start the installation procedures? That's what I would normally suggest, but when I did the initial Web server testing and configuration, I found it was already installed, just not activated. Of course, I load and unload software quite frequently on this system, and no doubt I loaded it earlier and just forgot about it. On the off chance you're at least as distracted and forgetful as I am, I suggest you view the Currently Installed Products screen before starting your Web server software installation. If Novell Web Server is not listed as one of the installed products, press the Insert key and start installing it by referencing the proper source for the new product files.

You've been through this a few times before, so I won't bore you with common installation details. Unless you have a good reason to change where the files are stored, accept the default file placement values of SYS:\ INW_WEB for the program files. You will specify a different directory for the actual files running your Web server when asked to choose a server root directory. The default value, SYS:\WEB, goes against my preference for placing growing and expanding directories on a non-SYS: volume. Although the \WEB directory can grow quite large, you can leave the \WEB directory on the SYS: volume and reference other volumes for the data files. After all, only the data files will grow as you add documents and images, and you allow other departments to control their own virtual directories.

I encourage you to pick a good password for use in Web server administration. Web server hacking is becoming a common way to embarrass companies, and using strict security inside your company will limit the opportunities for disgruntled (or mischievous) employees to "help" you with the look of your Web pages.

The WEBSTART command is inserted into your AUTOEXEC.NCF file during the initial program file load procedure. If you find the Web server software already installed, as I did, go to the server console, type **WEBSTART,** and see what happens. You may be surprised, as I was, to discover a fully functional Web server installation just waiting to be activated.

Once the Web server software is started, you can access the default page. Figure 12.1 shows the opening page, straight from Novell, running on my Gateway2000 IntranetWare server.

As the figure caption says, this screen was viewed within about five minutes from starting the LOAD procedure. Are there any questions about whether this is quick and easy?

Notice I referenced the IP address for my server, rather than a typical Web server name. It takes time for name servers around a company, and

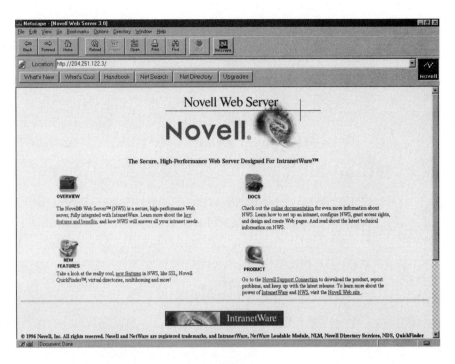

around the Internet, to learn of new Web server installations and add the DNS name to the tables. If you're building an intranet, you don't need fully qualified and descriptive server names to make life easier for those viewers unfamiliar with your Web page. Sharing a bookmark file listing all the intranet servers by their IP addresses allows you to get started quickly and spread the news easily.

As with the other products you install, you can remove the Novell Web Server software through the INSTALL program (Product Options ➤ View/Configure/Remove Installed Products). The utility won't delete all the file and directories, so rename the WEB directory for a few days to make sure that some important files haven't been placed there by accident. After a week or so, you can delete the files with a clear conscience. Reinstalling the Web server doesn't take long, if your managers change their minds yet again.

Updating NWAdmin for Windows 95

Getting started isn't too difficult, but the setup isn't completely automatic. Before you can use NWAdmin to configure some of the Web server access and control details, you must add the Web server information into the Windows 95 Registry.

Yes, there's a way to add this information to the version of NWAdmin running on Windows 3.1, but I'm not going to mention that option. If you haven't upgraded your management system to Windows 95, having to fight through the documentation is your penalty for ignoring my advice to use a Windows 95 workstation for management functions.

Here's what you must do on your Windows 95 management station:

1. Run the REGEDIT.EXE file from the \WINDOWS subdirectory.

2. Select Registry ➤ Import Registry File.

3. Choose WEBREGED.REG from \PUBLIC\WIN95 on the SYS: volume.

4. Click on OK to save and exit.

Run NWAdmin and verify that users have two new command buttons: Home Page and Photo, and Web Publishing. You can see these in Figure 12.2, as the bottom two command buttons on the right. Groups will have both new buttons, but containers will have only Home Page and Photo, so containers (especially those grouped in departments) can have their own home page. You must agree to extend the schema the next time you run NWAdmin.

The Web Publishing command button hides two radio buttons used to enable or disable Web publishing. If you want to encourage your users to put pictures of their children and pets on the company intranet rather than doing their regular jobs, feel free to enable publishing. Make sure each department manager gives approval, however, since that manager will be responsible for maintaining productivity while the staff tries to unravel the mysteries of HTML.

FIGURE 12.2

Personalizing a user's Web environment

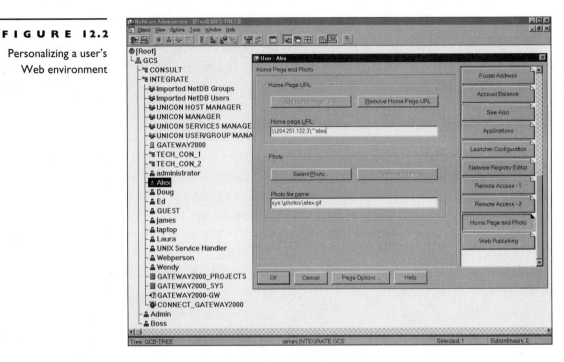

Multihoming with Virtual Servers and Virtual Hosts

One physical server can appear to the world to be many Web servers. This is often referred to as *multihoming*. There are two ways to do this: by using virtual servers and by using virtual hosts.

Virtual Servers

Virtual servers re-create the entire Web server directory structure, one for each virtual server, on the physical IntranetWare server hosting the Web servers. They must be differentiated by one of two methods:

- Separate IP address. If your server has two network interfaces, each IP address can have a separate virtual server. 204.251.122.10 can be gaskin.com, and 204.251.122.11 can be niksag.com. This method requires two interface cards in the server.

- Separate port number. A server with a single network interface can use separate port numbers for separate servers. For example, 204.251.122.10 can be gaskin.com, and 204.251.122.10:81 can be niksag.com. The Web server software will sort out which virtual server gets which packets by the port number (gaskin.com will use the default port number of 80).

You can stop and start virtual servers through the Web Manager utility program (discussed shortly) without stopping the main Web server software on the NetWare server. The world will see two separate servers, no matter which method you use to configure the virtual servers.

Virtual Hosts

Virtual hosts are partial implementations of the Web server directory structure. A virtual host has its own document and log directories, but it uses the configuration directory of the main server. You have slightly less flexibility with a virtual host than you do with a virtual server, but you're not limited in the content the virtual host can support.

You can specify virtual hosts via separate network interface addresses to the physical server hosting the Web server software, just as you can specify separate addresses for virtual servers. You can also separate virtual hosts by use of the DNS name.

Wait, you ask, doesn't an IP address get connected to the DNS name, one to one? Nope. I can list 204.251.122.10 as gaskin.com, and list 204.251.122.10 as the IP address for research.gaskin.com as well. The DNS routing will send packets for both virtual hosts to the same physical server, where the Web server software will read the destination address on each packet and deliver the packet accordingly.

If you're wondering if this is the way commercial sites, such as your ISP, support dozens of client Web servers on one Unix machine, the answer is yes. Each virtual host can be started and stopped via control software without affecting the other virtual hosts running on the same physical machine. Now you can do essentially the same thing, providing each department its "own" Web server to manage and control as those departments wish. This keeps you out of the Web server tinkering role, since the departments can access their own directory trees on the Net-Ware server acting as the physical host to their department Web servers. The department accesses its document tree, with access controlled by NDS so no other departments can get into those files, and you don't need to make the changes for them.

Managing Web Servers with Web Manager

Happily enough, there are only two operations where you must use the server console: to restart the Web server and to remove the Web server software. In other words, you won't need to listen to me whining about the C-Worthy interface, at least for the rest of this chapter. Type **WEBSTART** at the console to start the software; type **WEBSTOP** to stop the Web server from running.

For other Web server management, you can use the Web Manager program. This program lives in the SYS:\PUBLIC directory of the IntranetWare server running the Web server software. The WEBMGR.EXE program works just as well on my Windows NT client as on my Windows 95 system. Of course, the Windows NT client is running the NetWare Client32 software, as all your NT clients should as well.

Following the current rage of tabbed utility programs, Web Manager handles much of the Web server setup through one of six pages. The tabbed dialog box seems oddly ill at ease within the Web Manager, and refuses to fit neatly within the confines of the background program. Take a look at Figure 12.3 to see what I mean. I moved the foreground dialog box a bit so you can see all the menu and icons on the background screen.

You can easily see the tabbed pages, and the Server tab is the one that appears when you open this dialog box. Of course, if you don't think to check the File menu for the selection Select Server or use the keyboard shortcut of Ctrl+O, you'll never see this dialog box. (Clicking on the little icon on the far left of the Web Manager toolbar also pops open a dialog box to choose the Web server to configure.) When the Web server software is running, you will find it listed at the bottom of the File menu.

FIGURE 12.3

Web control central

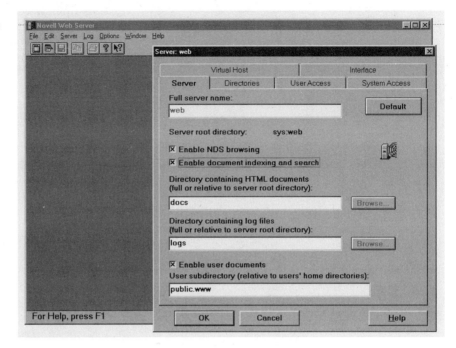

Is there anything here you must change to get your Web server going? Not really. The installation of the Web server takes care of all the pertinent details, at least if you keep all the default settings.

NDS Browsing

Do you see one interesting default, toward the top of the Server tab? I'm referring to the Enable NDS Browsing checkbox. Are you thinking that's some great new development that will revolutionize network management?

Well, yes and no. Frankly, it doesn't do much now, as you can see in Figure 12.4. However, the idea that Novell is moving ever-forward for better remote NetWare management is certainly good news. NDS management through a browser interface would make a neat addition to release as a counter to some Microsoft product, wouldn't it? Keep your eyes peeled.

FIGURE 12.4

Browsing for
directory services

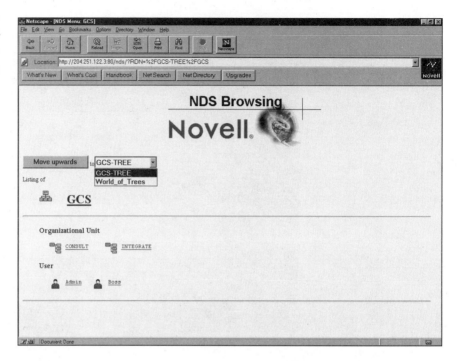

Doesn't this screen look great? Too bad you really can't do anything here. I suppose, to paraphrase the old line from Saturday Night Live, it's better to look good than to work good. Maybe in the next version of the Web server the NDS browsing will be read and write, rather than read-only.

In this browsing screen, you should recognize the top level of the GCS (Gaskin Computer Services) tree from earlier screen shots. I pulled down the pick list, showing which directory level lies above this level, and you can see only the World_of_Trees is listed as available. I suppose "World of Trees" is clearer than "Forest of Trees," which would be more semantically correct. Oh well, we certainly can't begrudge the Novell engineers a bit of whimsy now and then, can we?

User Directories for Storage

The last field in the Web Manager's Server tab (Figure 12.3) lists something interesting. Beside the checkbox is the label Enable User Documents. Immediately below that is a field named User Subdirectory (relative to user's home directories).

Do you have a clue what that is all about? This sets the default location of user directories that may be displayed by this Web server.

Remember when I spoke of allowing users to have their own home pages? Here we are, but I used this connection for something a little more work-oriented. Many users have home directories that are not used for anything of value. This makes these home directories great places to store large groups of files to share with all the Web server clients. If your users fill their home directories with lots of files, instead of using a real user's home directory, you can create a made-up user (or two), and make sure to give that imaginary user a home directory.

Figure 12.5 shows an example of this storage technique in action. Yes, Webperson is a made-up name and user. I was careful to make the name gender-neutral, in case this book falls into the hands of the Politically Correct.

FIGURE 12.5

Two views of a
home directory

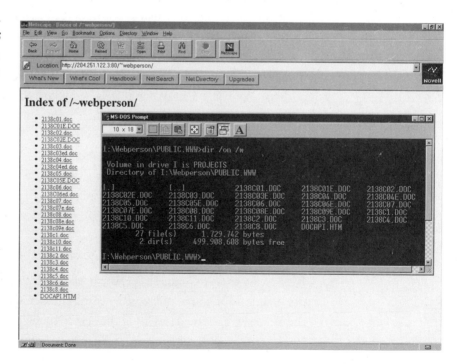

See the Web server page, which lists 27 files? Now look at the DOS screen, with the same directory displayed. How's that for verification of the browser screens versus the company security?

Notice the URL at the top of Figure 12.5. Notice what it includes: the IP address (along with the port number, which the software added itself and was not typed in the address to start), a tilde (that little "~" thing), and the name of the user. In this case, of course, I put in Webperson. I could have listed any user with a home directory.

When directed with this address formula, the Novell Web Server software finds the directory, builds an index if needed (it was), and displays the files therein. I did not list "index.htm" as some pages require. I did not convert those files from a Microsoft Word format to something else, so they show and load as Word documents. Graphic files are picked up automatically by the browser, if they have been configured properly in the browser's preferences.

The browser seems to make a difference. I could see this easily from several versions of Netscape, Quarterdeck's QMosaic, and the old WinWeb program. For some reason, almost like it was on purpose, Microsoft's Internet Explorer 3.0 won't work on these personal Web server files, but perhaps that's just a stray bug that is being corrected at this very moment.

Do you want your users putting their personal or possibly inappropriate files on the Web server? If the answer is "no," then create a pretend employee or two, as I've done here, and load the Web server by loading the files you want available into the home directories of these fake employees. Bingo, you've got an easy way to display tons of existing files to clients all over the company through a convenient browser front end.

Publishing with the Web Server Document Tree

Is there another, perhaps easier, way to publish an entire stack of electronic documents? Of course there is, by using the default "document tree" that the Web server provides. Under the server name chosen during installation (the default is *web*, remember), you can load files into the default root of the document tree, located in the SERVER-ROOT\DOCS directory.

On the server hosting the Web server software, this directory will be the \WEB\DOCS directory. Reach this by using the IP address of the server and the filename of the file you want to view.

No Web client can see any files in server directories above the \WEB\ DOCS directory, or any of the parallel directories from the server root. No amount of HTTP typing cleverness will allow a user to get to the \PUBLIC or \SYSTEM directories, because those directories are in different directory trees from the Web server.

Is this the way a smart Web master will tell you to find and organize your files? No, but I'm not a smart Web master. I am, however, clever at getting access on some limited level to a set of documents stored on a Web server through a client browser interface. My methods will make the Web masters among you shudder, but I have paved the way for you to look brilliant by comparison.

Configuring Web Server Access Security

As a NetWare administrator, you're used to limiting access to directory areas on the file server using NDS controls. Does NDS control access to files on the Web server?

Unfortunately, not yet. Novell is pushing NDS for use on the Internet and in TCP/IP networks, and it is making progress. Even if Novell succeeds in overlaying the Internet with NDS, it will take a few years to implement that system. In other words, don't hold your breath.

However, the Novell Web Server software does offer ways to control access to specific directory trees through the Web Manager utility. It's not the same as using NDS and NWAdmin, but it's considerably easier than blocking access through traditional firewall and proxy server means.

Restricting Global Access

Sometimes, you want to block access to the world while allowing only a few connections to your Web server. This can be done for Internet Web servers with subscription access, to limit access to the server to only those who are authorized. This is a good way to run an extranet Web server as well, since you can restrict the world except for the few other companies you have made partnership arrangements with for system access.

Open Web Manager, then pick the Web server to which you want to control access. If the server is running, you can click on the icon on the top left. If you look closely, I think the icon is a poor representation of the Server tab we looked at earlier. No matter what artistic interpretation you care to make, this icon opens the pick list dialog box for the configured servers. If you drop down the File menu, the active servers are listed and can be chosen there as well.

Click on the System Access tab. This page is somewhat sparse, but works well for our purposes. Check Figure 12.6 for the details.

Unlike the BorderManager Proxy Server settings, the system here assumes that you are listing the *only* addresses allowed to view the directory

FIGURE 12.6

Controlling Web
server access

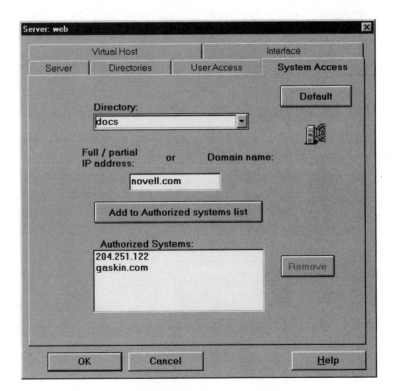

selected in the top field. You may list single IP addresses, IP networks, or domain names in the Authorized Systems list, as follows:

- **IP address:** Only the IP address listed will be allowed to view the directory.

- **IP network:** Any system on that network will be able to view the directory.

- **DNS name:** Only systems that are part of the named domain will be able to view the directory.

Yes, you may set different directories with different access restrictions. Your directory choices are DOCS, DOCS/IMAGES, DOCS/SSI, and MAPS.

Why would you want to limit access to certain directories? Actually, only the \DOCS directory should be available to the world at large. If you're building an intranet, you may be able to be less restrictive, but don't count on it. Keeping your SSI (Server-Side Includes, which are files pulling in other resources), images, and server maps out of the hands of "others" will make it more difficult for those with malicious intentions from spoiling your day. After all, if someone is going to spoil your day by trashing your Web site, you want the evildoer to work hard.

Allowing Exceptions to Restrictions

Let's say you want to keep access to the \DOCS\IMAGES directory blocked, for the very reasons mentioned in the previous section. So you set these blocks, and go home happy. Suddenly, halfway home, your beeper goes off. Laura, one of the two graphics designers in the company, tried to revise one of the images on the server, but she was locked out. Laura is not happy, and you make a U-turn and return to work, grumbling all the way.

Once back at your desk, you need to somehow block out the world from your images, but let Alex and Laura do whatever it is that those graphics people do. This can be accomplished through Web Manager, but through the User Access tab rather than the System Access tab.

Figure 12.7 shows how NDS can take over access control for your Web server directories, because these are directories on a NetWare server. You don't need to worry about IP addresses and domain names now, because you're on familiar ground.

The Directory field holds the same choices as the System Access tab: DOCS, DOCS/IMAGES, DOCS/SSI, and MAPS. The Authentication Method is Directory Services, although the field looks like there's a list of choices. This is optimistic on the part of Novell, since NDS still can't control the Internet. Maybe soon, but not today. The next field shows the NDS context for choosing the users to be allowed into the directory.

You can browse your entire NDS world, but you must type in the name of the context in the Browse Network Users At field. When you type a valid context, the names of groups and users pop up immediately in the pick list window below the context list field.

FIGURE 12.7

Allowing access to Web
server directories

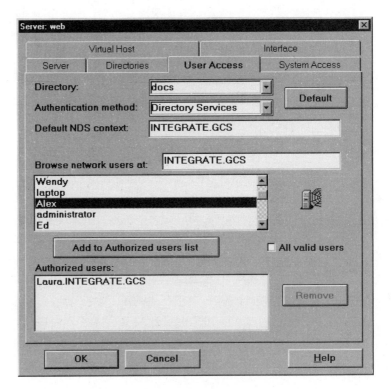

Highlight the user or group you want, or choose multiple names by holding down the Ctrl key as you select each name. Click on the Add to Authorized Users List command button to move the chosen names into the Authorized Users list. After you've put the names in the list, click on OK to save and exit this page. If you decide you want to take someone off the Authorized Users list, return to this tab, highlight the name, and click on the Remove command button.

Now, if you get a beep from Laura on your way home, it won't be because she can't get access to the \DOCS\IMAGES directory. Did you check to see if she needed access to the \DOCS\SSI directory before you left?

Third-Party Web Server Options

In previous chapters, we have discussed the phenomenon of third-party vendors rushing in to fill gaps left by market leaders, and particularly by Novell. The situation is the same in Web server software as in a variety of other niches.

In fact, Novell's short-lived Web Publisher product bundled third-party Web server software, since Novell's own product wasn't ready. Novell developers bought the rights to develop their own server software based on the code from American Internet, the company supplying the Web server software, and went about creating the Novell Web Server product we have been discussing.

One trade magazine editor asked me, during the writing of this book, if the rumors were true that Novell would dump its own Web server and ship a third-party server (Netscape, no doubt) instead. Those rumors have been circulating since before Novell started shipping its own Web server product, and I suppose they won't stop until Novell actually does dump its own server. If Novell never replaces its own server, then the rumors will continue.

Why would anyone want a third-party Web server when Novell includes a perfectly good Web server with IntranetWare? There are several reasons, not the least of which is the requirement to run the Novell Web Server product on NetWare 4.*x* or IntranetWare. Most third-party options support NetWare 3.*x*, meaning there are hundreds of thousands of file servers that the Novell offering won't reach.

Besides, some users already have a Web server running on other platforms. It's easier to keep the same Web server software if possible, especially when you start adding custom touches to the server.

I first thought I could list the few NetWare-based Web servers with a quick roundup of each. That was before I researched how many Web servers there are that run on the NetWare and IntranetWare server platforms. Frankly, there are too many to count, round up, review, and describe during the writing of this book. Instead, let's look at what Netscape and Novell are planning, and then see a tiny sampling of what else is available.

Novonyx: The Novell/Netscape Partnership

Created in early 1997 by Novell and Netscape, Novonyx is jointly owned by both companies but staffed primarily by former Novell employees. This partnership has at least slowed the rumors, for a time, of Netscape buying Novell.

Netscape shares a strong mutual interest with Novell: derailing the Microsoft freight train. Both Netscape and Novell have the majority market share in the Web and local networking areas, respectively, and Microsoft has them both on its hit list. Microsoft rarely targets a market area that it doesn't dominate within two years, and Bill Gates seems frustrated by both the "N" companies.

The most critical function of Novonyx will be to fit Netscape technology onto the NetWare and IntranetWare server platforms. This is why the rumors of Novell dumping its own Web server product became so widespread. After all, Netscape owns the lead in Web server operating systems, and Novell was late to the party with its Web server.

Why does Netscape need to work closely with Novell? Doesn't it make the SuiteSpot Web server software for every Unix platform under the sun, as well as for NT?

Here we have a great example of the old saying, "The enemy of my enemy is my friend." This was never so true as in the computer business today, with various groups partnering to attack Microsoft.

Netscape's Benefits

Look what Netscape gets with Novonyx:

- Faster server platform. NetWare runs faster and jumps higher than Microsoft Windows NT. Netscape's server will run faster on NetWare than on NT.

- Leading directory service. NDS has been running, and getting better, since 1992. We will see presidential hopefuls campaigning before the Active Directory from Microsoft sees a retail store shelf.

- Strong reseller channel. Novell's reseller channel is the best in the LAN business. Would you believe Novell has more resellers in the U.S. than there are 7-11 stores? Wrong. There are *twice* as many Novell resellers as 7-11s. Every company drools over the thought of sending their products to those resellers, and Netscape will soon be doing so.

Novell's Benefits

Now let's look at what Novell gets with Novonyx:

- Best of breed Web servers. No company can match the range of Netscape's Web servers, and the quality is high across the lot of them.

- Leading intranet position. Companies want to use the same server for their intranet as they do for the Internet, and Netscape is it. Novell won't need to put up with questions about Web server suitability running Netscape servers.

- NDS folded into SuiteSpot. Novell wants NDS to be the directory service of the Internet. Getting NDS integrated into the leading Internet Web server will help reach that goal.

- Leapfrog Web server features. Novell's current Web server is pretty good, as we've seen in this chapter, but Netscape has the lead in features, reliability, and customer acceptance.

From either angle, this pairing looks like a winner. Will Microsoft throw in the towel? Of course not. But if Novonyx takes off and fulfills even half the promises made to date, Novell and Netscape may become known as the "Big Ns" for their successful collaboration.

Other Third-Party Web Servers

As I said earlier, there are more than a few third-party Web servers out there. One of the first Web servers available was from GLACI, the Great Lakes Area Commercial Internet company. The GLACI-HTTPD Web Server for Novell NetWare came out about the same time as the original American Internet server, although the beta or even the released version from GLACI may have come first. Either way, these were the two pioneers. American is hard to find. Check out GLACI at www.glaci.com.

Process Software (www.process.com) ported its Purveyor Web server to the NetWare platform earlier than most of its competition. This company also has versions for Windows NT and 95, and for OpenVMS. They include advanced proxy services, as many of the high-end Web servers do.

One of the more interesting companies in the business of providing Internet-type tools to NetWare users is Puzzle Systems (www.puzzle.com). This was one of the first companies porting a reverse-engineered Net-Ware 3.*x* server to Unix hosts, bypassing Novell's licensing arrangements and code. The company's SoftNet WEBserv includes an e-mail, FTP, BootP-DHCP, and DNS server. Puzzle Systems has a long history of strong products, and its developers understand NetWare pretty darn well for a bunch of Unix folks.

Ukiah Software is another company doing lots of interesting things for NetWare servers. This company doesn't offer a Web server at this writing, but it does have a news server, firewall, and IPX/IP gateway. Check the Web site at www.ukiahsoft.com.

There are others, but I don't want to try and cover them all, because I'll forget more than I remember. Trust me, there are plenty of Web server options for NetWare and IntranetWare.

Should you consider a third-party Web server for your NetWare server? Sure, if the product does what you need and the developer will be around for the long haul. Try out whatever you want, because the method now is to download and try before you buy. Have fun.

Secure Web Services

There was no attempt to make the Internet "secure" during the early days. Remember, the pioneers were sharing every bit of information known to anyone about the developing network and the protocols, in order to make communications possible. The problem wasn't data security; it was sending and receiving data reliably.

Today, of course, reliable data communications are old hat, and we want to make life more difficult by demanding secure data transmissions. This desire overlooks the fact that open standards, the foundation of the Internet, do not fit neatly with security. In fact, if we look at the idea of standards (shared information), we see that security (private information) is about as opposite to it as the North Pole is from the South Pole.

Nonetheless, our consumer desires must not be thwarted, because then companies would lose business. The computer population, especially those of us in the U.S., have convinced ourselves that we have the right to use our credit cards safely across the Internet. Reality and technical details notwithstanding, we want to reach the opposite goals of security and standards immediately.

While technically not a part of BorderManager, Web security is important to most companies using BorderManager. That's why I brought up this subject. But realize that this book can't teach you all there is know about Web security. I'll give you some foundation and get you started, but your management must make a commitment of time and money to make Internet and Web security a reality.

An Overview of Web Security

Now that we have reconciled our competing and contradictory desires, and convinced ourselves that a standard, open network should also be secure, let's see what chance we have of achieving these goals with BorderManager. Fortunately, the Novell Web Server software supports an important security option: SSL (Secure Sockets Layer). We'll talk more about SSL soon, but let's cover some Web security concepts first.

Where Are the Web Police?

There are three security concerns the SSL client/server communication process eliminates:

- **Eavesdropping:** When confidential information is copied during the trip across the Internet and read by outsiders.

- **Data manipulation:** When data is captured and changed before reaching the destination.

- **Impersonation:** When conversation partners are not who they are supposed to be.

All these processes are criminal, in one sense or another. While some lawmakers may believe that the Internet is a wild new territory that requires new laws, most statutes dealing with fraud and other criminal acts cover the common data security issues. Federal wiretapping laws, however, have been expressly expanded to deal with data communications in the Electronic Communications Privacy Act of 1986.

Having a law on the books doesn't mean that the police in your area have the means to enforce that law. Many police departments and district attorneys are far behind in the computer area, and they are unable to identify, much less apprehend, computer criminals. There, don't you feel more secure already?

I hope that you believe in the old-fashioned Puritan ethic of self-responsibility, because computer security for your company will be up to you. There will be little or no help in any data communications area for several more years. If your data is important, you'll need to keep it safe, because the police can't.

Encryption for Temporary Security

The best way to keep information safe is through encryption. If someone is able to capture your data packets as they careen across the Internet, the encryption will stop the thief from doing anything with the packets for quite some time, but not forever.

Does it surprise you that I expect anyone with enough time and computer horsepower to be able to break whatever encryption method you use? It shouldn't. Historically, the outcome of warfare often turned on which side could break the code used by the opposing side. Military and government espionage moved into the corporate world years ago, and code breakers have moved from the side of good to the side of evil as well. Every month, some new computer hotshots break another unbreakable code, become famous for a few days, and then are forgotten by everyone outside the security business.

The laws on encryption are changing, as the computer industry tries to coerce the government into relaxing the ban on keys longer than 40 bits in software for export out of the U.S. If the ban isn't dropped by the end of 1997, I'll be surprised, because industry heavyweights are getting smarter about lobbying the government.

Keeping your data safe forever is not the goal, because that isn't possible. The goal is to keep the data safe in transit and for some amount of time after it reaches its destination. After all, if someone discovers your merger plan six months after the merger is completed, have you suffered any damage? No, and you won't, unless you leave the same security system in place for months and months, giving the bad guys time to catch up.

Certificates, Virtual Locks, and Keys

We keep physical things safe by locking them behind strong doors. We learn to trust people we don't know only if they come with verifiable references from someone we do know. Secure Web technology is based on similar ideas.

Public keys are readily available, and are what you see at the end of some e-mail messages. This key is mathematically related to the *private key*, which is kept, well, private. The message, created with the receiver's public key, is deciphered by the receiver's private key. Returning messages are handled in the same manner.

If your Web client doesn't have the key to connect to a secure server, the server will reject you. If your Web client is secure and the server sends the wrong information back to your client, you will be warned by the browser (Netscape) or the connection will terminate (Internet Explorer).

Does this sound like the old movies, in which only the people who knew where the speakeasy was and used the secret knock got inside? In a sense, we have exactly the same situation. You must know where the secure servers are, be able to perform the secret knock, and be verified and authenticated by an insider.

Certificates, issued by a recognizable and secure authority, are your passes through the locked doors of Web security. VeriSign (www.verisign.com) is the leading source of certificates used for Internet commerce, and that company's Web site contains many white papers and other helpful information. AT&T (www.att.com) is in this business as well. Xcert (www.xcert.com) is a newer company in the certificate business, and both Netscape and Microsoft Web servers can issue their own certificates strong enough for intranet use.

Did I say intranet use? Is there really a market for secure certificates inside companies? Yes, although I believe most of the demand is driven by the security system vendors rather than by users. After all, only a few companies really implement a card key system for access to physical resources. Why spend the money blocking employee access to company Web sites if you allow those same employees physical access to the information on the Web server?

WARNING   As you go deeper into the security issue, you'll find that paranoia overwhelms rational thought on a regular basis. Be prepared to suffer changing attitudes among managers, as they chase the latest security craze reported in the *Wall Street Journal* or the *New York Times*.

SSL and Your Web Server

As I mentioned earlier, the most popular method of Web security is the use of SSL, or Secure Sockets Layer. In this case, *Sockets* refer to programming sockets used by the developers to communicate between applications on the server and client.

Now at version 3.0, the newest SSL standard was completed in the spring of 1996, superseding SSL 2.0. SSL 3.0 added a thorough definition of client certificate requirements, updating the minimal support found in version 2.0.

Few commercial Web servers provide full support of SSL 3.0 (as of this writing). This makes Novell's support noteworthy.

SSL Session Details

Here is a brief description of how an SSL session works:

1. An SSL client sends a request to a secure server.

2. The server responds with its certificate.

3. If the server certificate comes from a certification authority (CA) that the browser understands, the browser will examine the certificate. If the server certificate is not from a known certification authority, the browser will ask the user if the connection should continue (Netscape), or the browser will terminate the communication (Internet Explorer).

4. If the server certificate matches the information of the server's domain name and public key, the server will be accepted as authentic.

5. The browser provides the server a list of acceptable ciphers.

6. If the server accepts client authorization, the client forwards its certificate to the server.

7. The server examines the client certificate to see if it came from a trusted source. If not, the server stops the dialogue.

8. Based on information provided by the client, the server chooses the strongest cipher in common, and then sends that information back to the client.

9. The client browser creates a session key based on the selected cipher.

10. The client encrypts the session key based on the server's public key.

11. The client sends the encrypted session key back to the server.

12. The server decrypts the session key using the server's private key.

13. The server and client encrypt and decrypt the continuing information sent and received based on the session key.

As you can see, there are lots of steps. Any slip up between any step, and the transaction is terminated. Do you see why I said this is a lot of extra overhead? Notice all the keys flying back and forth? Guess who has to deal with those keys. That's right, you do.

Are these sessions truly secure, even across the Internet? For now, the answer is yes. The longer the key, the stronger the key. As I mentioned earlier, the U.S. government has intentionally weakened security keys by not allowing keys longer than 40 bits to be exported. That restriction is loosening now, but the U.S. developers are all complaining that they're behind the foreign competition. Of course, U.S. developers lead the world in whining about the government, so there's nothing new there.

Configuring Your SSL Keys

Your NetWare or IntranetWare server hosting the Novell Web Server software has a new little NLM for you to examine: KEYMGR.NLM. Guess what KEYMGR stands for? If you guessed Key Manager, you're a clever network administrator and deserve a raise. Go tell your boss right now.

Now that your hopes have been crushed and you have updated your resume, let's get back to work. From the server console, or through RCONSOLE, type **LOAD KEYMGR**. This starts Key Manager, as shown in Figure 12.8. As you can see, you can't do anything until you specify the key database file location and create the file to track key pairs.

Must you put the key file in its own directory? No, but I thought it made a nice touch. This also helps by making it easy to control access to the key file. Several more people may have access to your SYS:\SYSTEM directory than the number of people who need access to the security keys. I told you that this stuff takes more effort than your managers imagined. Well, more work for you, anyway. They're not crunching any extra overtime, are they?

FIGURE 12.8

Starting your SSL journey

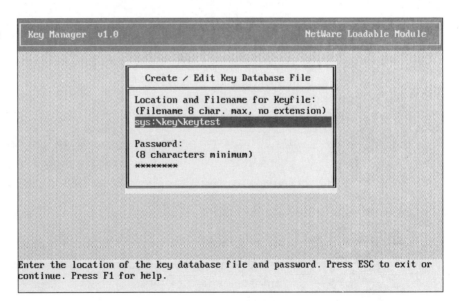

Please notice something critical on this screen: Your password must be a minimum of eight characters. If you don't use at least that number of characters, you will get an error message that provides no help whatsoever. Put in eight characters for your password, and you'll be in good shape.

You must go past this screen each and every time you work with your SSL configuration. Keep that in mind as you decide on a password. The password "my4dogshave72fleas" is a pretty good one, but it's a pain to type over and over.

What appears after this screen? The Key Datbase (sic) File Menu Option list comes next. As you can see in the menu below, you must now watch your datbase as well as your database. Life just keeps getting more complicated, doesn't it?

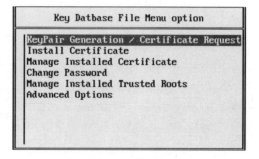

```
        Key Datbase File Menu option

 KeyPair Generation / Certificate Request
 Install Certificate
 Manage Installed Certificate
 Change Password
 Manage Installed Trusted Roots
 Advanced Options
```

Here's what each of the options does:

- **KeyPair Generation/Certificate Request:** Brings up the Request a Server Certificate screen. You may choose your certificate authority, but only VeriSign appears in the field automatically. Then choose whether you are asking for a new certificate or a renewal.

Certificates are issued for a certain amount of time, and will expire (at the most inopportune times, of course). Your request and all accompanying details are necessary for both new and renewal certificates.

- **Install Certificate:** Brings up the Certificate Install Option screen, which asks if the certificate you wish to install is part of a certificate chain or not. If you don't know, it's not. If the installation is part of a "trusted root," you will also know, because it's a lot more trouble to maintain connections with a trusted system. The last field asks for the location of the certificate.

- **Manage Installed Certificate:** Displays a screen that holds more work for you. Here, you can keep the details on the certificate and your certificate authority up to date. Name and contact information for certificate housekeeping isn't difficult to maintain, as long as you remember to make good notes the first time through.

- **Change Password:** A pretty straightforward choice, in case you kill some of those fleas on your dogs and want to lower the flea count down to 34 or so. (If you have no idea what I'm talking about, you obviously missed my witty account of how "my4dogshave72fleas" is a clever password, but probably not something you want to type in each time you need to work with your key database file.) You can't change the password if the HTTPD.NLM (the Novell Web Server software) is loaded, but the system warns you about that.

- **Manage Installed Trusted Roots:** Refers to the RSA (a public key encryption system, which is used for both encryption and authentication) and VeriSign connections maintaining the trusted root status for your SSL connections. Yes, this will cost money, but not too much. There are four options listed, one of which will be the company that you or your management has contracted to act as a trusted root. If and when a new trusted root reference is added, you'll need to type it all in yourself, or wait for the Web server software update.

- **Advanced Options:** In this version of Key Manager, the only "advanced option" is a Certificate Revocation List. If someone is really mean to you or your company, you can revoke his or her certificate, and that person won't be able to communicate with your secure server. However, it's best to let management make this decision, no matter how much some jerks deserve to be disconnected.

Configuring client systems falls under the varied and constantly changing Web client world. I have enough trouble keeping up with servers, much less the clients that change every two or three weeks. When it comes time to worry about trusted and secure clients, have a good time crawling through the client confusion. You really do deserve a raise if you get stuck with configuring all the clients as well as your server.

Turn Your Web Server into a Commerce Server

In my continuing quest to show you how IntranetWare, NetWare, and BorderManager relate to all the hot buzzwords you've been hearing, let's take a brief tour of the commerce server options. After all, since the Internet is generating money right and left for every company involved, you'll need a server to track all that commerce, right?

Unfortunately, Internet life is not all that wonderful. The Internet market yields riches grudgingly, and only to the same combination of good ideas and hard work that marks success in all markets. Nonetheless, the Novell Web Server software can function as a commerce server, and there are good reasons why you should check this out. But before we get to those reasons, we need to back up a little to define some terminology and put things in perspective.

What Is Electronic Commerce?

That's a good question, and one that's difficult to answer precisely. Perhaps it looks like pornography looks to the Supreme Court, and we'll know it when we see it. But let's look for another answer.

Depending on your viewpoint, you can make a strong point that all of today's serious commerce is electronic commerce. After all, do you think the bank sends a bag of money over to the car dealer when you take out a car loan? Does the travel agent convert your credit card number, taken over the phone, into dollar bills and physically take them to the airport to buy your plane ticket? Does your direct-deposit paycheck get converted into $20 bills and loaded in the ATM machine, waiting for you to suck them out, five at a time?

You understand that money is one of the more ephemeral notions in society today. The idea of billions of dollars floating around the country, none of it physical, can be disconcerting. If you consider how much easier it is to carry credit cards than to carry cash, you'll feel more comfortable with the idea of electronic commerce. Think of electronic commerce as companies using credit cards rather than cash, and you'll have the right idea.

But we need to put this notion into the context of the subject at hand: your networks and intranets. One book, *Electronic Commerce: A Manager's Guide*, by Ravi Kalokota and Andrew B. Whinston (published by Addison-Wesley in early 1997), doesn't even attempt to provide a single definition of electronic commerce. The authors define electronic commerce in four areas, with explanations for each, letting you pick the area that most closely resembles your own situation. Let me paraphrase:

- **Communications:** Electronic commerce is the delivery of information, products, services, or payments via computer networks, telephone lines, or other nonphysical means.

- **Business process:** Electronic commerce is the application of computer technology as a means of automating business transactions and workflow.

- **Service:** Electronic commerce provides quicker and faster delivery of information, leading to increased service.

- **Online:** Electronic commerce provides a safe means of buying and/or selling products, information, or services through the Internet or another network.

If you take a wide enough view, any transaction conducted over a telephone could be called electronic commerce. This inability to precisely separate normal business from electronic commerce shows how integrated the electronic processes have become in business-to-business commerce.

A Brief History of Electronic Commerce

EFT (Electronic Funds Transfer) activity started in the 1970s, and can be tagged as the beginning of electronic commerce. Big banks and federal bank clearing houses developed a proprietary network and employed high security in order to move money around. Today, more than $4 trillion (yes, trillion) changes hands through electronic means every day (yes, every day). Well over half of all payments by the U.S. government are made through electronic commerce.

EDI (Electronic Data Interchange) was the first wave of electronic commerce protocols and transaction standards. Through the late 1970s and 1980s, EDI support spread throughout all the large companies, enabling them to buy and sell products without sending paper back and forth. Electronic mail became an important part of EDI, but the need for security kept the protocols proprietary. These big companies and their suppliers tied EDI to mainframe technology in almost every case. There are some PC-based EDI software packages, but the traditional company network of PCs and medium-power computers has never been welcomed into the EDI world.

This effectively locked the consumer market away from EDI. In the 1980s, this wasn't a big deal, and electronic commerce stayed behind the scenes. The catalog company you called for product orders used EDI on the back end, but two people spoke and credit card numbers were exchanged verbally at the point of customer contact.

Once again, the Internet rips a traditional computer model to pieces. Consumers can now bypass the telephone catalog operator and simply click on their choices in Web pages. There are some consumers unwilling to trust their credit card numbers to a computer, but the trust issue is not new. This was a problem back in the 1970s, when catalogs became popular and people were wary about reciting their credit card information over the telephone. The acceptance of Web consumer commerce will develop more quickly than the catalog model, because consumers will transfer their trust of catalog telephone sales to the Web sales method more quickly than they made the transition from face-to-face sales to catalog sales.

What Defines a Commerce Server?

Although the term *electronic commerce* includes a wide variety of computer and network technology, let's stay focused on the Web side of the equation. After all, BorderManager is good, but it doesn't interface to your corporate mainframe (unless, of course, your mainframe starts speaking TCP/IP, and more of them are, every day).

Electronic Commerce: a Manager's Guide, the book I referred to earlier, includes several chapters about the Web in the world of electronic commerce. The authors see four areas of Web involvement (again, I paraphrase):

- **Marketing and advertising:** Strange turn for a network that effectively banned advertising at the beginning, isn't it? Now, the Web acts as a billboard to the world. Companies offer product and service information on Web servers, providing potential customers information in seconds. Customers no longer must wait days for brochures to wend their way through the mail. All too often, the information is provided with no more imagination than on the original paper brochure, but some companies are getting much better.

- **Customer service and support:** No need to tell those of us in the computer business about this, is there? No reputable computer products company can appear reputable without a support Web site. Now that same attitude is spreading throughout all businesses with customers who need support and have access to the Web. Depending on how you slice your demographics, that covers just about everyone, doesn't it? No wonder the Web designers are all driving new cars.

- **Distribution channels and new markets:** Every trade has trade magazines, and they are all moving to the Web. Again, the computer business blazed this trail, with all leading computer magazines offering an online version. It's tough to make money selling Web subscriptions, but it's tougher to look like a major magazine without a Web site. This doesn't begin to include the options for software distribution over the Internet, driven by the Web.

■ **New online information products:** If you can send your product through a fax machine, you can sell it on the Web. If your product is information, such as offered by the magazines, the Web and the Internet offer tremendous savings in production and distribution. Financial services, such as buying and selling stocks and bonds, benefit from the same advantages. Education is the favored government hook, and there are now a variety of online universities offering degrees. We'll never get to wide-scaled distance learning as described by some of the overexcited politicians, but anything printed, displayed, recorded, videotaped, or filmed can now come across your computer.

Need we mention entertainment? The only business making a real profit on the Web right now is the "adult entertainment" industry. These purveyors did a good job jump-starting the VCR industry, and they are repeating that success with the Web. What's more private than your "personal" computer?

This means that your Web server and supporting security architecture must help, rather than hinder, the attainment of these goals. Can your Novell Web Server software, along with BorderManager, help?

The answer is yes. What are the important parts of electronic commerce, and hence a commerce server, that we have described so far? There are three main parts: security, auditing capabilities, and authentication. Let's see how each of these work with your Web server.

Commerce Security

Commerce of any kind, long before electronic commerce, demanded security. Check and credit card fraud costs billions per year, but consider that this is only a fraction of the trillions that change hands in that same time frame. Commerce servers must have loss rates as low or lower than regular credit card transactions.

This level of security gets into all the SSL areas we covered earlier. Frankly, if the telephone operator copies your credit card number and shares it with a friend, they won't cause too much damage. However, if your credit card number is intercepted during a transaction across the Internet, it can be duplicated to a thousand users before you stop typing at your computer. This is unacceptable, and requires something special to eliminate the possibility. Encrypting transactions is one of those special things that might be done. Fortunately, BorderManager and the Novell Web Server cover that base.

Commerce Auditing

Log files make a virtual "paper trail" of what has happened. In case of any security problems, it's important to know who communicated with your system, when they did so, and the result of that communication. All those log files eating your disk space may have some value, after all. (See Chapters 8 and 9 for more information about BorderManager logs.)

Commerce Authentication

You may need to authenticate each and every visitor to your Web server, even if no money changes hands during the connection. Let's say you work for one of those clever Wall Street firms selling stock advice. Once clients pay the fee, they are given access to the current and historical information tracked by your systems and people.

Who grants and denies access? The BorderManager Proxy Server software certainly comes first, and it can take care of an entire network of systems if you wish. If you want to get more fine-grained than that, one Web server can be set aside for the "special" customers (who have paid the "special" fee). Remember when we discussed how to allow individual users access to Web server directories? (Look back at the section titled "Configuring Web Server Access Security" in this chapter if you don't remember.) This access can be controlled by NDS name or IP address. Either way, BorderManager and the Novell Web Server software make it all happen.

Why Use a Commerce Server from Novell?

The question of which platform to use for your commerce server is a fair one. After all, if you must pay $50,000 or more for a Unix-based commerce server from Netscape, isn't it much better than one based on NetWare?

Not necessarily. Granted, big Unix systems have more options, allow more customization, and have more third-party support than the Novell Web Server. Yes, you can nod your head in agreement when the boss asks if a SPARCserver with four processors and $100,000 worth of customized software is better than your IntranetWare server, BorderManager services, and the Novell Web Server software. But we're also talking about an investment in the neighborhood of $250,000, which is a darn nice neighborhood where I come from.

Face it—there's no sense using a vault with six-foot steel walls to guard $1,000. Save the heavy artillery for something with high value. Your Novell Web Server can be a great pilot platform to test the project. You'll have all the protection of SSL encrypted data, as well as strong security to control access to the server data, and spend only one-tenth or less than you would for the full system.

When the project is a success, you can spend the extra money and "upgrade" to Sun, HP, IBM, or whatever else you want. By then, however, your boss may start asking why you need to spend the extra money, when the IntranetWare system is working so well. If there is a good reason, say so. If not, remind management how much money you saved on this project when review time comes around.

Wrap

The Novell Web Server product offers excellent value for the money (it's free, remember?) and does a good job. Other Web server software will do a good job as well, and Novonyx wants to make Netscape the official NetWare Web server. This is not a bad idea.

Does this mean you'll be hopelessly confused when trying to choose a Web server? No, it means you will have many choices. The number of choices available today for the NetWare server platform tells me that Novell servers make a good platform for Web services. Novell's audited Web server performance numbers will tell you that a NetWare server can handle far more traffic without failing than any comparably priced system.

After all, since you trust your NetWare server for all your important company network file service and storage, why not take that next step and use NetWare as your Web server platform? All you have to lose is low performance and higher prices.

If you decide you need more security for your Web server, you can take advantage of the Novell Web Server software's support for SSL. But keep in mind that starting down the SSL road means increased security administration overhead, slower Web transactions, and constant network management. There is no sense in increasing the security profile of your Web transactions unless you make a corresponding commitment to upgrade the rest of your security. After all, what good is the best SSL system in the world if visitors to your office can take secure documents off desks or out off unlocked file cabinets?

Security precautions are mandatory for certain situations, such as some of the commercial server applications we discussed in this chapter. Just don't let your managers believe that they have a secure system because they use SSL. The biggest security holes in every system are the mouths of employees. Until each employee understands and abides by a well-designed security plan, your system is not safe.

CHAPTER

13

Applications Driving Your Network

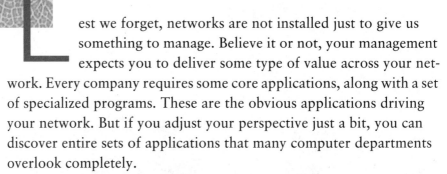

est we forget, networks are not installed just to give us something to manage. Believe it or not, your management expects you to deliver some type of value across your network. Every company requires some core applications, along with a set of specialized programs. These are the obvious applications driving your network. But if you adjust your perspective just a bit, you can discover entire sets of applications that many computer departments overlook completely.

You have a set of building blocks, described earlier in this tome, that can be arranged in a thousand different ways. You want to employ the security and protocol control of BorderManager by using the Proxy Server, the IPX/IP Gateway, and the IP/IP Gateway as necessary. Then you want to attack some corporate problem, solve this problem using your BorderManager and other IntranetWare tools, and graciously accept the Employee of the Year Award, thanking all the little people while smiling radiantly.

If you're into pop psychology, you realize we now have a Goal (pop psychology capitalizes lots of ordinary words, you know), and we must choose our Map to the Destination and Achieve Our Goal. For people unaware of the hyperbole in the self-help section of the bookstore, we need a *plan*.

Let's take a look at ten potential projects that are perfect for your intranet/extranet system. Then we'll review some of the software packages that you might find useful for your projects. Of course, I'll also offer some advice and warnings about all the application options.

What you must do now is take a step back, get your nose out of the network proper, and look for Opportunity (sorry, the self-help stuff crept back in for a second).

Top Ten Intranet/Extranet Projects

Top Ten lists are a staple of comedy monologues and e-mail jokes because lists are great organizing factors for many people. Your bosses (especially if they read the self-help books) probably have Top Ten Goal lists scattered around their offices. This Top Ten Projects list has something in common with the trendier types: It can help you to focus on your objective of getting extra value from your network.

Characteristics of Project Candidates

Your company has at least ten major areas your network can improve. Is there a common thread to these ten items? Yes, I think there is. All are paper-driven and are a major pain to organize, monitor, and control. Paper creation, storage, monitoring, and tracking dominate the time spent on these activities. There are ways to use your network that improve on what can be done with paper, especially when you don't limit yourself to simply replicating the existing paper-developed systems in electronic form.

Here are the areas in which you'll find good candidates for conversion from paper to the network:

- Great gobs of information, especially when most of the information is already gathered and organized electronically, should not be in the form of mounds of paper. Every company uses a computer database to record employee names, addresses, office locations, and telephone numbers. Why not skip the paper and put the information in an accessible and attractive electronic format?

- Data with set guidelines for content, layout, style, review procedures, and approval translates well to the computer. For example, public companies are required to provide certain financial information in specific ways. Paper is the least flexible method of providing this type of data.

- Databases that many employees need to reference belong on the computer system. Pick a winner for your first project. Identify that winner by finding the database that is the most inconvenient to produce and use in its current form; you'll also find the largest number of people who will benefit by moving that database to the computer system. Material that is printed and distributed on a regular basis makes a great starter project, because costs are strongly weighted toward paper. Replacing paper saves money every time.

- Any project that involves regularly changing information is usually a good candidate for translation to the network. After all, your Web pages change more often than your product brochures, right? That's because the computer version is easier to change than the printed version. Take the hint, and put the information on the computer so that you can get up-to-date information to the people involved— they are tired of waiting for paper.

And the Winners Are...

The characteristics list shows the reasons that particular types of functions will improve when they are moved from paper to your intranet. Now let's get to the specifics. These are the projects themselves:

- Company directories

- Policy and procedure manuals

- Online document services

- Calendars and schedules

- Electronic workflow support

- Access to corporate databases

- Electronic forms

- Rules and regulations

- Employee communications

- In-house training

Each one of these projects is paper-heavy. The few that aren't completely paper require access to information not normally shared through a Web server and intranet. That makes it all the better to push these projects, don't you think? After all, if your management is like some I've seen, the first comment about a new proposal is, "We tried that, and it didn't work." Resist the temptation to respond by saying that the first attempt was coordinated by brain-dead management trainees and a semi-trained monkey. Instead, reply that changes in the world of computing, such as the Web, eliminate many of the problems seen by earlier projects. This is actually true, so you can say it with a straight face.

Company Directories

I put this project first because this is a winner in every company large enough to run three file servers. Once you get past about 50 employees, paper sheets with employee names and extension numbers expand into little booklets. When you get into hundreds of employees, perhaps spread out over several locations, you have a quagmire. People come, go, change offices, get new phone numbers, change jobs, and generally create the need for constant directory updates.

There are two ways to produce paper company directories:

- Print and distribute complete employee directories. After all, a partial directory doesn't do much good, does it? Since you're making a complete directory, you must include each employee. Every employee in the company must get a copy. When enough information changes to make the directory more hindrance than help, you must reprint and redistribute it. This wastes enormous amounts of paper and time.

- Put pages in a loose-leaf notebook. By replacing, updating, and adding pages that employees can maintain themselves, you are spared the expense of printing an entire directory. You must still distribute the pages, however, at nearly the same cost as distributing the full directory. In fact, you may need to distribute the pages much more often than you would ever reprint a full directory. And after the new pages are distributed, you can't be sure that each employee updated his or her manual as requested.

There's no really good way to distribute this information, is there? Both choices require paper and time, which both cost money.

Try to track down the cost of producing your company directory. Once you find the cost of the directory, a light bulb should shine brightly above your head. "Wow," you'll say to yourself, "I can get all the upgrades I need for my network for the cost of one company directory." That moment, my friend, will seem like the end of your problems. It won't be, because you need to convince lots of other people the truth of what you have discovered, and that won't be easy. Some managers won't believe your figures, and other managers will be afraid that they'll lose some turf if they don't continue using the paper company directories.

For this reason, you'll need to expand on the company directory in ways that can't be easily duplicated on paper. Here are some ideas:

- Add employee photos. This is a common example, but be careful. The cost of obtaining and scanning photos may equal the cost of printing and distributing paper. If your Web server is visible to the outside world, display pictures of only the executives in the annual report.

- Add search capabilities. Searching through a paper directory is tough, because you're limited by the organizational method used by the printer. Normally, this is alphabetical, which is standard but doesn't help you find the payroll clerk who left a garbled message on voice mail. How about a predefined search listing by job function? Then if the purchasing manager is gone, for example, it will be easy to find the assistant's extension.

■ Create FAQ lists. To go one more step toward making life easier for employees, you could offer a page listing common employee questions linked to a FAQ list for each department that answers that question. What's your Social Security tax withholding so far this year? How can you file a claim for a lost laptop computer? Will that toy you bought for a client's child be accepted on your expense report? All these questions can be answered by the people listed in your company contact database, and you can make these folks as easy to find as possible.

You may be thinking that you could produce directories through NWAdmin, since it has space for user information, including physical location, mailing address, phone numbers, and the like. However, not every person in your company may have a NetWare client powerful enough to run NWAdmin effectively. But everyone probably has a Web browser, even employees carrying a Windows CD palmtop and cruising down the physical highway.

Policy and Procedure Manuals

If there are any company documents used less but needed more by company employees than the policy and procedure manuals, I can't guess what they are. Wait, I hear you, computer manuals for hardware and software are ignored more than personal advice from co-workers. But you must admit that the policy and procedure manuals, sometimes fondly called P&P manuals, rank right up there.

These documents start out small, and they arrive at about the same time you get your first real employee directory. By the time your employee directory grows thick, the policy manuals take up about a foot of shelf space. Does anyone read these? Not on your life. Does everyone need access to this information sooner or later? You bet.

One company productivity consultant discovered that the employee handbook (notice all the different names for this critter?) costs between

$10 and $15 per copy. Suppose that your company has 4885 employees and your purchasing department isn't too bright, so you pay $14 each for 4885 employees. The total comes to $68,390 before tax, shipping, handling, and distribution throughout the company. Like your company directory's cost, the dollars spent for your policy manual could fund your entire intranet system. You could buy four killer servers and load them all with BorderManager and IntranetWare for less than the cost of one printing of your manual. Quick, check to see if there's a bonus for employees suggesting cost-saving procedures. Where did you put that policy manual?

Procedure manuals tend to change more often than policies, since your company will probably change insurance carriers before the managers rework the vacation guidelines. When the insurance carrier information needs to be updated, which is easier: reprinting 5000 copies of your procedure manual or updating one Web server page and sending e-mail to each employee?

Employee handbooks are considered contracts in some states, so you need to print and archive a copy of each change made to the Web server. State laws totally disagree with each other concerning whether an employee actually must read the handbook for the regulations to become binding. Keeping track of those users hitting the employee handbook Web pages isn't difficult, and a paper trail of employees checking for loopholes may be useful if push comes to shove and a lawyer.

Online Document Services

Where do boilerplate paragraphs help more: printed on paper in the contracts office or stored on a central Web server for all employees to reference? How about old contracts, sales information, and letters? Should you keep them on paper in a locked filing cabinet in the basement or should you put them on the network?

The marketing and public relations departments create plenty of paper. Most of these documents can be displayed on your own Web server more cheaply than they can be photocopied and faxed to each office. Reviews and articles about company products, employees, and market plans make great morale boosters, as long as the employees know where to find them. Copy (with permission) anything printed about the company, whether it's good, bad, or indifferent.

Does everyone in your company know all about the company's products and services? Why not put copies of all the presentation materials used by the sales and marketing departments on your Web server? The more employees know about the company, the better able they are to hide from any real work. Oops, I mean the better they are able to help your wonderful customers.

Some departments in your company already have a document management system or two in place. Early versions of document managers were expensive, proprietary, and complex. All those problems disappear when the document management systems move to a Web-based model. Any client can search any server at any time. This is a much more efficient approach, don't you think? Cost isn't nearly as much of a problem when you can add the Novell Web Server software to the department Intranet-Ware server.

Calendars and Schedules

Why did I put calendars and schedules before workflow applications on the Top Ten list? Aren't they just about the same thing?

Sorry, but no, at least not in my opinion. Workflow systems normally rely heavily on scheduling software tied with e-mail. Novell's excellent GroupWise product can be considered just about the best combination of e-mail, scheduling, and task management software available. But it can be confused with a workflow system only if you've never seen a true workflow system. (GroupWise 5.2 promises to have workflow software, but I have not seen it yet; ask me next year how well GroupWise fulfills the workflow promise.)

Companies are integrating Internet (and hence intranet and extranet) support into PIM (Personal Information Manager) applications. Sidekick, the application that started all this PIM madness with the first TSR (terminate-and-stay-resident) program back in the middle 1980s, introduced Internet Sidekick in the middle of 1996. Sidekick 97, released about a half year later, folds the Internet hooks into the basic product. NetManage purchased ECCO (company and product) and transformed the application into an Internet-aware package by early 1996.

Will these work on an intranet? Of course, and they'll work on an extranet as well. We'll go into more details later in this chapter, when we talk about group communications applications, but rest assured that a variety of programs now can use TCP/IP as a transport for calendar and scheduling applications.

Department resources and schedules work great on Web pages. You can link any defined resource in the department to the front page, and tie calendars to any and all parts of a Web page. Resource scheduling systems are no longer a big headache to develop. Do you need a conference room? Check the intranet Web page, click once to pop open the calendar, click again to reserve your conference room if it's clear, and go about your business.

Does this save a ton of money over your current method of finding and tracking company resources and employees? No, it's not a big money saver, but it certainly is a time saver. Trying to make all the arrangements to cram six managers into a conference room can take more time than the meeting itself. The more automation and less secretary involvement, the less time wasted on all levels.

 Several scheduling packages have built-in capabilities for keeping track of resource and employee availability. For example, GroupWise has a "busy search" mode. But if you don't have one of those programs, and you have a programmer who wants to practice with some Web programming, you can build your own system fairly quickly, and you can make it available to every employee with access to a Web browser.

Electronic Workflow Support

Now that we know how to replace paper with Web pages and calendars with the same Web server, we're ready for electronic workflow support. Yes, *workflow*—sounds big, sounds expensive, and sounds executive.

All three parts of the previous sentence were true not long ago. Workflow systems were definitely expensive. They supported only certain client systems, and they didn't work well. Executives had to order them, because they were too expensive and too flaky for the computer folks to buy into them.

Look at the changes since the second stage of workflow applications, appearing in the early 1990s: Multiple types of client support aren't a problem, Web servers offer great value for the money, and the executives are too embarrassed by their stupid workflow and document imaging purchases early in the cycle to argue with you now about Web-based workflow. So take a deep breath and plunge into workflow if you're ready.

Oh, you say, your executives bought Notes (from IBM nee Lotus), never allowed anyone to examine the real costs of the system, and so kept it going until now. You're in luck, because Notes is racing to embrace the Web before the Web flattens Notes. The problems with Notes include client support (the Web has that covered), communication server hassles (the Web wins again), and developing Notes applications (Web servers run great on a variety of easy application development platforms, and that doesn't include Java). Look, the Web wins, and whether you replace Notes with the Web is less a question than how you can upgrade Notes using your new network technologies.

When you get started, take care to show value for your workflow applications. Here's an example: A North Texas hospital with 17 pharmacy locations now coordinates drug purchases through headquarters to gain volume purchasing power and better prices than each pharmacy can get on its own. The hospital intranet, spread across a WAN, and a workflow application replace a system that involved mailing envelopes full of purchasing documents. Now electronic documents and e-mail are used instead of face-to-face meetings and outdated paper copies. New contracts are offered, accepted, and ratified through the Web servers and workflow software in one month rather than six months. New contracts bring lower prices, and the faster a new contract gets started, the more money the hospital saves.

Someone (maybe you, since you've been tagged for everything else so far) should be the "Workflow Wizard" for the new system. Another Workflow Wizard, or perhaps Workflow Friend, should be in the executive ranks. Believe me and every workflow consultant when we tell you that executive support is necessary if your workflow project is to even get started, much less become a success.

Your entire workflow application will build upon your Web server and TCP/IP network foundation. Connecting the hundreds of PC users currently running only the IPX protocol for NetWare server communications can be easy, or it can be a deal-breaker. Options such as the IPX/IP Gateway make life easier for workflow designers, so make sure all the BorderManager features are well publicized during the workflow planning meetings.

Access to Corporate Databases

Every company develops databases of knowledge; some are official, and some aren't. While it's impossible to tap the smarts and experience of all the secretaries keeping the company afloat, electronic databases and file repositories are a different story. Putting these knowledge repositories online can improve your bottom line.

Each department in the company has sets of specialized databases as well. Accountants have tax books; lawyers have law books and recent cases; human resources people need new personnel guidelines; engineers need materials references; and the computer department technicians need drivers, documentation, and other support files.

Some of these databases already exist in your system, or they can be added by loading a CD-ROM or three onto some servers. Some of these systems require outside access, usually through the Internet, and BorderManager can control that access. Other collections may just be directories of letters, contracts, and associated files that should be indexed by the intranet Web server and made available to appropriate employees.

Do you have any old product files and information? Move those from dusty loose-leaf binders to your Web server, and make them accessible to employees supporting these older products. You also may want to make them accessible to outsiders, so long-time customers can see which replacement parts and upgrades are available for their existing products.

Sales and marketing departments will constantly bug you about Web client hit details. In other words, organize the names and e-mail addresses of all contacts (assuming the names are accurate) and sort them by company. Depending on your business, you probably care less about individuals visiting your Web site than you do about large companies looking for products or services. Handing the sales department the URL to listings of all the Fortune 1000 company e-mail addresses will gain you some major karma points.

How about your mainframe? Linking the wheezing old mainframe to TCP/IP networks is a big deal today, and one that pays dividends all around. One survey (no doubt run by a mainframe company) showed that 80 percent of corporate data resides on the mainframe. Whether that percentage is inflated or not, plenty of valuable information sits in a DASD (Direct Access Storage Device, those washer-sized hard disks tied to the mainframe). The easier that information is to find and use, the smarter your employees will appear, and the faster some work will get done.

Electronic Forms

For a good laugh, bring up the old "paperless office" concept around the break room one day. Old-timers especially appreciate the hearty laughs to be had when looking at document management brochures from the 1980s promising "no more dead trees." Today, it seems like the only people making money in the computer business sell paper or cables (yes, that's a knock on the wireless industry).

After laughing, take a moment to examine the options for cutting down on paper provided by your intranet. Isn't most of the paper cluttering your desk filled with administrative details demanded by power-mad bureaucratic drones? Of course it is. If it were important, it would be in e-mail. So take the next step, and use e-mail and your intranet Web servers to gather the necessary information, and skip the paper forms completely. Aren't there programs that have these features? Yes, there are. But if you construct your own, you can more easily tie it into the databases and employee records already available. Besides, you want to get funding to improve your intranet, not buy another proprietary electronic forms application.

Go to your forms-happy clerks and trade their printer for an electronic forms program that spits out HTML code. All the electronic forms programs I just disparaged in the preceding paragraph promise to produce HTML code in the next software update, so keep an eye on them.

Why not use the Web server to handle expense, vacation, purchase request, and address change forms? In fact, almost every paper form could be eliminated or moved to the Web server if you take the right approach.

Why move these forms? Here are a few good reasons:

- People can't write legibly, but they can type acceptably. Why introduce extra mistakes because no one can read anyone else's handwriting?

- Feed the information to a database, not into a manila folder. What happens to handwritten forms? They go in the file cabinet. Electronic forms go into a database and sometimes into the workflow system, which are other applications on the Top Ten list. Databases are easier to copy and distribute than paper forms. If you lose the original paper form, you're stuck. But if you mess up a record in the database, you can always retrieve another copy.

- Multiple users can view electronic forms concurrently. One paper form serves only one person well. Copies of forms, made to share information with others, don't reflect the different changes each person makes. Your Web server can track each response and make that response available to everyone else in the company with the proper authorization.

Real dollars and cents can be saved by replacing paper forms with electronic ones, but it won't happen overnight. If you can't convince the managers to convert the existing forms, at least get the Web server accepted well enough to be the source of new forms rather than continuing to print them on dead trees.

Rules and Regulations

You have them, you hate them, but you need to check them from time to time. If you dig around through your pile of unread memos, you're liable to come up with an old version of a rule rather than the current rule. Eliminate this problem for yourself and others by putting all the company rules and regulations on the Web server.

Are rules and regulations the same as the employee handbook? No, because the handbook provides guidelines for employees. Specific rules are contained in the rules and regulations book.

Geographically dispersed companies have a particular problem keeping this type of information current. Employees in small branch offices without human resources personnel on-site make long-distance calls to headquarters to get answers. This costs money and takes time, and the result is often mailing the remote employee a copy of the rules. Why not publish a URL for the table of contents for the rules handbook and be done with it?

As with other printed material, changing the rules in paper handbooks is expensive. Making changes in the electronic version on the Web server is little trouble. In fact, once you have the template organized, you can let the human resources folks change their own rules. This keeps you out of the loop and lets the human resources department employees control their own destiny (okay, it's just a little part of their destiny, but at least it keeps you off the hook).

Employee Communications

Several of the projects just explained have a direct bearing on this project. Your co-workers know the rules, have the knowledge you seek, and can often skip the paper trail. The trick now is to encourage employee communications across your new intranet.

You may need to reorient your thinking just a bit. Technical folks, such as you and I, may consider the intranet to be a technical system. Less technical folks, such as bosses, may consider the intranet as a communications system. You should encourage this attitude, because communication pathways get more, not less, money every budget cycle.

One goal for your intranet is to re-create the same information sharing seen on bulletin boards and around the break room. Let the employees take some Web page space and company time to post personal classified ads to each other. Not the "personal" personal ads, but the garage sales, used car, need baby-sitters, and tickets to the game on Sunday type of ads. The more reasons people have to use the system to get what they feel is important, the better they will know the system when they want to actually do some work. Besides, people looking for a car-pool partner will concentrate on learning the system more than bored people assigned to a training class on a system they don't know or like.

Moving up the ladder of importance, make the intranet Web server and e-mail the official location for all job postings. Direct interested parties to fill out an internal application for the job on the Web server, rather than sending paper through the interoffice mail. This results in less paperwork and hassle for everyone, and the response time will be quicker.

Your upper management can make all the difference here. If the CEO sends out the monthly morale message via e-mail directing users to the Web server, your intranet is a success. If your CEO sends out paper memos, your company will have trouble dealing with the competitive Internet marketplace. You should update your resume, or at least go to your association meetings for a little personal networking.

In-House Training

Small companies believe training is an overhead cost, never to be recovered. Those companies should look into making training materials available over the company intranet in order to save money. Employees can read the training materials when they have time, rather than going away from their desks (and work space) for hours or days at a time.

Large companies believe training is an investment in the future of their business and the success of their employees. Those companies should look into making training materials available over the company intranet in order to spread the knowledge to as many employees as possible. Every spare moment becomes a chance for employees to learn something new or brush up on a subject they studied earlier.

Yes, "stupid user" stories are great fun, but they don't help the company. Imagine how much free time you would have if all the users you support actually read the supplied material, help screens, and question-and-answer sheets passed around? You could play Solitaire, just like the executives. Okay, maybe you'll never have enough time to play Solitaire (besides, it cuts into the DOOM, Quake, and Duke Nuke'em 3D death matches), but putting training information at the fingertips of every employee makes it possible for your users to find answers to their basic questions without your assistance.

Your training department or human resources group will no doubt be in charge of training materials. As with rules and regulations, offering the group in charge a template on a prebuilt set of Web pages will save even more of your time. Besides, answering questions about Web graphics is more fun than fixing a "broken" monitor by turning up the brightness.

Training materials now routinely include CD-ROMs full of text, sounds, images, and video. Your intranet is a great transport mechanism for those training courses. Not only will new trainees be educated for less money, but prior trainees can review the material whenever they wish. This is another win-win situation delivered by an intranet and clever network managers like yourself.

Even more fun stuff is coming, as audio and video take more and more corporate bandwidth. Full-motion video clips with narration will be part of training materials in the near future. Interactive videoconferencing is farther away than vendors in this fledgling industry would have you believe, especially over WAN links. But your network upgrade plans must take into account these upcoming bandwidth hogs.

"Accounts" makes me think of funding your intranet again. Sun released information that in 1996, the company saved $2,200 for each salesperson trained over the intranet rather than transported to a classroom. Sandia National Laboratories saved $2.5 million annually by moving its Environment, Safety, and Health Awareness course from the classroom to the company intranet. Travel savings were the majority of the windfall, and the system cost only about $50,000 to build. Return on investment was immediate; the first batch of employees trained over the intranet saved enough money to pay for the entire system.

Group Communications Applications

All ten of the intranet/extranet projects you just read about have one thing in common: communications. You're probably tired of hearing me harp on this, but bear with me just a bit longer. After all, communication is the whole idea here.

Perhaps we should emphasize group coordination for this section, upgrading beyond just communications. Coordination implies more purpose than mere communications. Most people and companies I know can stand to be more coordinated, and I bet you and your company fit into that group as well.

Let's take a look at some of the more popular group coordination and groupware packages. Since everything we discuss can be used over the Internet, intranet, and extranet, BorderManager security features are important for your company's implementations.

BorderManager and Calendaring and Scheduling Applications

Interactive calendars and schedules are a great idea, but they bring up all sorts of protocol and security problems. First, you must have some way to allow others to read, modify, and delete information on your own calendars and schedules. This obviously requires some type of directory service. Then you must have a way to authenticate prospective clients to verify that they are on the list of approved users of your calendars and schedules. This definitely calls for a strong directory service, especially since you just realized some visitors should be able to read, but not modify or delete, your calendar and schedule entries. Wow, this is starting to get complicated. Where's the aspirin?

The first parts of this problem to tackle are protocols for communications and the directory service needs. The protocol part is pretty easy, since we're speaking of the Internet and related technologies. We're stuck with TCP/IP, aren't we? Don't forget all your existing NetWare clients who can use the IPX/IP Gateway in BorderManager, because that will be an important consideration for your installation time and budget.

This leaves the authentication details. NDS can handle all the details concerning lists of allowed visitors, varying degrees of access (just like access to NetWare volumes) to allow some people to change your information but limiting others to just reading, and tracking who comes and goes. (Oh yes, we want to know who came and went, just in case there's something wrong later—we need to have a villain and/or scapegoat, you know.)

Wait, you say, what about the possibility of non-NetWare clients getting into and out of your system? Looks like a job for Proxy Server, doesn't it? You have strong controls over external users via their IP addresses. Don't let the competition argue that NDS must be weak if it can't control IP addresses as NDS objects, because NDS matches the other firewalls and proxy servers functionality in that way. Each of them requires some manual address input to start.

After solving the problems of access and security, the problems of interaction and communication come up. The schedulers and calendar programs available for LANs were designed to control both the client and server sides of connections. If you checked your boss's schedule, the same program controlled both clients and the server database. That is not the case on the Internet.

What's needed is a standard for one calendar program client to communicate with the calendar server program written by a different vendor.

This is roughly the same as taking a Ford radiator and trying to hook it to a Chevrolet. Until recently, this was impossible. But technology trends (for software, not cars) suggest that new standards will allow interoperability of calendar and scheduling programs.

IETF Calendaring and Scheduling Standards Upcoming

You'll be glad to know that the Internet community has been working on the problems of calendaring and scheduling for some time. (Forgive me if I'm making a verb out of a noun with *calendaring*, but it has to be done. What good is all this computer jargon if we can't get back at our high school English teachers who were so inflexible?)

There's an IETF (Internet Engineering Task Force) working group called Calendaring and Scheduling (calsch) that has been active since the spring of 1996. Their first Internet Draft was presented in late November 1996, and the group expects to submit a Proposed Draft in August 1997, with all the work finished in April 1998. Of course, there's both software and committee work involved here, so don't get angry if some dates slip. (If dates didn't slip with software, we would all think something was wrong, and we were being lied to, wouldn't we?)

The calsch group has three objectives:

- Develop a standard content type for capturing calendar and to-do information.

- Develop a standard peer-to-peer protocol for common calendaring and scheduling transactions.

- Develop a standard access protocol to allow the management of calendars, events, and to-do list objects over the Internet.

Not surprisingly, the protocol the working group hopes to release is tentatively called the Calendar Access Protocol. The trick will be in developing the protocols and content descriptions to handle future growth and extensions while still making the largest possible allowances for current products. The results often make one or two of the participating companies angry, and they stomp off swearing to go forward with their own plans and to heck with the group.

Find the details at http://www.ietf.org (and continue down to /html.charters/ calsch-charter.html, if they don't rearrange their site by then), where you can also read the seven papers released as I write this. If you read these papers, you'll suddenly gain much more respect for products such as GroupWise, which are able to keep all the details straight. You may also despair of getting every vendor in the market to agree on the standard and convert their proprietary code for the good of the group.

As you would expect, there are competing protocols in development. Try these on for size: Calendaring Interoperability Protocol and Calendaring Interoperability over HTTP. Sometime near the end of 1997, the winner should emerge victorious, the vanquished slink away, and some companies start "extending" the standard before the ink is dry. So goes the world of Internet standards and protocols.

GroupWise and Some Competitors

As a consultant, one thing I always steer customers toward is using Internet e-mail servers and clients for all their internal and external communications. It's cheaper and easier to set up some new e-mail servers than it is to coerce some of the Internet gateways shipped by some LAN e-mail vendors to actually communicate with the Internet.

The exception to this recommendation is when the customer is using GroupWise. After GroupWise, customers won't settle for basic e-mail any longer. As I mentioned earlier, GroupWise is Novell's excellent e-mail, scheduling, and task management software. Today, the only competition for GroupWise in the opinion of many experts is Notes from Lotus/IBM.

InfoWorld reviewed centralized messaging solutions in March 1997, and judged GroupWise both the best universal inbox of those reviewed and the least expensive. The competition was Microsoft Exchange with RightFax and CallXpress3 for fax and voice, and Notes with the Lucent Technologies Intuity Multimedia Messaging Server. Teamed with GroupWise was Cheyenne/CA's FaxServe and CallWare from CallWare Technologies, Inc.

GroupWise Internet Access Options

GroupWise can use the ubiquitous TCP/IP to connect clients to servers if you wish. This sounds like a great way to connect GroupWise NetWare-based clients over an extranet or intranet, doesn't it? Guess what, you can even connect across the Internet with proper configuration of your Proxy Server filters (the subject of Chapter 9).

GroupWise is moving to add non-NetWare clients through its Web-Access software. This allows any Web browser client to access its GroupWise Universal Mailbox and view messages. The interface doesn't look quite the same in a Web browser as it does in a GroupWise client, but that's part of the "charm" of Web clients, isn't it? Frankly, the GroupWise interface seems somewhat inflexible to me, but the latest version is far better than the earlier GroupWise versions. Figure 13.1 shows the opening GroupWise WebAccess installation screen. Once you have the software installed, your login screen will look similar to Figure 13.2.

I'm happy to see GroupWise use Web browsers as interfaces to the user database, because this client support philosophy goes back to the roots of GroupWise. In the days before GroupWise, when the product was called WordPerfect Office, it supported a variety of Unix clients. Of course, it was all DOS and ASCII graphic boxes, but it shared databases just fine. Hey, I even go back to the beginning, when this product was called Library, and the WordPerfect company was still named SSL. I'll move onto the next subject as soon as I find my cane.

GroupWise has had an SMTP gateway for years and years, and it actually works most of the time. That sounds like a slam, but the GroupWise gateway seems more reliable and easier to configure than most of the other LAN e-mail application gateways. There are a variety of choices for your gateway pleasure. Do you prefer an NLM? GroupWise has it. Do you want OS/2 (for some strange reason)? GroupWise has it. You can even run the GroupWise gateway on the same Unix system running your Internet e-mail server software.

F I G U R E   13.1

Beginning GroupWise
WebAccess installation

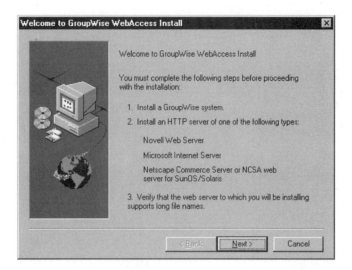

F I G U R E   13.2

Logging in with
GroupWise WebAccess

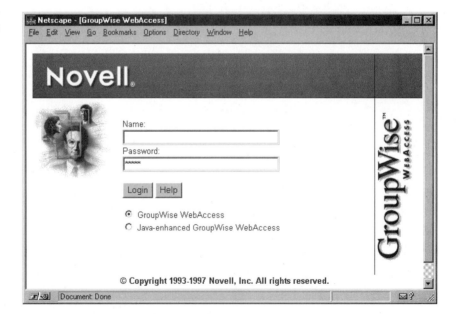

You should have a full-time Internet connection, but it may not be absolutely necessary. For example, a friend of mine sets his system to dial the ISP every 30 minutes to pick up mail messages. So far, the ISP hasn't complained about that arrangement, but talk to your ISP before trying something like this. Messages should address the Internet as a foreign domain, using the format of INT:USER@HOST. Of course, you can put those addresses into the address book, so you won't need to type them each and every time.

Is GroupWise Internet and intranet friendly? Yes, I believe it meets all the requirements. Having an e-mail gateway option running on the majority of the Unix platforms available makes that statement, as does the WebAccess software. It looks like GroupWise has integrated TCP/IP network access as well or better than any other LAN e-mail application.

Sidekick 97 (Starfish Software)

Sidekick is another program from the depths of PC history. Yes, I remember the original Sidekick, in all its primary-color splendor, back on the original PC XT platform. It was fast and smooth then, and it still is fast and smooth. Well, not on a PC XT anymore, but it's still fast and smooth under Windows 95 running on a decently configured system.

Why am I talking about a single-user program in a network book? Excuse me, but Starfish Software (www.starfish.com) released Internet Sidekick in 1996, and rolled all the Internet features into Sidekick 97. What are those Internet features, you ask? Take a gander:

- Communicate with other Sidekick 97 users via Internet e-mail.

- Designate calendars for resources such as conference rooms, vehicles, and computers.

- Schedule meetings, conference calls, and online events via Internet e-mail.

- Publish the Sidekick Cardfiles directly to your Web server (requires the optional Sidekick Web Publisher).

- Launch Web browser from URLs in contact files.

- Import contact information from Netscape, Microsoft Exchange, and Eudora Pro e-mail address books.

Figure 13.3 shows an example of the Sidekick 97 Internet Scheduling Wizard in action.

The trend here is for a PIM (Personal Information Manager) to coordinate with other users of the same PIM over the Internet. All the IETF (Internet Engineering Task Force) work for calendaring and scheduling protocols should take open communications to the point where one PIM can coordinate with another. Until that time comes, Sidekick 97 will do the trick (as will GroupWise, of course).

FIGURE 13.3

Scheduling an event
with Sidekick 97

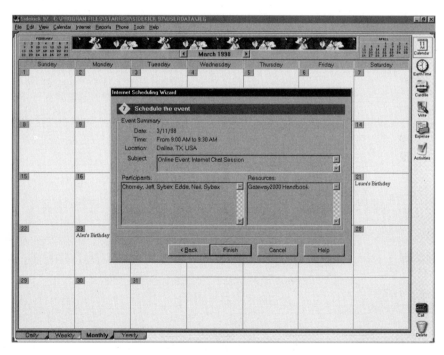

ECCO Pro (NetManage)

ECCO Pro was developed by a small company in Bellevue, Washington, named Arabesque. I first looked at the product in the summer of 1994, and it was version 2.0 then. Bought in 1996 by NetManage, Inc. (www .netmanage.com), the makers of Chameleon PC TCP/IP software, ECCO Pro is now up to version 4.01 and fully Internet-enabled. NetManage also bought the popular Z-Mail Pro client from NCD (Network Computing Devices), and ECCO Pro coordinates well with the e-mail client and all of the other NetManage TCP/IP utilities.

Going down the road of "the outline controls the world," ECCO creates folders and links for every bit of text entered. Outlines can be expanded and contracted at will, and up to 250 users can share a database through peer-to-peer (over TCP/IP) networking without designating a server.

How serious is ECCO for project management? It includes a Gantt chart as part of the product (and has since the beginning). Tie your project to your laptop or PDA (Personal Digital Assistant) to take it with you anywhere. You can even download information to your Timex Data Link watch (if you're that anal retentive or paranoid, or both). I guess if you really like the outline view of the world, the Data Link watch containing outlines of your project notes makes sense to you.

ECCO Pro includes a complete directory of more than 1000 Internet resources, organized into nearly three dozen categories. Take a look at Figure 13.4 for an example. When you find an address of interest, simply highlight it and pick Launch Internet from the Tools menu to start the NetManage Chameleon browser.

There is a small but thriving group of consultants, developers, and trainers following ECCO Pro. Do you need templates made to order for your business? The developers are ready to fill your order. Do you need to pull a Web site into ECCO Pro? You can do that, too. There's little you can't do with ECCO Pro, once you get the hang of it and mold your work patterns to the way of ECCO.

FIGURE 13.4

A handy ECCO Pro listing
of Web addresses

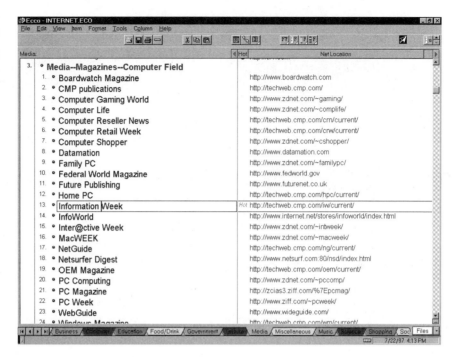

FIGURE 13.4

A handy ECCO Pro listing
of Web addresses

Intranet Genie (Frontier Technologies)

Up in wild Wisconsin, a company called Frontier Technologies (www
.frontiertech.com) is quietly trying to rewrite the story of intranets and
secure transactions. Long a provider of PC TCP/IP products (best known
is its SuperTCP Suite) and the first desktop TCP/IP vendor to provide an
IPX/IP gateway (CyberJunction), Frontier Technologies has a strong suite
of client applications with centralized administration. Its other high-
profile product is CyberSearch, a Web-oriented database and information management and retrieval tool. Check the Web site for information
and free software.

Intranet Genie is literally an intranet in a box. The CD includes the
SuperWeb, CyberSearch Information Retrieval, DNS, Mail, News, and
Network Time Servers. Is there anything left out of the server package?
Not that I can see. Well, maybe an FTP server, but that functionality is

included in the SuperWeb Server software, so there's little need for a separate FTP server.

Clients include Windows 3.*x*/95/NT, and you get all the necessary software to connect the clients to the intranet servers. If you don't want TCP/IP on each workstation, get the CyberJunction IPX/IP Gateway and run it on the same Windows NT server hosting Intranet Genie.

What? Did I say to run it on a Windows NT server? Is this heresy? Maybe, but it is also a good way to put your Windows NT servers to work. You have them hanging off your NetWare network, and most are still running pilot projects while your programmers hack their way through the mysteries of Microsoft's SQL Server, so you may as well put them to work doing something useful. Intranet Genie is only one of several e-mail and Web server packages available for NT. More vendors have written these applications for NT than for NetWare, primarily because Microsoft's marketing juggernaut keeps gaining momentum.

Of course, you can use the BorderManager IPX/IP Gateway in place of the CyberJunction product. You can also use the Novell Web Server software in place of the SuperWeb Server. More likely, however, if your intranet gains acceptance, you'll need all the above.

The combination of BorderManager and Intranet Genie works well together. Using BorderManager's VPN services along with Intranet Genie's e-Lock security modules for Web and/or e-mail access may give some paranoid managers more peace of mind. This way, two companies are providing encryption services, doubling your security value. Intranet Genie's bundled approach may make your system easier to install, configure, and manage, especially for smaller sites without adequate support staff on-site.

Client Software Options

Back in the old days (no, I didn't have to walk to school barefoot through the snow), you had few choices for desktop TCP/IP software.

Now you have many, including minimal built-in TCP/IP support for Windows 95 and somewhat better TCP/IP options with Windows NT.

This doesn't cover the multitude of IPX/IP gateways, all using their own WinSock software tailored to getting your clients on a TCP/IP network as easily and transparently as possible. Do you need more options? Your adventurous clients will find plenty available for downloading all over the Internet.

When you have too many options, life becomes more complicated. Most people chafe at a single source, are happy with three or four choices, but overwhelmed by ten. That's where we are now, with ten or more choices for Internet/intranet/extranet connections.

Recommendation: Focus on Security and Management

I know, you're looking to me for some type of recommendation regarding your client software. Here's my guiding philosophy in this area: Make life as simple for yourself as possible, while answering the needs of your clients.

You may think I'm taking the lazy way out, by putting "make life as simple for yourself as possible" before "answering the needs of your clients." I prefer to regard this method as the most efficient, as well as the most considerate of the company's resources, rather than lazy. I do realize, however, that the harder or more distasteful a task is, the more likely it is to be avoided.

The areas that are avoided most often during planning and early installation are security and management. No project planners include enough management time for active projects, leaving you overworked and underpaid after the project gets rolling. This is tough on you. Lacking enough security, however, can be tough on the entire company.

During the planning stages, put your foot down as hard as possible (without obviously stomping on your boss's toe) about security. Why focus on security? Because, frankly, managers don't care how hard you must work to maintain their poor design. They do care about security leaks, holes, and possible hacker attacks. Play your trump card of security control whenever necessary to ensure that your project will be controllable and that your network clients can be monitored adequately.

The security angle is one of the best reasons to use BorderManager. NDS is still the premier enterprise directory available today, and all the BorderManager parts fit right into NDS. Integrated security and management are two of the big reasons to try the BorderManager IPX/IP Gateway and other products before looking to third-party solutions.

Systems with a single point of control are always better maintained than systems requiring multiple control points. Does your house alarm system arm each door and window separately, or do you set one code for the whole house? How many times do you think you would forget to arm the garage door alarm if you had to set it separately? Managing network systems follows the same hassle rule as anything else: The more hassle, the more mistakes. Try to cut down the hassle factor by emphasizing the management needs of your network.

Client Connection Problems

During testing of a new beta Windows 95 client for BorderManager, my e-mail and newsreader software on my PC quit working. I couldn't connect to my ISP no matter what I did. "Stupid beta software," I said, "I wonder what Novell did to screw me up this time?"

As it turns out, it wasn't Novell at all; it was my mistake. Aren't you glad that I make all these mistakes so you won't have to? The problem was in my DNS configuration.

If you remember all the way back to the NetWare/IP discussion (Chapter 3), I said you can access the Internet over NetWare/IP if your name server is hooked into the Internet. Setting your NetWare server as the DNS name server works great for a closed NetWare/IP system that doesn't get to the Internet, but this setup may cause problems later.

When I dug into the problem with my client software, I found I had reset my DNS name server listing in NWIPCFG to the local NetWare server to help with NetWare/IP. The local NetWare/IP server was not configured to reach the Internet, for a variety of reasons. That's why my e-mail and newsreader client software couldn't see the Internet and my ISP.

Here's a hint for you: If clients start having problems reaching the Internet, check your DNS client and DNS server settings through NWIPCFG and UNICON, respectively. No doubt you changed something and messed it all up. Shame on you. Now go fix it.

Web Server Add-Ons

There's not enough room in this book, or a half-dozen others, to talk about all the plans some people have for new Web server goodies. None of them may apply to your network today, but don't bet that will be the case tomorrow. Never underestimate the fervor of a vice president after reading *Forbes ASAP*. The next time one of the executive-type magazines has an article on Web-based videoconferencing or a way to push corporate propaganda out of the Web server to a set of dealers or customers, you may get a visit. Unlike with alien visitations, you won't wind up in the tabloids. Also unlike with alien visitations, you can't escape from the nightmare by waking up.

Start your plan now for the next "great" idea to roll downhill from the executive offices. After all, they will have no idea about how to implement a Web-based global positioning system tracking each and every field salesperson, but they will expect you to figure it out.

Let's take a look at a couple of "executive" flights of fancy, and see what you and BorderManager may need to support. If the situation is hopeless, remember to list the job search Web servers as "permitted" under the Proxy Server, so you can decide which way to go when you bail out.

Wireless Communications

Ethernet is defined by the IEEE (Institute of Electrical and Electronic Engineers) under the 802.3 label. Token Ring comes under the 802.5 heading. Get ready for 802.7 and 802.11.

The 802.7 specification defines broadband networks carrying voice, data, and video traffic. Did you ever see the old CATV networks popular within large companies back in the 1980s? These were essentially cable TV systems, with various radio frequencies set up for each channel. The idea of using this setup for internal company network transport has pretty much died. Why bring it up? Because all the cable modems and Internet-over-cable projects hark back to 802.7. Be prepared, but don't be too concerned. You shouldn't need to worry about the cable TV company in your area keeping you waiting for two days to hook up your server to HBO and ESPN. Pilot projects are losing money, and no full-scale rollout has been scheduled.

The 802.11 specification is a different story. Wireless LANs now have a standard, and that standard is 802.11, formalized in the summer of 1997. While you will be able to avoid cable LANs for a few more years, wireless LANs are becoming big news once again.

Luckily, you won't have to break out your ham radio books to configure your Web or IntranetWare server for wireless communications. What you will have to do, however, is get involved with some serious design considerations when the executives decide to implement a wireless network for your company.

You will need to configure the system so the wireless network segment stays within the address range inside your Proxy Server and firewall. The majority of wireless systems available or in development connect to traditional Ethernet 10Base-T concentrators. You will be able to treat these wireless segments just as you treat a network segment for a department or floor of your network now.

Although your executives won't consider this, wireless networks are much less secure then traditional cabled networks. The wireless vendors have the burden of proof to ensure signals between the detached clients and your wired network are safe and encrypted.

Let's say your company has a campus headquarters, and your bosses want each and every security officer's golf cart to be connected to your main network. Since radio waves from the golf carts are omnidirectional, the signals go off the campus as well as to the antenna on your main building. Non-encrypted signals can be captured by competitors sitting legally on the sidewalk, monitoring channels and hoping to grab a password or two. Is this far-fetched? Yes, a little, but security will be a problem everywhere with everything from now on. Companies that don't consider all security angles may wind up as the example of bad planning in the next magazine article.

Voice over IP

With the voice-over-IP concept, we get into a whole batch of network problems. The first one is bandwidth. A spoken message takes 500 times more bandwidth than the same message written in an ASCII e-mail message. If your executives want to start running the office intercom over the computer network rather than the telephone system, upgrades are in order.

The next problem with voice communications through your Web server and over your network is "quality of service," sometimes referred to as QOS. If your e-mail message gets delivered in six pieces spread out over four seconds, there's no problem whatsoever. By the time you get the e-mail at your client, all the packets have been assembled by the e-mail server so that they are shuffled down to your client in one piece.

But imagine trying to understand a sentence or two fractured and split over four seconds. The result is worse than the announcements at the airport that no one can understand. In fact, the airport announcements are better, because they aren't interrupted by a two-second delay twice during the reading. Your voice over IP may be.

This means that not only will you need a lot of bandwidth, you will need a way to ensure that voice messages are handled with special consideration and delivered in one piece. I don't know exactly what that method will be, but I guarantee it will take much more server and network resources than anything you're doing now.

What's the moral of this story? When an executive brings up voice over the network, point to the telephone. If that doesn't work, realize your Web and IntranetWare servers are going to work ten times harder than they do now. Budget appropriately.

Wrap

This chapter should help you in selling your project to recalcitrant executives who don't understand that the network is only valuable when it helps people communicate. At least one of the ten projects listed here will make any intranet a success. Pick the idea that gives you the most bang for your effort, and push that project first.

Lack of use will doom your intranet/extranet to failure. Interestingly, overwhelming success may turn the system into a failure as well. The new applications and projects envisioned by developers and executives will swamp your network if you're not prepared. Even in your executive staff members have no clue where they are going, you must. That's the only way you can stay one jump ahead of them.

CHAPTER

14

E-mail in the Internet Era

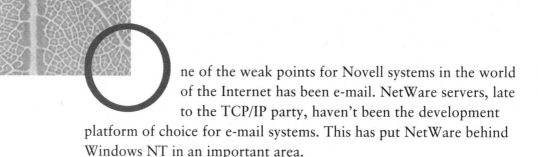

One of the weak points for Novell systems in the world of the Internet has been e-mail. NetWare servers, late to the TCP/IP party, haven't been the development platform of choice for e-mail systems. This has put NetWare behind Windows NT in an important area.

We begin this chapter with a bit of e-mail background and some insight on Internet-based e-mail systems versus PC LAN e-mail systems. However, your users and bosses will demand Internet e-mail, not insight. One way or another, you will need to add some e-mail service to your IntranetWare and BorderManager network. We'll take a look at some e-mail server options, including using your IntranetWare server or your NT server, as well as a few of the e-mail software packages that may meet your requirements.

Once you have decided on your e-mail server and software, you need to consider where it belongs on your network. We'll wind up this chapter by talking about e-mail server locations for intranet and Internet connections.

E-Mail History and Overview

E-mail used to be a simple choice. NetWare included basic DOS e-mail from the early days. Competitor choices included a slew of long-gone companies offering e-mail clients for DOS PCs with a central database on the file server. Some of the companies remaining in the market include cc:Mail (now owned by Lotus/IBM), DaVinci, and Microsoft Mail. As I mentioned in Chapter 13, GroupWise started as WordPerfect Office, and it included e-mail, scheduling, and calendar functions from the beginning.

Early E-Mail Packages

There were a few things missing from the early LAN e-mail packages. Standards, for one, were nonexistent. Your e-mail system talked to itself, period. Connections between your e-mail system and another department using a different brand of e-mail were initially limited to exchanging printed copies of e-mail. Gateways between vendors required one or both vendors to write special applications to convert the format of one system to a format understood by the other. When either vendor revised a version, the gateway had to be rewritten.

Another thing missing from those early e-mail packages was client variety. Of course, for a long time, only PCs could communicate with a NetWare server, so having only a PC client wasn't considered a weakness. When Novell started supporting Macintosh systems back in 1988, e-mail vendors scrambled to develop Macintosh client software.

Has the word "Internet" been seen anywhere yet? No, because during the early days, there were no LAN-to-Internet communications. This link wasn't possible until the early 1990s, and only on a small scale then. E-mail was an intra-company phenomenon only, and limited at that. Linking offices using different e-mail programs was tough to impossible. Linking remote offices, even when those offices were using the same e-mail program, was tough as well, but possible. PCs with dialer programs and queue software saved messages for remote systems and dialed in to those remote servers at predetermined intervals.

This is a fairly bleak picture of the dark ages of e-mail, isn't it? It's no wonder fax machines became embedded into the company communication framework. Take a snapshot of 1990, and you see e-mail struggling and fax machines doing all the important business.

E-Mail and the Internet

What a difference a half-decade makes in the computer business, right? Take the same snapshot at the end of 1995, and you see e-mail systems spawned by the Internet invading corporate LANs on all fronts.

This is as it should be, when you think about it. The purpose of e-mail is communication, and Internet e-mail developed standards, interoperability, and global reach long before the LAN e-mail packages could spell RFC 822 (the e-mail addressing standard).

Since early 1996, the push to replace LAN e-mail systems with Internet-savvy products has become a steamroller. Every LAN e-mail vendor still viable in the market has tried to develop a simple and robust e-mail gateway from the LAN to the Internet. Companies now believe e-mail communicates with people around the world first, and down the hall second. Easy Internet e-mail connections are demanded, and LAN-based systems are being eyed for replacement by Internet-based systems used both inside and outside the company firewall.

These new requirements make sense, but take plenty of extra work for you and the other network managers. Finding, installing, configuring, and supporting an e-mail system is a big job. If your boss insists that you convert all the existing address books (public and private) and prior messages into the new format, you should buy a pair of mittens immediately. Why? Because it's harder to pull your hair out wearing mittens.

Your hair is getting safer all the time, however, at least from being pulled out during an e-mail system upgrade. Each of the major e-mail players is making a big play for existing LAN e-mail customers wanting to upgrade and get into a full Internet mail system. The LAN e-mail vendors themselves are busy making connections easier and more reliable with the Internet, so you won't feel the need to upgrade. The race for your purchase order is on.

Behind Locally, Ahead Globally

It sounds contradictory, but Internet-based e-mail systems are lagging behind PC LAN e-mail systems in two areas:

- A proprietary e-mail system is easier to manage, especially when you are managing mail that is staying within the company.

- LAN e-mail systems handle fancy text formatting and attachments better than Internet e-mail.

It shouldn't surprise you that Internet e-mail vendors are still scrambling to match these LAN e-mail advantages. Let's take a closer look at these areas and see how long we'll need to wait for Internet e-mail to catch up.

E-Mail Management

Proprietary systems are often easier to manage, because one company developed all the pieces. If you have problems, you can call a single support department, wait on hold for a while, and then yell at whoever takes your call.

The downside of this system is that you are limited to the features the developer decides to implement. If all the pieces come from one developer and you have no way to add features yourself, what you see is what you get.

Internet e-mail systems are catching up on the administration front. E-mail server software, once limited to Unix servers, is now available on Windows 3.*x*, 95, and NT servers and workstations, and NetWare servers. Easy-to-use installation and management utilities are becoming commonplace, and integration with NDS is a feature supported by several e-mail server applications.

E-Mail Formatting and Attachments

Another advantage of a closed e-mail system is the control over message format. Since the e-mail developer wrote the client and server software, fonts and formatting will be consistent from one client to the server and back to the recipient. With a single developer, there's no translation between the interpretation of formatting codes of one developer and different codes supported by another developer.

Matching this formatting and attachment control across the Internet is a little more of a problem than providing LAN-equivalent management features. There's no one place to "fix" this problem with Internet e-mail systems, unless you're willing to wait a few more years.

Internet e-mail standards originally supported only ASCII text messages. Remember, this stuff was all being worked out in the early 1970s, and GUIs and fancy fonts were listed under science fiction. This wouldn't be difficult to overcome, except for the development of the Internet routers during the same time. Extended characters, out of the range of normal ASCII text, were used for control characters for the routers. This was a safe way to go at the time, but now we're caught on the sharp end of the dilemma.

Many routers do support extended characters in messages today, and some e-mail software clients can support fancy fonts. Several major client packages now use HTML as the formatting mechanism, a clever choice indeed. HTML uses ASCII codes to request the reading device (Web or e-mail client) to interpret the formatting and font instructions. Simple ASCII codes go across the network, but fancy bold fonts come out the far end.

The HTML feature points to another hitch in transferring formatting between clients: The two clients and servers are often from three different developers. Yes, each client is written to the same set of specifications, but not every programmer reads the specs the same way. Internet e-mail assumes that the two client software packages will be from different developers, and so the message formatting follows the "lowest common denominator" method of programming. Hence, ASCII text is chosen, because every system developer uses the same ASCII text codes.

Attachments suffer the same problem as formatting, since attaching a binary file of any kind requires the inclusion of non-ASCII characters. Early systems started using utilities to convert binary files to ASCII text (UUENCODE) and converting the file back to binary at the receiving end (UUDECODE). Mail systems today often make these adjustments behind the scenes, leaving the user free from the decisions of configuration. System administrators can set the defaults for the installed clients and servers.

New routers in a private TCP/IP network, such as your corporate WAN, won't have these problems. Private networks can use binary attachments without fear, and format to their heart's content, especially when the client software on both ends comes from the same developer. As the software gets better and the routers improve, communicating to remote users over the Internet will pose no more limitations than sending e-mail within the office. We're not there quite yet, but we're getting closer every day.

E-Mail Server Options

As you know, for PC LAN e-mail systems, you had an easy choice when selecting the server to host the e-mail system: Whatever the developer demanded, you had to supply.

When you move into the world of Internet-style e-mail, you find almost the exact opposite situation. The POP3 (Post Office Protocol version 3) and SMTP (Simple Mail Transfer Protocol) server software were developed on Unix systems. There are literally dozens of choices available for every flavor of Unix operating system, including Linux.

For our purposes, we will ignore all the e-mail server options for the world of Unix servers. This may not offer the most complete list of options, but that's not the goal. Since you're reading a book about BorderManager, you most likely have a large NetWare network, not a TCP/IP network full of Unix hosts. There is a chance you run only NetWare servers, and have so far avoided adding Windows NT or OS/2 servers to the mix. (Okay, avoiding OS/2 servers hasn't been too hard, but the Windows NT boxes seem to be spreading like the sniffles at a crowded day care center.)

There's hardly a platform you can name that doesn't have at least one e-mail server package available. My friend David Harrison discovered, in early 1997, Web server software written for the Amiga. So never doubt the existence of software for even the most unlikely platform.

Some ISPs offer e-mail server hosting services, allowing you to skip the choice of an e-mail server platform altogether. However, there are several problems with that setup:

- Lack of security (remember, play on your boss's paranoia when it suits your purposes)

- One-step-removed server management

- The need to route all mail, even from adjoining cubicles, through your ISP

Unless your network is amazingly small and your technical resources are extremely limited, I suggest that you spend the small amount of time and money necessary to set up your own e-mail server.

In most cases, an e-mail server on your site requires a full-time connection to your ISP. In fact, your ISP may (erroneously) insist that is the only way possible. However, there are ways to let e-mail messages queue on the ISP mail router until you connect and download the files. You should talk with your ISP about these details, but you want your e-mail to come to your own domain name if at all possible. Having a full-time Internet connection may be a requirement for your ISP, but not technically for the privilege of retrieving e-mail. Fortunately, prices are dropping for these connections, so a full-time connection may be a good option anyway.

Unless your ISP is very small with limited technical resources, it will offer consulting services, including e-mail server design, setup, and initial configuration. However, ISPs are traditionally extremely biased toward Unix systems, since Unix is what they run for all their Internet connections. If you don't mind adding a Linux or BSD-based (Berkeley Software Distribution) server, your ISP will be an excellent resource. If you want an e-mail server to run on your NetWare or Windows NT system, you may need to take the lead in reaching this goal.

Using Your IntranetWare Server

Your first step in putting an e-mail server on your NetWare or Intranet-Ware server will be to convince your ISP that it is, indeed, possible. Most ISPs don't know how to deal with NetWare, so their tech support people will try to change your mind. Be strong in your decision, and you will convince them to help you arrange the configuration between their e-mail server and yours. You won't change their opinion about the "best" choice, but after a while, they won't moan and complain too much.

Your second step in putting an e-mail server on a NetWare platform is to find the software you wish to use. There aren't a lot of choices, although the list is growing. Let's take a look at some of the e-mail server software options currently available.

N⊘TE   Keep in mind that Novonyx may weigh in with an e-mail server product before long. Novonyx was created to leverage Netscape programs with NetWare's installed base. Its focus is the SuiteSpot Web Server from Netscape (see Chapter 12 for details). However, Netscape makes a pretty decent e-mail server itself. I wouldn't be at all surprised to see a Novonyx e-mail server for sale before the middle of 1998.

GroupWise for E-Mail

First choice among the group of e-mail servers available for your Intranet-Ware server should be GroupWise, if the Novell folks have any influence on your purchasing decision. True, GroupWise isn't a full Internet e-mail system, but the SMTP gateway works well and the addressing back and forth between GroupWise and other e-mail clients is reliable. The ability of GroupWise to support the Web client interface for e-mail gives you flexibility for non-NetWare clients, such as any Unix systems (UnixWare, maybe?) you have. Word is that GroupWise 5.2 will have even friendlier connection options, including POP3 and SLIP.

I'll understand if you think that suggesting GroupWise is stretching things a bit. I just thought I would throw that in, on the off chance that you want to add strong calendar, to-do lists, and beginning workflow features to your network (see Chapter 13 if you're interested in more details). Check out the newsgroup comp.groupwar.groupwise for ongoing discussions and expert opinions. If you want plain vanilla e-mail, there are cheaper options than GroupWise.

Pegasus Mail

Speaking of cheaper, how about free? You're awake now, aren't you? Yes, I said free.

Pegasus Mail, by David Harris (www.pegasus.usa.com) is freeware, although the free license doesn't include spamming. If you spam, you violate not only this license, but the sensibilities of everyone on the Internet. But if you don't plan on spamming (sending tons of e-mail messages to people you don't know to try and sell them something they don't want), the price is zero.

Download the server software from the URL in the previous paragraph, and look at the options available for your system. Quite a body of technical support information has been built up over the years that Pegasus Mail has been available. Questions and answers about Pegasus Mail systems within pure and mixed NetWare environments appear in the Novell newsgroups comp.os.netware.connectivity and comp.os.netware.misc. Check these groups for help in a variety of areas. If you already know what you're doing, you can offer help to those less experienced than you. The good karma points will be worth the time spent reading and answering a few questions.

There are freeware e-mail clients that go along with the freeware server software. Check out Mercury mail and Charon utilities to upgrade your server's abilities. If you already have POP3 e-mail clients, they will work fine with the Pegasus Mail server, and it will connect upstream with your ISP without problems.

IPConnect and WEBserv

Two products from Puzzle Systems (www.puzzle.com) are not free, but they're not expensive either. Puzzle Systems has been in the NetWare-to-Unix/TCP/IP world for a while, and I first covered the company's SoftNet Utilities (emulating a NetWare 3.*x* server on Unix hosts) back in the middle of 1992. Not only did these products prove that the developers understand NetWare and Unix, they also had the easiest configuration and setup of all the systems I tested at the time.

The folks at Puzzle Systems have extended their product line to include two products that provide e-mail server software for NetWare servers:

- IPconnect offers an e-mail server along with IP-to-IP network address translation, IP routing, and firewall services. This competes somewhat with what BorderManager provides, but doesn't include any type of cache server.

- WEBserv includes a Web server (you guessed that, right?) along with an e-mail server, FTP server, firewall, BootP-DHCP server, and last but not least a DNS server. This feature list again overlaps much of what you get with IntranetWare and/or BorderManager.

Both of these products work with NetWare 3.*x* as well as 4.*x*, a feature BorderManager can't match. There are lots of NetWare 3.*x* servers in regular use, especially in small networks and branch offices, that may benefit from either of these Puzzle Systems products. For that matter, you can take an orphaned NetWare 3.*x* license, put it on a 486 system laying around, and support quite a few users with basic e-mail, FTP, and Web server capabilities.

Puzzle Systems programmers have figured out NDS, so when you're running the e-mail server software on a NetWare 4.*x* server, you automatically plug into NDS. Initial configuration is easier that way, since you don't need to type in the names and e-mail addresses of all your users. NetWare 3.*x* servers suck the information out of the bindery, so you still have some advantages over a non-NetWare server platform.

Firefox Mail Server

As I said in Chapter 6, one of the first companies to provide an IPX/IP Gateway was Firefox, started in England. This company's NOV*IX for NetWare was a favorite gateway solution, which was pushed into many accounts by Novell people themselves. The company also produced an e-mail server for NetWare to go along with its other offerings.

FTP Software was one of the very first providers of TCP/IP for the PC world, and buying the Firefox company is an interesting statement about the value of IPX/IP gateways in the late 1990s. The revamped gateway is now sold under the label Internet Gateway Suite version 2.0 for NetWare, which isn't particularly imaginative but does convey the proper information.

Firefox had one of the coolest front screens for system setup, and FTP wisely built upon this platform. Full interaction with Novell directory information is included, and FTP Software uses its own TCP/IP stack.

Firefox always did, because it made its stack before Novell's stack was on the market, and FTP Software has continued in that direction.

For details about the Firefox mail server, check out the Firefox and FTP Software Web sites at www.firefox.com and www.ftp.com.

Using Your Windows NT Server

You might expect that Microsoft's marketing minions have been busily convincing developers of all types of traditional Unix applications to port those applications to the Windows NT platform. You are correct. Microsoft promoters have made pushing Windows NT into the same server space as Unix a top priority. They haven't achieved this yet, and probably won't for the rest of this century, but they continue to focus on the long term.

Having a few extra billion laying around the company vaults and a lock on the extremely lucrative PC operating system market, not to mention a majority of the office productivity suite business, allows Microsoft to take the long-term view. Moving Windows NT servers into the prominent (and critical) position of enterprise servers requires numerous small steps. Each small success for a Windows NT server application is another loss for a Unix server. Each small success of a Windows NT server over a NetWare server moves Microsoft another step toward its goal.

Since you have Windows NT servers around, and there are more options for e-mail server software on the Windows NT platform, you may wind up providing e-mail from a Windows NT server. That's not a big problem, although few of the NT e-mail server applications can read your NetWare directory. Typing the names and addresses into the e-mail application certainly isn't a deal-killer for your boss. After all, you're the one doing the typing.

Is there a problem using a Windows NT server for e-mail? Not at all. The TCP/IP stack in Windows NT is decent, if not complete, and far better than the one shipping with Windows 95. Your NetWare and IntranetWare TCP/IP stack will communicate easily with a Windows NT server. In fact, some of the tests I did for this book used a Windows NT station to test the Novell Web Server software. As far as I can tell, the two systems work well together. Of course, using Novell's Client32 for Windows NT makes for easy communications to NetWare servers from Windows NT stations (see Chapter 15 for details about this client software).

E-Mail Server Location Recommendations

The question of "where to put the e-mail server" has many answers. Smart-aleck readers will instantly reply, "In the server room," and go on to the next section. Physically, they are correct. However, the world we (network administrators and consultants) live in is no longer just physical. Virtually, where you put the e-mail server on your network can make a big difference in security and performance.

Here are the requirements: You want to put the e-mail server where it will be accessible to everyone on the Internet who may wish to send your users e-mail, but where it will also be protected. I believe this is called an oxymoron, meaning a term that contradicts itself, such as "honest politician." In other words, you want to be open, accessible, and completely safe.

Bringing BorderManager into your network may make a difference in your comfort level, since handling the proxy server has not been part of the NetWare experience. It's not too difficult, once you get the hang of it. Just start you configuration a day or two before you need to have it working.

You must create little, tiny security holes in the firewall services of BorderManager to connect users on the inside of the firewall from any e-mail server on the outside. Configure only SMTP, using the system-assigned port 25, and no other protocol.

Ah, you're thinking ahead. Yes, other people know that port 25 is the magic port for SMTP. That's why you must also tag the source address to be *only* the e-mail server. Verify that all other ports and IP addresses are blocked. If your e-mail server requires more connections, remember to tag each one to that IP address only.

For Intranet Connections

For a purely local intranet, e-mail server placement is not a problem. If you have a dedicated e-mail server, which is a good idea if you have hundreds of active e-mail users, then you should put that server on the same backbone as the other file servers. Yes, put it in the server room, and plug it into the same concentrator as the other servers use. There, you're done. Figure 14.1 shows this, just in case you need a basic diagram to help you visualize what I'm talking about here.

Of course, if you have a WAN connection as part of your intranet, you need to put the e-mail server on the network segment that includes the router connection to the remote networks. Your regular NetWare servers should be on this same segment as well, so the advice to put the e-mail server with the file servers is still good advice.

If your intranet is large enough to have multiple servers at multiple sites, you might consider putting multiple e-mail servers around the network as well. It doesn't make much sense to route e-mail between two colleagues in the Dallas office through Chicago. However, if you have plenty of bandwidth between Dallas and Chicago, the delay will be small. But moving e-mail servers closer to the groups they serve keeps them out of your hair, as well as facilitating connections. That may be worth the move right there.

FIGURE 14.1

Put servers with servers

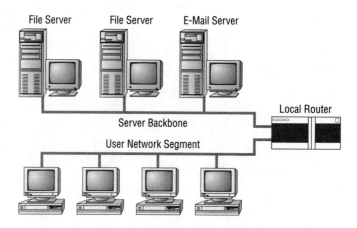

For Intranet and Internet Connections

The real considerations come when you have intranet and Internet connections, all served by one e-mail server. This is typical in traditional TCP/IP networks, and such a setup is no cause for alarm. Your only real concern is to safeguard your e-mail server and the pathway through your firewall that outside e-mail uses.

Stout Unix servers often run TCP/IP routing and firewall software on the same system running the Web, e-mail, and FTP servers. One box does it all. This works well, if your trust your box to stay up and the box is sturdy enough to handle the load.

You may, using BorderManager and e-mail server software running on your IntranetWare server, do the same thing with your network. One IntranetWare server can run e-mail and the BorderManager Proxy Server controls, including all the firewall filtering (covered in Chapter 9), without breathing too hard. Of course, if you are setting up a proxy cache for thousands of users, all going to and from the Internet and sending mail about their adventures, you will need to spend a few bucks on that server. But IntranetWare and BorderManager can handle this scenario, and the diagram is shown in Figure 14.2.

This does illustrate the old saying, "if you put all your eggs in one basket, *really watch* that basket." Good advice in many ways.

Yes, the design in Figure 14.2 does have a single point of failure, and many network designers start hyperventilating when you say those words.

FIGURE 14.2

All the eggs in one basket

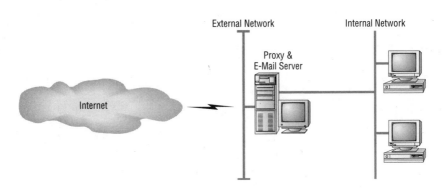

Of course, your boss may start hyperventilating when you budget the cost of redundant networks, routers, firewalls, and access servers of all kinds. Let your management team members pick the hyperventilating component of their choice. You can't have full redundancy and low price on the same network.

Dual-Homed Servers

A more expensive option, perhaps necessitated by high-usage demands, would allow both the e-mail server and the proxy server to link the internal and external networks. Another term for these servers is *dual-homed* servers, since each has two network connections. This network diagram appears in Figure 14.3.

Your e-mail clients on your company network address the e-mail server by the IP address of the connection linking the server to the internal network. The external e-mail servers forwarding messages use the IP address of the connection to the external, or lobby, network. Neither group needs to know about the other IP address on the e-mail box.

Adding details, such as the IP/IP Gateway for network address translation, throws an entirely new level of fun and games into the network design exercise. E-mail servers usually have some type of routing software included, in order to set up their dual-homing designs. Both the e-mail server and the BorderManager Proxy Server have enough smarts

FIGURE 14.3

Dual-homed dual servers

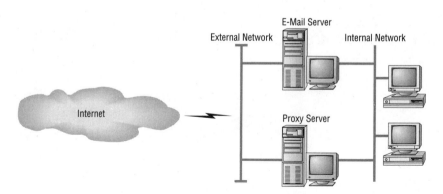

to separate the two networks and keep them separate. And you now have enough smarts to make this work, assuming you actually read the book to this point and haven't skipped to this paragraph. If you did, thumb back and read the parts you missed, with particular concentration on Chapters 8 and 9, where we cover the Proxy Server and security.

Wrap

We could spend a book on e-mail, and many people have. E-mail is becoming more critical for companies every day. Bob Frankenburg, when he was President at Novell, said it best: "You're nobody if you're not somebody at somewhere dot com." Never more true than today. Well, maybe more true tomorrow, but that ruins the catchy saying from my grandmother.

Your company needs to be using an Internet-aware e-mail system. If you already have one, you are to be congratulated. If you don't have one, you have your job cut out for you. Just don't cut too many corners, or you'll leave a big security hole. That's why the e-mail server and proxy server must work together.

C H A P T E R

15

Using Windows NT
with BorderManager

icrosoft has decided that Windows NT Workstation software should be the corporate desktop operating system of choice. This makes some sense, because Windows 95 and 98 (Memphis) don't have the crash protection and separated memory model used in Windows NT. Since many in-house corporate programs use serious databases and handle critical data, the most secure desktop operating system should be used.

Many of those corporate databases are connecting to Microsoft's BackOffice server application suite, which mandates the use of Windows NT Server. This makes sense from Microsoft's point of view, of course, but overlaps into traditional NetWare territory.

The same overlap occurs when companies are deciding which systems to use for intranet Web servers and other servers for intranet- and Internet-style communications and applications. Windows NT Server provides a stable, reliable platform for these applications, and it appeals strongly to companies not versed in Unix servers. Yes, some of these server applications are now available on NetWare servers, but Novell was late to the party and currently has only a small market presence.

For network administrators, this means that you need to accommodate many non-NetWare clients and servers. Because it is very likely that some of those clients and servers are Windows NT machines, in this chapter we focus on integrating NT into your network.

NT versus NetWare: History and Overview

There's no getting around the fact that Microsoft has pulled a clever flanking maneuver around Novell and NetWare with Windows NT. Microsoft spent years going head to head with NetWare, using LAN Manager as its main weapon. This was akin to betting on me in a tennis match versus Pete Sampras. Yes, I can play, but I'm not in that league. (Okay, LAN Manager was closer to NetWare than I am to Pete Sampras, but I'm trying to make a point using an exaggerated analogy—humor me.)

The Battle Plans

While Novell concentrated on improving NetWare, Microsoft concentrated on changing the battle to match its strengths. If Pete and I changed our contest to computer and network trivia, for instance, my chances suddenly improve dramatically. I may not win, because Pete's the champion until beaten, even in a new contest area. But if I get to choose the contest, I can pick my strongest area relative to Pete's weakest area.

So far, Pete is still ahead of me, and NetWare is still ahead of Windows NT. However, there are two battles being fought: the technical battle and the political battle. Microsoft's marketing machine has run unencumbered through the network playing field, declaring Windows NT the winner in the new contest area. Novell's marketing lags far behind, so the political battle goes to Microsoft and Windows NT.

Microsoft's new battle plan moved the contest from network operating systems to application server platforms. Oh, file and print services are still important, but the most important attribute, according to Microsoft, is the ability to support applications. Forget fast file and print service, because Microsoft can't win that battle. Forget directory services, because Microsoft developers are so far behind that curve that they have yet to introduce their answer to Novell Directory Services (NDS) six years after Novell put the technology on the street. Concentrate on application services, says Microsoft, and judge our success there.

Of course, Windows NT has become the corporate application server of choice, by hook, crook, or default. Novell has a poor answer for application services on the server, because the NLM (NetWare Loadable Module) environment is very different from most programming environments. So far, the NLM option has had good luck with network utilities, such as backup and license metering, but bad luck pulling many traditional business applications onto the NetWare server platform.

Windows NT leapt to the forefront of Web server applications, trailing Unix by a wide margin but leading NetWare by the same wide margin. Since most companies that don't have Unix hosts already are hesitant to install them, Windows NT is getting more and more attention in corporate networks.

Your network no doubt has at least one Windows NT system. If it doesn't today, it will tomorrow. You have no hope of converting those NT boxes to NetWare; in fact, you will have to fight to stop management from converting the NetWare boxes to NT. Such is Microsoft's marketing muscle.

I should tell you where I sit with all this. My first job as an independent consultant, after four years of supporting and selling NetWare, required me to use LAN Manager (in the guise of 3Com's 3+ Open) rather than NetWare. I was alternately excited and appalled at the differences between NetWare and LAN Manager at that time. That is still a good description of my feelings, I think. Window NT 4.0 looks familiar because of the Windows 95 interface, but the networking portion still drives me to ecstasy and depression, depending on what I'm doing at the moment.

Novell keeps the enterprise network crown, but Microsoft has stolen the application server/intranet leadership role. There will be an uneasy alliance between the two competitors for the rest of this century, at least. So, our job here is to accommodate both as much as possible, and keep your network from looking like the battle zone it really is.

NDS on NT?

Despite Microsoft's claims to the contrary, I believe an active, distributed directory is essential to networking today. NDS is the only real choice. Microsoft's Active Directory has been announced but won't see the light of day until summer (or later) of 1998. If Active Directory matches all the promise in the Microsoft announcement, it will be on par with NDS circa 1993—yes, five directory generations behind.

Novell is constantly working to pull Windows NT into the network fold. The developers have announced plans for, and will no doubt succeed in, making Windows NT act as a full NDS server by the next major release of NetWare. In fact, they may get NDS ported to Windows NT before the Moab release of NetWare. This means that if you're reading this page anytime in 1998 or later, you may already have the option to run NDS on Windows NT.

I think this is a great way for Novell to turn the tables on Microsoft. Making Windows NT a server for a real, live, distributed database directory service with the Novell name, while waiting for Microsoft to migrate Active Directory from slideware to software, is the perfect trick.

The delay in putting NDS on NT has probably been more political than technical. After all, NetWare 4.1 shipped with a few different drivers that allowed NetWare 4.1 to sit on top of OS/2—NDS and all. Microsoft used to make noises about forcing all Windows NT software to run on the various CPUs that NT supported, but Microsoft has alrady dropped all the CPUs except for the Alpha chip from Digital. (Funny, there weren't nearly as many press releases when they dropped multiple CPU support as when they announced it.)

Suffice it to say that Windows NT isn't so much worse a server platform that it would take the smart folks at Novell three or four years longer than it took to support OS/2 to translate the necessary code from the NetWare operating system to Windows NT. Remember, most of the initial development of Windows NT happened on IBM's tab while Microsoft and IBM were officially "operating system partners." The lower levels of OS/2 and Windows NT are enough alike that the software for OS/2 should be at least two-thirds of the way toward Windows NT support.

NOTE Rumors have always swirled that Novell had a version of nondedicated NetWare that ran on Windows 3.1. Why, for heaven's sake? Because some huge customer (always unnamed, but assumed to be a bank) needed NetWare systems to support less than half a dozen stations for branch office use. The expense of using a dedicated NetWare server for the 10,000 or so branches (the number varied, but was always substantial) far outweighed the hassles of trusting something critical to a Windows 3.1 PC.

Of course, running an NDS client is different (and much simpler) than running the full NDS application on Windows NT. And this is the software we are going to deal with right now. The client part is included in the BorderManager package; you'll find the Windows NT client software grouped along with all the IntranetWare/BorderManager client software on the CD-ROM.

How Does the NT Client Fit with BorderManager?

This looks like a trick question at first, doesn't it? After all, doesn't Windows NT act like any other NetWare client?

Well, yes and no. Novell and Microsoft have gone around and around about this whole client business. Windows 3.1 wasn't a problem, but when NDS became a big deal, Microsoft developers knew that they had nothing to counter with in their own network. So, when Windows 95 came out, the default Microsoft client for NetWare didn't support NDS.

People blasted Microsoft for being so short-sighted. Then they blasted Novell for not having their own client. Then the Novell folks blasted Microsoft for not providing the needed information. Then the Microsoft folks blasted Novell for not providing the information that they needed. Then the circle was unbroken, and people blasted Microsoft some more.

We were all witness to a computer industry action movie: explosions everywhere, but no substance. Meanwhile, network managers like you and I were stuck in the middle, waiting for the smoke to clear.

Fortunately, Novell has taken matters into hand and released a complete Windows NT, NDS-aware client with BorderManager. You can also check the Novell Web site (www.novell.com/intranetware/ntint/) for all the information you need about newer clients, patches, and the like. Novell will no doubt need to release fixes for each one of Microsoft's NT Service Packs (especially if the Service Pack is as bug-ridden as Service Pack 2.0 was).

Installing and Configuring the NT BorderManager Client

The easy way to install the Windows NT client is to use the BorderManager CD-ROM holding all the clients. This is especially fun if you have a sound card in your Windows NT system. You can hear an electric piano (set on vibraphone) chord rolling through all seven notes into a nice fat dominant seventh chord, daring you to continue. If you don't have a sound card, never mind.

Another way to install the Windows NT client is to run the SETUPNW .EXE program from the \PUBLIC\CLIENT\WINNT\I386 directory. This method assumes that you have some means to reach the file server, of course. Your existing Windows NT clients won't have a problem with this.

I'm sorry to report that the client installation process is pretty boring. A welcome screen appears, files are copied, the binding configuration for the Windows NT system gets updated, and finally, a screen says that the installation worked so hit the button to reboot. (I already had TCP/IP configured on the Windows NT Server machine in the lab, so I didn't try to enable any of the BorderManager IPX/IP Gateway features.)

A new login screen appears in place of the Windows NT login screen, but it still has that idiotic Ctrl+Alt+Delete key sequence demanded by Microsoft. This time, however, the logo behind the command is from Novell, not Microsoft.

Login Options

There is a cute little icon with an illuminated packet flashing across the wire, through the computer, and to the monitor (then back again) during the login process. Unfortunately, there's no way to load the screen capture program until after the login process, so I can't show you a picture.

The login page has five tabs:

- **Login:** Lists the current NDS tree at the top of the page, followed by fields for login name, context, and password. A line at the bottom of the screen says, "Network Status," and it should say "Ready." You must fill in your name and password on this screen, regardless of which network system you are using.

- **IntranetWare:** Presents NDS login information, including the tree name, a pick list if you wish to log in to another tree, and a preferred server pick list. In the Bindery Login section, there is a blank field and a radio button labeled Server. Click on that button to see all the available bindery servers appear in a pick list.

- **Windows NT:** Includes a field for the local username, followed by the From field for a domain or workgroup name. There is also a checkbox for Windows NT login only. If you check this box—guess what—you only log in to Windows NT.

- **Script:** Includes fields for Login Script and Profile Script, both filled with <DEFAULT> automatically. There are also two checkboxes: Run Scripts and Close Scripts Results Automatically. Both of these are checked by default.

- **Variables:** Lets you put in up to four login script variables, labeled %2 to %5. If you've always wanted to load up some variables, here's the place to do it.

When you connect to NetWare, after giving your password but not the Windows NT password, you get a chance to check a box to "Change your Windows NT password to match your IntranetWare password after a successful login." A nice touch, don't you think? I'm not quite sure if that makes a lot of sense security-wise, but Novell makes it quick and easy to modify the Windows NT password. On second thought, that's not a good idea, unless you're the only one with access to the physical systems. (Hmm…I wonder how hard it was to write a program to rewrite the NT password?)

Utilities for the Client

You may have noticed some IntranetWare utilities on the CD-ROM, and were curious what they were and if they helped. First is the Windows NT version of NetWare Administrator, called NWAdmnNT (yes, that's how they spell it), and it works fine. According to Microsoft marketing, this should work better on Windows NT than on Windows 95. Unfortunately, all the NWAdmin versions aren't quite on the same revision cycle. It may take a patch or two for the NWAdmin 16-bit version to catch up; Group-Wise users hang on.

The fact that today you can run the NetWare Administrator utility on a Windows NT station seems to indicate Novell has come farther in this forced partnership than Microsoft has. People in Redmond may complain, but I feel that Novell requiring its own Client32 software to support the NetWare Administrator program on Windows NT isn't too much to ask. Of course, I'm not locked in a bitter feud that makes the Hatfield and McCoy unpleasantness seem like an afternoon picnic.

During the addition and configuration of the NWAdmnNT program, a dialog box will pop open asking you to update the NDS schema. At least, it did with mine, and my schema was pretty current, so I'm assuming this message will appear for you. All this is to say that if it does pop up, hit the button to modify the schema. This updating shouldn't take long.

Another neat utility you'll find on the CD-ROM is Workstation Manager. With this program, you can manage Windows NT and Intranet-Ware user accounts.

We'll take a closer look at both NWAdmnNT and Workstation Manager later in the chapter, in the section about managing your Windows NT clients.

Netscape version 3.01 ships on the BorderManager CD-ROM, and you can install that along with everything else. Unlike the Netscape software that shipped with the IntranetWare IPX/IP Gateway, this version of Netscape isn't stylized for Novell. The earlier Netscape version added a nice little Novell *N* in place of the Netscape *N* in the upper-right corner. To indicate the system is working (slowly downloading a file, until you activate your Proxy Cache Server), the Novell balls change from white to black. (No jokes; we're almost finished with this book, and I don't want to get started now.)

Configuring NT as a NetWare Client

When running Client32 (another name for the BorderManager client software you'll see in Novell documentation) on a Windows NT system, whether NT Workstation or NT Server, you may as well be running Windows 95. Things are a bit different under the hood, but the activities seen by users map well with the activities from other clients. Well, there is that little detail about mapping the search drives to Z:\ rather than Z:\PUBLIC, even though the Z:\ is a false root stuck at \PUBLIC.

Windows and DOS search drives are mapped to Z:, which always points to the SYS:\PUBLIC directory. This is where all the NetWare utilities, such as MAP and NLIST, live. Windows NT, for some reason, doesn't support this mapping technique, meaning it won't allow you to treat a subdirectory like a root. Therefore, you have Z:\, instead of Z:\PUBLIC.

NT as a Non-NetWare Client

Here we run across one of the really adventuresome areas of Border-Manager: control of non-NetWare clients. We discussed many places where non-NetWare clients, namely TCP/IP clients, are controlled by Border-Manager's different services, depending on the job. For instance, the Proxy Cache Server doesn't care who or what uses the cache, just that the system has a valid IP address and is authorized as much as necessary to get connected.

You can control Windows NT systems with Novell utilities now, as you'll see in the next section. But you may not want to make your Windows NT stations full NDS members and suck them into IntranetWare; you may just want to cut off their Internet surfing during work hours. You may just want to treat them like any other TCP/IP-based system—no more and no less.

Check back in Chapter 8 to see how to configure Internet Explorer to use the BorderManager Proxy Cache Server (select Options from the View menu, go to the Connection tab, and fill in the IP address of the Proxy Cache Server). Once you have control of the IP packets flowing through the BorderManager server, you have better control than you have with any other proxy server or firewall product.

Be careful in the Internet Explorer setup if you are using Border-Manager in an intranet setting. Version 3.02 of Internet Explorer has an option to ignore the proxy server for local intranet addresses. This may change when Microsoft ships a proxy server with the same level of control that the BorderManager services have.

What about those Windows NT systems, and any other IP systems for that matter, that you can't physically reset to use the Proxy Cache Server. Are those completely out of your reach?

Oh, no, there's always a way. Of course, you must set the BorderManager system at the border between your network and the other networks, such as at the ISP link, that these non-NetWare clients will use.

Look back in Chapter 9 to see where the circuit-level filters are set. It may mean that you need to start blocking FTP, HTTP, and Telnet for network clients that have never had any limits before, so make sure that you and your management are clear on what you're doing. You don't need to block them all out entirely, of course. Even the most wide-ranging circuit-level filter works on a time basis, so you can block out work times, but leave the gates open after hours. Users can't do anything illegal or obscene after hours using company equipment, of course, but they will be able to read their newsgroup messages and visit their favorite fantasy baseball and football league Web sites after 5:00 PM.

Managing NT Clients

After you have your Windows NT clients up and running, how will you manage them? You have several options, including third-party products, the Workstation Manager utility for BorderManager clients, and good old NetWare Administrator.

Third-Party Management Products

Well, if Novell developers can't turn Windows NT into a newer NetWare server, at least they can embrace (and encompass) Windows NT clients as just more NDS clients. And if Novell can't do it, there is at least one third-party vendor that already has a product to merge Windows NT networking into NDS.

Synchronicity for NT, from NetVision, Inc. (www.netvisn.com) helps fill the directory service void left by Microsoft's underpowered Windows NT domain services. Synchronicity for NT ties Windows NT domain user management into Novell's NDS. Using Synchronicity for NT, network administrators use Novell's NetWare Administrator program running on a Windows 95 station to manage Windows NT domain and workgroup clients. Managed users may be a combination of NetWare and NT clients or NT-only clients.

Many Windows NT application servers are guests on NetWare networks, and those NT network clients are subsets of the NetWare world. Providing a single management point for all network clients, as Synchronicity for NT does, makes good sense. Make that point of management

NDS, and you have an even better idea. NetVision may be primarily comprised of ex-Novell people, but at least those developers have a different look and approach to some of the problems in NetWare.

Using Workstation Manager

A nice new little program from Novell is the Workstation Manager for Windows NT systems running as clients on NetWare networks. The utility, included with the Novell Windows NT client software in Border-Manager, allows administrators to manage both Windows NT workstation user accounts and IntranetWare user accounts from a single point of control, using NDS. Yes, NetWare managers can avoid dealing with NT domains using this tool. It's worth twice the price, which means twice nothing.

Download this from the Novell Web site (www.novell.com/ intranetware/ntint/) at your earliest convenience if you have many NT clients to support. It's cheaper than Synchronicity, but it doesn't offer all the benefits of that utility—you still have the straight-line Novell approach.

Running NetWare Administrator on NT

Let's take a look at something just a bit more traditional. Say your boss decides you should have a Windows NT station from now on. Can you work with this?

Figure 15.1 shows that you can. Here's NetWare Administrator running on Windows NT Server, believe it or not, setting up an application for the Novell Application Launcher (NAL).

If you don't have the Windows NT version of NetWare Administrator, the BorderManager installation disk does. You may also download sparkling new versions of Windows NT client software from the Novell Web site at www.novell.com/intranetware/ntint/.

FIGURE 15.1

NetWare Administrator
running on NT

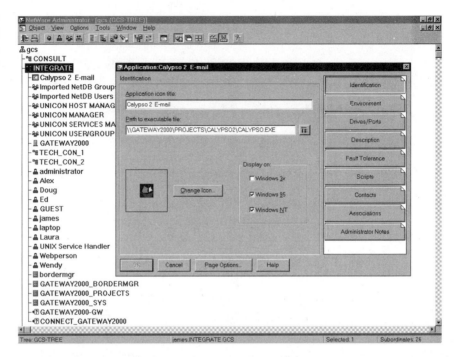

Notice the nice, normal look of NetWare Administrator, even running on an NT station. Do you see any difference from the earlier NetWare Administrator screen shots earlier in the book? Okay, I forgot to back the context up all the way to [Root], which I have as the default on my Windows 95 system. Besides that, do you see anything different?

There are plenty of ways to modify the application command-line parameters, ports the program uses, and even scripts to run before and after the program executes. If you haven't checked out the NAL in a while, you may be surprised.

My favorite page in this dialog box is Contacts. Get there by clicking on the command button that is third from the bottom on the right side of the dialog box. On this page, you can list the names of product support personnel, in case your users have a problem. For a good laugh, be sure and put the newest member of the staff on the hook for the most complex and demanding application. In fact, do your users a real favor, and put the rookie's home address in the contact information as well. Then erase any evidence that you did this, because even rookies know how to spell revenge.

See where the Display On choices are, right about the middle of the dialog box in Figure 15.1? I didn't fill those in; NetWare Administrator did, reading the details of the program.

Calypso, the e-mail client software highlighted in Figure 15.1, is a good product to check out for both Windows NT and 95 users. Get Calypso from my friends at MCS on their Web site www.mcsdallas.com. Tell them I sent you, and you'll get to download an evaluation copy for free.

How does the new version of NAL look? Figure 15.2 shows it looks pretty good. This new version offers various views. In Figure 15.2, I have the hierarchical view on the left, balanced by the detailed view on the right.

FIGURE 15.2

Do you feel lucky? Pick an application.

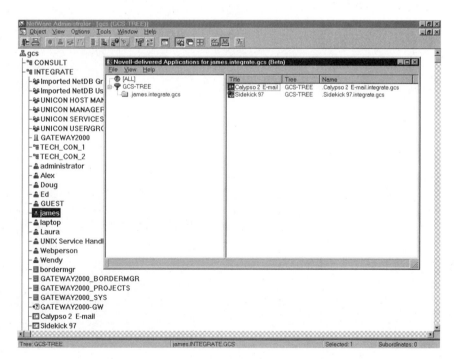

Can you think of anything you can't do with an NT user, after seeing some of these tricks? Full NetWare clients that happen to run on Windows NT fit perfectly well. Users with a foot in Windows NT domains and the other foot in NDS cause more problems, but there are easy answers. Keep an eye on the Novell Web site (cached with Proxy Cache Server, of course) for new and better ways to usurp control over Windows NT network users and slide them into NDS.

NT System Access and Security

The more militant among you may think this title is some sort of riddle. After all, there is no Windows NT in security, because there certainly isn't any security in NT.

You're not quite right, because Windows NT does have security. It doesn't have as good a security system as Novell does with NDS, but no one does. Windows NT security isn't as good as Unix, or OS/2, or AS/400, or HP/UX, or UnixWare, or…. Just because the Windows NT administrator can see the clear text passwords of all users, something Novell fixed in 1989, doesn't mean that there isn't some security in Windows NT systems.

Let's not spend time here trying to figure out how to implement a Windows NT network security policy. There are plenty of NT books out there (several from Sybex, in the Network Press series) that cover security and everything else about NT networking. Rather, let's see how we can integrate Windows NT Web servers into your BorderManager security system, and see if we can protect Windows NT from its own weak (and somewhat confusing) security.

NT Web Servers and BorderManager Security

Windows NT security for its IIS (Internet Information Server) is based on the Windows NT file access security rights. This means your IIS servers must all be running the NTFS (NT File System) format on your IIS disks. You can't restrict users and directories using the FAT file system.

IIS creates an anonymous Web user, based on the name of the host NT server. This user carries the default security profile for all Web clients. Be aware that this user is also a member of the GUESTS group, so any extra authority for that group will create Web server problems.

You can create entire lists of users allowed to view the Web server on a Windows NT system, but that's a lot of extra trouble. If you're going to restrict access in that way, it's better to fold everyone into NDS so you have only one directory service to track. If you can't do that, then at least use the BorderManager Proxy Server controls to limit access to the Windows NT IIS system, rather than maintaining two directories.

Take a look at Figure 15.3. You'll notice the familiar NetWare Administrator screen back on a Windows 95 system once again, where I'm adding some outgoing rules to block traffic from non-NetWare clients. If some non-NetWare clients are driving Window NT machines, all the better for our illustration.

FIGURE 15.3

Controlling non-NetWare clients

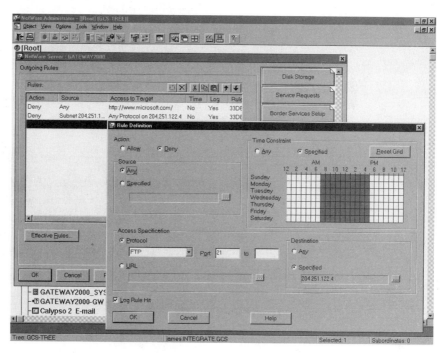

There are three rules illustrated here; two are finished and one is being written as you watch. Notice the background dialog box, labeled Outgoing Rules in the upper-left corner. This shows the two rules already written:

- Block access to microsoft.com. Novell road-show people tell me that during every demonstration, at least one person tries to connect to Microsoft's Web site through the Novell Proxy Server. This human tendency to bite the hand that fed you a continental breakfast is so universal that Novell folks don't even mention this blocking ability until someone tries to reach Microsoft, because it always happens. Other attendees to the session pay more attention after they see the message blocking Microsoft than they do when you just tell them about the feature.

- Deny any station on the 204.251.123.0 subnet to reach the Windows NT server hosting the Web server at address 204.251.122.4. All stations from the listed network, 204.251.123.0, are permanently blocked from reaching this Web server; that is, if the only route from their network to this one passes through the proxy server (and it should, or your network has more problems than I can address here).

The dialog box in the foreground, labeled, Rule Definition, is doing exactly that: defining a rule. This rule again limits access to the Windows NT Web server. Makes you wonder why I have a Web server if I won't let anyone see it, doesn't it?

Here, the rule limits FTP connections to the Web server, listed by IP address in the lower-right corner, during the work day. Notice the flow from the upper-left corner from left to right, then down, then left to right once again, used to create the rule:

1. Define the action (Deny).

2. Set the time (blocked 7:00 AM to 5:00 PM daily).

3. Set the protocol (FTP).

4. Set the blocked destination (204.251.122.4).

5. Activate the logging of failed attempts (Log Rule Hit checkbox).

That's how easy it is to create a rule. Our rule here blocks all access using FTP to the Windows NT Web server during work hours, including Saturdays and Sundays. Once this rule is saved, the Windows NT box will serve no FTP clients during the day. Yes, I realize you can set these same rules on the Windows NT box itself, but one of our goals is to manage only one directory service.

Short of absorbing your Windows NT network into your NDS structure, these are the options you have. Replacing the NT domains with a real directory service isn't a bad idea, but your boss may not give you that permission. At least you now know how to control access to the Windows NT Web server, even if you can't absorb the Windows NT server into a real network.

Coordinating NetWare and NT for Your Intranet

One of the better books around describing how to build an intranet out of a mixed bag of servers and clients is *Building Intranets on NT, NetWare, and Solaris: An Administrator's Guide* by Morgan Stern and Tom Rasmussen, available from Sybex (the Network Press series). My quibble with this book is that the authors ignore the idea of IPX/IP gateways. This means I've read their book, but they haven't read any of mine. I'm a big believer (in case you hadn't noticed) in the values of an IPX-to-IP gateway, whether from Novell or a third party. Any gateway is better than no gateway, if you have more than a handful of NetWare clients to introduce to TCP/IP.

In spite of the obvious oversight, this book makes a nice addition to your reference shelf if the intranet is your new goal. One of the helpful portions is the listing of all sorts of software available by platform. Do you need a new e-mail client for your UnixWare systems? The authors list the options. Do you need to learn how to install a new server on your Windows NT system? The book has a chapter just on installing Windows NT intranet services.

Intranet Security

Organize your network using BorderManager for all security. A diagram of a simple intranet, with a single connection to the Internet, is shown in Figure 15.4. For the sake of this chapter, let's agree that the intranet Web server is a Windows NT server.

Notice the two Windows NT servers in Figure 15.4, one at each end of the network. You probably don't need separate servers for intranet Web and e-mail servers, but this helps illustrate the flexibility of network design options. In fact, since I didn't put an IntranetWare server anywhere in the picture, this could even be a Windows NT network using BorderManager for connection to the Internet and for security. Most likely not, but this idea would work. In a lightly loaded network, the IntranetWare server hosting the BorderManager software can easily handle all the file, print, and security traffic.

All the internal traffic will stay on the inside of the BorderManager server. Even if you used the IPX/IP Gateway function on the Border-Manager box, all the intranet traffic would go back out the same

FIGURE 15.4

Applications on NT, but security and gateways on BorderManager

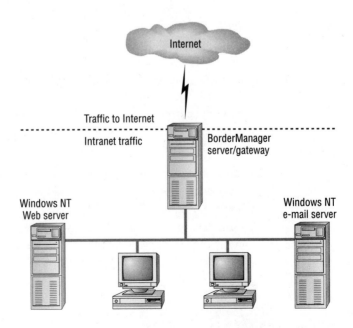

network connection it came in. Only traffic that was addressed to outside network resources, and was allowed to do so by the BorderManager software, would go out to the Internet.

Windows NT Intranet Software

Windows NT has plenty of software options for intranet products, including several complete intranet suites such as Frontier Technologies' Intranet Genie. One Windows NT server loaded with Intranet Genie becomes a complete hub of intranet software, powerful enough to run almost any imaginable software-based project. The Intranet Genie package includes:

- SuperWeb Server

- Document Indexer

- News Server

- POP3 E-mail Server

- Domain Name Server

- CyberJunction IPX to IP Gateway

- Serial Number Server

The client software includes clients for all the above servers, of course, plus Web page creation and administration tools. Add Frontier Technologies' handy CyberSearch utility, and there's little or nothing you can't do with your intranet. For more information about these products, check out the company's Web site at www.frontiertech.com.

My opinion is simple: use the Windows NT systems you're stuck with for application servers, but not file servers. Put products such as Intranet Genie, or various Web server software, on the Windows NT boxes, but don't put any other network functions on your Windows NT machines. Don't trust a Windows NT server for your network security, unless you add an expensive firewall package. Then you'll just be wasting your money, because BorderManager offers more features and better performance for less money.

Wrap

Can you get the encroaching Windows NT servers thrown off your network? Probably not. Can you integrate them into NetWare in a variety of ways? Yes, you can. Can you bypass Windows NT for all the important network operating system functions, such as security? Absolutely.

Make your peace with Windows NT. You won't stop it, and you will be required to support more and more systems running Windows NT unless you quit the business to grow sweet potatoes in East Texas.

Just do what you can to keep critical functions on the appropriate server platform for your network. Windows NT and NetWare can coexist, if each refrains from taking bites out of the other. Whether these two long-time competitors can stop the war long enough for the market to stabilize for a bit is up to them. Knowing human nature, however, I would always bet on conflict and against stability.

APPENDIXES

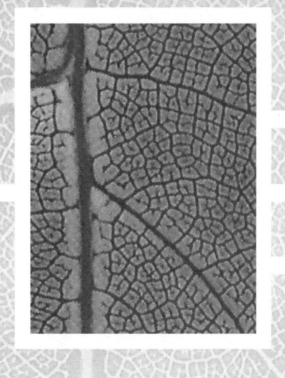

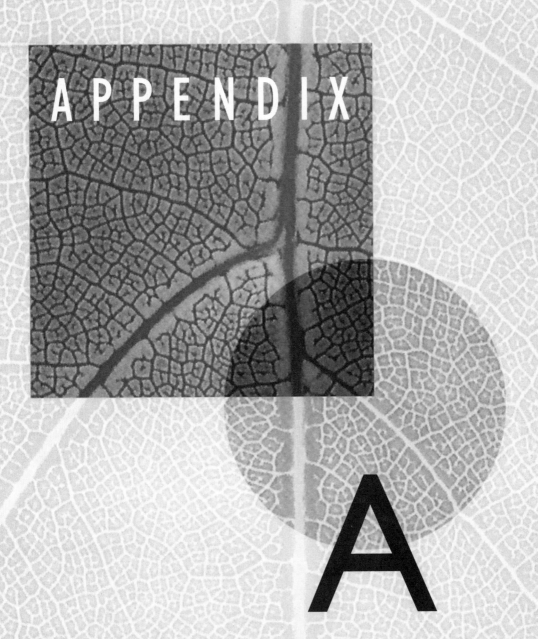

APPENDIX

A

BorderManager Case Studies

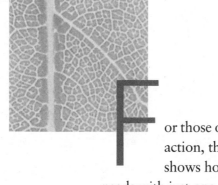

For those of you who want some examples of BorderManager in action, this appendix presents two case studies. The first one shows how a smaller network adds all the Internet services it needs with just one BorderManager server. The second case study is the true story of a well-known company's use of BorderManager services.

Case Study 1: A Small Network

This isn't a single case study; it's what the journalists call a composite, made of several cases all put together neatly to eliminate the messy details. You know, those messy details in life, such as cheap bosses and incomplete shipments from your vendors (here's your computer, complete except for the hard disk that's back-ordered for five weeks).

The Initial Setup

A small network can be supported easily by a single BorderManager server. In fact, as you'll see later in this appendix, a large network can also be supported by a single BorderManager server. This server can provide all sorts of benefits, including acting as your firewall, Web server, IPX/IP gateway, and even e-mail server with third-party software.

Let's start with a nice little network of about 60 users, supported by two NetWare servers. There are two servers so that the programmers can have their own and quit overloading the main server with compile sessions that suck CPU cycles faster than an industrial-strength Hoover.

The two servers support the office automation, accounting, and sales departments on Server 1. This server and users have their own wiring concentrator, connected to the wiring concentrator supporting Server 2. This side of the network, and Server 2, handles the aforementioned programmers, developers, and database users. The two wiring concentrators are separated by a physical-layer bridge, which helps keep the traffic loads on the programmer side from bleeding over into the "office" network. Figure A.1 shows this somewhat typical network arrangement.

The office users can get access to Server 2 without a problem, but the traffic on Server 2's network doesn't get on the office network. Physical bridges used to be a hot item, but they have lost popularity in favor of switches and routers. The one in our test network still works perfectly well, however, and does segment the traffic as desired.

FIGURE A.1

A small but separated network

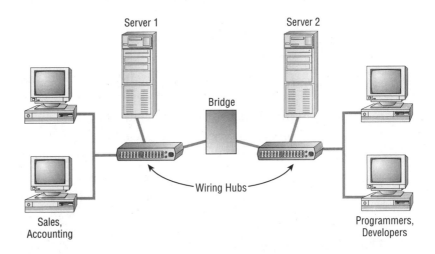

The Goal

The goal is to add a Web server, e-mail server, and Internet access for all network users as inexpensively as possible.

Now the trick becomes where to add the BorderManager suite of Internet access tools for the best protection. Should the company scrap the bridge and buy a switch or local router, no matter how much it costs? Can the company avoid buying TCP/IP software for each user workstation? Does the company need to buy Windows NT to get the Web server?

Our mythical company could do everything with the two servers already in place, but the president of the company vetoed that idea. He didn't have enough patience to listen to the whining of whichever vice president "lost" her network server to the project. So, a third network server, supporting as many of these extra pieces as possible, was introduced into the mix.

With the budget in mind, the server selected wasn't a high-end super-server, but a regular Pentium 166 in a tower case, with 64MB of RAM and a 1.5GB hard disk. Another wiring concentrator was bought, bringing the total to three. The company's ISP convinced the customer to use an external Ascend ISDN router for its 128Kb network connection to the Internet. This connection needs to support incoming e-mail and Web server traffic, as well as outgoing Internet traffic. Unless the managers allowed everyone to surf the Web at the same time, they should have plenty of bandwidth.

In order to get the Novell Web Server software, a five-user version of IntranetWare was obtained by upgrading an unused NetWare 4.11 operating system license. Using the BorderManager software by itself, with a third-party software package like Puzzle Systems WEBserv, would work just as well. There are no plans to use the BorderManager server for any file and print services, so the two-user IntranetWare runtime shipped with BorderManager can handle everything.

The Configuration

Here's how the BorderManager server was configured:

- Enable the BorderManager IPX/IP Gateway.

- Start the Proxy Cache Server for Web client acceleration.

- Program the Novell Web Server.

- Load the Pegasus e-mail server software.

The BorderManager IPX/IP Gateway software is necessary to run all the various Web-derived software, such as the Netscape browser included with BorderManager, e-mail client software for communication to Internet e-mail users, and other utilities. As you saw back in Chapter 6, any TCP/IP-based software you need will run on the client software provided by the BorderManager IPX/IP Gateway.

Even if one BorderManager server provides your IPX/IP gateway and Web server host, you still gain performance with the Proxy Cache Server because it caches the material perused by clients, no matter where those clients originate within your network. If our sample company adds internal TCP/IP systems in the future, it will also be able to reference the Proxy Cache Server for better performance.

Loading the Novell Web Server software enables any file on any NetWare or IntranetWare server to be offered to Internet clients. There is some work to be done for organization's sake, of course, but all the power of a Unix Web server is now available on the IntranetWare server.

For network clients, getting to the Internet means getting Internet e-mail more than using the Netscape browser. Adding the Pegasus e-mail server software to the BorderManager server makes the most sense, because that way only one NetWare server has TCP/IP software loaded. All of the local clients can reach the BorderManager server, as you can see in Figure A.2.

Another matter of importance: The use of the BorderManager IPX/IP Gateway makes the security for this network absolute. Server 2 acts as a router for the BorderManager server, as you can see in Figure A.2. Since there are no TCP/IP clients on the inside of the network, no firewall services are necessary.

However, to placate a paranoid boss, the network manager had to add filters and block all TCP/IP packets at Server 2. This is overkill, perhaps, but it doesn't cause any problems. Only IPX traffic goes from the clients out to the BorderManager server, and only IPX packets will return, since the BorderManager IPX/IP Gateway converts the TCP/IP from the Internet into IPX packets. If some local TCP/IP clients are added, then this network

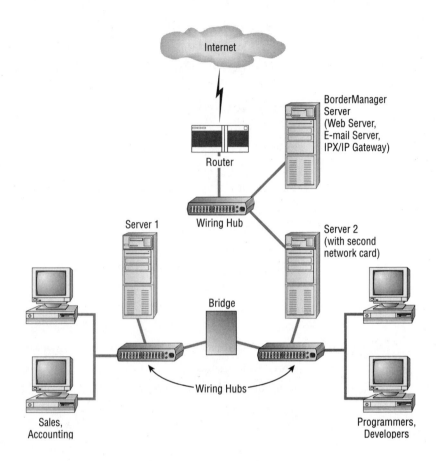

needs to have the firewall and firewall proxy services enabled and start actively blocking packets from unknown sources.

Here we have solid network security, an IPX/IP gateway allowing every client access to the Internet, and a Web server—all set up with BorderManager. See there, I told you a few tricks would be picked up reading this book.

Does this design work? Every NetWare client has access to the Web, using BorderManager's included Netscape client software. Every NetWare client has e-mail access, using the Netscape client e-mail software, or any other e-mail client software that communicates with a POP3 server. The

Web server for the company is available for all internal and external users to view. No TCP/IP packets get past the BorderManager server and the second network interface card in Server 2. Yes, this design, and several variations, work perfectly well.

Case Study 2: www.novell.com

Novell has taken plenty of lumps in the computer trade press over the last few years for being too "product"-centric rather than "customer"-centric. In other words, Novell is accused of making products that are easy to make rather than giving customers want they want.

The primary problem with "giving customers what they want" is that they often, truly, don't know what they want. If you are a consultant, you know exactly what I mean. If you work for a company in network support, you know exactly the type of requests made by non-technical management on a regular basis. If you are a member of non-technical management for a company, shame on you. And why are you reading this book, anyway?

No, people don't know what they want—they want what they know. Almost all "solutions" requested by companies are extensions of the types of tools they already have, and won't solve their long-term problems at all. There is great value in having a company such as Novell, with years of technical product development experience, drive the market with certain products. In fact, our case study of www.novell.com shows exactly what happens when new approaches are applied to existing problems.

Novell itself is an excellent example of Web site development, growth, false starts, redesign, and rescue. In this case, Novell has been rescued by BorderManager's suite of Internet technologies. In fact, a strong case can be made that the Proxy Cache Server component of BorderManager was written to solve a specific problem for Novell's own Web site. After all, for 15 years, Novell has dominated the LAN marketplace, not the Web server marketplace.

The Initial Setup

The problem facing Novell grips many companies today, large and small. A Web server is strategic, providing visitors and potential customers up-to-date information about products, services, solutions, and sales. Like many successful sites, www.novell.com handles large amounts of traffic, and demand is growing.

Web sites must be available 24 hours per day, 7 days a week, usually expressed as 24x7. After all, you never know when a potential customer will look for information. In addition, global companies must find ways to provide the best possible performance for customers all over the world. This problem is compounded by poor telecommunications infrastructure in many countries outside the U.S. Links between some countries and the U.S. are poor and slow in many cases, so the wait for Web page updates from halfway around the world to Provo, Utah (Novell headquarters), can be painfully long.

A significant investment of time and money is required to keep a large and dynamic Web site up and running, but no one likes to spend more than necessary. Yes, Novell is a large and successful company that understands that computers are a necessary expense for business, especially technology businesses. However, upper management everywhere can be just as obtuse as your upper management, and Novell departments face many of the same struggles you face. Take heart.

Novell recognized the value early on in providing a strategic online corporate presence. Starting in the mid-1980s, Novell maintained a large set of forums on CompuServe. Interested parties worldwide received product, marketing, sales, and support information through multiple CompuServe forums and file download sites. For a long time, you could buy a Novell membership for CompuServe, and get access to the NetWare forums and download areas for less money than what was charged for full CompuServe membership. (I didn't check, but I don't believe those deals are still available.) As the Web developed, Novell realized a corporate Web site could provide better service to more people around the world than any other alternative. (Those with CompuServe stock are put on notice: If you haven't already seen this coming, you should lose money on your investment as a "stupid" penalty for not paying attention.)

All Novell departments moved from CompuServe to an outside Web hosting facility (with the exception of Support, which moved in-house). This actually makes sense, and many of the most popular Web sites are hosted by large (often national) ISPs. The hosting services usually have lots of hardware to throw at a Web site, although you are sharing a server with several other companies in almost every case. Novell's Web site ran on multiple UnixWare 1.1 servers, probably provided by Novell.

NOTE The good news is that ISPs are at least one, and sometimes two, steps closer to the Internet backbone than you are. Hosting your own Web site automatically delays client response the length of time it takes requests and responses to come to your ISP, down to your site, and back up to the ISP.

Early Web publishing limitations required many departments within Novell to create separate Web servers. (Yes, the same lack of coordination and intelligent management you put up with each day hinders large, successful companies as well.) Each department and connected server had their own content information, style, and presentation method. Everyone did things their own way, regardless of every other department.

The Goal

Coordination was necessary. Novell hired a corporate Web master, who reevaluated the Web design. The redesign goals were to maintain 24x7 reliability, support ever-growing demand, and streamline content development and presentation. Facing this new Web master were multiple NetWare sites all under the Novell umbrella, such as corp.novell.com, network.novell.com, and education.novell.com, along with a few others, all renting space on an outside Web hosting firm.

Novell started two projects:

- Centralize the Web content for manageability. Hosting the Web at Novell funneled information distribution and updating to a single site, rather than multiple servers around the world. In-house Web servers also meant that redundant servers for fail-over support were close at hand and under Novell's control. Since Novell already had internal 24x7 support, this made sense in its situation.

- Distribute access to Web server information internationally. A way had to be found to improve performance to users and potential customers in remote countries. Novell is a multinational corporation, and customers everywhere need quick and easy access to hosts such as those that hold the support files for patch updates.

The Configuration

Using UnixWare 2.1 servers for the updated Web hosts, the central Web master had two adjacent mirror servers to provide redundancy. All had their IP addresses registered as www.novell.com, so all three would share the load.

Originally, only the home page ran on the three servers and referred all links to the outsourcing location. Yes, it seemed like overkill to have three stout servers to supply a single page to Internet clients. Statistics were needed to see the traffic levels generated by a single Novell site for worldwide Web queries. Figure A.3 shows the physical locations of the servers and the bulk of the corporate information.

Novell started with a single T1 line, but the traffic levels soon demanded two. After several more months, six T1 lines were needed, and the demand curve still headed skyward. (See what I mean about managers not providing the necessary tools until you show them page after page of statistics detailing how your inadequate funding impedes progress to the assigned goal?)

The Web server content was (painfully) reorganized to follow a common design style, authoring template, and filenaming conventions. It was

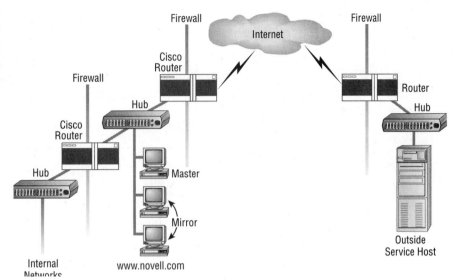

FIGURE A.3

Home page here, but other content still at Web hosting service

impossible to copy the existing Web servers onto one new Web server because the filenames were constantly duplicated. Combining site content had to be done by hand.

Once organized a bit better, the content was split 50–50 between the outsourcing host and Novell. Server utilization suddenly became a critical problem. The choices became clear: buy a larger server or balance the load with other servers. Traditionally, hardware vendors start circling like vultures, waiting for your performance to die so that they can swoop down and offer upgrades.

Novell managers didn't fall for that one, but they didn't control things well enough anyway. The Support department set up mirror sites of support.novell.com in the United Kingdom, Germany, and Australia. Performance improved, but content coordination became a problem. Replicating information around the Internet is difficult, especially since connection speeds across the oceans can be slow.

The search for speed, hopefully not hardware-driven, was on. Novell's Web master found references to the Harvest and Squid research, and checked their use on several large Web sites. Check back in Chapter 8 for details on how these technologies were developed. Still available under public GNU license at the time, the Squid caching software was downloaded, compiled, and placed on one of the outsourced servers, but the software was installed between the network connection software and the Web server software. The load on that server dropped dramatically.

> The GNU is a group of volunteer programmers who make software available for free, for which you promise to provide upgrades and new programs for free as well.

Wondering about caching remote servers, the Web master put the Squid cache on a system in San Jose, California. Again, the Squid software was placed between the network connection and the server software, but this time the placement was physical. The test Squid server was placed at the border between San Jose and the link to Provo.

The Squid software was configured to cache the corporate www.novell .com server in Provo. The response times for San Jose Web requests drastically increased, and the San Jose site suddenly had near-instantaneous access to Novell's content. What was the system that made this tremendous improvement? It was a 486/66 PC with 16MB of RAM and 100MB of disk space allocated to the cache. Was this a big capital expenditure? No. The Web master had found Web management Nirvana: an inexpensive system that cut the server load by more than half.

After a year of running a large and successful Web site, the Web team realized the two goals of central management and distributed performance weren't mutually exclusive. Advanced caching technology helped clients from everywhere when the caching server was placed near the Web servers. When placed a far distance from the Web server, the cache servers kept track of requested information and provided that information to nearby users at local access speeds, rather than the slow speeds of international access.

Novell engineers in Provo had been working on their own caching server software, as you might imagine. NetWare has the best file and directory caching in the LAN business, and the engineers wondered if that lead could include Web cache software. BorderManager now includes routines developed by Novell engineers based on years of NetWare and IntranetWare caching algorithms.

Can I give you some performance figures? How about the combined product of Harvest, Squid, and NetWare cache technology now supports up to 3800 connections per second. This translates into 32MB of throughput per second. That figure is roughly the actual throughput you get from a T3 (45mb per second) line.

These performance numbers are an order of magnitude greater than competitors. In other words, BorderManager is more than ten times faster than existing Windows NT and Unix solutions.

Novell now uses BorderManager and Web server acceleration (Proxy Cache Server) to cache the huge central site in Provo. This takes the load off the physical servers and provides extra protection for the Web servers.

Setting the Web accelerator outside the corporate firewall, yet inside the outer firewall, gives Novell extra security and ease of administration. Most Web server designs call for the server to be outside the corporate firewall, in the lobby area of the network. There is a router/firewall connection to the Internet, the Web servers, the internal network firewall, and the internal network.

Novell puts only the BorderManager servers in the lobby network, and the Web servers themselves are inside the company firewall. This design makes access to the Web servers simpler, since the Web master and other developers need not go through the firewall to reach the Web server. The only requests honored by the Web servers from outside the firewall are those from the BorderManager servers. Only the BorderManager servers are contacted by Web clients, since the BorderManager servers proxy the Web servers themselves, and answer all requests for Web services.

Figure A.4 shows the final result of all the network changes. Notice how the Web servers are all inside the internal network firewall. This is not typical, because no products heretofore allowed this combination of security and performance.

Remote BorderManager servers running the Web accelerator cache software provide close connections for remote users. All the material that users

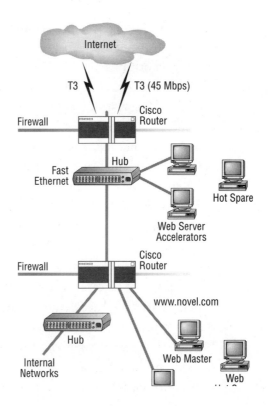

want and have requested in the near past are provided to these remote users at local speeds. Since each Web server packet request hop takes time, the more hops you can eliminate the better. Using a cache model rather than replicated remote servers keeps the information current. Any changes at www.novell.com are quickly filtered back into remote cache, without the Web master controlling a replication process.

According to Novell, the internal Web servers supported by Border-Manager are relieved of 90 percent of their processing load. This speaks loudly, because Novell gets more than 1,000,000 hits per day.

Expensive hardware upgrades were postponed initially, and are now canceled. Web response for clients all over the world is faster than ever. In this case study, WWW now stands for Win Win Win.

APPENDIX

B

Patrolling the Web with Cyber Patrol

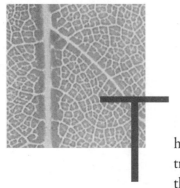

The Internet, being wild and woolly, is considered a giant distraction by most companies. They hesitate to let users reach the Internet because they fear the loss of productivity.

Other companies hesitate to allow Internet access for legal reasons. When companies install Internet access, they are assumed to know the type of material on the Internet. This material includes hate speeches and obscenities, both of which have created what the lawyers call a "hostile working environment." In other words, posting certain material offensive to specific groups, such as minorities, women, and sane and rational members of society, creates an atmosphere in the workplace that is unacceptable. Lawyers specializing in these areas often have multiple Mercedes' in their driveways. In other words, if you put up Internet access, you better put in some protection to stop some employees from downloading and displaying inappropriate information.

Microsystems Software, Inc. developed the Cyber Patrol program to work along with individual Web browsers. Using lists of known sites specializing in all sorts of material offensive to most people, Cyber Patrol became one of the leaders in assuring parents that they didn't need to watch over their children's shoulders every minute those kids were on the Internet.

It wasn't long before Cyber Patrol and its competitors were designing network-based software for company use. This makes sense, because the things most attractive to 12-year old boys are generally inappropriate for the business day (sometimes extremely inappropriate, depending on the 12-year old boy).

With the defeat of the Communications Decency Act during the Supreme Court appeal, the government agents may (finally) get off their censorship kick on the Internet and focus more on filtering technologies. Companies such as Microsystems Software, Inc., should make a bundle as more people realize Internet connections are mandatory, but so is a controlled and productive work environment. Including a copy of Cyber Patrol with BorderManager is a smart move on the parts of both vendors, Microsystems and Novell.

> If you haven't decided how to deal with the "distractions" of Internet access, do so before you connect your user community. I could also tell you to check out my book, *Corporate Politics and the Internet: Connection Without Controversy* to help you define an acceptable use policy for Internet access, but that could be misconstrued as an attempt to coerce another commercial transaction. Oh, go ahead, it really will help keep the lawyers out of your hair and off your doorstep. And it's darn near as funny as this book, believe it or not, before you get to the lawyer jokes.

How Cyber Patrol Works

Your copy of BorderManager has all the necessary tools to configure your filters to match the performance of Cyber Patrol. But the time you would need to spend is enormous. What Cyber Patrol and competitors (Net Nanny, SurfWatch, Watchdog, and others) sell more than their software is their lists of good and bad sites, broken down by category.

You've heard of "giving away the razor, but charging for the blades" haven't you? These companies work on the same principle: Give away the filtering software and charge for the ever-changing lists of inappropriate sites. That's a great way to build in customer loyalty over the long term, which is a polite way of saying you've got them by their, ahem, pocketbooks.

Checking URL Requests Against Lists

Let's look at how all this restricting and allowing happens in Border-Manager (which is about the same as it happens with other proxy servers and firewalls with proxy features). For our purposes, let's consider how a URL request is checked against a list of denied sites:

1. The request comes in to a proxy server supporting Cyber Patrol.

2. Is this an authorized user?

- Yes—continue.

- No—deny request.

3. Read the site address (URL) requested.

4. Check the NOT list.

- On the NOT list? Request denied.

- Not found on the list? Continue.

5. Route out the proxy server to the Internet.

Do you see anything unusual here? A request, if it's from an authorized user, is checked against a list of known inappropriate sites. If the requested URL matches an address on the list, the request is denied. If no match is found, the request is passed on to the router for further transmission. The software in question could block intranet and extranet sites as well as the Internet, but in most cases, the Internet is the packet's transport to the destination.

If you are in the school and/or education business, you may be glad to find out that Microsystems has a CyberYES list to go along with its CyberNOT list. The CyberYES list is filled with fun and educational sites suitable for children. Load this list in your proxy configuration, and you can turn the little darlin's loose with a clear conscience.

The list changes regularly, as do the sites that different vendors track. Some products can filter down to the page level, meaning you can block some pages of a site but not all pages. (That doesn't make much sense to me, honestly—if a site has some pages inappropriate for the work day, block the entire site and don't look back.)

Again, you can set BorderManager to filter out addresses you want to block from your users (as I explain in Chapter 9 of this book). However, the time spent configuring the "block" list would be enormous, and each day more new inappropriate sites will appear that must be tracked and added to the "block" list. Cyber Patrol is worth the money, because you and the other network managers don't need to do this yourself.

CyberNOT List Definitions

Since we're on the subject of creating lists of inappropriate sites, let's see what the developers of Cyber Patrol put on their lists. You can see all the categories within the BorderManager configuration, but not many details. Here, copied with permission, are the list definitions, directly from Cyber Patrol's Web site at www.cyberpatrolcom:

Microsystems Software has used what we believe to be reasonable means to identify and categorize CyberNOTs, but we cannot guarantee the accuracy or completeness of our screens and we assume no responsibility for errors or omissions. Please report errors and omissions using the Site Investigation Report.

Category Definitions - 5/7/97

Any on-line content that contains more than 3 instances in 100 messages. Any easily accessible pages with graphics or text which fall within the definition of the categories below will be considered sufficient to place the source in the category.

- Violence/Profanity (graphics or text): Pictures or text exposing extreme cruelty, physical, or emotional acts against any animal or person which are primarily intended to hurt or inflict pain. Obscene words, phrases, and profanity defined as text that uses, but is not limited to, George Carlin's 7 censored words more often than once every 50 messages (newsgroups) or once a page (web sites).

- Partial Nudity: Pictures exposing the female breast or full exposure of either male or female buttocks except when exposing genitalia. (Excludes all swimsuits, including thongs.)

- Full Nudity: Pictures exposing any or all portions of the human genitalia. Please note: Excluded from the Partial Nudity and Full Nudity categories are sites containing nudity or partial nudity of a wholesome nature. For example: Web sites containing publications such as National Geographic or Smithsonian Magazine. Or sites hosted by museums such as the Guggenheim, the Louvre, or the Museum of Modern Art.

- Sexual Acts (graphic or text): Pictures or text exposing anyone or anything involved in explicit sexual acts and or lewd and lascivious behavior, including masturbation, copulation, pedophilia, intimacy involving nude or partially nude people in heterosexual, bisexual, lesbian or homosexual encounters. Also includes phone sex ads, dating services, and adult personals, CD-ROMs and videos.

- Gross Depictions (graphic or text): Pictures or descriptive text of anyone or anything which are crudely vulgar or grossly deficient in civility or behavior or which show scatological impropriety. Includes such depictions as maiming, bloody figures, or indecent depiction of bodily functions.

- Intolerance (graphics or text): Pictures or text advocating prejudice or discrimination against any race, color, national origin, religion, disability or handicap, gender, or sexual orientation. Any picture or text that elevates one group over another. Also includes intolerant jokes or slurs.

■ Satanic or Cult (graphics or text): Satanic material is defined as: Pictures or text advocating devil worship, an affinity for evil, or wickedness. A cult is defined as: A closed society, often headed by a single individual, where loyalty is demanded, leaving may be punishable, and in some instances, harm to self or others is advocated. Common elements may include: encouragement to join, recruiting promises, and influences that tend to compromise the personal exercise of free will and critical thinking.

■ Drugs/Drug Culture (graphics or text): Pictures or text advocating the illegal use of drugs for entertainment. Includes substances used for other than their primary purpose to alter the individual's state of mind, such as glue sniffing. This would exclude currently illegal drugs legally prescribed for medicinal purposes (e.g., drugs used to treat glaucoma or cancer).

■ Militant/Extremist (graphics or text): Pictures or text advocating extremely aggressive and combative behaviors, or advocacy of unlawful political measures. Topics include groups that advocate violence as a means to achieve their goals. Includes "how to" information on weapons making, ammunition making, or the making or use of pyrotechnics materials. Also includes the use of weapons for unlawful reasons.

■ Sex Education (graphics or text): Pictures or text advocating the proper use of contraceptives. This topic would include condom use, the correct way to wear a condom, and how to put a condom in place. Also included are sites relating to discussion about the use of the Pill, IUD's and other types of contraceptives. In addition to the above, this category will include discussion sites on how to talk to your partner about diseases, pregnancy, and respecting boundaries. Excluded from this category are commercial sites wishing to sell sexual paraphernalia.

- Questionable/Illegal & Gambling (graphics or text): Pictures or text advocating materials or activities of a dubious nature which may be illegal in any or all jurisdictions, such as illegal business schemes, chain letters, copyright infringement, computer hacking, phreaking (using someone's phone lines without permission) and software piracy. Also includes text advocating gambling relating to lotteries, casinos, betting, numbers games, on-line sports or financial betting, including non-monetary dares.

- Alcohol & Tobacco (graphics or text): Pictures or text advocating the sale, consumption, or production of alcoholic beverages and tobacco products.

Note: All of the above categories pertain to advocacy information: how to obtain inappropriate materials and or how to build, grow, or use said materials. The categories do not pertain to sites containing opinion or educational material, such as the historical use of marijuana or the circumstances surrounding 1940's anti-Semitic Germany.

Copyright Microsystems Software, Inc.

Installing Cyber Patrol

From your administrative console, go to the SYS:\ETC\CPFILTER directory. You didn't know about that one? It's new with BorderManager, that's why.

In that directory is a program called CP_SETUP.EXE. You'll also see a file called CPFILTER.NLM. You don't need to copy that to the server, because the system will take care of it. Actually, the installation process leaves the file in this directory and points here rather than copying the file. Keeping all the Cyber Patrol files together makes things run much smoother, believe me. But I'm getting ahead of myself.

If possible, run the installation program from a system with a sound board. You'll hear the thrilling strains of "Hawaii Five-O" as the screen in Figure B.1 appears.

You're doubly unlucky, since this book has neither sound nor color. The screen is a vibrant red, dark at the bottom and getting lighter toward the top. You must hear to believe the incredibly cheesy sound for the Hawaii Five-O theme song.

As license screens and legal statements go, these are pretty short and sweet. If you cross your fingers behind your back when you click on OK, it won't count if you change your mind.

The next screen will ask for the location of your SYS: volume by drive letter. It will not assume that drive F: is your SYS: volume, because while F: is often the SYS: volume, it may not be the SYS: volume of the server hosting BorderManager. You must type the letter in yourself, but heed my warning: NO COLON! If you do put in the colon, such as **H:**, you

FIGURE B.1

Book'em, Dano.

will get an error message and feel stupid. Since life and my children make me feel stupid enough on a regular basis, I prefer my software to treat me with more respect. If you feel the same, don't put in the colon.

Now we get to some registration information. All the gory details are listed in Figure B.2.

None of this is difficult to fill in. The name of the registered owner should be easy. Don't put yourself—put your boss, in case some junk mail comes in response to the registration. The serial number is filled in automatically, based on the serial number of the Cyber Patrol software and your IntranetWare files as well.

Next comes the Unlock Code field. If you have a regular license to Cyber Patrol, put your real authorization code here. This will unlock the software for regular use.

If you are evaluating the software, as I am for this example, don't put anything here. Go now, while this screen is still displayed on your

FIGURE B.2

Your evaluation period
starts now.

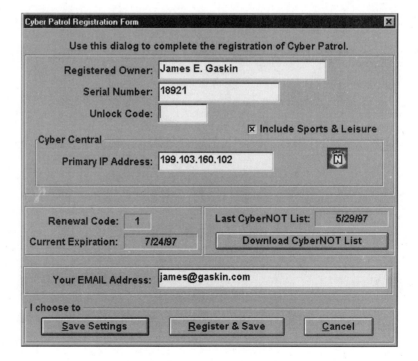

administrative workstation, and type on your server console (or RCONSOLE, of course):

```
LOAD SYS:\ETC\CPFILTER\CPFILTER.NLM.
```

Loading this file allows the software installation to continue, starting your meter for an evaluation term of 45 days.

During this 45 days, you are eligible to download a new CyberNOT list each week. This is how you keep your system current with the new inappropriate sites Microsystems finds. Once a week, do a quick download, and you're current.

On day 46, however, you are no longer allowed to receive the file. Your Cyber Patrol system will still work, but the listings will gradually go out of date. Before long, so many new inappropriate sites will be available that you and your bosses will effectively have no protection. That's when you call Microsystems directly, provide some method of compensation, and get your real Unlock Code. Then all is right with the world, and you may download the new CyberNOT list that very day.

The Include Sports & Leisure checkbox is an interesting item, isn't it? As you can see in the category explanations listed previously, no one is particularly worried about obscenity or hate speeches and the like from sports Web sites, but these sites are distracting. You have the chance here to block them or leave them accessible.

The Cyber Central Primary IP Address is also configured automatically. The same goes for the Renewal Code and Current Expiration entries; they are set automatically. The Last CyberNOT List changes based on the last list downloaded. Get current by clicking on the Download CyberNOT List command button to—guess what—start the download process.

Be sure to put your own e-mail address in the field, not mine. I get enough e-mail already, and the Cyber Patrol people already know how to find me.

You may Save Settings or Register & Save as your heart and financial arrangements dictate. Start this registration program anytime you wish by running SYS:\ETC\CPFILTER\REGISTER.EXE.

Configuring Cyber Patrol

With Cyber Patrol before BorderManager, you had a separate configuration and user control program. The beauty of the Microsystems and Novell partnership in this case is that the Cyber Patrol settings are integrated into NWAdmin.

Remember when we covered setting restrictions on users and groups earlier in the book (in Chapter 9)? If you wanted to set specific URL restrictions, you needed to type each and every one in by hand. Now, as you can see in Figure B.3, Cyber Patrol is one of your URL specification options.

Here, I have taken my opportunity to block Doug from visiting any inappropriate sites, mainly because I'm mad he beat me at tennis. Normally, I'm strongly against managing single users, but I'll make an exception in this case.

Here we are in NWAdmin, showing the Outgoing Rules page for the file server, GATEWAY2000. I can build rules on the organization or organizational unit level if I wish, but now I don't. Notice that the rule I'm building runs this way: Action (Deny) Source (Doug) access to (specific URL). It gets interesting when we hit the URL setting for the Access Specification.

FIGURE B.3

See Doug get restricted.

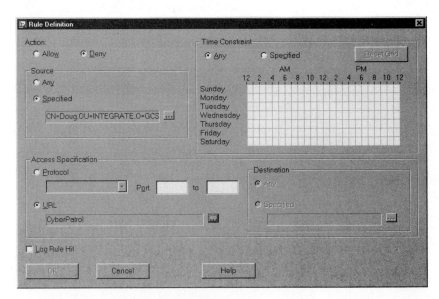

Normally, when you click on the browse box at the right side of the field, you have a blank field awaiting the input of a specific URL. After installing Cyber Patrol, however, there is actually something to browse in the browse box, and you can highlight and choose Cyber Patrol. When you do so, you will see something like the screen in Figure B.4. Notice that the listing at the bottom in the URL Specifications dialog box is for Search Engines. That isn't one of the categories Microsystems designers felt they needed to explain, but there is some value in blocking search engines for certain users or groups. After all, if you can't search at all, you can't search for inappropriate materials. The most common search term is "nude" if that clues you into the problems with allowing some users to search.

Any combination of categories may be chosen. If you're in a typical business situation, you might want to check them all and be done with it. Once you make your picks, simply click on the OK command button, and the rule is saved. If you wish to edit or delete the rule later, it is easy to do so. To change the rule, merely double-click on the rule after highlighting it.

FIGURE B.4

Pick your inappropriate category.

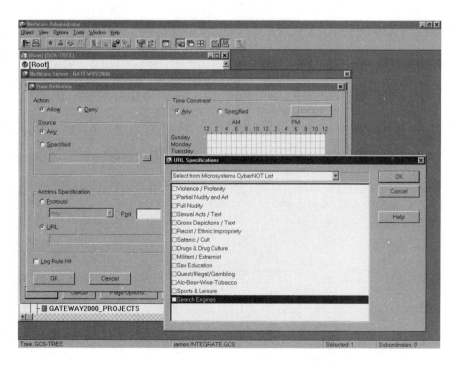

You can see from the full-screen capture that this is a normal copy of NWAdmin, modified by the BorderManager installation, and further modified, of course, by the Cyber Patrol installation. But everything works the way you would expect. If you can handle NWAdmin as it comes out of the box with NetWare 4.11, you'll be able to handle the extra stuff that is added during the BorderManager installation without any problems.

Finally, you can see the rule that I have created using the CyberNOT list. Figure B.5 shows that I am denying Doug access to Cyber Patrol. Unlike the display if you type in some URLs, using Cyber Patrol points the proxy server to the CyberNOT list in the SYS:\ETC\CPFILTER directory on your BorderManager server. Since that list is updated each week, you want the system to point to the list, not a particular list or particular set of URLs.

The rest of the information for this rule is fairly self-explanatory. There are no time restrictions, and I didn't set the log file to track each and every time Doug attempted to reach an inappropriate site and was

FIGURE B.5

Doug is denied.

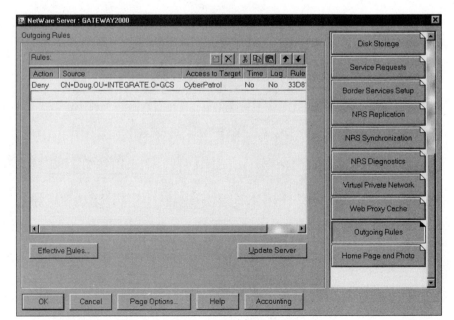

blocked. After all, log files can get pretty big with someone like Doug involved, don't you think?

See the last column title, disappearing off the right side? The full title is Rule Number, and it refers to a unique and system-assigned rule number. You don't need to worry about that, but NDS will. Different rules have different designations, so NDS can track where they came from and other details.

Using the CyberNOT List

This heading is a bit of a misnomer, since no one on your network "uses" the CyberNOT list in a traditional sense. Nothing is required of the user when the Cyber Patrol software is installed and running, except that the user reference the proxy server hosting the Cyber Patrol software. This aspect should certainly be out of the reach of the users, so the few who figure out what's going on won't bypass your security system and go surfing off to who knows where.

After installing and configuring your Cyber Patrol system, you must add the references necessary to use the list at the NWAdmin utility. The easiest way to do this is just to block everyone's access to the entire CyberNOT list all the time.

What will happen? You'll get a few calls or e-mail messages about problems with the browser software and/or the network, depending on how intelligent the users are. Of course, you have no doubt set your firewall and router to accept only the proxy server IP address for outgoing traffic, right?

One by one, you'll get some strange questions, and people will buttonhole you in the hall or break room. "Hey," they'll say, somewhat sheepishly, "sometimes I have trouble reaching certain Web sites."

This will be an important moment in your network management career. If you say something ill-considered such as, "Well, we blocked all the naughty sites," you'll fail your momentous test. Don't say anything like this whatsoever. Merely ask, "Which sites are giving you trouble?"

Your co-worker will probably say he or she doesn't remember any particular site, and perhaps mumble that you should just forget it altogether. Then you'll know exactly what is going on, won't you? The Cyber Patrol installation is working as it should, blocking sites, and your co-worker has been trying to waste some company time.

The reason I say not to admit you have blocking software installed is to avoid long, pointless arguments about free speech and this is America and people can, by golly, view what they want to view. Even if you win those arguments, you really lose, so don't start them.

Smile, offer to check for them next time they have a problem, and go away quietly. They were busted, and you know it, and they know it. Check the log file for ammunition in case your boss doesn't want to pay for the full version of Cyber Patrol. One or two log file perusals should convince even the cheapest boss that a good proxy-access-list-control application like Cyber Patrol is valuable.

APPENDIX

C

Web Addresses

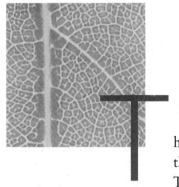

This appendix gathers all the Web addresses mentioned throughout this book into one place for easy reference. The resources are grouped as follows:

- IPX/IP gateway products

- Web server products

- Web security certificate providers

- Group communications products

- E-mail products

- Windows NT/NetWare integration products

- Harvest/Squid technology information

Here's one usefual address that doesn't fit into any of the above categories:

Novell manuals online   http://occam.provo.novell.com/

IPX/IP Gateway Products

Product	Company	Address
CyberJunction	Frontier Technologies	http://www.frontiertech.com
Inetix	MCS	http://www.mcsdallas.com
Instant Internet	Bay Networks	http://www.perftech.com and http://www.baynetworks.com
IPeXchange	Cisco	http://www.cisco.com
IWare Connect	Quarterdeck	http://www.quarterdeck.com
LANlink	FEL Computing	http://www.tic.net
Netra	Sun	http://www.sun.com
NetRoad FireWALL	Ukiah Software	http://www.ukiahsoft.com
NOV*IX	Firefox–FTP Software	http://www.ftp.com.
WebRamp IPX Gateway	Ramp Networks	http://www.rampnet.com

Web Server Products

Product	Company	Address
Cyber Patrol (Web-access control software)	Microsystems Software	http://www.cyberpatrol.com
GLACI-HTTPD Web Server for Novell NetWare	GLACI (Great Lakes Area Commercial Internet) company	http://www.glaci.com
Purveyor Web Server	Process Software	http://www.process.com
SoftNet WEBserv	Puzzle Systems	http://www.puzzle.com

Web Security Certificate Providers

Company	Address
AT&T	http://www.att.com
VeriSign	http://www.verisign.com
Xcert	http://www.xcert.com

Group Communications Products

Product	Company	Address
ECCO Pro	NetManage	http://www.netmanage.com
GroupWise	Novell	http://www.novell.com/groupwise
Intranet Genie	Frontier Technologies	http://www.frontiertech.com
Sidekick 97	Starfish Software	http://www.starfish.com

E-Mail Products

Product	Company	Address
Calypso (e-mail client software)	MCS	http://www.mcsdallas.com
Firefox Mail Server	FTP Software	http://www.firefox.com and www.ftp.com
IPConnect	Puzzle Systems	http://www.puzzle.com
MIMEsweeper (e-mail virus checker)	Integralis	http://www.mimesweeper.com
Pegasus Mail	David Harris	http://www.pegasus.usa.com
WEBserv	Puzzle Systems	http://www.puzzle.com

Windows NT/NetWare Integration Products

Product	Company	Address
BorderManager software for NT	Novell	http://www.novell.com/intranetware/ntint/
Synchronicity for NT	NetVision, Inc.	http://www.netvisn.com

Harvest/Squid Technology

Technology	Address
Harvest	http://harvest.cs.colorado.edu/
Squid	http://squid.nlanr.net/

APPENDIX

D

Glossary of Terms

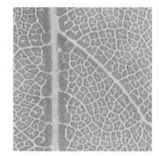

802.7

An IEEE (Institute of Electrical and Electronic Engineers) specification that defines broadband networks carrying voice, data, and video traffic. This specification relates to cable networks, modems, and Internet-over-cable projects.

802.11

An IEEE (Institute of Electrical and Electronic Engineers) specification for wireless networking.

A

abend

For ABnormal ENDing; a computer crash.

access controls

A set of access rules and control lists that work with the BorderManager's application-, circuit-, and packet-level filters. The most critical design guide for access controls is that what is not explicitly allowed is denied.

ACL (Access Control List)

Database kept within Novell Directory Services (NDS) listing which objects are allowed to use which network resources.

ACU

See *Automatic Client Upgrade*.

address

A unique identifier on the network, most often the number assigned to the network card by the manufacturer. *Address* may also refer to memory location in an operating system.

Other addresses becoming newsworthy now include IP addresses and e-mail addresses. IP addresses (such as, 204.251.122.48) are identifiers for systems on the Internet or other TCP/IP (Transmission Control Protocol/Internet Protocol) networks. E-mail addresses use the *domain name* after the @ sign, such as james@gaskin.com.

Address Resolution Protocol

See *ARP*.

Anonymous FTP server

An FTP server that accepts the username "anonymous," and an e-mail address as the password. No other user identity verification is done.

application-level filter

See *filters*.

ARP (Address Resolution Protocol)

The IP (Internet Protocol) protocol that provides the physical address when only the logical address is known.

authentication

A security procedure that verifies that a Novell Directory Services (NDS) user has permission to use the network service requested. NetWare 4.1*x*'s authentication is based on the public key encryption system, and it is extremely reliable and safe.

Authentication on the Internet and intranets is based on IP address, and it is administered (not nearly as strictly as within NDS) primarily by Domain Name Services (DNS) to find addresses and tables of accepted addresses stored on systems.

AUTOEXEC.NCF

The script of commands used by a NetWare server when booting and setting up the NetWare environment. This file is similar in purpose and organization to the AUTOEXEC.BAT file of a personal computer.

Automatic Client Upgrade (ACU)

A method to upgrade Novell client software during the login process, powered by four different executable programs called during the login script. This method is handy for mass upgrades when your client population uses consistent workstation configurations. Improvements include the ability to upgrade client software when starting programs from the Novell Application Launcher (NAL).

automatic rollback

A security feature of the Transaction Tracking System (TTS) that, when engaged, guarantees a database transaction is completed. If the network, client, or server fails during a TTS transaction, the database is returned to the state existing before the transaction started.

B

bindery

A security database controlling user privileges in earlier NetWare versions. NetWare 4 uses Novell Directory Services (NDS).

Bindery Services

A NetWare 4 feature that mimics bindery databases for software that requires the bindery of earlier NetWare versions. Many existing third-party print servers, for example, require Bindery Services.

binding/unbinding

Binding is initiating protocol-support software for a network board. *Unbinding* is removing protocol-support software from a network board. A single physical network board may have multiple protocols bound, such as the NetWare server boards supporting both IPX and TCP/IP.

block

The smallest unit of disk space controlled by the NetWare operating system. Size ranges from 4KB to 64KB. Smaller blocks require more server memory. The best utilization is achieved by using the 64KB block size with block suballocation.

block suballocation

A process that divides one block into 512-byte units that store fragments of other files. This greatly reduces the amount of disk space required, especially when many small files are stored on the disk.

BOOTP (BOOTstrap Protocol)

Early configuration protocols used by TCP/IP (Transmission Control Protocol/Internet Protocol) systems to provide IP address and other configuration details to diskless workstations. Enough code was placed in a chip on the system motherboard to find the BOOTP server and request information. BOOTP has been superceded by DHCP (Dynamic Host Configuration Protocol).

BorderManager

IntranetWare software for Internet, intranet, and extranet connections.

bridge

A powered network device that connects two or more network segments and passes packets based on physical addresses only. Routers use protocol-supplied addresses.

buffer

Memory area set aside to hold temporary data until the data can be accepted by either the workstation or network.

C

cache buffer

A server memory buffer that improves performance by keeping recently used files in server memory.

cache buffer pool

The total amount of memory available for server cache operations. The cache buffer pool is used to cache volume FATs (file allocation tables), volume directory tables, recently used files, directory names, and FAT indexes for large files.

cache memory

Another name for a *cache buffer* or *cache buffer pool*.

caching

Directory caching is a NetWare technique of keeping directory names in server memory for quicker access, rather than reading the directory from the disk.

File caching is caching recently used files in server RAM to speed file reading and operations.

BorderManager adds *Web Client Acceleration*, where a Proxy Cache Server stores Web pages viewed by users to improve the response for other users. Web Server Acceleration (reverse proxy) uses the Proxy Cache Server to hold information requested by outside viewers of your Web servers, to improve performance for subsequent outside viewers.

certificate

Issued by a recognizable and secure authority as a pass through Web security. VeriSign is the leading source of certificates used for Internet commerce. Netscape and Microsoft Web servers can issue their own certificates strong enough for intranet use.

channel

A logical memory connection point between workstation memory and hard disk controllers. *Channel* also refers to a pathway through a communications medium, such as a channel on a multiplexer, or the B (bearer) and D (data) channels on an ISDN (Integrated Services Digital Network) line.

circuit-level filter

See *filter*.

client

A machine that uses any of the network services provided by a network server. In NetWare, clients may be DOS, MS Windows, OS/2, Macintosh, or Unix systems.

Today, *client* also may refer to Web clients (browsers) partaking of a network server resource, locally or across the Internet. Because of this, some people feel that the Web is merely the latest incarnation of the client/server model introduced by the mainframe/terminal relationship.

Client32

Client software that takes advantage of 32-bit technology and expanded memory availability, developed primarily for Windows 95 and Windows NT. In NetWare 4.11, Client32 can also be used for DOS and Windows 3.1x clients.

commerce server

A Web server that handles electronic commerce transactions. This server must have strong security, auditing, and authentication capabilities.

connection number

A NetWare server-assigned number for each workstation, print server, process, or application that requires a server connection. The connection numbers are assigned on a first-come, first-served basis.

context

Shorthand to represent the specific container of an object within the NetWare Directory tree.

D

DARPA (Defense Advanced Research Projects Agency)

From the original ARPA, founded in the early 1970s, expanded to reflect the source of early Internet development money.

data protection

In NetWare, duplicate file directories and the process of moving data from bad blocks to known good blocks.

To protect data-location information, NetWare 4.1*x* uses duplicate DETs (directory-entry tables) and FATs (file allocation tables) to provide fault-tolerance on the hard disk. Having copies of each of these tables reduces the risk of loss due to a bad block or two.

To protect data against surface defects, NetWare 4.1*x* uses the following methods:

- *Read-after-write verification*: Verifying every bit written to the disk before the copy is erased from server RAM (NetWare default).

- *Hot Fix*: Separate area of the hard disk used to copy data from bad blocks on the disk. The bad block is then marked as bad so no other data will be written there.

- *Disk mirroring*: Placing data on two disks connected to the same controller.

- *Disk duplexing*: Placing data on two identical disks connected to two separate controllers.

default server

The server that responds to a workstation's "Get Nearest Server" request when the user first starts the login process. In earlier NetWare versions, the default server name was often specified in the NET.CFG file on the workstation. Novell Directory Services (NDS) has replaced the need for the default server destination with the default *context*.

DET

See *directory-entry table*.

device sharing

Allowing more than one person to use a device, and a great excuse for a network. Shared devices include hard disks, printers, modems, fax servers, tape backup units, and communication gateways.

DHCP (Dynamic Host Configuration Protocol)

A protocol update of *BOOTP*. Used to provide IP address and other configuration details from a central server to connected workstations. Novell's DHCP ships with NetWare 4.11, IntranetWare, and BorderManager as part of TCP/IP (Transmission Control Protocol/Internet Protocol) support.

Directory/directory

The *Directory* is the database supporting the hierarchical structure of Novell Directory Services (NDS), the upgrade from the bindery.

A *directory* is a file-system organization method. A directory may contain both files and other directories.

directory-entry table (DET)

Basic information concerning files, directories, directory trustees and other entities per volume are tracked in the directory table. Maximum entries per directory table is 2,097,152, since each of the 65,536 maximum directory blocks per volume can each hold 32 entries. A directory entry is 32 bytes long.

Directory Services

The distributed security and network-resource-locating database released with NetWare 4 to replace and upgrade the bindery. This database works on the network level, not per server.

Directory Services request

A user or an administrator request to the Directory database to read or modify the database contents. There are three types of requests:

- *Directory-access requests* are user requests to create, modify, or retrieve objects.

- *Directory-access control requests* are administrator requests to allow access rights to the Directory database for users.

■ *Directory-management requests* are administrator requests to manage the physical Directory database, such as to perform partitioning operations.

Directory tree

Container objects and all the leaf objects that make up the hierarchical structure of the Novell Directory Services (NDS) database. Also known as an *NDS tree*.

disk driver

Software that connects the NetWare operating system to the disk controller. The four Novell-supplied disk drivers are ISADISK.DSK (ISA disks), IDE.DSK (IDE disks), PS2ESDI.DSK (ESDI controllers in an IBM MicroChannel Architecture system), and PS2SCSI.DSK (SCSI controllers in an IBM MicroChannel Architecture system). Third-party vendors often supply their own disk drivers.

NetWare 4.1*x* now uses the Media Manager, a database that tracks storage devices and associated media attached to a server. This is part of the NWPA (NetWare Peripheral Architecture). Components include the HAM (Host Adapter Module), which is adapter-specific; the HAI (Host Adapter Interface), providing software programming interfaces; the CDM (Custom Device Module), device-specific for the storage device; and the CDI (Custom Device Interface, the programming interface for the storage device.

DMA (dynamic memory access)

A method of transferring information from a device such as a hard disk or network adapter directory into memory without passing through the CPU. Because the CPU is not involved in the information transfer, the process is faster than other types of memory transfers. The DMA channel must be unique for each device.

DNS (Domain Name Service)

A service that works across the global Internet to facilitate communication between systems near and far from each other. Normally invisible to users, DNS is used by applications to locate systems across the network using the TCP/IP protocol components. Developed in the early 1980s to automate the previously manual editing of host files on Internet-connected systems. DNS allowed the number of hosts to double each year, and is still the directory service in use on the Internet and the Web.

DNS server

Used in a network to find and connect to systems within and outside a company. NetWare needs a DNS server to maintain compliance with the TCP/IP method of operation. The primary function of the DNS server is to find a special DSS (Domain SAP server).

Domain SAP server

See *DSS*.

drive

A *physical drive* is a physical mass storage device that supports the reading and writing of data.

A *logical drive* is a network disk directory addressed as a separate drive with a drive-letter prompt.

drive mapping

The process of assigning various network disk directories as separate drives, each with a unique drive letter.

DSS (Domain SAP server)

NetWare software running on a NetWare/IP-enabled server to track the information normally distributed via IPX (Internetwork Packet eXchange) SAP (Service Advertising Protocol) broadcasts. Since TCP/IP (Transmission Control Protocol/Internet Protocol) networks dislike broadcasts, NetWare/IP clients must query the DSS for network configuration details, such as the nearest server during login.

dual-homed firewall

Firewall using two network interfaces, one to the internal network and one to the external network, normally the Internet. This funnels all network traffic through the firewall so all security rules are applied to all traffic. Your BorderManager server can become a dual-home firewall if you place two network interface cards in the server.

dual-homed server

Servers equipped with two network interfaces. One network connection goes to the internal network, and the other to the external network, just like a dual-homed firewall.

dynamic configuration

The ability of NetWare to allocate resources from available server processes first, and to allocate new processes if an available process fails to answer the request in a timely manner.

dynamic memory

Memory chips that require constant electrical current to hold the information written to them. Dynamic memory is used for RAM.

dynamic memory access

See *DMA*.

E

effective rights

A user's access rights to a file, directory, or object based on the combination of trustee assignments, inherited rights, Group object rights, and any security equivalence. NetWare calculates a user's rights before every action. Effective rights are based on a combination of the following:

- The object's direct trustee assignments to the directory or file in question.

- Any inherited rights from parent directories.

- Rights to the object gained from being a member of a group with trustee rights to the object or file/directory.

- Rights from a listing in a User object's security equivalence list.

encryption

The technique of scrambling information so only certain people and systems can read the information. As privacy concerns increase, so does the prevalence of encryption.

The VPN services from BorderManager encode packets that transverse the Internet to make them readable to only authorized users, for maintaining security even across the most public of networks. There are two major encryption standards, and BorderManager uses them both:

- The RSA (Rivest, Shamir, and Adleman, the three inventors of the security algorithm) system is a public key encryption system, used for both encryption and authentication.

- The Diffie-Hellman system (named for Whitfield Diffie and Martin Hellman, who wrote a paper on public key cryptography two years before RSA was released) has no point to attack the algorithm, and is considered more secure than RSA. Of course, it also requires more overhead.

Ethernet configuration

The Ethernet standard followed by network connections. NetWare 4.1*x* supports four Ethernet configurations:

- Ethernet 802.3: Raw Ethernet frame, used as the default for Net-Ware 3.*x* and earlier.

- Ethernet 802.2: NetWare 4.*x* default frame type.

- Ethernet II: Frame type for TCP/IP, AppleTalk Phase I, and DECnet.

- Ethernet SNAP (Subnetwork Address Protocol): Frame type for AppleTalk Phase II.

extranet

Adds the *extra* modifier to designate an outside company gaining access to an intranet. The other company's clients can see inside the firewall, with access to some of the network resources. Think of this as a partnership network, where only trusted partners are allowed to access your network resources, and vice versa.

F

fake root

A NetWare function that has applications accept a subdirectory as the root of the drive. Network-aware applications don't require tricks such as the fake root.

FAT

See *file allocation table*.

file allocation table (FAT)

The DOS index that tracks disk locations of all files and file fragments on the disk partition. NetWare uses the DOS FAT, accessed from the directory-entry table (DET). Files that exceed 64 blocks are listed as a *turbo FAT*, and indexed with all FAT entries for that particular file. This speeds access to the complete file.

file compression

A method of replacing repeating characters in a file with shortened characters, reducing the file length. NetWare 4.1*x* supports file compression, enabled by volume, directory, or file.

file indexing

NetWare's means of indexing FAT entries for better performance while accessing large files. Any file larger than 64 blocks is indexed automatically.

file locking

The process of limiting access to a file so the first user or application can modify the file before a second user or application makes changes.

file server

A machine used to run the network operating system. Referred to as the NetWare server when speaking of a machine running the NetWare operating system.

file sharing

An operating system feature that allows more than one user concurrent access to a file.

File Transfer Protocol

See *FTP*.

filters

Methods used by firewalls and proxy servers to control networks. BorderManager supports three types of filters:

- *Packet-level filters:* Use router technology to monitor and filter information coming into and leaving a network. Unknown packets are blocked for security against outsiders. Each packet from a known source is checked against the access controls set up by the network administrator.

- *Circuit-level proxies:* Control the connection between applications and the Internet or intranet at the Session layer of the network. The most common use is to compare the user request for a protocol service, such as FTP, HTTP, Telnet, and Gopher, against that user's authorizations to use that particular service. Circuit-level services include the IPX/IP and IP/IP Gateway.

- *Application-level proxies:* Relay all the data from Internet or intranet sources to the user application. During that relay, they examine the traffic packet contents and apply authorization rules concerning time of day, source address, and need for encryption. Application-level services primarily deal with Web access and control.

firewall

A security mechanism to protect private networks from unauthorized users gaining access through the Internet or any other network. Connecting to the Internet without a firewall is just as safe as doing electrical work without turning off the electricity while standing barefoot in a puddle of water. In other words, a firewall is now mandatory. Border-Manager performs all the necessary firewall functions. See also *filters*.

frame

A packet-format specification. NetWare supports Ethernet 802.3, Ethernet 802.2, Ethernet II, Ethernet SNAP, Token Ring, and Token Ring SNAP frames.

FTP (File Transfer Protocol)

IP (Internet Protocol) protocol that specifies rules for file exchange between two systems.

FTP server

Server software included with IntranetWare and BorderManager that allows remote clients to place and retrieve files from the server, generally over the Internet. Only a few limited FTP (File Transfer Protocol) commands, such as PUT file and GET file, are supported by any FTP server or client. Most FTP servers allow anonymous users, similar to the traditional Novell GUEST user, to have access to some files without needing a password. The majority of Internet file distribution happens through FTP servers and anonymous clients, although often the transfer is initiated by the Web client software

G

gateway

A link between two or more networks allowing dissimilar protocols to communicate. See also *IPX/IP Gateway*.

Gopher

An indexing and file presentation method that adds a friendlier face to an FTP server. Somewhat obsolete now that the Web server interface rules the file management world.

H

Hardware Specific Module (HSM)

See *Open Data-link Interface (ODI)*.

Harvest/Squid technology

A combination of the Harvest and Squid caching algorithms used by the Novell Proxy Cache Server. Harvest is used to gather, extract, organize, search, cache, and replicate information across the Internet. Squid is a proxy caching server for Web clients.

hashing

An index file in server memory calculating each file's physical address on the hard disk. By skipping the sequential disk directory reads, file operations can be serviced much more quickly.

home directory

A user's private area on the server hard disk. The user has full control over the home directory.

hop count

The number of network routers a packet passes through. NetWare allows only 16 hops between the packet source and destination. NSLP (NetWare Link Service Protocol) supports up to 127 hops.

HSM (Hardware Specific Module)

See *Open Data-link Interface (ODI)*.

HTML (HyperText Markup Language)

A subset of SGML (Standard Generalized Markup Language, developed by the government and roundly ignored by industry), used in Web pages.

Tim Berners-Lee took the most usable pieces of SGML and made HTML, allowing presentation formatting to be described by the server but implemented based on the intelligence and flexibility of the client.

HTTP (HyperText Transfer Protocol)

A lightweight, connectionless protocol developed primarily to support HTML document transport between clients and servers. Built upon TCP/IP, but inefficient because of the constant reconnections needed between client and server to facilitate the transfer.

hub

A physical wiring component that splits or amplifies the signal. The word *hub* is generally used with ARCnet cabling; *concentrator* is used in Ethernet 10BaseT, MAUs (media access units), and Token Ring.

I

ICP (Internet Cache Protocol)

A standard being developed to provide performance improvements by caching Internet traffic. ICP version 2 is under development as you read this.

identifier variable

A login script variable. For example, the identifier variable LOGIN_NAME is replaced with the login name supplied by the user when logging in.

IIS

See *Internet Information Server.*

INETCFG.NLM

Internetworking Configuration, the utility used to enable TCP/IP (Transmission Control Protocol/Internet Protocol) on the server, and configure your IPX/IP Gateway. Run this from the console by typing LOAD INETCFG.

Inherited Rights Filter (IRF)

The list of changes in a user's inherited file access rights as the user moves down the file directory tree. The IRF only revokes rights. You must have the Write property right to the Access Control right to a file or directory to change the IRF.

To allow flexibility in file systems and Novell Directory Services (NDS) design, there must be a way to lock some users out of areas below areas where they have access. The IRF blocks rights by revoking rights at directories or containers. This allows the network supervisor to freely grant access to higher levels, thereby saving time by granting rights to many people at once, while retaining the ability to lock users out of sensitive areas. An example is allowing everyone rights to the \ACCOUNTING directory, but using the IRF to limit access to \ACCOUNTING\PAYROLL.

Internet Cache Protocol

See *ICP*.

Internet Information Server (IIS)

Web server software included with Windows NT 4.0 Server software.

internetwork

Two or more smaller networks that communicate with each other through a bridge, router, or gateway. Also called an *internet*.

interoperability

Support for one user to use resources from two or more dissimilar networks. Advances such as ODI (Open Data-link Interface) and TCP/IP (Transmission Control Protocol/Internet Protocol) support in the server make interoperability easier, but not automatic.

intranet

Your local network infused with Internet technology. For most companies, this means Web servers and clients used for connections within the company network, rather than outside to the Internet. IntranetWare supports this function well, and the fact that your existing LAN may become an intranet with the addition of some Web server software just shows how smart you were to install NetWare in the first place.

IntranetWare

Novell's bundle that includes the operating system (NetWare 4.11), the Web Server, NetWare/IP, the Multi-Protocol Router (MPR), and the IPX/IP Gateway (Novell Internet Access Server). The name emphasizes the value of your existing NetWare network, now infused with Web and Internet technologies.

BorderManager builds upon the TCP/IP and Internet support provided by IntranetWare and adds the security, speed, and savings missing in most other intranet offerings from companies such as Microsoft and Sun.

IP (Internet Protocol)

Part of the TCP/IP (Transmission Control Protocol/Internet Protocol) protocol suite similar to IPX (Internetwork Packet eXchange). IP makes a best-effort attempt to deliver packets, but does not guarantee delivery. TCP is required for that step, as SPX (Sequenced Packet eXchange) is required in NetWare.

IP address

The 4-byte address, which must be unique in the entire Internet if connected, that identifies host network connections. Normally seen in the dotted-decimal format, such as 204.251.122.12. Internet committees oversee IP address coordination and distribution.

IP spoofing

A way to breach network security. An outsider discovers one of your valid internal network addresses and tacks it onto the packets coming from outside. If the only protection is your IP filtering, then your security is breached.

IPX (Internetwork Packet eXchange)

The Novell-developed and XNS (Xerox Network Services) derived protocol used by NetWare. Addressing and routing for IPX is handled by NetWare, unlike the corresponding functions in TCP/IP (Transmission Control Protocol/Internet Protocol).

IPX external network number

The unique network number that identifies a single network cable segment. The IPX (Internetwork Packet eXchange) network is defined by a hexadecimal number of from one to eight digits (1 to FFFFFFFE). A random number is assigned during installation, or the installer can specify the external network number.

IPX internal network number

The unique network number that identifies a NetWare 4 server. Each server on a network must have a unique IPX (Internetwork Packet eXchange) internal network number. A random number is assigned during installation, or the installer can specify the internal network number for each server.

IPX internetwork address

A 12-byte number (24 hexadecimal characters) made up of three parts: a 4-byte IPX (Internetwork Packet eXchange) external network number, a 6-byte node number (derived from the interface card's unique address), and a 2-byte socket number.

IPX/IP gateway

Generically, any software that converts datagrams from IPX (Internetwork Packet eXchange) to IP (Internet Protocol). There are at least a dozen vendors that sell IP translation gateways, most of which are focused on the NetWare market.

Specifically, the name of Novell's IP translation software running under NetWare 4.11 and included as part of IntranetWare and Border-Manager. See also *Novell Internet Access Server*.

IPXODI (Internetwork Packet eXchange Open Data-link Interface)

The client software module that accepts data from the DOS requester, attaches a header to each data packet, and transmits the data packet as a datagram.

IRF

See *Inherited Rights Filter*.

ISDN (Integrated Services Digital Network)

An all-digital voice and data service developed in the early 1970s by the telephone companies, which escaped into the consumer market only by accident, if you judge by the support provided by some of the telephone companies today. Rather than sending an analog signal over the wire as does a voice telephone connection, ISDN sends a digital signal that is more immune to noise and interference. With ISDN, analog voice is translated to a digital signal; computer and data communications can keep the same digital format as is used inside the computer system.

ISP (Internet service provider)

A company that buys large amounts of bandwidth (T1 minimum) from an Internet connection service provider and resells access to that bandwidth to consumers and businesses. Large ISPs can provide many local companies with high-speed links by sharing the available bandwidth. Smaller ISPs often focus on the consumer dial-up market, and resell modem access to small businesses and consumers.

K

key

Encryption uses public and private keys. A *public key* is readily available, and is what you see at the end of some e-mail messages. This key is mathematically related to the *private key*. The message, created with the receiver's public key, is deciphered by the receiver's private key. Returning messages are handled in the same manner.

L

LAN (local-area network)

A network connected by physical cables, such as within a floor or building.

LAN driver

Software in the server and workstation that interfaces the physical network board to the machine's operating system.

Large Internet Packet (LIP)

The NetWare 4.1*x* feature that allows packets going through routers to have more than 576 bytes. The small packet size was a limitation of ARCnet packets, and NetWare defaulted to the small size in case ARCnet was on the other side of the router. Because the use of ARCnet is dwindling, this restriction has been lifted.

Link Support Layer (LSL)

The client and server software between the LAN drivers and the communications protocols. The LSL allows more than one protocol to share a network board.

LIP

See *Large Internet Packet*.

loadable module

An executable file with the extension NLM (for NetWare Loadable Module) that runs on the server. NLMs can be loaded and unloaded without taking down the server.

lobby network

One term for the design goal of providing some network resources, such as a Web or an e-mail server, behind the minimal security of a router's Internet connection. The back door of the lobby network goes to the internal network, and is protected by a firewall such as BorderManager.

local-area network

See *LAN*.

log in

The process by which a user requests and receives authentication from the operating system, and is then able to use network resources. Login scripts configure details such as printer setup and drive assignments.

LOGIN directory

SYS:LOGIN, a default NetWare directory, created during installation. The directory contains LOGIN and NLIST utilities to support users who are not yet authenticated.

login restrictions

User restrictions that control certain network security parameters. Login restrictions include the workstation a user is allowed to log in from, the time of day, and whether the user is allowed to have more than one active connection to the network.

login security

An aspect of NetWare security. The NetWare supervisor establishes login security by using the LOGIN command to control who can access the network. Users must be authenticated by Novell Directory Services (NDS) by use of the login name and the correct password (although they are optional, passwords are strongly recommended). Passwords travel between the client and server in encrypted mode, so network protocol analyzers cannot capture any passwords.

login script

An ASCII text file that performs designated commands to configure the users' workstation environment. The login scripts are activated when the user executes the LOGIN command.

Container login scripts set general parameters for all users in a container, and execute first. *Profile login scripts* also set parameters for multiple users, but only for those users that specify the Profile script. This script executes after the Container script. User login scripts set parameters for individual users, and are the least efficient for administrators to use.

log out

To disconnect from the network (erasing all mapped drives). The LOGOUT command does not remove the NetWare client software from workstation memory.

LSL

See *Link Support Layer*.

M

Macintosh client

A NetWare desktop client using a Macintosh computer. By enabling the NetWare for Macintosh software included as part of NetWare 4.1*x*, Macintosh clients can become a full partner in the network.

MAIL directory

SYS:MAIL is a default NetWare directory, created by the system during installation. Earlier NetWare versions stored each user's login script in his or her personal mail directory; now login scripts are a property of the User object. Users created under NetWare 4 don't get personal mail directories.

MAP

A command-line utility that checks drive assignments and allows users to modify those assignments. The login script MAP command is used to assign drive letters to directory paths during the login process.

Media Manager

NetWare functions that abstract backup storage device control, allowing applications to address different storage devices without using device-specific drivers.

memory allocation

Segmenting RAM (random-access memory) for specific purposes such as disk caches, extended memory, and application execution space. NetWare 4 has replaced the five memory allocation pools with a single, more efficient memory pool.

memory protection

An operating system control function that allows you to lock NetWare Loadable Modules (NLMs) in a memory domain called OS_PROTECTED where the NLM can't access memory used by other NLMs or the operating system.

message packet

A packet, which is a basic unit of transmitted network information.

message system

The set of APIs (Application Program Interfaces) running on top of IPX (Internetwork Packet eXchange) that facilitates messages between nodes on the network.

MHS (Message Handling Services)

Early (NetWare 2.x through 4.10) e-mail integration and coordination software. MHS provided a standard means of connecting disparate e-mail systems. The focus on Internet technologies, including the IntranetWare and BorderManager products, has moved the e-mail world to Internet standards, leaving MHS behind.

MLID (Multiple Layer Interface Driver)

See *Open Data-link Interface (ODI)*.

MSM (Media Support Module)

See *Open Data-link Interface (ODI)*.

multicast IP packets

A new method of addressing IP packets halfway between an individual IP address and a broadcast. Used by "push" server technologies, where subscribers supporting multicast are listed on a particular address on the multicast server.

multihoming

One physical server can appear to the world to be many Web servers. This is often referred to as *multihoming*. There are two ways to do this: by using virtual servers and by using virtual hosts. Virtual servers re-create the entire Web server directory structure, one for each virtual server, on the physical IntranetWare server hosting the Web servers. Virtual hosts are partial implementations of the Web server directory structure. A virtual host has its own document and log directories, but it uses the configuration directory of the main server

Multi-Protocol Router (MPR)

Expansion of Novell's long-time ability to route multiple protocols through the NetWare server operating system. MPR is now included with Intranet-Ware and BorderManager. Any currently available WAN connection, up through T1 lines, may be controlled by WAN boards in a NetWare server running the MPR software.

multiserver network

A physical network with more than one server. Internetworks have more than one network connected by a router or gateway.

N

NAL

See *Novell Application Launcher.*

name context

Context; the location of an object in a Directory tree.

name space

The ability of a NetWare volume to support files from non-DOS clients, including Macintosh, OS/2, FTAM (Open Systems Interconnect), and Unix (NFS) systems. Each client sees files on the file server in its own file format. A Macintosh client will see a file as a Macintosh file, while an OS/2 user will see that same file as an OS/2 file.

Name space support is enabled per volume. NLMs with an extension of NAM are loaded to provide the file name translations. The ADD NAME SPACE command is necessary for each volume, after the appropriate name-space NLM is loaded (for example, LOAD NFS, then ADD NAME SPACE). This process creates multiple entries for each file in the name space of the volume's file system.

Name spaces cannot be removed without using the VREPAIR utility, or by deleting the volume and creating a replacement volume without the name space.

NAT (Network Address Translation)

The process of converting an internal IP address to a different IP address when a packet leaves the local network. Developed for security, since the actual internal network addresses are hidden, and also to accommodate internal addresses that are not unique, and therefore not allowed on the Internet.

NCP

See *NetWare Core Protocol*.

NCP Packet Signature

The NetWare security feature that allows each workstation to add a special "signature" to each packet going to the server. This signature changes with every packet, and this process makes it nearly impossible for another station to pretend to be a station with more security privileges.

NDIS (Network Driver Interface Specification)

A process similar to ODI (Open Data-link Interface) that allows a workstation to support multiple protocols over one network interface card. This was developed by 3Com, Microsoft, and Hewlett-Packard and released before Novell released the ODI drivers. ODINSUP (ODI NDIS Supplement) supports NDIS drivers under ODI when necessary.

NDS

See *Novell Directory Services*.

NDS Manager

A graphical utility included with NetWare 4.11 and IntranetWare that includes parts of the older Partition Manager client application and the DSREPAIR console NLM application. All partition and replica operations, except major repairs, are supported by NDS Manager.

NETBIOS.EXE

The client networking file that emulates NetBIOS, the peer-to-peer network application interface used in IBM or IBM-inspired networks. The INT2F.COM file is necessary when the NETBIOS.EXE file is used.

NET.CFG

The client workstation boot file that contains configuration and setup parameters for the client's connection to the network. This file functions like the DOS CONFIG.SYS file, and is read by the machine only during the startup of the network files.

NetWare Administrator (NWAdmin)

The primary program for performing NetWare 4.1*x*, IntranetWare, and BorderManager supervisory tasks. This application is fully graphical, and it can be executed from within MS Windows, Windows 95, Windows NT, or OS/2. BorderManager adds many new features and capabilities to NWAdmin.

NetWare Client32

See *Client32*.

NetWare Core Protocol (NCP)

The NetWare Presentation layer protocol and procedures used by a server to fulfill workstation requests. NCP actions include manipulating files and directories, changing the Directory, printing, and opening programming connections (*semaphores*) between client and server processes. The process of starting and stopping a connection between the workstation and server is indelicately called creating and destroying a service connection.

NetWare DOS Requester

Client software for DOS and MS Windows computers. The DOS Requester replaces the earlier NetWare shell software. Modules of the DOS Requester provide shell compatibility for applications.

Rather than intercept all software function calls before they reach DOS, as the shell did, the DOS Requester works with DOS. When DOS requires a network service, it passes the function call to the NetWare DOS Requester.

NetWare/IP

Server modules and client software product that replaces IPX (Internetwork Packet eXchange) as the transport protocol between NetWare clients and NetWare servers. Requires multiple NLMs (NetWare Loadable Modules) and new client software. Gateways between the IPX and IP (Internet Protocol) networks allow NetWare clients from either side to see and use the resources of the other network.

NetWare Licensing Services (NLS)

A new Novell Directory Services and management feature that tracks application use to ensure that you have enough valid licenses for the number of concurrent users for each application. This feature has been available from third parties in the past, but it makes sense for Novell to include more application management features along with the Novell Application Launcher (NAL).

NetWare Link Service Protocol

See *NLSP*.

NetWare Loadable Module (NLM)

A program that executes at the NetWare server. NLM programs are loaded at the command line, by one of the configuration programs, such as AUTOEXEC.NCF, or by another NLM.

There are four types of NLMs in NetWare 4:

- Disk drivers (DSK extension) control the hard disk and other mass-storage devices.

- LAN drivers (LAN extension) control the network interface boards in the server.

- Name space NLMs (NAM extension) add non-DOS file name support to a volume.

- Utilities or applications (NLM extension) execute at the server for client support, for management, or to provide applications to users.

NetWare NFS Services

The collection of NetWare Loadable Modules (NLMs) that allows a NetWare server to participate in Unix networks as both an NFS (Network File System) client and server. Additional features are bidirectional printing between Unix and NetWare, and FTP (File Transfer Protocol) server capabilities for the NetWare server.

NetWare operating system

The operating system developed by Novell in the early 1980s to share centralized server resources with multiple clients. The seven important features of the NetWare operating system are directory, file, print, security, messaging, management, and routing services. NetWare currently owns the majority market share among all PC-based network operating systems. More than a million new computers a month become NetWare clients worldwide.

NetWare server

An Intel-based PC running the NetWare operating system. A software NetWare server is created in Unix systems running the NetWare for Unix product available from a number of third-party vendors. To the NetWare client, the Unix-hosted NetWare server is exactly like any other NetWare server.

Servers for NetWare 3 are always dedicated machines. NetWare 4 servers can only be nondedicated when running on an OS/2 host machine; otherwise, they are also dedicated.

NetWire

The online information service accessed through the Novell Web server (www.novell.com). Marketing and product information (propaganda) is available, as are patches, fixes, and helpful technical support files.

network acceleration (hierarchical caching)

A result of technology outlined in the ICP (Internet Cache Protocol), an advanced technique that benefits large sets of clients, Web servers, and proxy installations. BorderManager advances the technology being developed for ICP version 2 in its own Network Accelerator, including peer-to-peer and parent-child caching communication.

Network Address Translation

See *NAT*.

network backbone

A special network generally connecting only specialized devices such as servers, routers, and gateways. The backbone is a separate cabling system between these devices, isolating the backbone from regular client/server traffic.

network board

An interface card, or NIC (network interface card in earlier NetWare-speak) that fits into a workstation or other network device and connects the device to the cabling system.

network communication

Data exchanged in packet format over a defined network.

Network Driver Interface Specification

See *NDIS*.

Network File System

See *NFS*.

network interface card (NIC)

A network board, card, or adapter (choose your term) that connects a device with the network cabling system. More recent Novell documentation favors "network board" rather than NIC or adapter; other companies and references are less restrictive.

network node

An intelligent device attached to the network. Traditionally, nodes are servers, workstations, printers, routers, gateways, or communication servers. However, other devices, such as fax machines, copiers, security systems, and telephone equipment may be considered network nodes.

network numbering

A unique numbering scheme to identify network nodes and separate network cable systems. IPX (Internetwork Packet eXchange) automatically adds the node number for the client, while the server installation process sets the network cable segment number (IPX external network number) and the address of the server (IPX internal network number). TCP/IP (Transmission Control Protocol/Internet Protocol) networks require the installer to set and maintain all network addresses.

network supervisor

A traditional term for the person responsible for the network, or a portion thereof (subadministrator). Also called the network administrator. Truly, a hero for the modern age.

Network Support Encyclopedia (NSE)

The CD-ROM based information resource which includes patches, fixes, drivers, bulletins, manuals, technical bulletins, compatibility testing results, press releases, and product information. Produced by Novell, the NSE is available by subscription by calling 1-800-NETWARE.

NETX

The VLM (Virtual Loadable Module) under the client DOS Requester that provides backward-compatibility with the older versions of the NetWare shell.

NFS (Network File System)

A distributed network file system developed by Sun Microsystems, where remote disk contents appear to be subdirectories on your local file system. It is pervasive and well accepted. Attempts are constantly being made to better adapt NFS to the Internet and vice versa.

NIAS

See *Novell Internet Access Server*.

NIC

See *network interface card*.

NIS (Network Information Services)

A distributed database that provides common information for network use, such as user and group information. Similar to Novell Directory Services (NDS), NIS uses the database of users and groups to validate access to network resources, especially NFS. The tables of information are called *NIS maps*, which are controlled by the master NIS server.

The NIS domain is controlled by this NIS server. NIS domains consist of local network connections only and generally cover a single network. The domain names are flat, rather than hierarchical as in DNS (Domain Name Service), and the rules for these names are not as strict.

NLM

See *NetWare Loadable Module*.

NLS

See *NetWare Licensing Services*.

NLSP (NetWare Link Service Protocol)

A routing protocol designed by Novell that exchanges information about the status of the links between routers to build a map of the internetwork. Once the network map is built, information is transferred between routers only when the network changes.

RIP (Router Information Protocol), the previous method for routers to exchange information, requires regular broadcasts that add network traffic. Using NLSP reduces routing traffic across WAN links. NLSP does use RIP to communicate with NetWare clients.

node number

Similar to a network number, a node number generally refers to a client machine only. Under NetWare, node numbers are based on the unique, factory-assigned address (Ethernet and Token Ring) or the card's configurable address (ARCnet and Token Ring cards supporting LAA, or Locally Administered Addresses).

Novell Application Launcher (NAL)

A utility for managing applications presented to NetWare clients. The NetWare Administrator (NWAdmin) program defines which applications are available for the users and provides an icon group for the users. Different startup and shutdown scripts may be used for extra application control. NAL uses the Universal Naming Convention (UNC), reducing the need for more drive letters and their attendant management.

Novell Directory database

Sometimes abbreviated by Novell documentation as NDD, the Novell Directory database stores and organizes all objects in the Directory tree. The objects are stored in a hierarchical structure, mimicking the hierarchical arrangement of Novell Directory Services (NDS) itself.

Novell Directory Services (NDS)

A NetWare 4-specific database that maintains information on, and access to, all network resources for all network clients. NDS replaces the bindery in earlier NetWare versions. The database in NDS is distributed and replicated among multiple servers for fault-tolerance and high performance. Network resources controlled by NDS include users, groups, printers, volumes, and servers.

NDS allows access to network resources independent of the server holding those resources. With the bindery, each user was required to know the server responsible for each network service. NDS allows users to access resources without knowing the server responsible for those resources.

Users no longer establish a link to a single server in order to log in. Users are authenticated (logged in and verified) by the network itself through NDS. The authentication process provides the means for the client to communicate with NDS, as well as to check the security profile of each user.

Novell Internet Access Server (NIAS)

The server software module that translates data requests from a client running on IPX (Internetwork Packet eXchange) to TCP/IP (Transmission Control Protocol/Internet Protocol) for connection to the Internet or TCP/IP host.

There are two pieces to this technology: one at the client and one at the server. The client software includes a special version of WinSock that "spoofs" the TCP/IP client software, such as Netscape, into believing the client is running the TCP/IP protocol stack. In reality, only IPX is running at the client.

The server portion of the WinSock software converts the data transport protocol from IPX to IP for connection the TCP/IP systems. Outgoing packets are assigned port numbers in addition to the IP address of the NIAS, which is shared by all systems. Incoming packets, identified by their port numbers, are routed back across IPX to their original stations.

NSE

See *Network Support Encyclopedia.*

O

object

Any distinct, separate entity; in NetWare 4.1*x*, a Novell Directory Services (NDS) database entry that holds information about a network client or another resource. The categories of information are called *properties*. For example, a User object's mandatory properties are login name and last name. The data in each property is called its *value*.

NetWare 4.1*x* network objects include users, printers, servers, volumes, and print queues. Some of these are physical; some are virtual, like the print queue and groups of users. Container objects help manage other objects.

Leaf objects, such as users, printers, volumes, and servers, are the end nodes of the Directory tree. Containers (called *branches* in some other systems) are Country, Organization, and Organizational Unit objects. A container object can be empty. Leaf objects can't contain any other objects.

Object names consist of the path from the root of the Directory tree down to the name of the object. The syntax is *object.container.container .root*. There may be one or more containers in the middle section.

Typeless names list just the names (as in JAMES.INTEGRATE.GCS). Typeful names list the designators as well (as in CN=JAMES.OU= INTEGRATE.O=GCS). An advantage of NetWare 4.1*x* over earlier versions of NetWare 4 is that it allows the constant use of typeless names.

object rights

Rights granted to a trustee over an object. An example is the Create object right for a container object, which allows the trustee to create new objects in that container.

ODI

See *Open Data-link Interface*.

ODINSUP

For Open Data-link Interface/Network Driver Interface Specification SUPport, this strained acronym refers to the interface that allows both ODI and NDIS protocol stacks to exist on a single network interface card.

Open Data-link Interface (ODI)

Novell's specification, released in 1989, that details how multiple protocols and device drivers can coexist on a single network interface card without conflict. The ODI specification separates device drivers from protocol stacks. The biggest advantage of ODI over NDIS is speed and size; ODI routes packets only to the appropriate frame type, rather than to all frame types as in NDIS. The major components of the ODI architecture are:

- *Multiple Layer Interface Driver (MLID)*: A device driver that manages the sending and receiving of packets to and from a physical (or logical) network. Each MLID is matched to the hardware or media, and is therefore unique.

- *Link Support Layer (LSL)*: The interface layer between the protocol stacks and the device driver. Any driver may communicate with any ODI-compliant protocol stack through the LSL.

- *Media Support Module (MSM)*: The interface of the MLIDs to the LSL and the operating system. This module handles initialization and run-time issues for all drivers.

- *Topology-Specific Module (TSM)*: The software layer that handles a specific media type, such as Ethernet or Token Ring. All frame types are supported in the TSM for any media type supported.

- *Hardware-Specific Module (HSM)*: The software layer that handles adapter startup, reset, shutdown, packet reception, timeouts, and multicast addressing for a particular interface card.

open systems

Technically, a goal of guaranteed interoperability between disparate operating systems. Marketing has recast this term to mean any system that can be coerced to communicate with TCP/IP (Transmission Control Protocol/Internet Protocol). Realistically, open systems utilize Internet and Web technologies to support any client connecting to any server.

optical disk

A high-capacity disk storage device that writes or reads information based on reflecting laser light for bits, rather than reading magnetic fluctuations as on a standard hard or floppy disk. Disks may be read-only (a CD-ROM), read-once (a WORM, for Write Once Read Many), or fully rewritable.

P

packet

A block of data sent across the network; the basic unit of information used in network communications. Service requests, service responses, and data are all formed into packets by the network interface card driver software before the information is transmitted. Packets may be fixed or variable length. Large blocks of information will automatically be broken into appropriate packets for the network and reassembled by the receiving system.

Packet Burst Protocol (PBP)

The NetWare version of TCP/IP's (Transmission Control Protocol/Internet Protocol's) *sliding windows*. Rather than send one packet to acknowledge the receipt of one packet, PBP acknowledges multiple packets at one time. This improves the performance of NCP (NetWare Core Protocol) file read and writes, especially across WAN connections.

NetWare 3.1 requires additional NLMs (NetWare Loadable Modules) loaded at the server and some configuration at the client. NetWare 4.1*x* has PBP built into both server and client software automatically.

packet-level filter

See *filters*.

packet receive buffer

The memory area in the NetWare server that temporarily holds arriving data packets. These packets are held until the server can process the packets and send them to their proper destination. The packet receive buffer ensures the server doesn't drop arriving packets, even when the server is heavily loaded with other operations.

paging

A NetWare 4 performance feature that takes advantage of the Intel 80386 and 80486 processor architecture to group memory into 4KB blocks of RAM. The NetWare operating system assigns memory locations in available 4KB pages, then uses a table to allow the noncontiguous pages to appear as a logical contiguous address space.

parity

A simple form of error checking in communications.

partition

In a hard disk, a section treated by the operating system as an independent drive. For example, there are DOS and NetWare partitions on a server hard disk.

In Novell Directory Services (NDS), a partition is a division of the NDS database. A partition consists of at least one container object, all the objects therein, and all the data about those objects. A partition is contained in a replica. Partitions contain only NDS information; no file-system information is kept in a partition.

Partitions are useful for separating the Directory to support parts of the network on different sides of a WAN link. Multiple partitions are also advised when the network grows to include many servers and thousands of NDS objects. More partitions keep the NDS database closer to the users and speed up lookups and authentication.

The [Root] object at the top of the Directory tree is the first partition created during installation. New partitions are created with the NDS Manager (NetWare 4.11), NetWare Administrator (NetWare 4.10), or PARTMGR utility. Each partition must contain contiguous containers. The partition immediately toward the [Root] of another is called that partition's *parent*. The included partition is referred to as the *child* partition.

password

The most common security measure used in networks to identify a specific, authorized user of the system. Each user should have a unique password. NetWare 4.1*x* encrypts the login passwords at the workstation and transmits them in a format only the NetWare server can decode. Web servers can demand passwords, but most accept all clients. Password schemes for Internet use require encryption coordination between the server and a multitude of potential clients, and no common, workable standard has become popular.

path

The complete location of a file or directory, listed from the root of the drive through each directory and subdirectory and ending with the filenames.

PBP

See *Packet Burst Protocol*.

physical memory

The RAM (random-access memory) in a computer or server.

Point-to-Point Protocol

See *PPP*.

Point-to-Point Tunneling Protocol

See *PPTP*.

POP3 (Post Office Protocol version 3)

A protocol defining the connections between an e-mail client and e-mail server. All Internet e-mail clients communicate with POP3; LAN e-mail systems require translation to reach the Internet.

port

A *hardware port* is the termination point of a communication circuit, as in parallel port.

A *software port* is the memory address that specifies the transfer point between the microprocessor and a peripheral device.

Post Office Protocol version 3

See *POP3*.

PPP (Point-to-Point Protocol)

Upgrade of the earlier SLIP (Serial Line IP) used first by asynchronous modem communication links. PPP is faster than SLIP, and it supports multiple protocols, including IPX.

PPTP (Point-to-Point Tunneling Protocol)

A secure PPP connection between two devices adding some encryption method to the standard PPP communication. PPTP is used by Microsoft for remote-client connection over the Internet to Windows NT servers, and a modified version is used by BorderManager's VPN software.

Primary time server

The NetWare 4 server that provides time information to Secondary time servers and workstations. Primary time servers must synchronize time with at least one other Primary or Reference time server.

private key

See *key*.

privilege level

The rights granted to users or groups by the NetWare Administrator program. These rights set the level of network access for that user or group.

Privilege level also refers to the microprocessor access level determined by the Intel architecture for 80386 and higher microprocessors. Four levels are defined: 0 through 3. NetWare uses the 0 and 3 levels. These levels, also known as *protection rings*, are controlled by the NetWare memory domains. The OS_PROTECTED domain, used for ill-behaved or suspect NLMs (NetWare Loadable Modules), provides memory protection for the server's other NLMs and operating system memory.

property

A piece of information, or characteristic, of any Novell Directory Services (NDS) object. For example, User object properties include login name, last name, password restrictions, and similar information.

property rights

Rights to read, create, modify, or delete properties of a Novell Directory Services (NDS) object.

protected mode

The mode in 80286 and higher Intel processors that supports multitasking and virtual memory management. This is the mode that processors use by default. They switch to real mode only when forced to emulate the earlier 8086 processor functions. In protected mode, 80286 processors can address up to 16MB of memory. 80386 and higher processors can address up to 4GB of memory.

protection ring

See *privilege level*.

proxy

A firewall mechanism that hides the internal IP addresses from outsiders. The official definition of *proxy* is one who is authorized to take the place of another, and that fits the use of proxy IP addresses by firewalls. By substituting the IP address of all internal clients with the address of the proxy server or other address, security is enhanced.

Proxy Cache Server

A server that caches Web pages. Novell's Proxy Cache Server applies the same file-caching intelligence used at the NetWare server. It delivers up to ten times the performance of traditional Web connections.

Other proxy server caching services are based on the CERN caching guidelines. While the CERN folks are the originators of the Web protocols, they are still using first-generation caching technology. The Proxy Cache Server is based on the next-generation Harvest/Squid cache research, developed to maximize performance in an open standards environment.

The Novell Proxy Cache Server supports HTTP versions 1.0 and 1.1, FTP, and Gopher protocols. Files are transferred from Web servers with FTP as the underlying protocol in most cases. The Proxy Cache Server increases the performance of FTP, as well as the Gopher search and directory listings. When files are transferred using HTTP, the prefetching of full pages and related links speeds local performance even more. Many companies rely on the same few Web pages or network resources for most of their information. By caching those requested pages on the proxy server, performance jumps for each local network client.

proxy server

A generic name for all software and hardware servers that support caching or filtering for network access. Proxy servers help with performance and security when they hide the real IP address of internal servers.

PUBLIC directory

One of the NetWare system directories created during installation. PUBLIC stores NetWare utilities and files for use by all clients. The default login script for DOS users maps a search drive to SYS:PUBLIC, with Read and File Scan rights granted automatically.

public files

Files kept in the SYS:PUBLIC directory, placed there during NetWare installation. These include all command-line utilities, help files, and printer definition files.

public key

See *key*.

Public trustee

A special NetWare 4 trustee, used only for trustee assignments. It allows objects in Novell Directory Services (NDS) that don't have any other rights to have the effective rights granted to the [Public] trustee. This works similarly to the user GUEST or group EVERYONE in earlier NetWare versions. [Public] can be created and deleted, just like any other trustee. The Inherited Rights Filter (IRF) will block inherited rights for the [Public] trustee.

Rather than use the [Public] trustee to grant rights to large groups of objects, it's more secure to grant those rights only to a container object. The difference between the two options is that rights granted to a container object are only passed to those objects in the container, while [Public] rights go to all objects.

R

real mode

The 8086 emulation mode in 80286, 80386, and 80486 Intel processors. Real mode is limited to 1 MB of RAM address, as the 8086 itself is limited, and no multitasking is possible. Contrast this with *protected mode*.

record locking

The operating system feature that prevents more than one user from modifying a record or file at the same time.

Reference time server

A NetWare 4 server that provides the network time to Primary and Secondary time servers and workstations.

remote boot

The process of booting a workstation from the files on a NetWare server rather than from a local drive.

remote-control system

A remote-computing system that sends only screen information and leaves all the processing power on the network. Remote-control systems need a PC to run the processing. All the remote PC must do is display images echoed from the host PC. The advantage of remote control is speed. The processing is done where the programs and data live, so there's no delay while you copy program and data files across a slow modem link. The disadvantage is cost. Two complete PCs are being used to support one user.

remote-node system

A remote-computing system in which a user dials in to a modem, attached somehow to the network, and runs the regular LAN operating system over this link. Speed is the main disadvantage of remote-node computing. No matter how fast the analog modems get, and how widespread ISDN support is, no remote option is as fast as your LAN connection.

remote workstation

A personal computer linked to the LAN by a router or through a remote asynchronous connection. Remote workstations can be either stand-alone or part of another network.

replica

A copy of a Novell Directory Services (NDS) partition, used to eliminate a single point of failure, as well as to place the NDS database closer to users in more distant parts of the network. There are three types of replicas that can be managed:

- *Master replica*: The primary replica, created during installation. A Master replica of the [Root] partition is stored in a hidden directory on the SYS: volume of the first file server installed.

- *Read/Write replica*: Used to read or update the database. Actions such as adding or deleting objects or authenticating users are handled by the Read/Write replicas. There should be at least two Read/Write replicas for each partition, to ensure that the Directory will function if one or two of the servers that hold replicas are unavailable.

- *Read-Only replica*: The least powerful replica, used to access or display NDS database information, but unable to support changes. (Read-Only replicas are generally not very useful.)

Subordinate Reference replicas are maintained by the system. They cannot be modified by a user (even the supervisor).

Replica synchronization is the process of a partition's replicas exchanging information to stay up-to-date. When a change is made to one replica, the synchronization process guarantees all other replicas obtain the same information as soon as practical.

resource tag

An operating system function call that tracks NetWare server resources. Screens and memory allocated for various tasks, as well as the memory resources used by NetWare Loadable Modules (NLMs), must be tracked so the resources can be made available to the operating system once the NLMs are stopped or no longer require the resource.

resources

Technically, any part of the network, including cabling, concentrators, servers, gateways, and the like. Practically, resources are the components on a network that are desired by the network clients. Under this definition, resources tend to be server volumes, gateways, printers, print queues, users, processes, and the security options of a network.

ribbon cable

Flat cable with each conductor glued to the side of the other conductors rather than twisted around each other. This type of cable is used most often for internal disk and tape drive connections.

rights

Privileges granted to NetWare users or groups of users by the Admin user (or equivalent). These rights determine all operations the user can perform on the system, including reading, writing, creating, deleting, and modifying files and directories.

Trustee assignments grant rights to specific directories, files, or objects. An object with a trustee assignment to a directory, file, or another object is called a *trustee* of that directory, file, or object.

Each object maintains a list of which other objects have rights to the object in the ACL (Access Control List) property.

Directory rights apply to the directory in the NetWare file system to which they are assigned, as well as to all files and subdirectories in that directory. Rights can be reassigned, or the Inherited Rights Filter (IRF) may remove some of the rights passing down the file-system directory tree. These rights are part of the file system only, and have no relevance to Novell Directory Services (NDS) objects.

The following types of rights apply to a NetWare 4.1*x* network:

- *File rights* apply to only the file to which they are assigned. Trustees may inherit file rights from the directory containing the file.

- *Object rights* apply to only NDS objects. These rights do not affect the properties of the object, just the object itself.

- *Property rights* apply to only the properties of NDS objects. These rights may be assigned to each property, or a default set of rights may be assigned to all properties.

A trustee must have the Access Control right to a directory or file before granting directory or file rights to other objects. A trustee must have the Write, Add or Delete Self, or Supervisor right to the ACL property of the object before granting other objects property or object rights to the object.

Rights flow downhill. By granting trustee rights to the top level of a directory, the trustee has the same rights to all files and subdirectories. The two ways to change inheritance are to reassign rights or use the Inherited Rights Filter (IRF) to block the rights. Inheritance applies equally to the file system and to the objects in the Directory tree.

RIP

See *Router Information Protocol.*

root container

The topmost container in a Directory tree partition. The partition and replicas are named after the applicable root container.

root directory

The topmost directory level in a directory structure. The root directory is the volume in NetWare, and all directories are subdirectories of their volume.

router

An intelligent device that connects two or more networks. A router sends packets from one network to another network, based on the address contained in the protocol rather than the physical address listed at the beginning of the packet. Router functions are included in NetWare servers, or may be stand-alone workstations or specialized computers developed for high-speed routing operations.

Since routers use the address in the protocol portion of the packet, they are able to connect different cabling topologies. This is how a NetWare server can contain up to four different network boards and send all packets to their proper destinations.

Routers are often connected to high-speed modems to support geographically separated networks. These devices are sometimes referred to as *remote routers*.

Router Information Protocol (RIP)

The protocol based on TCP/IP (Transmission Control Protocol/Internet Protocol) that maintains a table of reachable networks and calculates the difficulty in reaching a specific network based on the number of intervening routers (referred to as the *hop count*). Workstations can query the nearest router to locate the least hop count route to a distant network by broadcasting a request packet.

RIP has a reputation for creating lots of network traffic based on the periodic broadcast packets containing all current routing information. These packets help in keeping the routing tables of all routers in the internetwork synchronized. Broadcasts are also sent when a network configuration change is detected, such as when a new router is added or a router goes offline.

S

SAP

See *Service Advertising Protocol.*

schema

NDS (Novell Directory Services) database design components, hidden from direct manipulation. Vendors writing applications to utilize NDS may modify and expand the schema, such as when the IPX/IP Gateway adds new objects to the NDS database.

SCSI (Small Computer Systems Interface)

Pronounced "scuzzy," SCSI is the industry standard that sets guidelines for connecting peripheral storage devices and controllers to a microprocessor. SCSI defines both the hardware and software requirements for the connections. The wide acceptance of the SCSI standard makes it easy to connect any disk or tape drive to any computer.

SCSI bus

Another name for the SCSI (Small Computer Systems Interface) interface and communications protocol. Make sure connected devices are properly terminated and addressed.

SCSI disconnect

A feature in NetWare 4 that allows communications with SCSI (Small Computer Systems Interface) disks to be more efficient by informing the disk to be ready for upcoming I/O (input/output) requests.

search drive

A designated drive used by the operating system to look for a requested file that is not found in the current directory. Search drives allow users working in one directory to access application and data files in other directories. NetWare 4.1*x* allows up to 16 search drives per user, normally defined in one or more login scripts.

search mode

A specification used to tell a program how to use search drives when looking for a data file. When an EXE or COM file requires support files, the file-open request is made through the operating system. This request may or may not specify a path to the support files. When a path is specified, that path is searched. If no path is specified, the default directory is searched first. If the files are not found, the NetWare client software uses the search mode of the executable file to determine whether or not to continue looking in the search drives.

Secondary time server

A NetWare 4.1*x* server that requests and receives time information from another server, then provides that time information to requesting workstations.

Secure Sockets Layer

See *SSL*.

security

The operating system controls used by the network administrator to limit user access to the network's resources. The six categories of security are login security, trustees, rights, inheritance, attributes, and effective rights.

semaphore

A file-locking and control mechanism to facilitate control over the sharing of files. Semaphores with byte value 0 allow file sharing; byte value 1 locks the file while in use. Semaphores are also used to limit the concurrent number of users for applications. When the user count is reached, the semaphore blocks any more users from gaining access until a current user closes the file.

Sequenced Packet Exchange

See *SPX*.

serial port

A hardware port. IBM PC and compatible computers generally come with COM1 and COM2, which transmit data one bit at a time. Serial ports are primarily used for a modem or a mouse on the workstation. In the past, these ports were used on file servers for serial printers. Today, most printers are parallel printers, so it's rare to see a serial printer attached to a file server.

serialization

The process of branding each NetWare operating system with a unique serial number to prevent software piracy. If two NetWare servers discover (through non-filterable broadcasts) that both are using software with the same serial number, copyright violation warnings are shown at the server console and each connected workstation.

server

A *NetWare server* is a PC providing network resources through the use of the NetWare operating system.

A *print server* is a device that routes print jobs from a print queue and sends them to a printer. The print server may be software in a file server or workstation, or a stand-alone unit attached to the network cabling. The Novell Directory Services (NDS) object that represents this device is referred to as a Print Server object.

A *time server* is a NetWare server that provides time to network clients and is capable of providing time for other servers. All NetWare 4 servers are time servers of some type (Primary, Secondary, Single Reference, or Reference).

A *Web server* is a software system based on HTTP communications to send HTML-enabled documents to Web client systems. Novell's Web Server software is included with IntranetWare, as is a DNS server and an FTP server.

Third-party products for IntranetWare include a variety of e-mail, FTP, and Web servers.

server console

The information screens for the NetWare server operating system. Monitoring traffic levels, setting configuration parameters, loading additional software (NetWare Loadable Modules, or NLMs), and shutting down the server must be done at the server console.

The physical keyboard and monitor on the file server are the primary server console. The RCONSOLE utility allows a DOS session on a network client to echo the server screen and redirect keyboard input across the network.

server protocol

An inaccurate shorthand method of referring to NCP (NetWare Core Protocol). (NCP is used on more devices than just the server.)

Service Advertising Protocol (SAP)

The NetWare protocol that allows servers of all types to broadcast their available services across the network. Routers and other NetWare servers receive and track these broadcasts to keep their router information tables up-to-date.

NetWare clients begin each login process by broadcasting a "Get Nearest Server" SAP packet. The first server that responds will become the server the workstation attaches to before continuing the login process.

Because of the traffic generated by SAP, most WAN routers now offer the capability of filtering SAP broadcasts. SAP filtering can also be activated on the NetWare 4 server.

Simple Mail Transfer Protocol

See *SMTP*.

Simple Network Management Protocol

See *SNMP*.

Single Reference time server

A NetWare 4.1*x* server that provides time to workstations and Secondary time servers. The Single Reference name comes from the fact that a server so designated is the single source of time for the network. This is the default for the first server in a Directory tree.

sledgehammer

A last-ditch tool to convince misbehaving servers to change their ways. My personal favorite is the four-pound hand sledge, small enough for a desk drawer yet heavy enough to threaten even the largest servers. Some may say it's only coincidence, but I believe computers work better under threat of dismemberment.

SLIP (Serial Line Internet Protocol)

Internet Protocol running over a serial connection, usually a dial-up asynchronous modem. Only IP is supported, which is why PPP and its ability to support multiple protocols has replaced SLIP in most situations.

SMS

See *Storage Management Services*.

SMTP (Simple Mail Transfer Protocol)

Internet standard for communications between e-mail servers across a network, usually the Internet. Any e-mail server following the SMTP specifications can communicate with any other e-mail server also following the SMTP rules, at least in theory (some tweaking is necessary in practice, but the vendors do it). E-mail servers communicate with e-mail clients using POP3.

snap-in

Novell's name for added feature pages incorporated within Novell Directory Services (NDS) and managed by the NetWare Administrator program (NWAdmin). BorderManager adds several snap-ins, including the Web Proxy Cache, Border Services Setup, Virtual Private Network, and Outgoing Rules command buttons.

SNMP (Simple Network Management Protocol)

Protocol developed in the late 1980s to manage Internet routers that has now expanded to manage almost any network device equipped with the proper agent software. Novell servers and clients respond to SNMP consoles (administration programs) when configured to do so.

socket

The destination point within an IPX (Internetwork Packet eXchange) packet on a network node. The socket number is part of an IPX internetwork address. Many sockets, such as those used by NCP (NetWare Core

Protocol), are reserved by Novell. Third-party developers may also reserve socket numbers by registering their intentions with Novell.

source routing

The IBM method of routing data across multiple networks by specifying the route in each frame. The end stations determine the route through a discovery process supported by source-routing bridges or routers.

There are two types of source routing:

- In *single-route broadcasting*, designated bridges pass the packet between source and destination, meaning only one copy of each packet arrives in the remote network.

- In *all-routes broadcasting*, the packet is sent through all bridges or routers in the network. This results in many copies of the same frame arriving at the remote network—as many frames as there are bridges or routers.

spam

Messages received via e-mail or in newsgroups from someone you don't know offering something you don't want. Also refers to any Usenet newsgroup message sent to more than 20 newsgroups, since no one message would apply intelligently to that many newsgroups. Some people hate spam with a passion; others just delete the message and go on.

SPX (Sequenced Packet Exchange)

The part of NetWare's transport protocol suite that guarantees packet delivery at the protocol level. The use of a check on each packet not only guarantees that the packet reaches its destination, but that it arrives intact.

If an SPX packet is not acknowledged within a specific amount of time, SPX retransmits the packet. In applications that use only IPX (Internetwork Packet eXchange), the application program is responsible for ensuring packets are received intact.

Because of the guaranteed nature of SPX, this protocol is often used for backup systems based in workstations.

Squid

See *Harvest/Squid technology* (and http://squid.nlanr.net).

SSL (Secure Sockets Layer)

A method of Web security. *Sockets* refer to programming sockets used by the developers to communicate between applications on the server and client. Now at version 3.0, the newest SSL standard includes a definition of client certificate requirements, updating the minimal support found in version 2.0. The Novell Web Server software provides full support of SSL 3.0.

STARTUP.NCF

The first of two boot configuration files on a NetWare server. The STARTUP.NCF file primarily loads and configures the disk driver and name space support. Some SET parameters may also be set through this file.

stateful inspection firewall

The newest firewall service level, not fully implemented in most products. An advanced device that carefully matches incoming packets with an outgoing packet address and reads packet content if necessary. This requires more intelligence than other firewall services.

station

Usually, station is short for *workstation*, but it can refer to any intelligent node connected to the network.

Storage Management Services (SMS)

NetWare services that support the storage and retrieval of data. SMS is independent of file systems (such as DOS, OS/2, Unix, or Macintosh) and the backup and restore hardware.

SMS NLMs and other software modules that run on NetWare servers include:

- SBACKUP: Provides backup and restore capabilities.

- SMDR (Storage Management Data Requester): Sends commands and information between SBACKUP and Target Service Agents (TSAs).

- Storage Device Interface: Sends commands and information between SBACKUP and the storage devices.

- Device drivers: Control the mechanical operation of storage devices and media under orders of SBACKUP.

- NetWare-server TSAs: Send requests for SBACKUP-generated data to the NetWare server where the data resides, then return requested data through the SMDR to SBACKUP.

- Database TSAs: Send commands and data between the SBACKUP host server and the database where the data to be backed up resides, then return the requested data through the SMDR to SBACKUP.

- Workstation TSAs: Send commands and data between the SBACKUP host server and the station where the data to be backed up resides, then return the requested data through the SMDR to SBACKUP.

- Workstation Manager: Accepts "I am here" messages from stations available for backup. It keeps the names of these stations in an internal list.

STREAMS

The common interface between NetWare and transport protocols that need to deliver data and requests for services to NetWare. STREAMS makes protocols, such as IPX/SPX, TCP/IP, SNA, and OSI transport protocols, transparent, allowing services to be provided across internetworks.

NetWare can install the protocols of your choice (if your applications support these protocols), and the service to the user will be unchanged.

NetWare 4 STREAMS and related NLMs are:

- STREAMS.NLM: The STREAMS application interface routines, the utility routines for STREAMS modules, the log device, and a driver for ODI (Open Data-link Interface).

- SPXS.NLM: Access to the SPX (Sequenced Packet eXchange) protocol from STREAMS.

- IPXS.NLM: Access to the IPX (Internetwork Packet eXchange) protocol from STREAMS.

- TCPIP.NLM: Access to the TCP (Transmission Control Protocol) and UDP (User Datagram Protocol) protocols from STREAMS.

- CLIB.NLM: Function library required by some NetWare Loadable Modules (NLMs).

- TLI.NLM : The API (Application Program Interface) that sits between STREAMS and applications.

subnet mask

IP address technique used to differentiate between different TCP/IP (Transmission Control Protocol/Internet Protocol) networks. Each client must have a subnet mask, so it will know its exact network address range. The format is in dotted decimal. The most common subnet mask is 255.255.255.0.

subnetwork

Term for a network that is part of a larger network and connected by a router. From the outside, the subnet identity is hidden, and only the main network is visible, making addressing simpler.

Supervisor right

The file-system trustee right that conveys all rights to directories and files. The Supervisor object right grants all access privileges to all objects, and all rights to the property when speaking of property rights.

Misuse of the Supervisor right may be the single largest security hole in many networks. Grant Supervisor privileges rarely.

synchronization

Replica synchronization is the process of ensuring that Directory partition replicas contain the same information as that of the other replicas in the partition.

Time synchronization is the process of ensuring all servers in a Directory tree agree on the time.

SYSTEM directory

The directory created during installation on each server that contains the NetWare operating system files. Also included are NetWare Loadable Modules (NLMs), the AUTOEXEC.NCF file, and many of the NetWare utilities used by the Admin user to manage the network. The name of this directory is SYS:SYSTEM and should not be changed.

T

TCP/IP (Transmission Control Protocol/Internet Protocol)

The primary, industry-standard suite of networking protocols, and the only protocol allowed on the Internet since 1983.

TCP/IP is built upon four layers that roughly correspond to the seven-layer OSI model. The TCP/IP layers are process/application, host-to-host, internet, and network access.

NetWare TCP/IP refers to the collection of NetWare Loadable Modules (NLMs) that add support for TCP/IP onto the NetWare server. Routing can be enabled, as can RIP (Router Information Protocol) to support that routing. One advantage of TCP/IP support in the NetWare server is the ability for IPX (Internetwork Packet eXchange) packets to travel across a TCP/IP-only network by using IP (Internet Protocol) tunneling.

The NetWare TCP/IP suite of protocols is a necessary foundation for all NFS (Network File System) products from Novell. The NetWare TCP/IP suite provides both the 4.3 BDS Unix socket interface and the AT&T Streams TLI (Transport Layer Interface).

With the release of IntranetWare and BorderManager, the TCP/IP support at the NetWare server becomes even more important. The Web Server relies on TCP/IP to communicate with the Internet and intranet clients. NetWare IPX clients using the IPX/IP Gateway require TCP/IP at the gateway server to provide the TCP/IP protocol stack necessary for connection to TCP/IP hosts, either locally or on the Internet.

Telnet

Internet protocol providing terminal emulation to remote systems using TCP/IP. All TCP/IP applications today use fancier emulations, but basic Telnet functionality provides the foundation for them all.

termination

The process of placing a specific resistor at the end of a bus, line, chain or cable to prevent signals from being reflected or echoed, causing transmission problems. Typical devices that need terminating resistors include hard disk drives and SCSI (Small Computer Systems Interface) devices.

TFTP (Trivial File Transfer Protocol)

Subset of the FTP suite, used without any security measures such as passwords. Rarely used by people today, but a mainstay of automated file transfer functions, such as e-mail message transfer.

time synchronization

The method of guaranteeing that all servers in a Directory tree report the same time. Any Novell Directory Services (NDS) function, such as a password change or renaming of an object, requires an NDS time stamp.

The *time stamp* is the unique code that includes the time and specifies an event. The NDS event is assigned a time stamp so the order of events may be recounted.

NDS uses time stamps to do the following:

- Establish the order of events (such as object creation and partition replication).

- Record "real-world" time values.

- Set expiration dates on accounts, passwords, and other items.

The time server software specifies each NetWare 4 server as either a Single Reference, Primary, Reference, or Secondary time server. (See the individual entries for more information.)

Time source servers must find each other. The two ways to do so are SAP (Service Advertising Protocol) and custom configuration. Primary, Reference, and Single Reference servers use SAP to announce their presence on the network by default. Primary and Reference time servers also use SAP packets to determine which other servers to poll in order to determine the network time. Secondary time servers use SAP information to pick a time server to reference. SAP is easy to install and works without regard to the network layout. It does create a small amount of network traffic.

Alternatively, you can set up a custom configuration. Specific time servers that a particular server should contact may be listed. You can also specify that a server should ignore SAP information from other time sources, and that it shouldn't advertise its presence using SAP.

The network supervisor retains complete control of the network time environment using this method. However, the custom configuration method does require extra planning and installation time.

topology

The physical layout design of network components, such as cables, workstations, servers, and concentrators.

There are three design options when planning your network topology:

- *Star network*: End nodes are connected directly to a central concentrator but not to each other. Used for ARCnet and 10BaseT Ethernet.

- *Ring network*: All nodes are cabled in a ring; a workstation's messages may need to pass through several other workstations before reaching the target station or server. Used by IBM's Token Ring network and followers.

- *Bus network*: All nodes are connected to a central cable (called a *trunk* or *bus*). The electrical path of a 10BaseT Ethernet network is really a bus.

Transaction Tracking System (TTS)

A standard, configurable feature on NetWare 4 servers that protects database applications. By "backing out" of any incomplete transactions resulting from a network failure, the system guarantees to return the database to the state that it was in before the interrupted transaction.

trustee

A User or Group object that has been granted access to an object, a file, or a directory. This access-granting method is called a *trustee assignment*, which says, "This user can access this object, directory, or file in the following ways." The following relate to trustees:

- Trustee list: Kept by each directory, file and object, the trustee list includes those objects that can access the object, file, or directory. The trustee list is kept in the object's ACL property.

- Trustees of groups: Rather than granting trustee rights to multiple objects one at a time, they can be granted to a group of users. Trustee assignments granting access for the group enable each individual user to have the same trustee rights as the group.

- [Public] trustee: A special case that grants the trustee rights of [Public] to all users. Users who try to access an object, directory, or file without explicit rights still have the rights granted to the [Public] trustee.

Rights are the access levels allowed an object to a directory, file, or object. Trustee assignments grant to an object the rights to other objects. Assign the right to the trusted object, not the trustee. For example, to grant LAURA the right to delete a Print Queue object, make LAURA a trustee of the Print Queue object, not the Print Queue object a trustee of LAURA.

TSM (Topology Specific Module)

See *Open Data-link Interface.*

TTS

See *Transaction Tracking System.*

tunneling

Creating a proprietary, closed connection across a public network. Virtual private networking (VPN) is an advanced example of tunneling across the Internet.

turbo FAT index table

The special FAT (file allocation table) index file created when a file exceeds 64 blocks and the corresponding number of FAT entries. NetWare creates the turbo FAT index to group all FAT entries for the file in question. This turbo FAT index allows a large file to be accessed quickly.

typeful name

The complete Novell Directory Services (NDS) path name for an object, including the container specifiers. An example is CN=JAMES.OU= INTEGRATE.O=GCS. This was the default in earlier versions of NetWare 4.

typeless name

The complete Novell Directory Services (NDS) path name for an object, excluding the container specifiers. An example is JAMES.INTEGRATE.GCS.

U

unbinding

Stopping and removing a communication protocol from LAN drivers and the network board.

UNC (Universal Naming Convention)

A file resource naming convention, popularized by Microsoft but now supported by many companies including Novell, that replaces drive letters with two backslashes (\\). This is handy if you keep running out of drive letters for some users, which is why NetWare 4.*x* started supporting UNC. As an example, f:\apps\email\calypso could become GATEWAY2000_SYS:\\ apps\email\calypso. This is longer, but it doesn't require a letter for the drive connection.

Unicode

A 16-bit character code, defined by the Unicode Consortium, that supports and displays up to 65,536 different unique characters. With Unicode, multiple language characters can be displayed with a single code. Unfortunately, not every character created using a given code page will display correctly on a workstation using a different code page. Different Unicode translation tables are needed when you change code pages.

All objects and their attributes in the Novell Directory Services (NDS) database are stored as Unicode representations. Clients use only a 256-character code page made of 8-bit characters.

These Unicode files are necessary for each language and translation table:

- 437_UNI.033: Translates the specific code page to Unicode.

- UNI_850.033: Translates Unicode to the specific code page (page 437, supporting English, French, and German, among others).

- UNI_MON.033: Handles the proper display of upper and lower-case letters.

The Unicode pages and translations are one of the reasons you must define a country code for different locales.

UNICON

Short for UNIx CONsole, UNICON is the server utility used to configure and manage NetWare/IP, the DNS server, start and stop NetWare/IP and other services, and includes file operations to FTP host tables from other systems.

Universal Naming Convention

See *UNC*.

Unix client

A NetWare client running the Unix operating system. Originally, Novell's Unix hopes were pinned to UnixWare, but Novell has now sold that product to SCO and HP, both of whom promise to continue the strong ties of UnixWare to NetWare. Yeah, right. Other Unix systems are starting to provide better NetWare integration for their clients, including the ability for the Unix client to use IPX/SPX as its transport protocol. The good news is that 85 percent of all shipping Unix systems now support NDS.

upgrade

The process of converting your network operating system from an earlier version of the operating system to a more current version. Many customers will upgrade from NetWare 3.*x* to NetWare 4.*x*, just as most customers upgraded from MS Windows to Windows 95.

Migration refers to the process of upgrading NetWare 2.*x*, 3.*x*, or another network operating system to NetWare 4 using one of the following two methods:

- The Across-the-Wire upgrade transfers the network information from an existing server to an existing NetWare 4 server on the same network.

- The Same-Server method upgrades the network information on the same server hardware.

The In-Place upgrade method is a three-step process that converts NetWare 2.1*x* or 2.2 to NetWare 3.1*x* using the SERVER.EXE program. Then you continue the upgrade to NetWare 4 from NetWare 3.*x*. With an In-Place upgrade, you begin with a file system upgrade. Then you install the new operating system, giving you a NetWare 3.1*x* file system. This has not upgraded the system and public files on SYS: volume SYS yet. Finally, you can complete the upgrade to NetWare 4.

UPS monitoring

The connection between a NetWare server and an attached UPS (uninterruptible power supply) that allows the NetWare server to know when the UPS becomes active after power has been lost.

When the UPS becomes active, the system sends a signal to the NetWare server, and the server notifies users of the backup power situation. A timeout may be specified, giving the users time to close their files and log out. When the time expires (and the power has not returned), the NetWare server closes all open files and shuts itself down properly.

utilities

Programs, usually small, that have a specific purpose and add specific functionality to an operating system. NetWare 4 utilities are included for DOS, MS Windows, and OS/2 clients.

Utilities that execute on the server and are listed as NetWare Loadable Modules (NLMs) are run from the console colon prompt. Examples of NLMs are MONITOR, PCONSOLE, and SERVMAN. The server NLMs add LAN drivers, disk drivers, name space support, and other low-level network utilities to the NetWare operating system. Workstation utilities execute on a client workstation and are COM or EXE files.

UTP (unshielded twisted-pair)

Cable with two or more pair of wires twisted together and wrapped with a plastic sheath. Each individual wire is twisted around its mate; the more twists, the less interference.

Originally used for telephone wiring, UTP is now the LAN wire of choice. Various grades of cable run from the low end (Level 1 is awful; Level 3 is telephone wire) to the high end (Level 5), supporting high-speed data transmissions.

V

Virtual Loadable Module (VLM)

The modular, executable client program that connects each DOS workstation with the NetWare server. There are many VLMs called by the VLM.EXE program, some adding new NetWare client features, and others ensuring backward-compatibility.

There are two types of VLMs: *child VLMs* and *multiplexor VLMs*. Child VLMs support particular implementations of a logical grouping. For instance, there is a child VLM for each NetWare server type:

- NDS.VLM: Novell Directory Services (NetWare 4) servers.

- BIND.VLM: Bindery-based servers (prior to NetWare 4).

- PNW.VLM: NetWare desktop-based servers (Personal NetWare).

Multiplexor VLMs are the multiplexing modules that route network calls to the proper child VLM.

virtual private network (VPN)

A way to securely combine various remote networks into your existing enterprise network, using the Internet for connections. Multiple LANs can be connected via a VPN. Encryption between servers keeps the packets private during their Internet trip. Some pure firewalls support VPNs as well, but they don't support IPX as does BorderManager.

VLM

See *Virtual Loadable Module.*

voice over IP

Voice communications where special software packetizes voice input, stuffs the packets onto TCP/IP, and routes the packets across a TCP/IP network. Early attempts were not very successful, but the quality is getting better and you can't beat the price, which is free as part of your flat-rate Internet access. Large companies are now investigating connecting branch telephone systems across the Internet to bypass local and long-distance telephone charges altogether.

volume

A logical grouping of physical hard disk storage space. A NetWare volume is fixed in size and is the highest level in the NetWare directory structure, similar to the DOS root directory. Each volume is represented by a Volume object in the Directory.

A NetWare 4 server can support as many as 64 volumes. These volumes may be divided logically on a single hard disk, be a single volume per hard disk, or be a single volume spanning multiple hard disks.

The first, and only mandatory volume, is labeled SYS:, and it includes the NetWare system and client support files. Other volumes can have names between 2 and 15 characters in length.

A volume must be "mounted" by NetWare, and this is the sequence:

- The volume becomes visible to the operating system.

- The volume's FAT (file allocation table) is loaded into memory. Each file block of data takes up one entry in the FAT. Because of this, volumes with a smaller block size require more server memory to mount and manage.

- The volume's DET (directory-entry table) is loaded into memory.

volume definition table

The table that tracks volume-segment information, including volume name, volume size, and the volume segments on various server hard disks. The volume definition table is required for each NetWare volume, but it is created by the system during volume initialization.

volume segments

The physical division of a volume. A volume may be composed of up to 32 volume segments, and the maximum number of volume segments on a single NetWare disk partition is 8.

Volumes can have multiple physical segments spanning multiple hard disks. This allows you to create large volumes, with NetWare maintaining the volume definition table to track all the segments. Be aware that if one drive of a volume fails, the entire volume must be re-created. For this reason, some networks prefer to stick with a one-disk, one-volume philosophy.

VPN

See *virtual private network*.

wait state

The period of time a microprocessor does nothing but wait for other processes. For instance, slow memory forces many wait states on a fast CPU.

WAN (wide-area network)

A network that communicates over a long distance across non-physical media, such as public or private telephone lines, satellites, or microwaves. Traditionally, a WAN includes modems connecting different LANs (local-area networks) across leased telephone lines.

watchdog

Packets sent from the server to make sure a workstation is still connected. More watchdog packets are sent until the workstation responds or the server clears that connection.

Web browser

Client software that communicates over TCP/IP to a Web server, accepting Web pages written in ASCII and coded to dictate the display characteristics on the client system. Bloatware is rampant, as Web browsers now include e-mail, newsgroups, address books, graphics display, and electronic forms applications.

Web Client Acceleration

The software service within BorderManager that allows your Border-Manager server to cache received network information while it passes the information downstream to the clients. Subsequent clients receive the information from the cache rather than across the Internet, speeding response. Novell's intelligent caching also pre-fetches links within pages, since those are the pages most likely requested by the client.

Web Manager

The WEBMGR.EXE program that is installed during Web server installation in NetWare 4.11 and IntranetWare. This allows a Windows client to configure and modify settings on Web server systems.

Web server

A software system based on HTTP communications to send HTML-enabled documents to Web client systems. Novell's Web Server software is included with IntranetWare, and works extremely quickly, as you might expect.

Web Server Acceleration

A way to "turbo-charge" access to your Web servers. Heavily loaded Web servers benefit from offloading repetitive page queries to the proxy server, using the Proxy Cache Server. This is one of the biggest performance boosts for Web content providers that is included with BorderManager.

wide-area network

See *WAN*.

WinSock

Short for WINdows SOCKets, WinSock software is the result of a vendor group meeting in 1991 to provide a single, standard application platform separate from the underlying network transport protocol. The top part of the WinSock software residing on a client machine interfaces with a TCP/IP application, such as Netscape. The bottom part of WinSock interfaces with the TCP/IP protocol stack on the machine, regardless of the TCP/IP developer.

wireless network

Simply, a network without wires. Proponents lean toward either radio frequency networks or infrared transmitter/receiver systems. Standards now in place (IEEE 802.11) bode well for more options for the mobile users straining against their cords.

workstation

A personal computer connected to a NetWare network. The term *workstation* may also refer to a Unix or OS/2 machine. Synonyms are client, station, user, or end node.

XCONSOLE

Utility included with server TCP/IP (Transmission Control Protocol/Internet Protocol) support that allows a remote vt100 or equivalent terminal or terminal emulation program to run RCONSOLE.

XON/XOFF

The handshaking protocol that negotiates the sending and receiving speeds of transmitted data to ensure no data is lost.

X/Open

Group formed by competing/cooperating vendors in 1984 to ensure standards were fair to all companies, not dictated by market share. As Unix has waned in public consciousness, so has X/Open. Novell granted the UnixWare name and reference code technology to X/Open in 1994 for continued sharing of Unix standards.

Index

Note to the Reader: First level entries are in **bold**. Page numbers in **bold** indicate the principal discussion of a topic or the definition of a term. Page numbers in *italic* indicate illustrations.

O

P

X

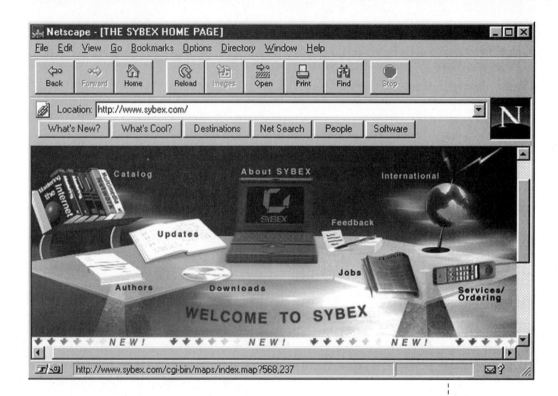